QUANTRILL *at* LAWRENCE

Colonel William Clarke Quantrill. This image of Quantrill is one he gave to Lydia Stone while living in Lawrence before the war. (Emory Cantey Collection)

QUANTRILL *at* LAWRENCE

The Untold Story

PAUL R. PETERSEN

PELICAN PUBLISHING COMPANY
Gretna 2011

Library of Congress Cataloging-in-Publication Data

Petersen, Paul R., 1949-z Quantrill at Lawrence : the untold story / Paul R. Petersen.
p. cm.
Includes bibliographical references and index.
ISBN 978-1-58980-909-3 (hardcover : alk. paper) 1. Lawrence Massacre, Lawrence, Kan., 1863. 2. Quantrill, William Clarke, 1837-1865. 3. Kansas—History—Civil War, 1861-1865—Underground movements. 4. United States—History—Civil War, 1861-1865—Underground movements. I. Title.

F689.L4P37 2011
978.1'03—dc22

2011008243

Printed in the United States of America
Published by Pelican Publishing Company, Inc.
1000 Burmaster Street, Gretna, Louisiana 70053

This book is dedicated to my brother warriors of the United States Marine Corps. In tender memory of the dead and with affectionate greetings to the living. My proudest thought is that I was one of you. May you live forever. Semper Fidelis.

I have a rendezvous with death
In some flaming town.
When summer comes again this year,
And I to my pledged word am true,
I shall not fail that rendezvous.

Contents

Acknowledgments

I would like to express my appreciation to Rick Mack, Patrick Marquis, Claiborne Scholl Nappier, Greg Walter, Robert C. Stevens, Joe and Shirley Wells, Anne Jacobberger, Marian Franklin, Armand DeGregoris, Thomas C. Molocea, and Emory Cantey of Our Turn Antiques for their friendship and encouragement and also for their assistance in allowing me to use their Civil War photographs.

Introduction

The true story of the day's terrible work will never be told.
—John Newman Edwards

The most heinous and barbaric act committed by either side during the Civil War was undoubtedly the premeditated murder by Kansas Jayhawkers of five young Southern girls who were close relatives of members of Colonel William Clarke Quantrill's partisan ranger company. All other acts, whether civilian or military in nature, pale in comparison to this one incident. Occurring on August 13, 1863, this solitary deed was the catalyst for the great 1863 raid on Lawrence, Kansas, by Quantrill and his men. There were those who should have been truly sorry for the actions that precipitated the retaliatory Lawrence raid, but such men could not be found in Kansas. Instead, those who were responsible refused to accept blame for their actions and pointed fingers at others while continuing to pursue their own self-interests and political ambitions.

As a result, the most misinformed and controversial campaign of the entire Civil War became Quantrill's August 21, 1863, raid on Lawrence, Kansas. Compared to Ambrose Burnside's fiasco at the "crater" at Petersburg, Virginia, or Nathan Bedford Forrest's episode at Fort Pillow in Tennessee, the Lawrence raid was even more maligned because it was misunderstood and incorrectly reported. An objective viewpoint has never been given of this incident taking into account the brutal and treacherous actions leading up to the event in order to fairly explain the causes and reasons behind it. In simple audacity, planning, and performance the raid was considered one of the most daring light cavalry raids of the war. No other leader but

Quantrill could have possibly carried off the raid successfully.

The only comprehensive accounts of the raid were those offered by Northern writers taken from separate narratives of the survivors. Publisher J. S. Broughton, who attempted to compile an account of the raid, stated, "It is a fact not generally known that no complete account of this massacre has ever been published."[1] The separate accounts that were compiled unfortunately painted an unfair and inaccurate picture of what transpired. Far more questions arise from these accounts than can be explained by any knowledgeable historian. Skeptics have observed that these similar accounts reflect collusion rather than accuracy. In an effort to justify their wartime conduct and make themselves appear innocent of any inciting actions, those responsible wove into their narratives fantastic stories that defy contemporary logic. A local newspaper reported shortly after the war that the "Quantrell raid[,] for that is what it is popularly called, [contained] many details of which have been historically inaccurate, or pure fiction. Writers have drawn on their imagination, or used statements of participants designed to mislead, until only a few grains of truth appear in the stories told."[2]

Even Cole Younger, who often conversed with the Kansas raid survivors, commented, "The murders, destruction of property, and outrages committed generally, by Quantrill and his men, were bad enough when the truth is told, yet we learn from those who were there at the time, that the facts were largely magnified by the newspaper accounts gotten up immediately thereafter." He continued by saying, "There is nothing that ever happened that was so misrepresented in literature and in history." Adding to the charges of unjust reporting Professor Burton J. Williams of the University of Kansas wrote, "In the place of fact one finds fiction, for in Kansas history has often been distorted by fancy. Kansans have historically 'bled' for nebulous 'causes' and have fought for vague ideologies; consequently her heroes and heroines often appear more like villains."[3]

Discovering the reason something happened may be uncomfortable for many, especially after the truth has been ignored for so long. What this book will prove is that Lawrence was a viable military target. It was a Northern recruiting center. It was a way station for numerous Federal units traveling through the region.

It housed a vast amount of military stores and supplies. It was headquarters of the noted Redlegs, and in many instances Kansas Jayhawker regiments started from and returned there with their "spoils of war." Jayhawkers hid behind a façade of patriotism to fulfill their desire for pillage and plunder. Cities in Kansas grew up overnight and prospered from the ill-gotten gains from the farms and plantations of Missouri. Though accused of murder and robbery Quantrill's guerrillas in fact directed their operations solely against military targets; conversely, there are no historical facts supporting the claim that any guerrillas under Quantrill's command ever benefited financially from their wartime experiences.

At the time there was reasoning behind the falsehoods coming from Kansas. Responding to the fabrications, guerrilla Lee C. Miller expressed his view on the matter: "Kansas men at the time swore up and down that we killed women and children. That was done with the expectation that the Confederate Government would have us withdrawn from the border."[4] This report from one who was there appears to suggest that the distortions circulating after the raid were politically motivated.

In keeping with this accepted fact, purely fictionalized accounts that were neither believable nor even logical were printed without hesitation. One particular historical figure was quoted as saying that if the lie is big enough, people will believe it. With the North effectively controlling the propaganda war, it was able to control history. Stories such as citizens outsmarting the guerrillas by ingenious means, guerrillas being drunk, men escaping detection dressed like women, and narratives of victims' last words when no eyewitnesses were present to record the event are but a few examples. One such story is the last account of Lawrence citizen Lemuel Fillmore. During the attack Fillmore's first reaction was to hide his horse in a ravine. He then went back to his house to retrieve his weapons. He was apprehended as he stepped back outside. His guard enticed him to escape by saying, "Now is your time to make your escape. Now is your time to run." When he bolted away he was shot and killed. Fillmore was completely alone when he was killed. Who his executioner was or who was supposed to have heard and reported the guerrilla's enticing words and observed Fillmore's death has never been satisfactorily explained.[5]

The credulity placed in these accounts is the result of the fact that they have never been seriously questioned in a significant forum. As a result, many of the victims' accounts of the raid have been proven to be patently false. Accounts from Lawrence survivors specifically include the version of the camp of recruits being unarmed, which was apparently constructed in an obvious collusion with other witnesses who collaborated on their mutual stories about what transpired during the raid. To reveal the brutality of the guerrillas it was necessary to show that the camp of the recruits were "unarmed" and "too young to be in the service," and as a consequence most of those who investigated such accounts tried their best to point out these disingenuous facts.

Another obvious attempt to sway public opinion was included in the testimony of Mrs. Louis Wise who repeated that "many of the women were brutally assaulted" and "only a few escaped." In truth, there were no women assaulted whatsoever during the raid. To do so would have resulted in instant death by Quantrill himself. Accounts that have been historically established favorable to the guerrillas have been ignored, while those that cannot be verifiably proven are habitually repeated until they are taken as actual fact. The collective narratives of the raid survivors took on a surreal account of its own. With repeated tellings, their stories added exaggerations until finally the exaggerations became legend, and after time the legend became accepted truth.

To a trained historian who takes all facts into account there is a preponderance of complicity associated in the explanations covering the Lawrence raid. There has only been one view concerning the Lawrence raid, and that has been from the Northern perspective. There has never been an accounting of the Jayhawker's bloody deeds leading up to the raid. In all their accounts written after the war, their murders, their atrocities, their rapes, their pillaging and house burnings have been conveniently omitted. Official records fail to mention the atrocities, but a gleaning of personal records and diaries at the time give a glimpse into what actually transpired on their Jayhawking expeditions.

Lawrence citizens never admitted to participating or acquiescing in Jayhawker atrocities. Lawrence militiaman Richard Cordley tried to prove that the guerrillas did not carry "Death Lists" or lists of buildings slated to be destroyed. Somehow he unwittingly thought that the contrary facts would never be challenged or discovered. Cordley wrote, "It was not the shooting of a few obnoxious persons. The killing was indiscriminate and mostly in cold blood, the victims being quiet, peaceable citizens. None of them, as far as I know, had taken any part in the early disturbances, and none of them were connected with the border troubles during the war. I do not now recall a single military man among the killed. . . . The guerrillas shot the men they found, without knowing who they were or caring what they were." With the archival of historical records and the development of modern databases now available it has been discovered that at least 40 percent of the victims in the Lawrence raid were in the Federal military with the rest being in the Kansas militia. Attempts have been made to determine their military titles, which are provided when known. Also, their affiliation with the early border troubles is well known and is also documented despite Cordley's denial of the fact.[6]

Every story told by the survivors excludes any detailed report of a heavily armed citizenry. Yet acknowledged accounts before the raid indicated that "almost every man in town owned a Sharps carbine," the most deadly and accurate weapon of its day. When the raiders went door to door looking for wanted men, one of their first demands was that the residents throw out their guns. Besides trying to turn their horses out of their stables to keep them from being recognized as stolen from Missouri, the citizens of Lawrence also tried to hide their weapons, for a Sharps carbine found in their home would be a prime indication that they were a member of the local militia. There were very few men in Lawrence who were not in the town's militia. Whether young or old, they could all be found in uniform drilling and doing daily patrols. A Federal officer, Colonel Francis B. Swift, was in command of thirteen companies of militia in and around Lawrence. With an average of eighty men in each company, that made approximately 1,000 soldiers who were anxiously waiting for an attack by Quantrill. Besides having a large militia, Lawrence had defensive embrasures and artillery ready and waiting for Quantrill and his men. Cordley admitted that there were defensive block houses stationed along the likely avenues of approach to the town.

The cowardly measures taken by the citizens during the raid corresponded to their prewar actions. As a result, these Kansans have left this generation a "legacy of lies," the most shameful example being the glorification of John Brown's actions and those of his followers. When irresponsible individuals make statements that there was a "moral justification" for John Brown's murder of five unarmed Kansas settlers in the middle of the night along Pottawatomie Creek in 1857, then there must be an equal consideration for the Missouri guerrillas' "moral justification" in their raid on Lawrence, Kansas.

Alice Nichols, author of *Bleeding Kansas,* concurred with the fact that Quantrill's raid was simply an act of retaliation. "There is considerable evidence to support the contention that this bushwhacker's fiendish sack of Lawrence in 1863 added up to no more brutality than had been imposed on Missouri and Arkansas civilians by Jim Lane's unauthorized brigade and by that flying squadron known as the Kansas Redlegs, a brutal band that flaunted its identity by wearing red morocco leggings."[7]

One eyewitness account of the raid that receives little notice is by Mrs. Harriet M. Jones who tended to concur on the subject of the survivors' inaccurate stories. She remarked, "They have in too many cases exaggerated trivial things and passed over affairs of great pith and moment."[8]

No one will deny that the Lawrence raid was a terrible undertaking. That it was an act of war directed on those who had perpetrated the same genocide on a daily basis along the Missouri border for the preceding two years must be acknowledged before the raid can be judged in all its truth and horror. The author does not wish to offend the naivety and sensitiveness of those who have never experienced the terror of war and its accompanying bloodshed, but he does reserve the right and liberty to show the dark side of wrong, so that he may illuminate the reason for retaliation. The history of the Lawrence raid will be studied for generations. There will oftentimes be disagreements and differences of opinions. Some will believe totally the stories that emanated from the survivors after the raid, and some will empathize with the guerrillas and the plight of their families who were hanging precariously to life along the Missouri-Kansas border. The reader must necessarily withhold judgment until all the facts are in. There are many stories about Quantrill's guerrillas. Some portray them as exceptional partisan fighters just trying to protect their homes and families. Others portray them as ruthless marauders with no good in them at all. What is set forth in this book is the untold story.

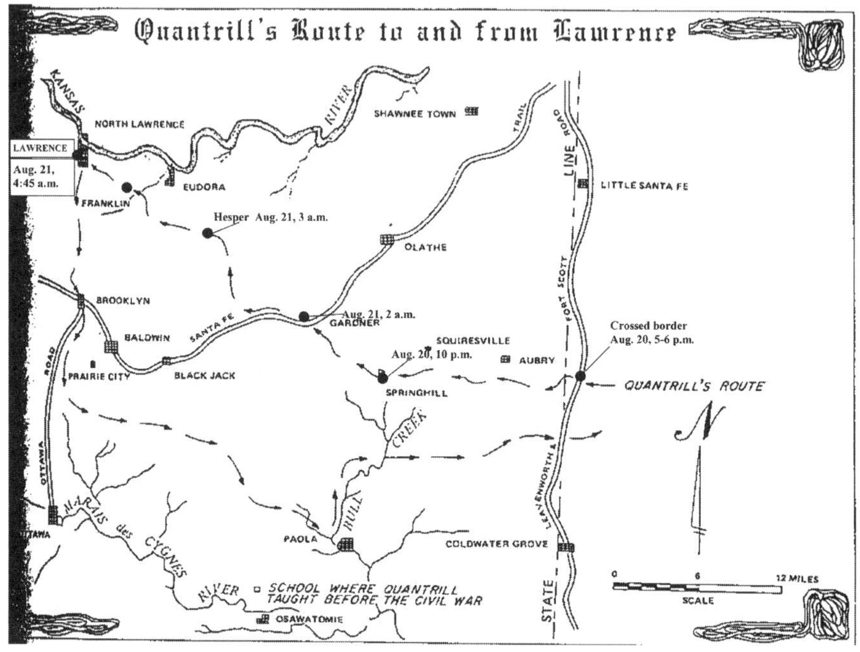

Map of Quantrill's Route to and from Lawrence. (William E. Connelley, *Quantrill and the Border Wars,* Cedar Rapids, IA: Torch Press, 1909, 1978.)

Time Line—1863 Lawrence Raid

August 13—A female prison collapses in Kansas City, Missouri. Five women relatives of Quantrill's men are murdered when the building in which they are confined is undermined by Federal soldiers.

August 14—Quantrill sends scouts into Lawrence, Kansas, to spy out the town and orders his officers to gather their men together.

August 18—7 p.m. At sundown the guerrillas meet at the Perdee farm near Columbus in Johnson County, Missouri, and make camp. Bands of guerrillas keep arriving all evening. By nightfall most of the guerrillas have arrived.

August 19—4 a.m. After breakfast the spies return and brief Quantrill's officers.

August 19—5 a.m. Following the council of war Quantrill has his men saddle up and start for the Kansas line. It is daybreak when the guerrillas leave Perdee's.

August 19—4 p.m. It is sundown when the guerrillas ride past Walnut Grove in Johnson County, Missouri, on their way to Lawrence.

August 19—5 p.m. The guerrillas take supper at Marion Potter's farm in Lone Jack, Missouri. They stay at the Potter farm until dark.

August 19—8 p.m. The guerrillas begin their ride toward the Kansas border.

August 20—5 a.m. The guerrillas travel all night, reaching the headwaters of the middle fork of the Grand River in Cass County, Missouri, at 5 a.m. Confederate Colonel John Holt and 100 new recruits from Clay County, Missouri, join them along with 50 guerrillas from Cass and Bates Counties. Quantrill tells the rank and file about their intended target. The men rest in the heavy timber during the day. Late in the afternoon Quantrill gives the order to mount up.

August 20—6 p.m. The guerrillas cross the Kansas line. Quantrill leads his men four or five miles due west, where he strikes the road leading from Aubrey to Paola. This he crosses, and then strikes out on a northwestwardly course, toward Squiresville. The column travels in this direction for three to four miles. Two and one-half miles from Squiresville, Quantrill halts his column at dusk to rest and allow the horses to graze for one hour. The house of a Captain Sims is nearby.

August 20—9 p.m. The guerrillas ride past Spring Hill, Kansas.

August 20—11 p.m. Quantrill's scouts ride through Gardner. The houses of Captain Andrew Jennings and Private Joseph Stone are searched and wanted men are shot.

August 21—2 a.m. The guerrillas pass by Hesper, picking up the trail that runs between Olathe and Lawrence, three miles south of Eudora and fifteen miles from Lawrence.

August 21—4:45 a.m. The guerrillas enter Lawrence.

August 21—9:00 a.m. Guerrilla lookouts on Mr. Oread spot Union troops approaching.

August 21—10:00 a.m. Quantrill assembles his men and withdraws from Lawrence, heading back to the safety of Missouri.

QUANTRILL *at* LAWRENCE

1

Knee Deep in Blood

The art of war is simple enough. Find out where your enemy is. Get at him as soon as you can. Strike him as hard as you can, and keep moving.

—Ulysses S. Grant

Between the Washington and Blue Townships in Jackson County nine miles south of Independence, Missouri, a small band of mourners made their way to the Smith Cemetery, a small plot of ground just east of the abandoned farm of Jordon R. Lowe. Darkness had already settled in, and a slight rain was starting to fall. A Union picket nearby was sitting around a campfire, but no one made a move to inquire about the heavily armed men in the cortege moving ever so slowly down the dirt lane. The men were leading an ox-drawn wagon. Three small wooden caskets containing the bodies of three young girls were seen loaded in the back. Accompanying their caskets was a satchel of trinkets and dry goods the girls had earlier bought in Kansas City. There was at least a company of guerrillas escorting the pall. Also accompanying the group was a number of civilians, friends, relatives, and neighbors of the slain. Muffled cries could be heard coming from the wake following the wagon.

The group had been quickly assembled. On August 13, 1863, Federal soldiers retrieved the bodies of the young girls from the rubble of their former prison and placed them in rough-hewed coffins. Early the next day relatives of the young girls rode to Kansas City and retrieved their remains from the Union authorities. The girls were hastily buried in one mass grave, laid together side by side, with only wooden markers to note the date of their death. Two weeks earlier, the girls had been delivering a wagonload of produce in Kansas City and were returning home when they were arrested for "aiding and abetting enemy forces." The girls' husbands, brothers, and cousins all rode with Quantrill. Other girls were also imprisoned. Two of them were sisters of Jim Vaughn, who had been executed by Gen. James G. Blunt on May 29 in Kansas City. Vaughn's sisters had been imprisoned at Fort Leavenworth but brought to Kansas City and put with the rest of the women prisoners. Guerrilla Bill Anderson had just removed his sisters from Kansas where for a year they had lived at various places, stopping finally with the Mundy family on the Missouri side of the line near Little Santa Fe. The parents of the Mundy family were dead. One of their sons was in General Sterling Price's Southern army, and three daughters were at home: Susan Mundy Womacks, Martha Mundy, and Mrs. Lou Mundy Gray, whose husband was probably with the guerrillas. The Mundy girls and the three Anderson sisters were arrested as spies.

They were confined in a building that served as a jail. Later the building was undermined by soldiers of the Ninth Kansas Jayhawker Regiment who served as provost guards in town. "The first guard was a detail from the 12th Kansas Regiment and was strict with the women." Captain Frank Parker and Sergeant George M. Walker with Company C, Eleventh Kansas Jayhawker Regiment, were stationed in Kansas City and were given orders to have their men serve as the prison guards. Many of these soldiers were found to be from Lawrence, which later helped precipitate its destruction. In only a few days after the supporting structure of the prison was cut away by the soldiers, the building collapsed. Five girls were killed: a Mrs. Wilson, Josephine Anderson, Charity McCorkle Kerr, and sisters Susan Crawford Vandever and Armenia Crawford Selvey. The last three girls were carried back to the Smith Cemetery for burial. Fourteen-year-old Josephine Anderson was taken to the Union Cemetery, less than two miles from her place of death and only a short distance from where she had formerly been living with friends. Mrs. Wilson, mortally wounded in the jail collapse, died from her injuries a few days later and was laid to rest elsewhere.[1]

The guerrillas had made this sad trip before. The Ninth Kansas

General Thomas Ewing, commander of the District of the Border, was in charge of Jayhawkers who plundered freely in Missouri. A board of Federal officers met, acknowledging that Ewing and his subordinate officers were all guilty of a conspiracy to rob and murder innocent Missouri citizens. Ewing was eventually transferred to another military department in Southeast Missouri. (Greg Walter Collection)

Regiment was the same regiment that had suffered a disastrous defeat by Quantrill's men south of Kansas City on June 17, just weeks earlier. Three of Quantrill's men had been slain during the skirmish. Quantrill had ordered Captain George Todd to take seventy men and attack a Federal patrol south of Kansas City. Major Luin K. Thacher, stationed in Paola, Kansas, was ordered by General Thomas Ewing to move three companies of the Ninth Kansas Jayhawker Regiment to his headquarters in Kansas City. Ewing had just been appointed commander of the District of the Border consisting of the state of Kansas and the two western tiers of Missouri counties north of the thirty-eighth parallel and south of the Missouri River. There were already 3,000 troops in the District of the Border and another 3,000 in the Department of Kansas. There were Union soldiers stationed north of Kansas City in Parkville, Leavenworth, Weston, Iatan, Atchison, and St. Joseph, and at nearly every county seat in Northern Missouri, and in the border counties between Missouri and Kansas south to the Arkansas line.

Previously Ewing had recruited and organized the Eleventh Kansas Jayhawker Regiment that was presently serving in Kansas City and had been the prison guards for the murdered girls. Almost as soon as Thacher received the dispatch instructing him to transfer his companies from Paola to Kansas City, spies relayed the news to Quantrill's headquarters. Captain Henry Flesher would be leading

Major Luin K. Thacher lived in Lawrence and was an officer in the Ninth Kansas Jayhawker Regiment. During the summer of 1863 he was in charge of three companies stationed in Westport, Missouri, where his unit suffered a humiliating defeat by Quantrill's men. Thacher's soldiers were responsible for the murder of five young Southern girls, just days before the Lawrence raid. (Kansas State Historical Society)

Company A and a portion of Company K along the Westport to Kansas City road. Ewing had only recently placed Federal companies every twelve to fifteen miles apart from Kansas City to Mound City, Kansas. These outposts were to pass patrols from post to post at hourly intervals and report any guerrilla activity to Ewing's headquarters. Ewing assured Union sympathizers along the border that he would have a thousand soldiers constantly patrolling every road and path and would make the roads run red with the guerrillas' blood. He assured the nervous citizens that these strategically placed outposts would secure Kansas from guerrilla attacks.[2]

Captain Flesher's men came leisurely riding down the lane. It was late afternoon and the soldiers had been in the saddle since morning. They were hoping to avail themselves of a short respite at Westport before continuing to Kansas City. The guerrillas under Todd were waiting behind a stone wall covered in thick underbrush that lined the road. Being only four miles from their main garrison in Kansas City the blue-coated soldiers relaxed and unwisely let down their guard. Many had their heads drooped over their saddles. Some were laughing and talking with each other, not realizing the dangerous trap they were entering.

Others had their legs thrown over their horses' necks, trying to find a comfortable position in the hot summer sun.

Quantrill's men had been sitting in ambush for most of the day and were becoming restless from inactivity. Only the discipline they had learned from years of guerrilla warfare and the confidence they had in their leaders kept the guerrillas patiently waiting for their quarry. Most of the time the intelligence information they received proved accurate, and today was no exception as they soon saw a long line of Federal cavalry coming up the road. Guerrilla horses began pawing the ground in anticipation. At Todd's signal the men stood to horse, mounted, and awaited his final order. When the Federal column came abreast of the ambush site Todd hollered out a familiar order for all to hear, "Charge! Kill 'em boys! Kill 'em!" The guerrillas didn't need further orders. They knew instinctively what to do next. With pistols in both hands they charged the startled Federal column.

After quickly attempting to fire a volley at the charging horsemen the Federal soldiers looked to their officers to see whether to make a stand or make a run for it. But fear took control, and the thought of safety in the garrison in Kansas City seemed more alluring than continuing the struggle. As horses reared and screamed and the cries from wounded men filled the air each guerrilla continued to take calm and careful aim at the enemy. In the ensuing skirmish thirty-three Federals poured out their blood on the dusty road. The Federal report stated, "The guerrillas were finally repulsed, but with very serious loss to Capt. Flesher's command."[3]

It was a close hand-to-hand encounter. Fletcher Taylor and his best friend Daniel Boone Scholl made the charge together. Scholl was the first man to fall. In horror Taylor watched Boone's horse, a new one he had only recently acquired, become unmanageable in the fight and charge through the enemy line. A Federal soldier turned to fire as Boone rode past, the bullet striking him in the back exiting through his belt buckle. Fellow guerrilla Frank James saw Boone's predicament but was too late to help. James did manage to shoot the Federal who had killed his friend. Next, Alson Wyatt, bravely firing his pistols at the blue-coated targets in the midst of the struggle, was also struck down and mortally wounded.

As the remaining soldiers fled the battle the guerrillas gave chase.

A short distance beyond a Federal infantry regiment heard the noise of battle and watched in horror as their fleeing comrades stampeded past them chased by gaily-dressed horsemen. When the guerrillas saw the infantry unit they drew rein, trying to decide what to do next. Captain Ferdinand Scott raised himself in his stirrups. As he was watching his prey escape a Federal sniper took aim, the bullet striking Scott in the neck. Both Scholl and Scott died quickly. They were taken to the Smith Cemetery and hastily buried in their saddle blankets. Wyatt was placed on his horse and carried to a friend's house where he passed away the next morning.

Quantrill was saddened when his men returned and relayed the news. Even though the ambush had been successful it had been a costly one. He had lost three of his best fighters. Quantrill was heard to comment, "One of my men is worth fifty of the enemy."

As was his custom Quantrill as the leading spirit among the band spoke some comforting words to the families of the deceased, honoring them for the sacrifice they had made for the Cause. When Quantrill spoke about Ferdinand Scott he described him as being devoid of fear. "Under fire no soldier could be cooler; he won the love of his men first, later, their adoration."[4] Commenting about Boone Scholl, Fletcher Taylor said, "Boone was one of the most gallant soldiers we had and the day he was killed we rode together four of us in the front. The last word I heard him say as he fell out of ranks [was] 'I am done for.'" His cousin Boone Muir and Dick Berry carried him from the field.[5] Boone was described as six feet, three inches tall. Author John Newman Edwards said that Boone was "destined to give up a dauntless young life early for the cause he loved best, won the respect of all by a generosity unstained of selfishness and the exercise of a courage that in either extreme of victory or disaster remained perfect in attribute and exhibition. None were more gentle than he; none more courteous, calm and kindly. When he fell, liberty never required upon its altar as a sacrifice a purer victim."[6] In honor of Boone's sacrifice Quantrill took one of his pistols, engraved it with his name, and presented it to the grieving Scholl family.

A Guerrilla Council of War

Now one month later the guerrillas were standing once again beside

This is a war-dated photo of guerrilla George T. Scholl who lost a brother, Daniel Boone Scholl, in a skirmish just a few weeks prior to the Lawrence raid. George T. Scholl rode with Quantrill in every operation up to the time Quantrill departed for Kentucky. (Patrick Marquis Collection)

the graves of their loved ones. But this time it was not to pay respect to a comrade lost in battle nor for a man who had braved bullets defending his home and family against cruel Jayhawker attacks. This time it was for innocent girls cut down in the bloom of life; arrested then murdered by Federal guards who were detailed to protect them, serving a government that had stooped to the lowest depths of depravity and brutality. This was the result of the Federal authorities who had recently stepped up their efforts and were now waging war against women.

Each one of Quantrill's men knew what was expected of him when he became a guerrilla fighter. They all knew that the brutality they had experienced from the Kansas Jayhawkers was intolerable to a free people and was the main cause for their joining the guerrillas. But now things had changed. Since before the war they had been fighting against Kansas Jayhawkers in an effort to protect their homes and families. Now in return their female relatives had been struck down in the most horrible manner imaginable. No longer would there be a merciful answer to the enemy's call for quarter. Guerrilla John McCorkle lost one sister killed and a sister-in-law seriously injured in the jail collapse. Three sisters of William Anderson were imprisoned, one sister was killed, one sister was crippled for life, and another would suffer terribly from her wounds to her dying day.

Guerrilla Nathan Kerr's wife Charity was killed. Brothers William, Marshall, Marion, and Riley Crawford lost two sisters killed. Guerrilla Thomas Harris's sister Nannie was mangled in the jail collapse. Guerrilla James E. Mundy's sisters Susan and Martha, and his married sister Mrs. Lou Mundy Gray, were imprisoned along with William Grindstaff's sister Mollie, but somehow each of them miraculously survived. The Federals arrested Susan Vandever because her husband and brother-in-law rode with Quantrill and because her husband was responsible for having personally killed a Captain Sessions during a skirmish in Richfield, Missouri, on May 19, 1863. As a result, guerrilla Thomas Vandever lost his wife in the jail collapse and his brother Louis lost a sister-in-law. The murdered girls and those who were injured were kin to many others of those riding with Quantrill. Thomas J. Hall was on Quantrill's July 6, 1862, roster. His sister was arrested along with the other Southern girls, but she survived the jail collapse.

Cousins John McCorkle, Thomas Harris, and George Wigginton stood with the rest of the mourners consoling each other. Standing with his head bowed McCorkle glanced up and saw the still fresh grave of his brother nearby. John had been on patrol with his brother Jabez several weeks earlier in the Blue Hills when Jabez' rifle accidentally fell from his saddle, going off and striking him in the knee. He lingered in pain for several days before finally succumbing to his wound on June 2, 1863. Now McCorkle was mourning his dear young sister who had been foully murdered after being arrested and held by Union authorities. As he pondered on the Federal atrocity McCorkle told those around him that he could stand no more.

The guerrillas were blind with rage. Many wanted to ride out on their own and strike the first Federal force they encountered. Only the mastery of Quantrill's leadership held the men together. Their lives meant nothing to them if they were not allowed to avenge their loved ones. With a calming voice Quantrill made them aware that he had been making plans for quite some time for a military operation that would bring the Federal authorities to their knees. He would need each man to keep a cool head and trust in his leadership. Quantrill's men knew "he kept his own counsel until the last moment, and even then he had but few confidants." One who was present stated, "Quantrill's raid on Lawrence was consummated in retaliation for the inhuman treatment of Southerners in Missouri by Kansas Jayhawkers. No Confederate, whether of Quantrill's command or not, ever fell in the hands of Kansans in any of the border counties of Missouri and came out alive."[7]

As the funeral service came to an end Quantrill instructed his adjutant to pass the word to every guerrilla and every Southern man old enough to carry a gun to meet at Captain James Perdee's farm on the banks of the Blackwater River in Johnson County, Missouri, forty miles southeast of Independence and sixty miles from the Kansas line. Everyone knew when Quantrill gave an order it would be immediately obeyed. Quantrill's adjutant Lieutenant William Gregg reported, "The men were scattered over three Missouri counties, the bulk of them being in Jackson. Captains of various companies were

The Perdee campsite is the place where Quantrill's three hundred guerrillas camped prior to the Lawrence raid. Here Quantrill formulated his plans and put together the "Death Lists" and the list of "Buildings to Be Destroyed." (Author's Collection)

called together and ordered to concentrate their forces."[8] They were instructed to bring their best equipment, all the guns and ammunition they could gather, and a good horse freshly shod. They were also to bring a three-day supply of rations. Quantrill's own company immediately rode to the Cummins' settlement, twenty-four miles southeast of Independence. The night of the rendezvous was dark and stormy as the guerrillas continued on to Captain Perdee's where all the men finally came together.

The next day Quantrill called a council of war with his officers. It was decided that he would send a letter to General Thomas Ewing in Kansas City, demanding that Ewing release the women who had escaped death in the prison collapse instead of sending them to the Gratiot Street Prison in St. Louis as Ewing had originally intended. Quantrill said that if his request was not immediately complied with, he and not the Yankees would be responsible for the consequences. Quantrill pressed a local citizen to bear the note to Ewing. It was said that when the officer to whom the note was addressed read it, he "threw it on the floor and rubbing it under his foot bade the bearer to go and tell Quantrell and his outlaws to go to Hades and do their worst."[9]

Guerrillas who had not been at the funeral began gathering the very next morning from orders they had received from those who had attended the funeral. Some came riding in by twos or in small groups of up to ten. They made their way into the dense woods surrounding the Blackwater River coursing its way past the nine-hundred-acre farm of Captain Perdee. The Reverend Theodore M. Cobb remarked that Quantrill's men "were all young and from the best families in the State, they were intelligent, fearless, and desperate. They had seen their homes burned, their families turned out doors and many of their kindred and friends murdered in cold blood."[10]

When the guerrillas of Johnson County, Missouri, gathered at Perdee's it was with a feeling of a just retaliation. Their county seat of Columbus and fifty homes had been completely destroyed by Captain Clark S. Merriman of the Seventh Kansas Jayhawker Regiment on January 9, 1862. The same sense of anger and resentment could be felt by the fifty guerrillas from Cass County who joined Quantrill along the banks of the Grand River bottoms before crossing the

James Morgan Walker was a wealthy Missouri farmer from Blue Springs, Jackson County, Missouri. Before the war, Kansas Jayhawkers raided his farm intent on plundering his thoroughbred horses, mules, money, and slaves. Quantrill foiled their plan, marking him as an enemy and putting a price on his head. Walker's home was later burned to the ground and all his property taken back into Kansas. This is the only photo of Morgan Walker known to exist. (Anne Jacobberger Collection)

state line into Kansas. Cass County before the war enjoyed a population of more than 10,000 people. By the start of the Lawrence raid there were only 600 surviving citizens.

As the guerrillas arrived they picked out a good campsite and built a fire in which to cook their meals. The Blackwater River provided water and a nearby gristmill provided both food and feed for the men and their horses. Quantrill was already there, and the guerrillas who began arriving observed him busily making plans and consulting with his subordinate leaders. The officers were quartered in tents, while the men slept on the ground. The campsite was a good one, surrounded by deep woods and an ample supply of water. Quantrill instructed some of the first men who arrived to ride to the Morgan Walker farm in Blue Springs and bring back several barrels of gunpowder he had hidden in a small cave in Walker's woods. The gunpowder had been placed there and kept ever since the guerrillas captured it during the August 11, 1862, victory over Lieutenant Colonel James T. Buel's forces at Independence. Now Quantrill had need of it. Anticipating that he needed more than just powder, Quantrill sent Andrew Jack Liddil into Independence in disguise to purchase more than two hundred big Colt revolvers, and a quantity of pistol ammunition and a large quantity of percussion caps from R. L. Fraser, an army sutler who kept everything that soldiers needed.[11]

Word of the atrocity in Kansas City had spread quickly. Every citizen within miles had already heard about the guerrillas' female relatives being murdered by Union troops. The Federals had never achieved a victory over the guerrillas. The arrest and confinement of the guerrillas' female relatives had come about because of the Union's failure to root out and destroy the guerrillas from along the border. Since organizing his first band of guerrilla fighters Quantrill and his men had proved to be as elusive as phantoms, disappearing into the timber whenever a Union patrol caught sight of them. Oftentimes the guerrillas would fire a volley and withdraw down narrow bridle paths before the Federal soldiers could consolidate their forces and pursue. If they were followed the guerrillas would divide their forces, forcing the Federals to do the same. As if by some prearranged signal the guerrillas would come together, circle around their pursuers, and strike their rear guard when least expected. All the Federals had time to hear was a wild Rebel yell and catch a glimpse of charging horsemen bearing down on them at top speed, pistols blazing from both hands. Without time to form line the soldiers usually sought self-preservation by spurring their horses into a full retreat back to the safety of their garrison. Few made it back. For those who stood to fight the end came quickly. Some of those who chose flight managed to make a mile or two before they were run down and shot from their saddles. Surrender was not an option.

When the guerillas returned with the barrels of gunpowder they made themselves busy preparing as much ammunition as each man could carry. Quantrill also made himself bullets with a bullet mold made for him by a local blacksmith from Oak Grove and given to him in 1861. The mold made six .44-caliber bullets at a time.[12]

Quantrill's Officers

Quantrill's main company, including the company of Captain George Todd who had just participated in the Westport skirmish, were the first to arrive in camp. By the evening of August 18, most of the men had arrived. Lieutenant Gregg remarked, "The command consisted of five companies under Captains Blunt, Pool, Jarrette, Todd and Anderson, with some other small contingents, amounting to 294 men."[13]

Captain George A. Todd. At the beginning of the war, Todd's father was put in prison for refusing to help build Federal fortifications. Todd had joined General Sterling Price, and when his enlistment was over he came home and was thrown in jail. When he was released, he joined Quantrill, becoming his second-in-command. (Emory Cantey Collection)

Others filtered in during the night. Also present were Colonels John D. Holt from Vernon County and Boaz Roberts from Barry County, recruiting officers from the regular army who joined in with a handful of men, along with other guerrilla leaders George Shepherd and Richard Maddox. Before this time Quantrill still enjoyed a reputation of renown. Author George Miller said, "Quantrill's peculiar methods of warfare, enabled him with fifty to one hundred men, to keep two or three thousand men on the special duty of watching for him; and even then he usually turned up where he was not expected."[14]

The officers who led the guerrillas were personally familiar with the Jayhawkers' atrocities. Captain George Todd was an early guerrilla recruit. George along with his father and brother were educated in the profession of civil engineering and bridge building. They were from Scotland and had come to Kansas City by way of St. Louis from Canada in 1859. The family consisted of five persons; the father, the mother, one daughter, and two sons, Tom and George, the latter being the youngest of the family. The father and Tom were practical stonemasons and worked at the trade while George, then about eighteen years of age, and of small stature, about 5 feet 8 inches, was a helper. He had blue eyes, auburn hair, and fair complexion. At the beginning of the war the Todds were building bridges and structures around Kansas City. When the war started the Federals asked George's father to help the army build fortifications along the border. When he refused he was thrown in prison and put on a diet of bread and water. The cold and dampness of the prison disabled the elder Todd, and he became unable to care for himself. Neighbors had to come to his cell and help feed him.

George had already joined Colonel William M. Roper's regiment in the Missouri State Guards, fighting at Carthage, Wilson's Creek, and Lexington in 1861 as an artilleryman, but when he returned home he was thrown into jail. After his release and seeing the treatment his father was given by the Federals he joined Quantrill in January 1862, eventually becoming Quantrill's second-in-command. It was this incarceration and that of his father that turned him against Union authority. An acquaintance remarked that he possessed a large amount of personal courage due to his early association in Price's army. It was said that he bore the mark of nine different wounds on his body. Todd wore a rich Federal coat, pants, top-boots, and cap, admirably set off by a belt containing a pair of elegant six-shooters. Those who personally knew him said, "He makes the best fighting captain in the whole command. He is chivalrous but not rash; prudent but daring, and always successful both in attack and strategy." Guerrilla Jim Cummins described Todd. "My beau ideal of a man was George Todd, who always seemed to me to be a great general."[15]

Lieutenant William H. Gregg was twenty-two when he joined Quantrill and had a reputation among the guerrillas for his skill in throwing a Bowie knife. He was known for the ability to open up a "Fed" at twenty paces with this weapon as a projectile.[16] Gregg was born near Stony Point in Jackson County between the upper reaches of the Sni-a-Bar Creek and the Little Blue River. He found that it was Colonel Charles Ransford Jennison, the leader of the Jayhawkers, who had shot his uncle, David Gregg, for being a Southern sympathizer. Gregg's own mother was also abused by Jayhawkers. She wore her watch and other jewelry concealed in the bodice of her clothing, but the Jayhawkers finally discovered the watch chain about her neck. They tore her dress open, robbed her, almost choking her to death in

Colonel Charles Jennison. Even before the war, Jennison murdered men who expressed sympathy for slavery. He personally killed several family members of Quantrill's men besides plundering throughout Missouri. In his own words, Jennison said he had "grown stoop-shouldered carrying plunder out of Missouri in the name of liberty." (Rick Mack Collection)

trying to release the chain. Written accounts state: "In January, 1862, seventeen of Jennison's Kansans had been at the senior Gregg's house, and had cruelly hanged and almost choked to death the inmates, and also poured out two casks of wine. Gregg was coming home that night. He had four men, only one of them armed. The seventeen men fought Gregg, captured two of the unarmed, and shot them after surrender. Gregg and the one man drove them back and saw the two men shot. The day after the two men were killed Gregg saw fourteen houses burned at one time."[17]

Gregg also found that the father of his fiancée Miss Elizabeth Hook had been jailed. In addition, the Federals who jailed him stole every one of the family's horses, slaughtered every pig they owned, and seized the family's slaves, money, jewelry, and even their bedclothes. After learning about this incident, Gregg immediately sought out Quantrill and joined his command. Elizabeth Hook later recalled:

> Everybody was happy and prosperous. . . . but it was not until 1862 that the horrors of war were realized. I had never known a sorrow or a care until one day a company of Federal soldiers came to our home with wagons in which they loaded the negroes and their belongings;

> the negro men were mounted on my father's horses and forced to ride them away. Colonel Jennison came down from Kansas, robbed, murdered, and burned everything in his way. Mother had spun and woven five pairs of blankets; had only recently before had them scoured, and these Redlegs took every one of them, placing them under their saddles.

During the summer of 1863 Jayhawkers again visited her neighborhood. "Our homes were ransacked and jewelry, money, in fact, everything they could carry away was taken."[18] Kansan William G. Cutler, who later wrote *The History of Kansas* in 1883, readily admitted, "The proslavery men suffered heavily; indeed, many of them were completely impoverished by the oft-repeated visits of their hungry, and rapacious neighbors."

The summer of 1863 saw the enemy more savage if possible than ever before. Jayhawkers killed numerous old men and boys. Lieutenant Gregg said, "There could have been no better argument for the people to flock to Quantrill than the dastardly acts of the enemy." Gregg told anyone who would listen the sobering facts about why the raid on Lawrence was being made.

> Jennison, Lane, Burris, and many other marauding bands under leaders of lesser border fame had visited various Missouri border counties, and never left the state without murdering, plundering and devastating the homes of a greater or less number of our citizens, and to kill, it was only necessary to know that a man sympathized with the south, but as to robbing, they robbed everybody without distinction, and they often laid waste whole districts. I counted thirteen houses burning at one time on the 28th day of January, 1862. This burning was done by Jennison's men, although government officials said Jennison was not a U. S. officer and had no authority, yet he carried the U. S. flag and was often assisted in his forays by troops stationed at Independence and other stations in Jackson and adjoining counties. These parties until early in sixty three did not haul away much household plunder, contenting themselves with such as blankets, quilts[,] wearing apparel[,] and jewelry. Such articles as they could carry on their horses, but they usually went back to Kansas well loaded with such articles as I have mentioned.

One Kansas lieutenant admitted, "Kansas was filled with horse and 'nigger' thieves."[19]

Like many others, Gregg initially joined Price's army and returned home when his enlistment expired. In 1862 when Quantrill headed to Richmond, Virginia, seeking a colonel's commission of partisan rangers, Gregg was put in charge of Quantrill's company and led the guerrillas during the battle of Prairie Grove, Arkansas. In the initial cavalry battle, just before dawn, Quantrill's guerrillas led a furious charge upon a 1,200-man column of Federal cavalry. Within thirty minutes the Federals were routed from the field, losing twenty-three wagons, three standards, including the regimental flag of the Seventh Missouri Cavalry, and 218 men captured from four different Federal cavalry regiments. Of the standards captured, all were taken by Quantrill's command. For his part, Lieutenant Gregg was recognized in General Joseph Shelby's official report for the manner in which he led his men. Gregg later recounted being in sixty-five battles and skirmishes during the war.[20]

Gregg's younger brother, Jacob Franklin Gregg, also joined Quantrill's company. It was said of him, "He shot equally well with each hand." After he and his father were released from prison because his brother was riding with Quantrill, seventeen-year-old Jacob joined Price in the Missouri State Guard. Returning to Missouri after his enlistment was over, he went to Clay County in April 1862 and met Frank James, joining John Jarrette's company, then rode with George Todd, where he was currently preparing for the Lawrence raid. Jacob became a lieutenant like his brother, and it was said of him that he was "true to his friends and implacable to his enemies." During one skirmish in Jackson County he and several other guerrillas were surrounded by Federals at the home of Richard White. When the Federals commanded them to surrender, Jacob answered, "Never," in a voice that might have been heard a mile, "Never, while there is a leg to stand on or a bullet to kill. Look out, for we are coming." Saying this, the five guerrillas shot their way out of the house and to safety.[21] William Gregg's brother-in-law, James A. Hendricks, served under him as a lieutenant. In 1860 Hendricks was listed as a merchant owning a store near Stony Point in Jackson County. While he was living there, Jayhawkers came through and pillaged his store of all its wares. He joined Quantrill in December 1861, becoming one of his earliest members.

Lieutenant James L. Bledsoe rode in with a number of Confederate soldiers recently returned from Price's army. Bledsoe had fought

James Anderson was a lieutenant in Quantrill's band of guerrillas. Jim and his brother Bill joined Quantrill after Federals hanged their father and uncle on March 12, 1862, in retaliation for Quantrill's raid on Aubry, Kansas, five days earlier on March 7, 1862. One year later Federals murdered Jim and Bill's fourteen-year-old sister Josephine and threw their other two sisters in prison. (Emory Cantey Collection)

alongside Quantrill's men at the battles of Cane Hill and Prairie Grove in Arkansas. Many guerrillas fought in the regular Confederate army but joined Quantrill's force for safety when returning home on furlough or on sick leave. Bledsoe was an officer in Shelby's Fifth Cavalry Regiment. His brother, Colonel Hiram M. Bledsoe, was Price's chief of artillery. Other officers also began arriving. Captain William Anderson rode in with about thirty to forty men. Jim Cummins said that Anderson was the most "desperate man I ever knew." Anderson was described as "nearly six feet tall, of rather swarthy complexion and had long, black hair, inclined to curl. He wore a big black hat with a plume in it. [His] shirt was black, with open breast and gold braid bordering it. He carried two revolvers in his belt and two on his saddle."[22]

An unusual event made a guerrilla out of William Anderson. He had been living in Kansas at the start of the war, selling forage to the government at Fort Leavenworth. Following Quantrill's March 7, 1862, raid on Aubry, Kansas, a Federal patrol rode to the home of the Andersons a few days later, knowing them to be Southern sympathizers. The soldiers wound up hanging William's father and uncle. By March 12, Bill and his brother Jim were both riding with Quantrill. All he had left was a brother and two sisters who had miraculously survived the jail collapse. His sister Martha's legs were horribly crushed and crippled

The William Anderson Family. Inscribed inside the photo case is the phrase "William Anderson family, Council Grove, T. K."(Territory of Kansas). Standing, left to right: Josephine, Jim, Mary, Charlie (baby), Bill, and Martha. Seated, left to right: Tom Anderson (Jim and Bill's first cousin and son of William's brother Thomas who lived in Council Grove as well. This boy went with the children to Missouri and was the one who ran and notified the guerrillas when the Anderson girls were arrested), William (father), and Martha (mother). The image is dated 1859-1860, just prior to the mother's death. It is the only image of the Anderson family extant. (Emory Cantey Collection)

for life, and Molly suffered serious back injuries and facial lacerations. Martha was only ten years old, while Mollie was sixteen at the time of the collapse. Both girls would carry their battered bodies and emotional scars for years to come. When asked why he joined Quantrill, Anderson replied, "I have chosen guerrilla warfare to revenge myself for wrongs that I could not honorably revenge otherwise. I lived in Kansas when this war commenced. Because I would not fight the people of Missouri, my native State, the Yankees sought my life, but failed to get me. [They] revenged themselves by murdering my father, [and] destroying all my property."[23] The Federals would soon regret their wanton actions against the Anderson family. Together with his brother James, William Anderson would cut a devastating path of death and destruction through Missouri, striking any and all Union soldiers and Federal outposts they could find.

Captain Fletcher Taylor was sent into Lawrence to spy out the city prior to the raid. After returning and reporting to Quantrill, Taylor was given the honor of leading the column on the expedition. (Emory Cantey Collection)

First Lieutenant Archie Clement was Bill Anderson's second-in-command and was said to be the brains behind the outfit. A Federal militiaman by the name of Harkness killed his youngest brother and burned down the home of his mother. Archie then rode off to fight with Quantrill. At age seventeen Archie became a lieutenant in Anderson's company. Archie originally hailed from Kingsville in Johnson County, Missouri. He was small of stature, blond with gray eyes, and sported a perpetual smile. Lieutenant Fletcher Taylor was also in Anderson's company and was the only officer who did not ride in with the rest to prepare for the raid on Lawrence. He had been given a special mission by Quantrill and had not yet returned. Taylor was described by his fellow guerrilla Jim Cummins who said, "Fletcher Taylor was one of the smartest of them all and it was he who piloted the way into Lawrence."[24] When Taylor returned from his mission, he was assisted by another scout, John M. "Doc" Campbell, who helped him lead the way into Lawrence.

Captain John Jarrette joined Quantrill early in 1862. Jarrette was born in Nelson County, Kentucky, and was living with a Charles Dawson in the 1850 census. By 1860 Jarrette was living in the Big Cedar Township in Jackson County, Missouri. He married Josephine Younger on May 8, 1860. He soon enlisted his brother-in-law Coleman Younger in his company because, as Jarrette told his brother-in-law, "Cole, your mother and your sister told me to take care of you." Jim Cummins said that Quantrill had utter confidence in Jarrette, and when extra work was to be done Jarrette was called on to take the lead.[25]

Besides being blood relations, many of the guerrillas were related by marriage. Captain Richard Yeager married Martha J. Muir, sister of Boone Muir, just before the war started. Yeager came from a prominent and wealthy family; his father was the presiding judge of the Jackson County Court and operated a freighting business. While returning from a freighting expedition on one of his father's wagon trains, Yeager found that Jennison and his Jayhawkers had pillaged his father's farm and stripped it of everything they could carry off. Afterward Captain James W. Christian, James Lane's business partner, held a public auction on his farm one mile northwest of Lawrence. He received $9,000 for 200 head of horses and mules, 300 cattle, and 400 sheep. The livestock was all "confiscated" from Missouri farms.[26] Yeager rode off to join Quantrill. His father was arrested and thrown into prison in St. Louis. Federals also arrested Yeager's wife and her parents' family with the understanding that they would be sent to Fort Leavenworth. Also in Yeager's company were brothers Dan and William Vaughn, with Dan serving as a first lieutenant. Their brother Jim had been recently executed in Kansas City.

In a few days Lieutenant Andy Blunt rode in with about one hundred men. Blunt joined Quantrill in April of 1862. His first battle as a guerrilla was against Captain Albert P. Peabody's forces at the Samuel C. Clark farm where he fought a hand-to-hand duel with a Federal cavalryman. A few days later he was wounded at the Lowe house fight where he was captured along with Joseph Gilchrist. After Lowe and Gilchrist were taken prisoners, the Federals lined the two guerrillas up and shot them. In the volley Gilchrist was killed and Blunt received a broken arm. Instead of finishing him off, the Federals carried him back to Independence where Dr. P. H. Henry, a Southern doctor, nursed him back to health then helped him to escape. Later Blunt participated in every skirmish and battle in which the guerrillas were involved, always in the forefront of the assault. Many of the men believed him a better shot than Quantrill. It was said of him that no one knew his history. He asked no questions, and he answered none. Some guerrillas found it offensive to have to shoot Yankee prisoners when given the order by Quantrill. Some only felt justified in taking

Dave Poole. Quantrill's company had grown to such proportions by 1863 that he divided his command under able leaders such as Captain Francis Marion "Dave" Poole. Jayhawkers had murdered Poole's uncle, plundered his property, then burned down his home and murdered his brother-in-law. (Emory Cantey Collection)

a life in open battle, but not Blunt. Blunt and his family had been so victimized by the Jayhawkers and their attacks that he took whatever opportunity he could find to seek revenge.[27] During the winter of 1862 Blunt accompanied Quantrill to Richmond where Quantrill sought a commission to operate along the border as a colonel of partisan rangers.

Another of Quantrill's officers, Captain Dave Poole and his brother John, joined after Jayhawkers killed their uncle Archibald Poole, plundered his property, then burned down his home and murdered their brother-in-law. Poole's full name was Francis Marion Poole. His parents were from South Carolina. One of Poole's best friends remarked of him, "He was one of the bravest men I have ever known. As a soldier he was as dashing as Murat, and the wilder the charge and the more desperate the odds the better it pleased him. He had many splendid qualities, and was as honest as he was brave."[28]

Captain George W. Shepherd and his brothers Frank and Oliver lived in Big Cedar Township in the Valley of the Little Blue, eight miles south of Independence, Missouri, when the war started. They were kin to James Pendleton Shepherd, Jr., who founded Independence and whose Negro slaves constructed the first courthouse. Like many other families they were set upon indiscriminately by Kansas Jayhawkers and robbed of all their possessions. George was twenty-one when he rode in to take part in the Lawrence raid. He had been with Sterling Price at the battles of Wilson's Creek, Prairie Grove, and Pea Ridge and later with Quantrill when he routed Union forces at the battle of Independence on August 11, 1862, and so joined Quantrill as an experienced officer. The brothers were all riding with Quantrill when he returned from Texas in the spring of 1863. They joined to avenge the murder of old men and young boys by Federals in Jackson County and were riding beside Quantrill when he was wounded in a skirmish near their home south of Independence.

Captain Richard P. Maddox and his brothers George, William, and Tom came from a well-to-do family. Their father Larkin owned two to three thousand acres of the best farmland in Jackson County, some two hundred to three hundred head of fine mules and horses, and about sixty Negroes. The elder Maddox took an active part in the hostilities before the war, which made him especially hated by the Kansans when the war started.

> Hence, when the rebellion broke out and the Kansas troops under Jennison and Lane marched into Missouri in 1861, old Maddox and his sons were early victims of their hatred and revenge. The "red-legs" made a descent upon the Maddox "ranch", carried off their mules, horses and other stock, burned their houses, barns, Negro quarters, cribs and out-houses of all descriptions and took away with them all the Negroes on the place. They would doubtless have exterminated the last Maddox on the face of the earth if they could have laid hands on them, but the sons fled to the brush and the old man found it convenient for him to make a certain visit to the "loyal" state of Kentucky. It is said that George Maddox joined Quantrill at Blue Springs in June of 1861 and fought with him in every fight until Quantrill left the State. George carried on his body the scars of thirteen wounds received while fighting under Quantrill. The elder Maddox ventured back to Missouri before the close of the war but was speedily nabbed and lodged in the Independence jail where he languished many months among the bushwhackers and lice.

Colonel John D. Holt, a Southern recruiting officer under orders of General Price, was camped with Quantrill and under his protection. Holt had been a regular officer in Elliott's Ninth Missouri Cavalry but had been ordered into Clay County, north of the Missouri River, to recruit. Quantrill had suggested to Holt that he continue on to Clay County to pick up his new recruits then meet him at a prearranged time and place along the Missouri border where they would join forces for the raid. Holt could use his recruits to bolster Quantrill's forces and to serve as lookouts and guards to cordon off the town once they arrived. Holt had his own reasons for seeking revenge on the Jayhawkers. Thirty days after being organized in Kansas City the Eleventh Kansas Cavalry ventured south and burned Nevada City in Vernon County on May 26, 1863. Captain Anderson Morton in command gave the citizens twenty minutes to vacate their homes and property. Holt owned a large hardware store in Vernon County, which was put to the torch and his home plundered and his family insulted. Historians have admitted, "Every raid meant a robbery and plundering, maybe a house-burning and a murder. The booty obtained was held to be property acquired and when these pirates of the prairies returned to their homes after a successful foray, they were greeted with joyful acclaim."[29]

Jayhawker Rampage

There has never been an estimate of the total number of innocent Missouri citizens killed, but community after community reported losses by the score. Throughout Missouri and Northern Arkansas, chimneys marking the sites of destroyed homes were called "Jennison's Monuments."[30] One Jayhawker in particular, Peter Jackson Bryant of Kansas, boasted of his illegal exploits. "In July our Captain raised a company and went into the army, and I mustered about 50 men and went into Missouri. All the difference between us [was] he jayhawked under cover of Uncle Sam and I under a lieutenancy from Governor Robinson. I marched when I damned pleased; he, when he was told to. I kept my plunder if I chose; he didn't. I took my pay as I went along; he, when he could get it. I have disbanded my squad; he has got to stick until war is over."

One guerrilla officer noticeably missing was Captain John Thrailkill. Thrailkill was originally from Holt County in Northwest Missouri. He could empathize with his fellow comrades who had

Captain John Thrailkill. At the start of the war, Federals invaded the home of Thrailkill's fiancée and killed her invalid father. As a result of this brutal assault, she went insane and died shortly afterward. To avenge her death, Thrailkill made a vow of revenge and joined Quantrill, but he was not part of the raid on Lawrence, Kansas. (Emory Cantey Collection)

just lost their sisters and wives in the jail collapse. At the start of the war twenty Federal militiamen invaded the home of his fiancée and killed her invalid father. As a result of this brutal assault, she went insane and died shortly afterward. To avenge her, Thrailkill joined Quantrill, but not before making a solemn vow at his sweetheart's grave: "Blood for blood; every hair in her head shall have a sacrifice." Thrailkill eventually killed eighteen of the twenty men who caused his fiancée's death but there were more of his enemies to be found in Lawrence. If it wasn't for the fact that he had recently been captured on July 19 and placed in prison Thrailkill would have undoubtedly been on the raid.[31]

William Gregg remembered that prior to the raid "the enemy had been more savage if possible than ever before. They had killed numerous old men and boys." Besides the remembrances of a large number of citizens killed during the summer of 1863 there were also the vivid memories and recollections of dozens of communities plundered in Western Missouri, many of them being wiped out of existence by the Jayhawkers from Kansas. Not only that, but Jayhawkers also destroyed entire families, killing every male in the household and completely destroying family lines forever. After Fort Sumter in South Carolina was fired upon by the Confederates in April 1861, beginning the Civil War, many Union men began to move out of Missouri. Many of them enlisted in Kansas regiments and returned as Union soldiers, leading Jayhawker attacks on their former neighborhoods.

While in Missouri on a Jayhawker expedition John A. Martin of the Eighth Kansas Regiment recruited in Lawrence wrote to his sister.

> The country around is a desolation; the ravages of war have laid waste the fields, and ruins mark the spot where once stood costly houses. I have seen since coming down here, the effects of civil war terribly portrayed. West Point [Missouri] was once a thriving town, with large stores, elegant private dwellings, and a fine large hotel. Now soldiers are quartered in the dwellings and horses occupy the storerooms. The hotel was burned down three days ago. The houses are all torn to pieces, plastering off, mantles used to build fires, and doors unhinged. I presume the place will be burned as soon as the troops leave. All around . . . the same scenes of ruin and devastation greet the eye. Large farms, with crops ungathered, barns and stables falling to pieces, houses deserted, fences torn down, and stock running loose and uncared for. From West Point to Jonesville I saw not a house occupied and I have been all over the country about here without meeting with a half dozen habited dwellings.[32]

The chief of all Jayhawkers, as everyone knew, was Charles Ransford Jennison. Born in New York, Jennison migrated westward, settling first at Osawatomie and then in Mound City, Kansas. Many abolitionist emigrants came to Kansas from New York though the state had known its share of slavery atrocities. Before the war one of every five New York families owned slaves. Slave traders were well known to the city's business community; some ranked among the city's most prominent members. More slave trade expeditions were organized and financed in the city than in any other place in the world. John Speer, a newspaperman from Lawrence, remembered Jennison as "a roisterer, a reckless, drinking man, and a gambler." Upon arriving in Kansas, Jennison immediately threw in his lot with the notorious John Brown. After first accompanying Brown on raids into Missouri before the war, he began conducting his own attacks on proslavery settlers on both sides of the border.

All too often, indiscriminate plundering characterized these attacks, as was the case when Jennison attacked Independence,

Missouri, in the fall of 1861. Independence provoked Jennison's enmity because the town was the first in the state to raise the Confederate flag. On the day it was raised a large group gathered. A cannon signaled the moment that the flag reached the top of the staff, and afterward a large celebration was held. For this seemingly innocent act of patriotism Jennison crossed the border with his Jayhawkers and pillaged the town. Jennison said of the citizens, "They shall be treated as traitors, and slain wherever found; their property shall be confiscated and their homes burned, and in no case will any be spared either in person or property."[33]

Something of a glamour surrounded Jennison in those days; he had been conspicuous as a leader in the early days of border troubles, and his Jayhawkers had inflicted damage on the proslavery sympathizers that ranged all the way from blood to loot; indeed, he carried the latter to such an extent that the pedigree of most Kansas horses, it was said, should have been recorded as "out of Missouri by Jennison."[34]

Lieutenant Colonel Basel F. Lazear, a Federal officer serving in Missouri, wrote to his wife, describing the conditions around Independence following several of Jennison's raids, saying that it was "one of the prettiest towns I ever saw and this is the finest country up here I have ever seen in Missouri but it is a waste now but few people living here and full one third of the houses burnt and I would not be surprised if by fall they would not all be burnt and the country entirely desolated."[35]

A year later Jayhawkers were still pillaging the town. Jacob Hall recounted what his family experienced from Jayhawkers while he was away on a trip to Washington, DC. They "cursed the whole family. Proceeded to take the two mules, all the oats, all the hay, 35 or 40 tons, all the old corn about 1,000 bushels, all the peaches, apples, grapes, sweet and Irish potatoes, cabbage and all the other vegetables in the garden." Mrs. Hall lamented, "There has been no improvement in the things here. Worse than ever. If I could leave home I would go to Kentucky and remain until the war was over."[36]

On November 4, 1861, Jennison issued a proclamation to the people of Jackson, Lafayette, Cass, Johnson, and Pettis counties, warning, "Every man who feeds, harbors, protects or in any way gives aid and comfort to the enemies of the Union will be held responsible for his treason with his life and property." In actual practice little or no distinction was made between loyal and rebel Missourians, and Jennison and his subordinate officers and men were said to have appropriated by far the greater part of the confiscated property to their private use or sale in the black markets of Leavenworth and Lawrence. Eventually Jennison was accused by Federal authorities and brought to trial after seizing "a large amount of forage and a number of horses for his brigade." He permitted his acting brigade quartermaster to prepare vouchers as if the forage and horses had been purchased, and that he had approved the vouchers, "knowing the same to be false and fraudulent," and that having captured about 140 head of cattle, "from alleged enemies of the United States," he permitted his acting brigade quartermaster to turn the cattle over "to unauthorized parties with the intention of converting the proceeds of such cattle to private use." Jennison received thirty dollars a head for the cattle. Part of the plunder was turned over to his brother, Alonzo Jennison, who accompanied the Jayhawking expeditions in an unofficial capacity.[37]

In late November 1861, Jennison's Seventh Kansas Jayhawker Regiment was stationed four miles south of Kansas City. When they were ordered to West Point, Missouri, thirty-five miles south, every house and barn along their line of march except one was burned. When they arrived in West Point, the town was plundered, thirty homes were burned, and twelve men were killed for being Southern sympathizers. Local citizens reported, "West Point fell an early victim to the Kansas raiders and the town was almost wiped out of existence. Its stores were looted and houses burned. The office of the *West Point Banner*, which had incurred the enmity of the Kansas men, was looted and type and machinery scattered and destroyed. The other towns suffered, but to a less extent."[38]

Quantrill's Reconnaissance and Intelligence

Quantrill was seldom in ignorance of the enemy's movements, and whenever it was apparent to him that he could engage them under advantageous circumstances he never failed to benefit from the opportunity. Even some strong Union men acted as his spies so utterly disgusted were the citizens with the conduct of the Federals who were carrying on indiscriminate murder and robbery.[39]

Acting on orders from General Shelby and General Price, Quantrill sent spies into Lawrence frequently during the summer of 1863 in anticipation of a planned raid on Kansas. Even Hovey Lowman, editor of the *Lawrence State Journal,* was aware of Quantrill's activities in the area. "For three months previously, Quantrell had been threatening Lawrence, and had gathered a force twice before with the well known purpose of leading it against the city."[40]

Quantrill's spies observed that there were periodic scares and musterings of the militia without the coming of the guerrillas; after the fears subsided, the militia was demobilized, and Union army units ordered elsewhere as the inhabitants reverted to a false sense of security. It was well known that "nearly every able bodied man served in the Lawrence Rifle Guards"[41]

There were even citizens in town who were known to keep in regular communication with Quantrill. Following the raid some staunch Union men went so far as to claim, "Spies were in town all night, indeed it is placed beyond peradventure that the mother of a certain Banker of Lawrence, who secured all his valuables the night before the raid, spent weeks with his family in Lawrence, and made a map of the town giving names, residences and location of those who were to be killed and their homes burned, marking them thus—'Kill and Burn,' or 'Burn,' as if the property belonged to a sympathizer only 'Kill.' This map was taken by this heinous woman to Kansas City, and Quantrall and his lieutenants entertained day and night in the greatest possible seclusion in her parlor, where they had the maps explained preparatory to the [raid]."

Others also affirmed this information. "Names and houses were marked prior to their coming in." Hovey Lowman later stated, "He [Quantrill] had spies going and coming constantly to and from the city, and knew much more accurately than most of its citizens just the preparations that were made for his reception. He was doubtless at all times in possession of as perfect a knowledge of the exact condition of the city, whether it was guarded or not, whether its citizens slept soundly nights and pursued their avocations through the day

General James Lane incited his fellow Kansans to invade Missouri for plunder. "When you march through a state you must destroy the property of the men in arms against the Government; destroy, devastate, desolate. This is war. Ours is an army of volunteers who must not be judged by the rules applied to regulars." (Greg Walter Collection)

undisturbed by a thought of danger, or whether they were aroused by rumors in the air, to such a state of watchfulness as to preclude the idea of a surprise, as were its chief officers."[42]

The citizen Quantrill most sought in Lawrence was Senator James Lane, said to be the "head devil of all the burning and killing in Jackson County." With Congress not in session Quantrill hoped that Senator Lane would be found in town. Lane led the first organized band of Union Jayhawkers into Missouri. It was also Lane who originally laid out the "Lane Trail" of safe houses located in Kansas so runaway slaves could escape from Missouri and avoid proslavery settlements. Quantrill was often heard to remark, "I would like to meet him, but then there would be no honor in whipping him. He is a coward. I believe I would cowhide him." Quantrill told others his intention was to capture Lane and bring him back to Missouri and burn him at the stake. Since before the war Lane had been offering a heavy reward for Quantrill's head. Some say it was as much as $50,000.[43]

After analyzing all of the intelligence information he had gathered Quantrill began laying his plans. Secrecy was paramount for a

John T. Noland was born in 1844. He was one of several black men who served under Quantrill. Noland showed himself a brave soldier by his conspicuous actions during the first battle of Independence and the battle of Lamar. At Noland's funeral all his pallbearers were white. He was described as "a man among men." His gravestone in Woodlawn Cemetery in Independence denotes his service with Quantrill as a scout. (Emory Cantey Collection)

successful campaign. There were at least three Negroes in Quantrill's company. All of them were highly trusted and respected. One in particular went through the entire war with the guerrilla company. John T. Noland was a black man who had been with Quantrill from the start. He was described as "a brave, resourceful fellow." Federals once offered him ten thousand dollars to betray Quantrill, but he replied with scorn. He served as Quantrill's hostler and gathered information for Quantrill from his contacts with other Negroes located around Jackson County. Noland sensed something big was in the works and asked Quantrill to let him ride along in the ranks as a private soldier. Noland admired Quantrill because he said that Quantrill trusted and depended on him. Quantrill pulled him to the side and confided in him. "John, if I let you go with us once, your usefulness will be gone. I want you for another purpose."[44]

Quantrill assigned his trusted aide to make a perilous journey. He asked Noland to go to Lawrence and spy out the situation. Noland did not cower from the responsibility, he welcomed it. Noland said,

> I being a colored man I had the advantage of any white man as a spy. . . . It was then the Col. [Quantrill] sent for me to meet him on the Little Blue River, and it was there that I received my final instructions, which was to find out the number of soldiers quartered in Lawrence, and if there were any in the vicinity. I started for Lawrence about the 12th or 14th of August, arriving there I found some colored people there but did not mix with them for fear of recognition. I only spent one day and one night in Lawrence. I counted one hundred and forty soldiers camped about the town.

Quantrill gave him a brace of Colt Navy revolvers, some money, and a good horse. He made his way from Independence and on into Lawrence.[45]

Noland was captured twice along the way. The first time was by some of Quantrill's own men who did not recognize him. Noland had a passport from Quantrill sewn in the lining of his coat but he disliked cutting it out, so they took him to the brother of his master who identified him. The second time was by some Union soldiers who caught him as he was returning riding a horse with a Federal saddle. He explained that during a skirmish some soldiers left the horse in a thicket and in his haste to get away he mounted it and rode off. It was lucky he was not searched for his pockets were full of pistol caps he had acquired for Quantrill's men. The soldiers did find a hundred dollars on his person. His master was summoned and questioned. Mr. Noland explained that John should have money because his master had always given him a good chance to prosper. In the years following, Noland was cautious in what he admitted to concerning the raid. He was afraid of public criticism if he were to admit that he returned prior to the raid so he often repeated, "I did not see the Colonel or make any report to him until after his return from Lawrence."[46]

Two other black men in Quantrill's company, Henry Wilson and John Lobb, were also sent into Lawrence to spy out the situation. Wilson served as Quantrill's bodyguard because he didn't drink, was dependable and a good shot, and because he promised Quantrill he would stick to the end. Wilson was kidnapped by Jayhawkers early in the war and was on his way to Kansas when he escaped. Wilson who lived near Independence chose to remain in Quantrill's band rather than accept his freedom. He told those around him, "I observed with my own eyes, the stealing, plundering and burning of homes of the people of this county by bands of 'red legs' even to the enticing of slaves into Kansas. I joined Quantrill when Master Wilson moved to Texas to run the blockade at Independence, carrying supplies to Quantrill and his men." He said he ran for miles without stopping until he found Quantrill.

Wilson was also one of Quantrill's best spies because he could slip into a village without alarming the occupants and secure significant information. Quantrill assigned him to go to Lawrence and find out the conditions as to the town's defenses. Wilson recalled, "I was really only a boy and small for my age when I went into Lawrence as a scout. I was barefoot and had my pants rolled half way to my knees. I begged cornbread for a poor nigger boy and got a good lay of things." It was said that Wilson was shot seven times during the war and always dressed his own wounds.[47]

John Lobb was also sent into Lawrence, but William Gregg remembered, "Lobb did not get back before we had started. He met us on the way and told us that Lane had left town."[48]

Because of his jocular personality and easy manner Quantrill asked Lieutenant Fletcher Taylor to also spy out the situation in Lawrence. Taylor's subterfuge was to pose as a land speculator and cattle trader. He was to stay several days at the Eldridge House Hotel, the most notable guest quarters in town, and spend his money liberally, playing the part of a wealthy hospitable gentleman, and gather names of those Federal soldiers making the hotel their headquarters. For years the hotel was used as a fort before it was even finished. Lawrence citizen Richard Cordley said, "It was used for military purposes, and was made quite comfortable as headquarters. Several of the companies used it as a 'barracks' for the accommodation of the 'army.'"

The Eldridge House Hotel itself was a formidable structure, three stories tall with an initial cost of $20,000. It was one of the largest and most luxurious inns west of the Mississippi River. The building was the principal hotel in town, holding sixty patrons at the time of the raid. After it was first destroyed in 1856, Shalor Eldridge employed Benjamin Johnson to rebuild it for a cost of $80,000. Situated on the corner of Massachusetts and Winthrop Streets, it was constructed as a fort ready for any emergency with a roof parapeted for defense and portholes every six feet apart built into the façade for firing. It extended one hundred feet on the east front and one hundred and seventeen feet on the north. The walls were eighteen inches thick and the basement walls two feet thick. It stood four stories tall and was the most imposing structure in all Lawrence. The ground-floor windows were all protected by iron grills. The rooms were large and imposing. The ballroom was big enough to hold a hundred persons and could accommodate forty-eight couples dancing at one time. The yard in the rear was enclosed with a strong fence eight to ten feet high. Across the street the Lawrence militia kept their cannon "shotted and ready for any emergency." If there were to be a defense of the town it would logically be the Eldridge House Hotel where the defenders would naturally muster. If even a small number of Lawrence citizens could arm themselves from the armory across the street and find safety behind its walls, getting to them inside the hotel would be costly.

James D. Faxon, a clerk in Brinton F. Woodward's drugstore located next to the Eldridge House Hotel, said, "During this period which was the time of the war business was good. Some army supplies were bought there and occasionally there would be quite a number of soldiers quartered there."[49] Lawrence newspaper editor and militiaman Hovey Lowman readily admitted, "Well filled, by efficiently, armed and resolute men, with a brave and cool-headed leader, such a building would, so it seems, be a fortress of most dangerous defensive power against two or three hundred cavalrymen armed with weapons no more efficient in assault than revolvers."[50]

Taylor's other mission while he was in Lawrence was to find out the names of any Jayhawkers and Redlegs in town, including the number of soldiers and what military units were stationed there and where they were bivouacked. Especially wanted were the Redlegs. There were never less than fifty of them, nor more than a hundred. Little was known of them until the spring of 1863. They were not enlisted soldiers. They dressed in citizens' clothes, and the red leggings were a sign of recognition to each other. They were employed by the generals in command, and were carried on the payrolls at seven dollars each per day. They gained prominence when Generals Thomas Ewing and James G. Blunt organized a body of scouts to operate on the Missouri border. They were recognized by the government as fully as any captain, colonel, or general. The Redlegs soon acquired an evil reputation. Their organization became one of professional thieves, robbers, murderers, and arsonists, attacking anyone who had sympathy for the South or anyone who had any type of wealth or possessions they coveted. Even General Blunt admitted, "The organization embraced many of the most desperate characters in the country, while the inducements of easy gain had allured into it many persons who, in ordinary time, would never have consented to be connected with such an enterprise. Officers, soldiers and citizens had become infected until the leaders became so bold as to defy interference with their operations."[51]

Lawrence, Kansas: Redleg Capital

Names of Kansas Redlegs are rarely found in official muster records. The organization was a loose one comprised of men who joined simply for adventure and plunder, wanting to operate under no military constraints. They were simply freebooters and criminals of the worst sort, who would kill and plunder knowing they would suffer no repercussions. Their headquarters were in Lawrence, and they were in close association with the citizens and other military units stationed there. A Lawrence citizen recalled, "We in Lawrence came into very close touch with the soldiers of the Union. We saw a great deal of them during the four years. Squads and detachments, regiments and brigades, were constantly passing through the state, often remaining for days and weeks in camp among us."

Most of Lawrence's citizens had served or were serving in the army or militia. "Whole neighborhoods were found without a single able-bodied man left." It was common knowledge that "half the men of Kansas were in the army, or at the front in some capacity, and that an overwhelming proportion of the home men were in office, either in the civil or military service of the United States or state government."[52] Even Kansas writer A. C. Nichols wrote, "Many Kansans were assigned to formal fighting, but others were incorporated under local commands and fought the war out in the same roles, now legalized, that they had played in the curtain-raiser."[53]

Next to the Eldridge Hotel the most notable hotel in town was the Johnson House Hotel located about a block to the southwest on Vermont Street. It was a large three-story stone building. Rates were one dollar a day or four dollars a week. The stage line arrived and left there daily to all parts of the territory. Everyone was aware that Colonel George Hoyt, the noted Redleg leader, made this hotel his headquarters, and his Redlegs filled the hotel's stable to capacity with stolen horses from Missouri. Stealing horses was a priority during a Jayhawker raid due to the lucrative market. A Jackson County citizen wrote a letter describing the practice. "Stealing horses is quite a common occurrence here, but by reason of the close proximity of the state of Kansas which furnishes them a place of retreat, as well as a market for such stolen stock their arrest and detection is exceedingly difficult." It was an easy matter for the Jayhawkers to obtain horses. C. C. Spalding from Westport remembered, "Every man and woman, especially young men and young ladies are supposed to have a saddle and bridle if no other personal property. On this border, traveling on horseback, to town, to church, to court, to school, and to the dance, is the favorite mode of traveling. It is not only a habit with the old and the young people, but it is an amusement, a luxury enjoyed by every one."[54]

George Hoyt was small of stature, only weighing seventy-five pounds. He came to Lawrence as a lawyer and was described as "a combination of ambition and cruelty." Hoyt started out as a lieutenant in Company K of the Seventh Kansas Jayhawker Regiment commanded by John Brown, Jr. He later served as Jennison's aide-de-camp, and the two became inseparable companions. Hoyt resigned his commission on September 3, 1862, to take up Jayhawking full time. The adjutant general of the state of Kansas remarked, "The company and regiment was well rid of him when he resigned."[55] Later at a public meeting in Paola, Kansas, Hoyt was seen "dressed in a suit of black velvet, red sheepskin leggin[g]s reaching to the knees, a red silk handkerchief carelessly thrown around his neck, and a military hat with a flowing black plume. At his waist was an embossed morocco belt carrying a pair of ivory-mounted revolvers." Other descriptions of him portray him as wearing a wampum skirt and fringes and Indian ornaments similar to his partner in crime, Charles Ransford Jennison

One eyewitness saw "[George] Hoyt without a word of explanation or warning, open fire upon a stranger quietly riding down Massachusetts Street. He was a Missourian whom Hoyt had recently robbed." Another eyewitness recounted, "The Lawrence livery stable was usually full of stolen horses. One day I saw three or four Redlegs attack a Missourian, who was in town searching for his lost property. They gathered about him with drawn revolvers, and drove him off very unceremoniously." A Lawrence citizen recalled, "Nobody dared to interfere with them because they did not hesitate to shoot inquisitive and troublesome people." Hoyt was especially hated by Southerners for having defended John Brown during his trial for treason. When not at the Johnson House Hotel, Hoyt could be found at the home of Lieutenant Henry S. Clarke.[56]

With General Ewing's blessing Hoyt was put in charge of a group of Redlegs known at the time as "detectives" to root out disloyal sentiments among the citizens. As Hoyt's Redlegs grew in size and scope, detective papers would become one of their most powerful tools. Lieutenant Cyrus Leland, Jr., an officer on Ewing's staff, admitted that Ewing always had fifteen Redlegs on his payroll, among them Theodore Bartles, George Kingsley, and J. G. Losee, who was Jennison's business partner in stolen trade operating out of Leavenworth. Bartles had already gained an unsavory reputation as a noted thief. In July 1862 many of the leading citizens of Wyandotte County, Kansas, formed a vigilance committee to stop an outbreak of robbery and horse stealing, which the civilian law enforcement officials were powerless to halt. The committee believed the "Six Mile House," owned by J. A. Bartles and his son, Theodore, had become a "den of thieves, operated by a gang of Red Legs." When citizens attempted to arrest Bartles he was protected by troops sent out by General Blunt. Afterward Bartles joined the staff of George Hoyt at the Johnson Hotel in Lawrence.

After selecting a crew of the most notable cutthroats along the border, Hoyt started plundering on a large scale. Historian Stephen Starr said, "The Red Legs were not the kind of military body that keeps records and makes reports," and added, they "stole, robbed, burned, and killed indiscriminately, and not in Missouri alone." Solomon Miller, a staunch Unionist, expressed his disgust over Hoyt's activities. "A system of terrorism was practiced upon loyal citizens by means of deputy marshals, so-called detectives, and desperate, irresponsible men under other guises, to keep them to the wishes of Lane. They first despoiled men of known disloyal sentiments and when that harvest was exhausted they began to make disloyal men, that is, they would trump up charges of disloyalty and proceed to steal their horses." Another method was to accuse unfriendly persons of owning stolen horses, then seize the animals and retain them for their own use or profit.[57]

Writing from Leavenworth, Kansas, C. M. Chase, a pro-Union journalist for the *True Republican and Sentinel* of Sycamore, Illinois, defined the Redlegs and the various forms of Jayhawkers who operated in Missouri and Kansas. "Jayhawkers, Red Legs, and Bushwhackers are everyday terms in Kansas and Western Missouri. A Jayhawker is a Unionist who professes to rob, burn out and murder only rebels in arms against the government. A Red Leg is a Jayhawker originally distinguished by the uniform of red leggings. A Red Leg, however, is regarded as more purely an indiscriminate thief and murderer than the Jayhawker or Bushwhacker."

Benjamin Johnson, known as one of the town's more strident abolitionists, owned the Johnson House Hotel besides owning a farm eight miles outside of town. He was also a man who split no hairs when it came to who he liked and who he allowed in his hotel. The year before when he learned that a number of Missourians had signed his registry and were in town looking for their stolen property, the irate innkeeper collared the men and kicked them into the street with the warning not to come back. John Speer, editor of the *Lawrence Republican,* laughingly wrote, "If you're from Missouri, and you're looking for strayed property, give the Johnson House a wide berth."[58]

When the Redlegs were in town, the men of Lawrence would come to the hotel to listen to them brag about the number of Missourians they had killed and the amount of plunder they had acquired from the wealthy slave owners across the border. At most any time there were usually a dozen men registered as guests; most notable among them being: John W. Blatchly; John L. Bridges, known mostly by his nom-de-plume "Beauregard"; and Joseph B. Swain, who had ridden with Lane during the destruction of Osceola, Missouri. Previously they had

Captain Henry E. Palmer was an officer in Lane's Brigade and took part in the destruction of Osceola, Missouri. (Kansas State Historical Society)

served as scouts, not on government payroll but simply as private citizens. In compensation for their service they were allowed to keep all captured property, including weapons, horses, mules, and other livestock, all of which could be readily sold for cash. Soon Swain and his men became less concerned with the political sympathies of their victims and more interested in their own financial gain. However, as long as they provided some service to the Union, sympathetic Federal authorities were willing to ignore their transgressions.[59]

Stories of Jayhawkers terrorizing the Missouri border were numerous. Redleg Joseph B. Swain, described as Jennison's "right-hand man," and seven of his followers made a nighttime raid on the home of a Missouri farmer named Lawrence. The party demanded the man turn over to them all his money and silverware. Lawrence said he could not comply with their demand as he had sent all of his money to a bank in Canada for safety. Dragged to a nearby tree with a rope around his neck, Lawrence was repeatedly hauled into the air and strangled as Swain tried to extract the location of his wealth. When Lawrence failed to produce the goods, the men ransacked his home, smashing open locked drawers, emptying trucks, and ripping open mattresses. In the parlor they found the coffin of Mrs. Lawrence, who had died that day, resting across two chairs. In the words of Jayhawker Henry E. Palmer: "One fellow suggested that maybe money was hid in the coffin, and with that he knocked off the lid of the casket and searched for gold. A ring on the finger of the dead woman attracted his attention, and whipping out his bowie knife he cut off the finger to release the ring. Before leaving, this gallant party of Union defenders said to the terror stricken daughters: 'If you want to plant the old lady, drag her out, for we are going to fire the ranch.'" Unaided they dragged the coffin from the burning home.[60]

Even some Union officers were disgusted at the Redlegs' activities. Ironically General Blunt, military commander for the District of the Frontier who employed several Redlegs in his command, stated, "I found the country on the border of Kansas and Missouri overrun with bands of marauders, thieves, and robbers, styling themselves 'Red Legs.' Their organization was so formidable, and their depredations committed with such impunity, as to have become the terror of all law-abiding and honest men. No man's life or property was secure for a moment. The civil law was powerless to arrest and punish them." Author William Connelley wrote: "Every thief who wanted to steal from the Missouri people counterfeited the uniform of the Red Legs and went forth to pillage." Captain Henry Palmer of the Eleventh Kansas Jayhawker Regiment summed up the Redlegs' activities by explaining that three hundred Redlegs were "sworn to shoot rebels, take no prisoners, free slaves, and respect no property rights of rebels or their sympathizers."[61]

Fortress Lawrence

Lawrence was a bustling recruiting center for the Union army, but many did not know the underlying hostility in the way men were recruited. Lane's speeches harangued men to enlist in his brigade. "Men, we want you to let your families take care of themselves. Let everything go: you have no rights that we are bound to respect." Another source reported, "Men were persuaded or driven into the service against their own inclinations, leaving their families destitute and dependent upon the precarious charity of neighbors for subsistence, and misery and starvation deplorable in itself and disgraceful to Kansas has resulted." Several Kansas regiments "had been organized by misrepresentation; and men enlisted in many cases at the point of the bayonet."[62]

Twenty-two men of the Fourteenth Kansas Jayhawker Regiment were bivouacked in tents on the east side of Massachusetts Street in the southeast portion of the city, and another twenty soldiers of the Second Kansas Colored Infantry were camped a little further south on the other side of Massachusetts Street. These soldiers were recruits who had enlisted in the service but had not yet been mustered into their respective units. They were expecting to be sent to the front any day. Captain Leroy J. Beam, the enrolling officer in charge of the white recruits, lived in town. Beam offered a five-dollar reward for anyone bringing in a new recruit. Samuel S. Snyder, serving as an officer in the Second Kansas Colored Regiment, was in command of the newly enlisted Negro soldiers. Union army chaplains were put in charge of escorting Negro contrabands taken in Missouri back to Lawrence and arming them for Lane's Black Brigade. As a result, Snyder was one of the most wanted men on Quantrill's list. It was Snyder who induced slaves to leave their masters while ordering them to take as much plunder from their owners as they could carry. Besides stealing horses and livestock they even took carriages and wagons to haul the plunder back into Kansas.

Missourians feared their former slaves more than the white Jayhawkers. One Missourian stated, "Our wives and daughters are panic stricken, and a reign of terror as black as hell itself envelops our county." When the war started, Missouri had one hundred thousand slaves, worth about thirty-five million dollars. Besides the slaves who were "enticed" to accompany the Jayhawkers back into Kansas, thousands of other slaves ran off, wandering the countryside, often in the train of Union troops who both cared for them and exploited them.[63]

Early on in the war Lane led his Negro brigade on a raid into Missouri. The October 13, 1862, *Philadelphia Inquirer* reported, "Last night a detachment of General Jim Lane's Free Negro Brigade attempted to cross the river from Wyandotte, Kansas, it is thought, for the purpose of making a raid upon the citizens of Clay County, Mo., when they were met on the Missouri bank by a company of the Missouri State Militia and driven back. Several shots were fired, but little damage was done to either party." Lane was trying to pay back Clay County for an earlier proclamation it had made: "The citizens of Clay County, are solemnly pledged one to another that they will not suffer traitors to her institutions to concoct and give utterance to their contemptible fanatical abolitionism to prevail, at any future time."[64]

A newspaper article in August of 1863 stated that Lawrence had a population between 2,500 and 3,000. Besides the regular soldiers who were expected to be encountered during the raid, almost the entire male population of Lawrence served in the local militia. Pastor Richard Cordley of the Plymouth Congregational Church was also in the Lawrence militia. He admitted that Lawrence had a "vigorous and effective military organization." Cordley acknowledged: "The company to which I belonged was a rifle company, and comprised a large portion of the business and professional men of the place. Instead of accepting the muskets furnished by the state, we had armed ourselves with the most improved repeating rifles, mostly Spencer rifles. . . . The ranks of the militia companies were full, and everybody rallied, and rallied promptly. There were merchants and ministers, lawyers and doctors, laboring men and men of leisure, all shouldering their muskets, and taking their place in the ranks." Cordley noted that even the previous pastor Samuel Y. Lum fought alongside the Lawrence militia. His members all attended church services heavily armed.

In fact at one time the Plymouth Church in Lawrence was turned into a barracks for the militia. The church was sixty feet long by forty feet wide. It could comfortably seat three hundred and fifty people and was often used as a station on the Underground Railroad. Cordley confessed that even his house was used as a meeting place for the military officers. One Union soldier in Lawrence recalled, "All that summer Lawrence had from two to three hundred militia, well drilled and well armed with plenty of ammunition. The militia was drilled every day; pickets were stationed on every road that led to town."[65]

Quantrill wanted Fletcher Taylor to find out the names of the main troublemakers in town plus the location of their residences. Many individuals were already known from previous years of Jayhawker raids into Missouri. Their businesses had prospered from the sale of stolen goods, and these businesses were to be marked for destruction as well as the homes that were well furnished with stolen Missouri property. Though at one time there may have been some honest merchants in Lawrence, it was hard to compete against businesses selling stolen property. Therefore the honest merchants fell in with their fellow tradesmen and succumbed to the temptation to profit from ill-gotten gains.

General George W. Collamore. Collamore was mayor of Lawrence at the time of the raid and secured arms from General Thomas Ewing for the city's defense. Before becoming mayor in March of 1863, Collamore served as the quartermaster general for the state of Kansas but was relieved of command by Governor Charles Robinson on suspicion of fraudulent practices with state funds. (Kansas State Historical Society)

Richard Cordley divulged, "Lawrence was more prosperous during the first three years of the war than she had been the three year's preceding," and the criminal activities of Jayhawkers were to be credited. Writer Lucien Carr called Lawrence a "mere fence-house for stolen property" once owned by Missourians. "Lawrence was a den of thieves, Jayhawkers, renegade Missourians, and abolitionists of every degree. Here lived and flourished on their ill gotten booty hundreds of depredators and plunderers of Southern men; here was got three million dollars worth of army stores and supplies."[66]

At night when Taylor got back to his room at the Eldridge Hotel he was to sit down and make a complete map of the area, targeting businesses and residences slated to be destroyed.

During the first part of August, Mayor George Washington Collamore received verifiable information that Quantrill was planning a raid on the city at any time. It had been rumored that Quantrill would arrive about the "full of the moon" which would have been near August 1. The word was relayed through General George Deitzler who had received a letter from Major Charles G. Halpine, chief-of-staff to Major General David Hunter. His younger brother had succeeded in getting into Quantrill's organization while camped on Sni-a-Bar Creek. Halpine wrote,

"Quantrill is coming at the light of the moon." Deitzler then relayed the information to Mayor Collamore. Josiah Trask called Collamore "our nervous mayor." Collamore was a small man described by fellow citizen Richard Cordley. "He [Collamore] was a very active man with a good deal of executive ability, and had an air of self-sufficiency which made him want to do everything his own way and made other people disposed to stand aloof from him." Others described him as being a very reticent, peculiar, and careful man.

Before becoming mayor in March of 1863 Collamore served as the quartermaster general for the state of Kansas but was relieved of command by Governor Charles Robinson on suspicion of fraudulent practices with the state's funds.[67] Whenever Collamore received news about an intended raid the citizens were quietly called out, armed, and converted into soldiers. Two or three militia companies were ordered from the country, and they, when joined with the armed citizens, made a formidable force. Collamore kept his information secret for if it was known that the city was in a perfect state of defense it would have kept Quantrill from coming, and the Kansans were anxious to do battle with the guerrillas. This last call-up of soldiers was well remembered since it was the last alarm sounded before the famous raid. Governor Robinson remarked that many militia members laughingly would say, "With one round the Missourians would fly like frightened hares."[68] Richard Hinton recalled the defensive posture of Lawrence: "The men and boys of Kansas, every one capable of carrying a musket, responded speedily to the call to arms."[69]

Five earthen blockhouses were built at different approaches to the town. Each militia company was given charge of one of these blockhouses, and a portion of the company slept in them every night. "There were, therefore, always fifty men or more ready for immediate service. These were intended as a nucleus around which the rest could rally as they came."[70]

The blockhouses commanded the entire business portion of the town. When they were first built the blockhouses were constructed by the soldiers who "spent their time during the day in throwing up earth works at the most exposed points. These earth works were circular, and some of them one hundred feet in diameter. The largest was at the crossing of Massachusetts and Pinckney streets. This was intended as a place of refuge for the women and children in case of an assault. It was built of hewn timbers, banked up with earth, and a deep trench dug all round it. It was five feet high. Another was at the crossing of Massachusetts and Henry streets arranged for cannon. A third was near New Hampshire Street, north of Henry. Another located on Kentucky Street overlooked the ravine and the last one on the corner of Massachusetts and Winthrop Street was equipped with a howitzer manned by Captain Thomas Bickerton and William Crutchfield.[71]

Each of these defenses was in the charge of an officer and had a contingent of troops assigned to its defense. During drill there were fully six hundred men within the entrenchments, and two hundred or more were armed with Sharps rifles. "When the men were in the trenches with their guns, the women were making bullets for them at home."[72]

"It was not considered possible that a force could pierce the lines of General Ewing, evade his scouts, and penetrate fifty miles into a populous region and attack the third town of the State, without notice of the raid being given in season to prepare for defense."[73] When the town first expected an attack editor Hovey Lowman remarked, "The cannon, full-shotted, watched for the enemy down Massachusetts Street. Pickets, both foot and mounted, were sent out, and they guarded the approaches to the town, both day and night, ten miles out. A large force, armed and equipped for the field was marching through its streets before those outside of the militia companies were aware of the import of the movement."[74]

The Mission of Quantrill and His Spies

Back at Quantrill's camp his spies were equipped and sent off on their mission. Quantrill left instructions for his remaining officers to keep well concealed and make sure the men were kept busy making cartridges and caring for their horses. An arduous journey lay ahead, and a good horse and a good supply of ammunition would be needed. The guerrillas' horses were fed chiefly on grain and were as gaunt and ready as greyhounds. Quantrill had been making contingency plans for quite some time, considering a raid on the "Yankee Town" of Lawrence. It was not that Lawrence had not been warned. In response to Jayhawker atrocities in the spring of 1863, "Quantrell issued a proclamation to the Federal forces of Kansas that if they did not stop burning and robbing houses, killing old men and women, he would in return come to Lawrence at some unexpected time and paint the city blacker than Hades and make its streets run with blood."[75]

If he were to strike Lawrence it would have to be soon. A telegraph line was being constructed by the Kansas Pacific Railroad and would be completed in a matter of weeks. Also construction of a bridge across the Kaw River, also known as the Kansas River, was begun in the spring of 1863 by a Chicago concern and was slated to be completed by December. Lee C. Miller remembered, "Quantrell was the quickest man to see a mistake on the part of the enemy I ever saw and to take advantage of it. It mattered not how difficult an undertaking might appear he went at it with full confidence of accomplishing it, and he seldom failed."[76]

Two weeks previously Quantrill with two of his most trusted men rode as far as Eudora, eight miles east of Lawrence, to reconnoiter the area and to spy out the situation himself in anticipation of a future raid. William Gregg said, "Quantrill didn't want to make [the] raid. He held off for months, but the old men clamored for revenge on the 'red legs' of Kansas. He told them of raids by the Redlegs on Missourians, insulting our mothers and our sisters and setting fire to our homes. Finally us boys were as strong as our fathers for revenge."[77]

The little town of Eudora was settled in 1857 by a colony of Germans who did not ingratiate themselves well with their fellow settlers. Additionally a large percentage of soldiers and citizens living in Lawrence were German. They had been induced by the New England Emigrant Aid Society through German agents to migrate to the new Kansas Territory. Most had never taken the oath of citizenship and did not speak the English language. One historian noted, "They [the Germans] associated with the English speaking people in so far as they were forced to do so in their business, but they never felt that they had the same ideals." Germans made up 15 percent of the Union army, and a large percentage of them could be found in and around Lawrence. Germans were one of the first groups to raise the Missourians' ire early in the war. When the first shots were fired in Missouri at Camp Jackson in St. Louis, it was German troops who fired on an unarmed crowd, killing twenty-eight men, women, and children, and wounding a hundred more.

The Germans were despised for being mercenaries and devoid of genuine patriotism, in direct contrast with Southern soldiers who were fighting for home and principle. A Saline County newspaper wrote, "The army of occupation is principally composed of German mercenaries, willing tools in the hands of aspiring demagogues who are building their fortunes from the fragments of the temple their own hands have destroyed, that of constitutional liberty." One Federal officer added, "My command is made up largely of Germans, and it has been very hard to restrain them from depredations on people known as Southern sympathizers."[78]

Because of his earlier days in Lawrence, Quantrill couldn't gamble on riding any farther west for fear that he might be recognized. He was well known in Lawrence and during his time there became unpopular with the straight-laced Massachusetts men, described as "hypocritical and mercenary" although the womenfolk remarked: "[Quantrill] had lovely manners, never forgot to remove his hat in the presence of ladies and always made himself agreeable to them. The townsfolk remembered that some of the girls missed [Quantrill's] pleasant smile and good manners. During his reconnaissance he reacquainted himself with the roads leading into town and was able to scrutinize any obstacles he would have to contend with."[79]

Quantrill determined that the easiest place to slip past the Kansas border would be between Aubry and Coldwater Grove. It would be a treacherous journey getting his men past the Federal outposts unobserved. He determined to ride mostly at night. During this lone expedition he made a determination how long the march would take, how much time his men could spend accomplishing their mission, and the route they would use to get back to the safety of Missouri.

The wooded Wakarusa River passes through the town of Eudora before emptying into the Kansas River. The Wakarusa, though narrow, barely twenty yards wide, is deep, and its bottom and high banks are composed of a stiff, sticky mud that renders the passage of a horseman a very difficult and dangerous undertaking. Before the raid there were only two bridges over the Wakarusa; one was at Eudora, and the other south of Lawrence called Blanton's Bridge. It was named after Napoleon Bonaparte Blanton who also had a blacksmith shop and sold groceries and whiskey next to his house, which also served as an inn. Before the war free-state forces built fortifications and rifle pits surrounding the bridge. Midway between the two bridges was a ford called Blue Jacket's Crossing. Quantrill knew there were only three avenues of escape out of Lawrence, and only one, Blanton's Bridge, could afford a quick withdrawal back to the safety of the wooded hills and deep ravines of Jackson County. Quantrill found a difficulty with crossing the Wakarusa River at Eudora as his escape route. It involved a wooden bridge that could easily be destroyed, and a nearby blockhouse might be a formidable object to pass; therefore Blanton's Bridge was the more desirable choice as a crossing. The surrounding country and its roads were thoroughly explored so that no unforeseen difficulty might delay the quick withdrawal that would be necessary. With his scouting mission completed, Quantrill and his escort easily slipped back past the Federal outposts.

There were at least a hundred Federal cavalry assigned by General Ewing located in each outpost along the border. Soldiers of the Ninth Kansas Jayhawker Regiment manned many of the posts. Most of the time Colonel Edward Lynde, commanding officer of the regiment, stayed with the headquarters element at the small hamlet of Trading Post. Major Luin K. Thacher was in charge of three companies of cavalry at Westport. Captain Joshua A. Pike with two cavalry companies was at Aubry. Company G was stationed at Harrisonville. Captain Charles F. Coleman with D Company was at Pleasant Hill; while three other companies of cavalry were in Little Santa Fe, Paola, Olathe, and Rockville. All had one company of infantry, while Coldwater Grove, thirteen miles north of Rockville, had Company E, a cavalry company of the Ninth Kansas Regiment commanded by Lieutenant Colonel Charles S. Clark. The outpost at Little Santa Fe was important because it consisted of two general stores, a shoe store, a blacksmith shop, a post office, and a saloon. Trails from Kansas City, Westport, and Independence met there coming through the Blue Valley. Its location on the state line made it possible to transact business in the public room of the main building either in Missouri or Kansas. One of the stores was built by Jim Bridger, the famous explorer, mountain man, trapper, and scout.

With the large number of men at his disposal Quantrill would require both the use of deception and boldness, knowing that the outcome of his raid was dependent on perfect timing. He planned on leaving his campsite posing as a large Federal force. Most of his men wore blue uniforms, and these he would have riding in front of the column. The men would ride leisurely so as not to arouse suspicion. Along with this deception he would assign a large number of pickets in front and on the flanks of his marching column with instructions to ride back to the main body every few minutes and report any suspicious activity. With the time constraints involved Quantrill knew he would have to ride through Missouri during daylight, but for safety's sake his ride to Lawrence would have to be made during the hours of darkness. If they could make it to the Kansas border unobserved the guerrillas would camp for a few hours and get some rest among the heavy timber along the Grand River in Cass County, four miles from the Kansas line. From there Quantrill and many of his men were familiar with this part of Kansas and if needed they could press guides to assist them for the remaining fifty-five miles to Lawrence.

Quantrill's Well-Laid Plans

Quantrill laid his plans well. He knew that this operation would be a "one-fell-swoop" on his Kansas enemies. He planned on striking any known individual Jayhawkers along the way who would not imperil his mission. If successful in Lawrence, he would withdraw fighting, striking at known targets along the way back to Missouri. Nothing on this scale had ever been attempted before for its daring and audacity. Finally the information about attacking Lawrence was divulged to his officers. When he learned of the intended target Lieutenant William Gregg told those afterward that if their women relatives had not died the raid would not have taken place. "You may imagine what a sensation this dastardly, heinous crime cast over the followers of Quantrill, and in my estimation, only for this cowardly act, the raid on Lawrence never would have occurred."[80]

Quantrill patiently waited for the return of his spies to hear their reports. On his way back to Missouri, Fletcher Taylor stopped at a farmhouse, four miles from Lawrence. The host believed Taylor to be a genuine, first-rate Federal, and soon became very communicative. He told Taylor the number of raids he had made into Missouri and the amount of plunder brought off, that he belonged to the gang of Red-legs whose only occupation was depredating upon Southern men and robbing promiscuously.[81]

John Noland at last returned a little ahead of Taylor and Wilson. They went directly to Quantrill and made their reports. Quantrill used the intelligence information to put together a list of guilty individuals and objectionable houses that would be sought out when they arrived in Lawrence. Taylor also had a map showing the residences of wanted men and a map of commercial buildings and businesses that had provoked so much trouble for Missourians over the past two years. Quantrill had enough copies made so that each assigned squad would have no trouble ferreting out the individuals and places marked for destruction. The list was long, but Lawrence had always been known as "the home of Jim Lane, the headquarters of the Red Legs, the chief station on the Underground Railroad, the Abolitionist capital of the West, the recruiting ground for Jayhawkers and Union soldiers. Lawrence had been the Free State fortress and Abolitionist capital since the first settlement of Kansas Territory." The Reverend Richard Cordley, who himself openly violated the Fugitive Slave Law by employing a runaway slave woman as his housekeeper and cook, readily admitted that Lawrence "had its soldiers and its officers, its arms and its unwritten laws."[82]

Taylor and Noland were each asked by Quantrill to brief the officers after breakfast on August 19. The sun had not yet risen when they finished eating their morning meal. The two men stepped to the middle of the group and began their report. Noland's mission had been to present himself as a free black man and gain the confidence of any runaway slaves in Lawrence, obtaining any valuable information he could from them. Lawrence citizen Major James Abbot claimed that Lawrence was the best advertised antislavery town in the world where fugitives were sure to receive sustenance, sympathy, and encouragement. Noland found out where the way stations were for the Underground Railroad in Lawrence and who was aiding the slaves to escape. Most of the stations for the Underground Railroad were located at farms just outside Lawrence, mostly in the heavily wooded Wakarusa bottoms.

Taylor was next to speak and was congratulated for having such an easy time accomplishing his part of the mission. He had made a successful foray into enemy territory and had gained a great deal of valuable information. It was said that he had "been in the city, through it, over it, about it, and around it."[83] Taylor also reported that there were many military units constantly passing through town. One of the main concerns was the number of soldiers the guerrillas could expect to find. There was a barracks for them located in the 800 block of New Hampshire Street. Quantrill's men were always able to overcome great odds on the battlefield, oftentimes fighting and winning stunning victories when the odds against them were overwhelming. The *Lawrence Journal* had recently reported that Lawrence held more than five hundred fighting men and that a guard had been kept for miles in every direction about the town for months past. The town companies were joined by those from the country. The article went on to heap praise on the citizens of Lawrence who served in uniform, running the patrols that were keeping the city safe

There were two companies constantly patrolling. One company was led by Lieutenant Tobias J. Hadley of the Fifth Kansas Jayhawker Regiment, and the other by Major Edmund G. Ross, a citizen of Lawrence leading Company E, Eleventh Kansas Jayhawker Regiment. The *Lawrence Journal* praised Hadley's efforts by stating, "No enemy can come within ten miles of Lawrence before we know it, with such men guarding us." Hadley received his orders directly from the mayor, General George Collamore, who also served as the commander of the local militia. Collamore organized an effective military company and secured arms for them from the state.[84] Hadley's brother, Major John M. Hadley of the Ninth Kansas Jayhawker Regiment, was on General Ewing's staff in Kansas City. In early August he received a letter from his brother stating, "Quantrill would descend upon Lawrence at the time of the full moon in August."[85] In response the Lawrence militia rolled out their cannon, and the town was picketed and patrolled for only a short time before they grew tired of the exercise and returned to their previous stations.

Colonel Francis B. Swift, who took part in the destruction of Osceola, Missouri, with Lane, was in charge of thirteen companies of militia in and around Lawrence. It was said by the local newspaper, "These

Frank B. Swift was a printer, a member of the New England Emigrant Aid Society, and a captain in the First Kansas Jayhawker Regiment. During the Lawrence raid he was killed as soon as he was discovered. (Kansas State Historical Society)

companies are well organized and armed, and are putting themselves in the best possible fighting trim by persevering in drill."[86] Swift had taken an early part in the border troubles. He belonged to Company A of the Kansas Rifles, an early militia organization put together to protect the extralegal abolitionist government in Topeka. The militia had often been called upon to respond to rumors of an intended invasion. Back in April, Swift had called out his militia companies but soon learned it was a false alarm. The papers reported, "The farmers left their work at a busy season of the year, and promptly responded to the order of Colonel Swift." Swift also excelled as a journalist, extolling the most virulent articles in the *Kansas Tribune*.[87]

The newly elected governor of Kansas, Thomas Carney, encouraged Kansas towns and rural communities to raise home guard militia units. On May 28, 1863, the governor toured the counties of Kansas, helping to raise military companies for home protection. He contributed his own money to fund an additional 150 mounted men to support the regular troops in patrolling the country. The sheriffs of these counties, as well as those in the second-tier counties along the border, were authorized to reorganize their militias and secure arms from General Blunt, the commander of the military District of the Frontier or from the governor. When the governor visited Douglas County the *Lawrence Journal* observed:

First Lieutenant George Ellis was in charge of Kansas troops across the Kaw River at Lawrence but was staying at the Redleg headquarters in the Johnson House Hotel during the raid. He ran away, managing to escape, but his clothes were full of shot holes as a result. (Douglas County Historical Society)

"It is gratifying to know that companies are to be armed in such a manner as to be able to compete with the best armed invaders. We hope our local organizations will at once reorganize, so as to be ready for any emergency."

The greatest fear of Kansans was an attack from Quantrill's raiders. There were thousands of men serving in the local militias around Lawrence, and once they received word of an impending attack they were to be quickly gathered for defense. William Gregg responded by saying that there were no citizens in Lawrence at that time. "They were all soldiers, armed, equipped and ready for the fray." On July 2, 1863, the *Lawrence Journal* announced how the men in town kept active: "Weekly meetings of the Lawrence Volunteer Militia were being held at the armory for the purpose of drill, prize target shooting, and the regular transaction of business."[88]

One Lawrence citizen, Lieutenant George Ellis, was in charge of a group of soldiers from Company I, Twelfth Kansas Jayhawker Regiment, guarding the north side of the Kansas River. If needed in town they would be expected to cross the ferry and join forces with those in Lawrence. The only other crossing of the Kansas River was either twenty miles above the town or thirty miles below it, too far for a rescuing force to arrive in time. For his own comfort Lieutenant Ellis stayed at the Redleg headquarters in the Johnson House Hotel in Lawrence each night and returned to his command on the north side of the river each morning. Guerrilla Captain Kit Dalton stated, "In garrisoned towns the commanding officers lived in the city, enjoying all the luxuries that could be obtained of the intimidated people, leaving the soldiers in tented village arranged in the most advantageous places in case of an attack from the enemy."[89] For the past two or three weeks recruiting was going on the north side of the river for a company of sharpshooters for Lawrence. They were camped by the old Baldwin Mill.

Quantrill's Plan of Attack

Regardless of the braggadocio coming from Lawrence, Quantrill continued with his plans. As Taylor and Noland spoke, the officers began to realize the overwhelming odds against them. The report from the spies lasted for quite some time. They had given a detailed house by house plan of the entire town. When Taylor and Noland finished speaking there was a hushed silence within the group. Quantrill's officers had just heard all the information that needed to be relayed. They had also heard Quantrill's personal report from his trip to Eudora two weeks earlier. Besides what Taylor and Noland had to say they also had information gathered from a myriad of other sources concerning Lawrence. As the discussion came to an end Quantrill broke in, telling his men, "You have heard the report, but before you decide it is proper that you should know it all. The march to Lawrence is a long one; in every town there are soldiers; we attack the town garrisoned by soldiers; we retreat through soldiers; and when we would rest and refit after the exhaustive expedition, we have to do the best we can in the midst of a multitude of soldiers."[90]

Quantrill had already expertly planned his withdrawal from Lawrence. Kansas was sparsely settled. It had no railroads, no telegraphs into the interior, and no thickly settled districts swarming with people. Most of it was prairie land with only scattered farms and settlements. Quantrill's retreat would be across open country, independent of roads. Many of Quantrill's men were familiar with the

Kansas prairies that were unobstructed by "any roads or fords, with a rolling country to traverse, as open as the sea."[91]

Lawrence was not a defenseless town. Four hundred soldiers were said to be encamped on the other side of the river opposite the town. Two separate camps of recruits were stationed in the middle of the town. Cannon were placed in strategic places within the city limits, and an armory centrally located north of Winthrop Street served as a rallying place in case of emergency. The armory bell would be rung to alert the militia and call the men together. Although modern Federal arms were kept solely in the armory, the militia living in town had their own personal weapons with them. It was known that almost every man in town owned a Sharps carbine. This was the weapon of choice used by the Lawrence militia. It could fire thirteen rounds a minute, and keep it up for thirty-eight rounds before having to put in a fresh supply of caps, which would take from twenty to thirty seconds. Armed guards patrolled the town prior to the raid but were discontinued out of laxity immediately preceding the attack. Even though the raid was sprung on the unsuspecting town at first light, many of the militia had on their Federal uniforms and were armed with sidearms. An added incentive to attack Lawrence was General Thomas Ewing's recent General Order No. 10 issued only four days after the murder of the female relatives of Quantrill's men. It forced all citizens and their families who were willfully aiding the guerrillas to leave the district and the state with only their moveable possessions.

In their own minds the guerrillas counted the numbers of armed men who would be arrayed against them before adding up the costs. The odds seemed insurmountable. Quantrill reminded them, "The Kansans [have] been murdering and robbing our people for two years or more, and burned their houses by districts, hauled their household plunder, farming implements to Kansas, driven off their cattle, until forbearance has ceased to be a virtue. Lawrence is the great hotbed of abolitionism in Kansas. All the plunder or at least the bulk of it, stolen from Missouri will be found stored away at Lawrence. We can get more revenge and more money there than anywhere else in the State of Kansas." Regarding the money they expected to get in Lawrence, Quantrill told them, "I want to compensate the people who have divided their last biscuit with us and are still willing to do so. Now, my plan is that whatever money may be gotten in Lawrence shall be divided among the men with the instructions to give to these needy people very liberally."[92]

Someone spoke up, commenting on the great distance and the thousands of soldiers in and around Lawrence, stating that the undertaking was simply too hazardous. To this comment Quantrill replied, "I consider it almost a forlorn hope, for if we go, I don't know if anyone of us will get back to tell the story, but, if you never risk, you never gain." Turning to his officers sitting in the circle in front of him, Quantrill addressed each one individually.

Looking each man in the eye Quantrill asked softly. "Come, speak out, somebody. What is it, Anderson?" Bill Anderson had been sitting quietly. His men remembered that Anderson "would become as wild as a maniac if the subject of Federals were brought up." It was said that Anderson was the first man to propose to Quantrill to go to Lawrence. Anderson shouted back his reply, "Give me Lawrence or give me hell, but with one proviso, that we kill every male thing. She has sown the wind, let her reap the whirlwind." Anderson told Quantrill that he "would take Lawrence or go to hell trying."[93] Quantrill next turned to Dave Poole who replied with only a few words. "On to Lawrence. An eye for an eye." George Todd finished his thought. "And a tooth for a tooth. Lawrence, if I knew that not a man would get back alive."

Quantrill next turned to his adjutant William Gregg who spoke what was in his heart. "On to Lawrence, because Quantrill wills it. It is the home of Jim Lane; the foster-mother of the Red Legs; the nurse of the Jayhawkers." Quantrill next pointed to George Shepherd who replied, "Lawrence, till Lawrence is no more." Captain John Jarrette spoke up in turn. "Lawrence, by all means. I've had my eye upon it for a year. The head devil of all this killing and burning in Jackson County lives there. I vote to fight it with fire, to burn it before we leave it, just like Lane did Osceola." Quantrill next asked for Dick Maddox's opinion. "Sack Lawrence. Destruction and death to everybody there. An eye for an eye and a tooth for a tooth; God understands better than we do the equilibrium of civil war." Colonel John Holt was next to speak. "Lawrence, and

Henry Wilson was a Confederate Negro soldier who served as one of Quantrill's bodyguards. Quantrill sent Wilson into Lawrence before the raid to spy out the town. (Emory Cantey Collection)

John Lobb served as a scout and spy for Quantrill. In this photo dated July 25, 1863, he is shown mounted shortly before the raid on Lawrence. (Emory Cantey Collection)

quick about it. Lawrence loves the black man. We'll give her a taste of the black flag." Following Holt's remark Dick Yeager had this to say. "Where my house once stood there is a heap of ashes. I haven't a neighbor that's got a house. Lawrence and the torch." Andy Blunt was next to add his opinion. "Count me in whenever there's killing. Lawrence first, and then some other Kansas town; the name is nothing." Surveying each face once again, Quantrill asked. "Have you all voted?" They answered in unison. "All." "Then Lawrence it is. Saddle up men!"[94]

Following the unanimous vote Quantrill laid out his method for the assault. On the ride to Lawrence they would dispatch any known Jayhawkers living along the way. If the outskirts of Lawrence could be reached they would determine at the last possible moment whether an attack could successfully be made. Any large bodies of soldiers camped in town would be immediately assaulted. A small arsenal kept inside the Eldridge House Hotel and the hotel itself would be the first and primary objective to be targeted. If they were successful there, the next target would be the Johnson House Hotel, headquarters of Colonel George Hoyt's Redlegs. Both hotels were understood to be rallying points if the citizens feared a raid. If those two objectives could be successfully gained, then each of Quantrill's separate companies would be assigned different parts of the city, and individual squads would then seek out those most wanted. Those running about the streets would be assumed to be militia members trying to rally at their assigned rendezvous. These men would be dispatched without inquiring their identities.

Ironically, on the same day that the raid took place Confederate president Jefferson Davis issued a proclamation asking all Southerners to observe a day of "fasting, humiliation and prayer." On this day the president invited his countrymen to go to their "respective places of public worship" and to pray for divine favor "on our suffering country."[95]

The reasons were obvious. The South had suffered a number of heartrending defeats during the year 1863. The exception was Fredricksburg and Chancellorsville, but the loss of Stonewall Jackson made the latter a bittersweet victory. Besides the audacious exploits of John S. Mosby in Virginia and John Hunt Morgan's daring raids into the states of Kentucky, Indiana, and Ohio, the remainder of the year was a humiliating concern. The South's land mass was rapidly shrinking as the Federal juggernaut rolled forward, and the Southern attrition in men and arms made some Southerners begin guessing how much longer the war could last. The defeat of General John S. Marmaduke at Springfield, Missouri, on January 8, and his dubious raid on Hartville followed by a Confederate defeat at Arkansas Post a few days later, made Quantrill's Lawrence raid and the stunning victories he achieved afterward the only victories the South could claim in the Trans-Mississippi Department during the year.

2

Brotherhood of the Blood

Dead Yankees look much better than live ones.

—Captain George Todd

After relaying his plans for the operation to his officers, Quantrill supplied his men with maps with each targeted house marked for destruction and "Death Lists" of individuals to be killed. The names and places shown came as no surprise. In its entirety it revealed the enormity of the opposition and the level of the Kansans' participation in waging war against their neighboring state.

The New England Emigrant Aid Society

The foremost movers against the institutions in Missouri were those from the East who had come to Kansas in military-styled companies associated with the New England Emigrant Aid Society. The society was created by New England abolitionists to establish antislavery settlements in Kansas and thereby vote for it to be a free state when the time came for the territory to be organized as a state. Upon establishing themselves in Lawrence the society's members organized a Lawrence town association. Without any opposition to office, all the leading members filled positions in their new quasi-legal government. In their first meeting they elected Charles Robinson chairman along with other officers before discussing what salaries each would receive after levying a tax on the existing settlers. Next came rules and regulations governing the people of Lawrence. Joseph Savage, who had emigrated with the second party of the New England

Emigrant Aid Company, commented that the association told them that they couldn't go back East to visit their relatives until the elections were over.

Besides threatening violence the abolitionists sought to restrict land claims to only free-state settlers. Responding to the abolitionists' armed takeover of land claims, a local newspaper, the *Kansas City Enterprise,* wrote, "No sooner was Kansas Territory laid open for immigration and settlement than this very faction, armed in the usual panoply of their warfare, have in the short space of time, which has elapsed since then, thrown the whole country, which was before the very embodiment of harmony and quiet, into a state of the most dangerous and irreconcilable commotion."[1] The first fifty-six town lots soon went on sale after being surveyed by A. D. Searle. Both abolitionists and proslavery settlers were able to bid. The bidding for each lot reached as high as $250. But strangely only members of the New England Emigrant Aid Society wound up as successful bidders. Afterward the money was never collected.

Their scheme eventually came to light. These New England abolitionists came to join in a revolution to overthrow established institutions supported by illegal shipments of smuggled arms supplied by wealthy radical abolitionists in Massachusetts. Proslavery forces saw the society as nothing more than a means for bribing antislavery voters. The society built reception facilities that doubled as fortifications should they need to defend themselves. Richard Cordley remarked, "They had come in many cases without any definite idea as to what they were to do or how they were to make a living. That was entirely a secondary consideration. They were ready to do anything that offered, their main purpose being to take part in settling the great question of freedom for Kansas. Whether they made a farm or not, and whether they made a living or not, they proposed to make Kansas free." Cordley continued by saying, "The country was full of the curious who came to see what was going on; of adventurers who came to join in the fray; of speculators who came to profit by the occasion."[2]

It was asserted by the proslavery forces that the New England Emigrant Aid Society was responsible for all the turmoil in Kansas. A congressional committee investigating the troubles agreed that the society had indeed incited the invasion into Missouri by

President Franklin Pierce. In a special message to Congress, Pierce declared that the prewar Kansas government was "revolutionary and operating in an act of rebellion." (Library of Congress)

its propaganda and activities. Senator Stephen A. Douglas and President Franklin Pierce held the same views. While no illegal weapons were technically shipped by the Emigrant Aid Society to the free-staters in Kansas, weapons were purchased and shipped by the directors of the company and funneled through company channels. Upset at the upheaval caused by the abolitionists, President Pierce issued the following condemnation: "I have never believed that actual disruption of the Union can occur without blood; and if through the madness of Northern abolitionists that dire calamity must come, the fighting will not be along Mason and Dixon's line merely. Do we not all know that the cause of all our calamities is the vicious intermeddling of too many of the citizens of the Northern states with the Constitutional rights of the Southern states, cooperating with the discontents of the people of those states?"[3]

The Kansas Troubles

On March 23, 1857, the Lawrence *Herald of Freedom* wrote, "The Kansas troubles are over. They were, from the beginning nothing but a war between Pro-slavery and free-state speculators. The question of slavery was simply a bugaboo, introduced to give character and acerbity to the contest." A Northern newspaper in Wisconsin agreed with the same assessment in one of its editorials: "A gentleman from

Madison has just called on us, and states that a reliable citizen of that place has just returned, who has spent some six months in Kansas and made himself well acquainted with the truth of all the difficulties in that Territory. When he went there he was a Republican Whig and favored the Black Republican side, but after witnessing their maneuvers and learning their object and end in keeping up the troubles there, he changed at once his political position."[4]

One such group of abolitionist emigrants was reported in the *Herald of Freedom* on October 21, 1854. "It is said there is a company established at Antwerp, for the purpose of forwarding convicts to this country, and that the authorities pay a premium on each one sent over by the company. Arrests have lately been made, but nothing definite could be proven, and so the newly arrived malefactors are let loose upon us. These are a sample of the 'settlers' to be forwarded to our States and Territories by the newly invented 'Western Emigrating Associations.'" Another Kansas paper, the *Kansas Pioneer,* stated, "Steamers have been landing at our wharf the past week, and filling over the gangway. We see men armed, not with axes and pruning hooks, or the instruments of husbandry, but each one with his patent revolving rifle, or double barrel shotgun in hand. Where do these foreign looking importations come from?"[5]

One such group of eighty abolitionists from Michigan arrived in Lexington, Missouri, heavily armed. They were confronted by local citizens who confiscated their weapons, but not before at least twenty of them threw their weapons overboard to keep them from being seized. The entire group was sent back from where they came. These foreign emigrants added much to the discord in Kansas and gave the state an unfavorable reputation. George W. Brown of the *Herald of Freedom* remarked, "The complete ignorance of our customs in which the foreign emigrant finds himself, and in more than half the foreign emigration, has complete ignorance of our language, subjects him to every fraud, and to constant accident. It is in the face of every conceivable inconvenience that the country receives every year four hundred thousand foreigners into its seaports, and sends the larger portion of them to its Western country."[6]

It was early recognized that "the Yankees did not bring the implements of agriculture of a bona fide settler, but came as minions of political schemers of the East to fill Kansas with free[-state] men." In 1858 Senator John J. Ingalls described in a letter the inhabitants of most Kansas towns, saying that they were "shabby, ill-dressed, unthrifty people like the inhabitants of the Irish quarter of a large city, wearing upon their countenances a look of discontent akin to despair." He observed that offices were filled with dolts, and posts of honor and profit were held by irresponsible persons because there were more positions than worthy candidates. Many came west with no thought of making the new state their home. An idea persisted of making a fortune and returning home in three or four years.[7]

Even the renowned Horace Greeley remarked on the character of Kansas men he encountered during the summer of 1859 as he was heading overland to California. Greeley was characteristically outraged to find isolated, improvident settlers more interested in drinking whiskey and buying and selling land than in the moral benefits of hard work and temperance. "It was enough," he wrote in his *Overland Journey,* "to give a cheerful man the horrors." Also part of the horrors in Kansas reported in the *Herald of Freedom* was this observation: "Among the mass of emigration to Kansas, has come the pickpocket, the thief and burglar. But few days elapse but we hear of some case of this character. Strangers seem to be in the greatest danger from these villains, and yet no class of our people is safe from their depredations." Richard Cordley even remarked, "There were rough and turbulent characters among them, and rash things and wrong things were done by them." In rare instances the Southern viewpoint concerning Kansas immigration was allowed to grace the pages of the *Herald of Freedom*. In one column it revealed, "The Abolition party at the north are at work sending their emissaries among us. Greeley now has a proposition to raise a fund for paying the passage of all pauper emigrants across the ocean, and colonizing them in Kansas. They are to work so many years to pay expenses. They thus make slaves of them, and voters too."[8]

If these early settlers had only come to Kansas Territory to work and to vote in free elections, hard feelings would never have surfaced. Unfortunately, the men who came under the auspices of the New England Emigrant Aid Society and their supporters were reactionary in their desire to make Kansas a free state through insurrection and violence if necessary. Missourians mostly agreed in their feelings toward these new settlers. "Their coming was regarded in Missouri very much as would have been regarded the coming of a foreign foe. Each new settlement in Kansas was viewed as a menace to the security of slave property in Missouri. The fear was not groundless. A fleet of hostile ships anchored outside the harbor of a city would create a feeling of alarm exactly similar to the feeling in Missouri caused by these settlements in Kansas."[9] A newspaper in the heart of Missouri, a region known as "Little Dixie," recalled, "One abolitionist agent was discovered at Brunswick, Missouri on Thursday last. He hopes to get to Chicago in time to ship an additional supply of abolitionists to Kansas before the election. They are fearful that they will be beaten in the election. He can get to Chicago, and send men to Kansas yet before the 30th, the day of the election."[10]

In 1855 the levee at Kansas City was the objective of one of the great national migratory movements. At the foot of the levee from Delaware and Main Streets to the foot of Grand Avenue dozens of steamboats came and went daily. The emigrants paid twelve dollars for the trip from St. Louis. The territory of Kansas had been opened to settlement the previous year, and every available steamboat was now bringing three to five hundred emigrants to decide its political status. The Lexington, Missouri, *Express* stated in March 1855: "Every steamer up the Missouri brings hundreds of abolition emigrants to Kansas." The numbers and purchasing power of the migration had transformed the town of a few hundred inhabitants in 1855 into an incipient metropolis of perhaps five thousand by 1860, seemingly overnight. Westport was headquarters for Southern emigrants to Kansas Territory, as Kansas City was for those from New England.[11]

Radical Abolitionists

Naturally many of the names listed on the guerrillas' "Death Lists" were radical abolitionists, as exhibited in their highly vocal stance against slavery. The abolitionists relayed their viewpoint quite clearly: "Our undertaking as radical political abolitionists, is to remove slavery from the national territories by means of our national political power, and to remove it from the States, also, by means of the same power."[12] Describing the men belonging to the Emigrant Aid Company, Joseph Savage said they were "willing, and perhaps anxious, to become martyrs to their principles."[13]

Recounting the differences in the radical elements in Kansas, one newspaper described an abolitionist as

> the most radical. He is opposed to the Constitution of his country, regards the Union conceived in sin and brought forth in iniquity, that there should be no union with slave holders or participation in the affairs of so corrupt a government as ours. Believes it the duty to incite Negroes to run away from their masters and take all the property they can with them. In comparison a Free-Soiler believes that all the soil in the Territory over which the central government has control ought to be forever free. They wish to confine slavery to its present limits. They hold that the Constitution does not recognize property in slavery and that it does not protect slavery in the territories. A Free Stater is different. He wants Kansas free, not from any sympathy for the Negro or regards for his rights but because of the pecuniary gain of the masses. All three examples can be spoken of interchangeably."

According to this newspaper, some new settlers even wanted to make Kansas a "free white state."[14]

Benjamin Franklin Stringfellow, an outspoken proslavery man from Platte County, Missouri, and former Missouri attorney general, explained the slave owners' viewpoint. "We do not regard Negro slavery as it exists in our country, as either a moral or political evil. The condition of the Negro is far better as a slave in our country, than it has ever been in this or another country in which the Negro has been free."[15] Stringfellow called a meeting on July 20, 1854, to deal with abolitionists stealing slaves or inducing slaves to run away. Four Negroes had run away on July 8 from their Platte County owners. The proslavery men in the county had no doubt that the fugitives had been lured away by Leavenworth abolitionists. The attendees organized the Platte County Self-Defensive Association and named Stringfellow as secretary. They passed resolutions asserting that the value of all slaves was being diminished by abolitionist activity and that therefore they had a right to investigate anyone suspected of free-soilism and refused to do business with them.

Most Missourians felt equally unanimous in their feelings. "We want to see the Constitution of this great Confederacy observed to the letter, by the enemies of our Union, the Abolitionists. They are causing all the disturbances in our land by their hellish and disunion loving maneuvers, and if a dissolution must take place, they will be the aggressors. Man's property is sacred, and his slaves are recognized as property. The protection of property is one of the invaluable rights of man. And if the laws fail to protect a man in this right, he will naturally seek redress."[16] Abolitionists called for the immediate, uncompensated, and universal emancipation of the slaves. In effect, the abolitionists were demanding "the confiscation of billions of dollars worth of private property, the ownership of which constituted the power of, and defined the nature of the slave-owning class."[17]

Illegal Activities of the Abolitionists

Often the abolitionists' uncompromising attitudes made them a nuisance even to their Northern neighbors. Abolitionists knew that their actions would inevitably cause a civil war, but in their own minds they believed they had to destroy the country in order to save it. If there was not enough animosity in Kansas when the first company of Emigrant Aid Society members reached Lawrence, the abolitionists made sure there was ample opportunity once they arrived. A Kansas Citian wrote on one occasion: "A company of about twenty-five abolitionists from Ottawa, Illinois was landed at our wharf on Wednesday last, from off the steamer *Arabia*. They had Sharps rifles and ammunition, most of them had no other baggage but black carpet sacks. They came to resist the laws of the territory and were destined for Topeka. The men came to fight and to stir up civil war in our territory. They were sent out and their passage paid by the Aid Society."[18] Once in the territory, the abolitionists turned their antislavery zeal on their Kansas proslavery neighbors. A. J. Hoole, who lived near Lawrence, said, "I never lie down without taking the precaution to fasten my door, and fix it in such a way that if it is forced open, it can be opened only wide enough for one person to come in at a time. I have my rifle, revolver, and old home-stocked pistol where I can lay my hand on them in an instant,

This is a photo of the old log Mineral Hotel, one of the three hundred buildings destroyed on September 23, 1861, during Jayhawker James Lane's destruction of Osceola, Missouri. (Emory Cantey Collection)

besides a hatchet and axe. I take this precaution to guard against the midnight attacks of the Abolitionists, who never make an attack in open daylight."[19]

Major James B. Abbot from Lawrence was a member of the first company of society members who left Boston on July 17, 1854. Once in Kansas, Abbot quickly returned to Connecticut to seek weapons for the New England abolitionists to use in overpowering the Southern settlers living in Kansas. Abbot was responsible for bringing Sharps rifles and a brass howitzer into Lawrence to start an insurrection by thwarting the laws of the Federal government. He was also accused of using his home as a station on the Underground Railroad in violation of the Federal Fugitive Slave Law. Abbot was known as a radical abolitionist. He longed for "one more big fight in Kansas" even if it should cost him his life or the lives of others as the "object is worth all it will cost." Abbot became the Shawnee Indian agent and was later implicated in stealing a large amount of Indian funds.[20]

Abbot's neighbor, Colonel Joel Grover, was also a radical abolitionist and lived with his wife Emily on their farm outside Lawrence. After coming to Lawrence with the New England Emigrant Aid Company he fought in Lane's Brigade at the destruction of Osceola, Missouri. Grover was an officer in a militia cavalry unit in Lawrence and used his stone barn as a station on the Underground Railroad.

Fugitive slaves who were hidden in various persons' homes in town could be brought to Grover's barn when the time was near to send a group on to Topeka or points farther north without anyone observing their activity.

These radical abolitionists conferred that it was "their stated purpose to shelter fugitives owing service in southern states, and to kill any who should assist in attempting to enforce the fugitive slave law." Most of the abolitionists were armed by their benefactors back East. The New England Emigrant Aid Society's organizer, Eli Thayer, helped to manufacture firearms that were sold only to free-state men. He donated $4,500 for the purchase of rifles and cannon from his own money.[21]

The Emigrant Aid Society and Kansas Jayhawkers

Many of the early emigrants from the New England Emigrant Aid Society became members of Kansas Jayhawker units. These early Kansas emigrants who graduated into the ranks of the Jayhawkers were a lawless set of men.[22] They were violent men intent on violent action. As early as 1855 Governor Reeder of Kansas appealed to the abolitionists through the *Herald of Freedom*: "Kansas must be a country of law and order. No man must be allowed to cast contempt upon the law, to unsettle the foundation of society, to mar our future destinies, to cause us to be shunned and avoided by good citizens, and to turn us upon the retrograde path toward barbarism by substituting his unbridled passion for the administration of justice, and by redressing his real and imaginary wrongs by the red and cowardly hand of assassination or the ruffianism of the outlaw."[23] Despite the pleadings of Governor Reeder to maintain law and order, the following year of 1856 saw the abolitionists receive fifty-four Hall military rifles, six breechloading cannon, and another one hundred Sharps carbines with saber bayonets. Knowing the weapons were illegal, the abolitionists had them shipped separately and packed in crates marked "tool chests."

The newspapers in Kansas often recounted the abolitionists' illegal activities.

> The fact is that open and avowed rebellion and treason exist in our territory. The abolitionists are in arms against the laws and authority

> of the Territory. For this they have received arms and ammunition from Massachusetts. For this they had formed months ago a grand secret organization in the Territory called the Grand Army of Kansas and they have commenced their work of rebellion, by rescuing criminals from the hands of the officers of the law, and have burned the houses of proslavery men, and driven their families into the wilderness, and have set all law and order at defiance, saying by their presses, by their speakers, in public and in private, we will obey no law, we recognize no laws in Kansas, no governor, no magistrates. Truly, a more infamous, lawless set of men ever assembled together than these men were. And yet look at their duplicity, dishonesty, falsehood and hypocrisy. But these are the cardinal virtues of an Abolitionist, together with stealing. But they are as bold and reckless as they are wicked; for if they persist in their rebellion they will be crushed and not one of them be left.

At the first appearance of John Brown in Lawrence he was immediately put in command of a company of abolitionist militia. Brown was recorded as telling a mob at Lawrence concerning the territorial laws, "Those laws we denounce and spit upon and will never obey." Brown told the abolitionists that he had come to the territory "to draw a little blood," as he described it. Many of them were in constant fear that he would precipitate a conflict by some rash deed.[24]

Lawless Lawrence

Lawrence had always maintained a reputation for lawlessness. From its very inception, its citizens had thwarted Federal law. As far back as 1855, the town had expressed open disdain for the law. The *Chicago Tribune* on February 15, 1855, stated: "Two men, named Calbert and Bagsby from Independence were in search of four runaway slaves. They were set upon by fifteen Negros who ran them back into Missouri. Missourians together said, 'We find these miscalled emigrants really negro-thieves, their purpose not to procure a home in Kansas, but to drive slaveholders there from; that they are not freemen, but paupers, who have sold themselves to Eli Thayer and Co., to do their master's bidding; who hesitate not to proclaim that they are expert in stealing slaves; that they intend to follow their calling.'" On another occasion on April 20, 1860, Deputy U. S. Marshal Leonard Arms was run out of Lawrence when he attempted to enforce the Fugitive Slave Law by reclaiming a Negro woman hiding in town. On his last assignment, as Arms came riding into Lawrence, he was shot dead by John Richey, a member of the Free State Party, who was charged a few days later of robbing the mails. Richey later joined Lane's Jayhawker brigade.[25]

For years troublemakers from the New England Emigrant Aid Society poured into Kansas Territory and headed straight for Lawrence. Many after arriving continued to reside there. Most of them were radical abolitionists who thought nothing too bad or wrong to do to a slaveholder or for that matter anyone residing in the slaveholding state of Missouri. But the quality of the character of these newly arrived emigrants left something to be desired by the more judicious class of settlers. A New York executive residing in Lawrence complained, "We are not exactly advocates of slavery, but would prefer it by far to a community composed of a people such as will soon occupy these new territories if they are to be populated by Western Emigration Associations."[26] The New England Emigrant Aid Society's aim as a powerful antislavery organization was to quickly promote a sufficient number of people casting a majority of votes favoring a free state. Those emigrating with the society were promised protection and cut-rate lodging while they traveled with the group. Kansas was promoted as a garden of nature. The first New England emigrants had a grand design: claim political legitimacy, whether they had it or not. The plan was simple enough; organize a quasi-legal organization; band together, elect leaders, and claim jurisdiction as a legal body. When confronted by the true legal authorities they were to ignore them when they could and fight them when they must. These Yankee emigrants aroused hard feelings from the settlers from Dixie, not exactly the kind of folks they wanted for neighbors.

When Kansas proslavery settlers established a proslavery legislature, New England settlers sought to circumvent the agreement by starting their own government. From their first inception in Lawrence emigrants from New England quickly sought to establish a perception of authority. The settlers met among themselves and voted for a governing body that excluded any thought contrary to their abolitionist philosophy.

They spent their time issuing high-sounding resolutions and proclamations but lacking any power whatsoever. They then raised two military companies complete with uniforms and armed with Sharps rifles. These maneuvers were illegal as the territory was under the authority and protection of the Federal government. Illinois Senator Stephen A. Douglas blasted the Kansas abolitionists by warning, "Those daring revolutionists in Kansas plot to overthrow by force the system of law under which they live." Wilson Shannon from Ohio, who was governor of the territory from 1855 to 1856, emphasized, "It is regarded as a revolutionary movement for the people of Kansas to organize a State government without permission of Congress."

Richard Cordley became a member of the Lawrence militia and wrote concerning the free-staters' threats on the territorial constitution being considered at Lecompton, Kansas. "They came to take possession of that stronghold of border ruffianism; they came prepared for emergencies; they came in squads and companies; they came from all quarters."[27] James Lane also got involved in the Lecompton troubles when he planned to assassinate all the delegates to the Lecompton convention.

Charles Carroll Spalding, a Unionist living in Westport, Missouri, testified on June 5, 1856, before a special congressional committee investigating the Kansas troubles. Spalding said that he had been a resident and publisher of a newspaper in Westport at the time of the controversial election in Kansas Territory on March 30, 1855, and had talked with emigrants there a few days earlier. His testimony supported the Southern contention that many New England emigrants, as had been charged against those from the South, were primarily interested in casting ballots and did not remain in the territory.[28]

The Kansas-Nebraska Act

All the troubles began on May 30, 1854, when the Kansas-Nebraska Act became law. It established the territorial boundaries of Kansas and Nebraska and opened the land to legal settlement. Included in the act was a declaration that the Fugitive Slave Act of 1850 was still in full force in the territory. The Fugitive Slave Act eliminated any safe haven for runaway slaves escaping to the Northern states.

Under no circumstances did proslavery congressmen want a free territory west of Missouri. Stephen A. Douglas, chairman of the Senate Committee on Territories, decided to offer legislation making concessions to the South. The act contained the provision that the question of slavery should be left to the decision of the territorial settlers themselves. This was the famous principle that Douglas called "popular sovereignty." The obvious inference, at least to Missourians, was that Missouri would be slave, and Nebraska free. The bill enraged the antislavery forces. Its effects were anything but reassuring to those who had hoped for a peaceful solution. The popular sovereignty provision caused both proslavery and antislavery forces to marshal strength and exert full pressure to determine the "popular" decision in Kansas in their own favor, using groups such as the New England Emigrant Aid Society. The society was formed with the sole objective of sending in, as soon as practicable, a large emigration from the free-states. Both Northerners and Southerners were aroused to such passions that sectional division reached a point that precluded reconciliation. A new political organization, the Republican Party, was founded by opponents of the bill.

Early Kansas had long been known for its troubles. "Repeated conflicts with the Indians over their rightful claim to virtually all the land were aggravated by the squatters' belief in their own moral superiority, as well as the unrestrained aggression of speculators, political hopefuls, and a host of lesser opportunists." Following the passage of the Kansas-Nebraska Act both Missourians and New Englanders staked claims in the new territory. The sentiment of the majority of the settlers was proslavery, but settlers from the New England Emigrant Aid Company illegally staked more than one claim for themselves. A New England man openly admitted that the settlers formed a pact to hold a claim independent of the one on which they resided. He said that they knew that they "had no support under the U.S. laws; but the settlers set up a 'higher law.'"[29] Erastus Ladd, who came to Kansas with the second party of the New England Emigrant Aid Company, said that the abolitionists were "scattered all over the prairie and wood land to keep claims from the Missourians."[30]

In response, an article in the *Missouri Republic* sought to defend the Southerners' constitutional rights. "They [the people of Jackson

County] have as much right to go into Kansas Territory with their slaves and other property as any fanatical son of New England[,] and this right they will assert at all hazards."[31] Another Missouri newspaper, the *Liberty Platform,* editorialized in the same vein. "Shall we allow cut-throats and murderers, as the people of Massachusetts are, to settle in the territory adjoining our own State?"[32] In the midst of all this turmoil, the names of those who were the most reactionary began to surface.

James Henry Lane

James Henry Lane was born in Lawrenceburg, Indiana, in 1814, and followed the footsteps of his father, an Indiana congressman, by becoming a lawyer and a Jacksonian Democrat. The father had the reputation of the trickiness of the wily politician. His son received only the barest rudiments of an education at home from his mother. Lane's service as the commander of two Indiana volunteer regiments in the Mexican War helped him to launch his own political career. He served as Indiana's lieutenant governor from 1849 to 1853 and then as a congressman from 1853 to 1855. His vote in favor of the Kansas-Nebraska bill in 1854 ruined him politically in his native state so he rode off to Kansas to salvage what was left and to start a new career. He began in Kansas as a Democrat, but when the Kansas legislature refused to grant him a divorce he attached himself to the Republican Party and did an abrupt about-face, aligning himself with the free-state forces. Whenever a general gathering took place in Lawrence, Lane was called upon to give a speech and "would work the crowd up to the fighting point." Only the coarsest of men seemed to enjoy Lane's speeches. One listener commented, "It has never been my misfortune to listen to a more vulgar and indecent harangue from the stump." Lane himself admitted, "The man who told the biggest lies, nowadays served his country best, and that God would pardon him of his sins."[33]

Senator John J. Ingalls characterized Lane as "a backwoods orator who never lost a chance to mount the stump, and his effusions lacking in any logic, polish, or consistency, he was a rabble-rouser who had an astonishing ability to stir mob action." A letter further described Lane: "A wiry, lank specimen of a backwoodsman, with prominent features, smooth face and erect hair. He is a nervous speaker, full of fire, and 'takes' with the people. Three years ago he would have spoken in St. Louis at the peril of his life. Now, his most radical utterances were cheered to the echo." Such praise of Lane often found its way into the pages of the *Lawrence Republican* newspaper. Lane fronted his friend John Speer $3,500 to buy the paper, then used both the paper and Speer as political tools. Thus Speer became one of the prime agitators in the early border troubles, and even used the paper to entice slaves to run away. Lane's early underling Charles Jennison eventually accused Lane of being a "villain of a darker hue, and more capable of treachery, deceit and corruption than I had at that time imagined." It was generally understood that Lane's policy was to control the state government or disgrace it. In order to get his own men into office, Lane would have opposing candidates arrested and locked up until his own men had been elected. As a result he developed an unsavory reputation in Lawrence, and it was heralded that "Lane rules the roost in the city of corruption."[34]

Lane became the acknowledged leader of the most radical free-state men, "often rousing them by his rough eloquence to such a furor of excitement as to lead to most serious apprehensions," especially when it came to stirring Kansas settlers to attack their neighbors across the border. Lane was quoted in the *Lawrence Republican* as saying, "A rebellious province or State must be visited by severe chastisement of war; Traitors must suffer the loss of property; and desolation must overwhelm them."[35] Another description of Lane noted: "[He] is hot-headed, rash, regardless of consequences, but not wanting in bravery. Lane looks only to the present, acts only for today, never gives a thought about how his acts will appear in history and considers a 'bird in the hand worth two in the bush.' Lane is a cross between a Western mountain-man and a Broadway dandy. Lane can't sit still long enough to write anything; if he can write at all. He has always been use to mounting a stump, whenever an idea struck him as worthy of notice, and 'letting off' extemporaneously." One of his Kansas contemporaries remarked about him, "He left behind him a family which he did not love, and a Democratic constituency too weak to serve his purposes. He was poor in

Robert S. Stevens served as Quantrill's lawyer before the war, winning a case against spurious charges brought against Quantrill by his Kansas enemies. Stevens summoned Quantrill while the Lawrence raid was taking place and obtained his promise for protection of the occupants of the Eldridge House Hotel. (Robert C. Stevens Collection)

purse, lax in morals, but not uncontrollably demoralized in his habits, and was possessed of a genius that neither poverty nor moral defects could conquer. Before Lane entered the senate he was so poor that he was refused credit for a loaf of bread in Lawrence and started to the capital on money he had borrowed."[36]

In 1858 William Weir was a captain of an early militia company. Weir, who became the regimental commander of the Fourth Kansas Regiment in Lane's Brigade, eventually discovered the truth about the man he once respected. Weir had gladly taken part in the destruction of Osceola, Missouri, but by the spring of 1863 told his friends, "Your worst enemy has been, and is, that mean, contemptible rascal, who pretends to represent the State of Kansas in the United States Senate, Jim Lane, the damnedest scoundrel that ever disgraced our state, or any other decent society."[37]

Robert S. Stevens, a lawyer from New York, often visited Lawrence trying to establish a railroad through the state. Stevens was an avowed enemy of Lane because he refused to join in Lane's criminal activities and despised his cunning, deceitful, and self-serving ways. Since Stevens had influence and prestige in Kansas, Lane feared him as a potential rival. At one point Lane accused Stevens of being part of a bond swindle, saying he was a thief and was stealing the treasury. As master of state politics, Lane worried that Stevens could influence Kansas legislators. Their votes were always important, and Lane was intent upon retaining his Senate seat. In one maneuver, friends of Lane who were delegates to the Topeka convention and who voted for Lane were later commissioned by him as officers in the Lane Brigade. Stevens wrote from Washington, DC, prior to the 1860 election commenting about ultra-radical abolitionists like Lane who were using the upheaval in Kansas for their own self-serving purposes. "Nothing is desired by the ultras in reference to Kansas, except to keep her 'bleeding' until 1860. Are they not finding active co-workers in the persons of Conway, Lane and company? Is Kansas ever to be kept as the arena of strife, rapine and bloodshed, merely to furnish capital for an outside party of greedy [persons] only to keep up and continue agitation, that they may perchance, gain a little notoriety or position?"[38]

Lane joined in the New England Emigrant Aid Society's preponderance for violence which became evident when its members boldly jumped claims belonging to Missourians, confronting them with armed bands of free-state settlers. The law stated that anyone could stake a claim. Many Missourians staked claims in the territory and made improvements to them, then returned to their established farms in Missouri to harvest their existing crops. The *Kansas Free State* encouraged newly arrived settlers not to honor claims laid out by anyone not actually living on them.[39]

It was said that many times "bearded men who wore no masks their identity was well known as the leaders of the Redlegs whose business was to rob settlers who had worked their claims, and forced them to leave the country. These improved farms were sold to newcomers by the leaders as abandoned claims, thus turning a pretty profit for the leaders." If the original owners returned to their rightful claims they were confronted by these armed bands of ruffians with drawn revolvers, threatening the owners to go back to Missouri. One abolitionist living in Kansas said that his neighbor, a

New Yorker, had gone back East and remained away for more than six months so his claim became "jumpable." He took over the claim illegally, admitting, "There was a great deal of jumping going on."[40]

Even free-staters suffered from the jealousies of land claims between themselves. Quantrill discovered firsthand the character of these Kansas settlers while he was residing in Kansas before the war. In a letter dated January 22, 1858, while living near Stanton, Quantrill wrote to his mother, "The claim north of mine was jumped last Monday by a young fellow from Indiana." At about the same time James Lane had his own problems with the rightful ownership of his claim when in 1858 he shot and killed a neighbor, Gaius Jenkins, another well-known free-state man, over a boundary dispute. Sensing that the disputed case was going against him, Lane attempted to bribe officials in the land office by offering them forty acres of land. After Lane was elected senator he had the case reviewed by the Secretary of the Interior who reversed the decision by the land office and the former Secretary of the Interior. Actions such as these led the *Lawrence Daily Republican* to denounce such treachery on its pages: "We obtain representatives who are very sound politically, but very rotten morally. Very honest Republicans, but very dishonest men."[41]

Lane continued his political intrigues, maneuvering to steal land from the sanctuary of his law office in Lawrence by canceling owners' claims, then putting them in his own name. It was noticed by all those living in the city. "Forty acres of the finest property in Lawrence is taken from its rightful owners and given to a vile demagogue. Jim Lane is no more the rightful owner of that property than is 'Jeff Davis.' It is understood that every owner of lots in the property referred to, must submit to an expensive law suit to secure again the title to his house and lands. Among those interested are several politicians, opponents of James Lane, which accounts to some extent for the outrage."[42]

William H. R. Lykins staked a claim for 160 acres in Lawrence, Kansas, as early as May 26, 1854, and built a cabin upon it. Lykins soon had trouble with claim jumpers from the New England Emigrant Aid Society. "From the first coming of the people of Lawrence, my claim has been trespassed upon and robbed of its timber." Abolitionists tried to steal his land by rendering his claim filing null and void. The New England Emigrant Aid Society's goal was to seize all town lots within the city limits, and if need be to run off any prior settlers or claimants to the land. Lykins filed his claim before the first members of the society ever arrived in Kansas, but they called him an intruder for trying to locate a farm claim in their town. The society's actions were illegal, and an appeal to the U. S. Congress affirmed the rights of the first settlers. Missouri newspapers recorded similar difficulties. "We learn that since the passage of the bill opening the Kansas Territory for settlement, some three thousand claims have been formed with many difficulties and furious quarrels are arising among the claimants."[43]

Charles Robinson

When the legal rights of Missouri settlers had to be protected by Federal troops, Charles Robinson, who had emigrated from Massachusetts to lead the Kansas troubles, was chosen as the leader of the free-state forces. As early as 1855 Robinson denounced all Missourians and spoke of making war on Missouri. Robinson was described as cool-headed, cautious, and calculative, and along with other society members unhesitatingly took up arms against the government. Robinson wrote to Amos Lawrence in Boston, "I have only time to thank you and your friends who sent us the Sharps rifles, for they will give us victory without firing a shot." The reputation of the Sharps was enough to cause consternation for any opposing force. The reason was that the Sharps had a fairly unusual pellet primer feed. This was a device that held a stack of pelleted primers. One was automatically flipped over the nipple every time the trigger was pulled and the hammer fell. This mechanism made the Sharps much easier to operate from horseback than weapons with individual percussion caps. The Sharps made a superior sniper weapon of higher accuracy than the more commonly issued muzzle-loading rifled muskets. This was due mainly to the higher rate of fire of the breech-loading mechanism, and the fact that the quality of manufacture was superior.[44]

Armed with the most improved weapons of their times these New Englanders were the chief troublemakers among the early settlers.

While some sought an honest living in farming or starting a business, many desired political position and the power and influence that came with holding office. Charles Robinson was selected as the leader of the first company of the New England Emigrant Aid Society because of his past experience in the early squatter wars in California. It was there he learned how to thwart the legal process in gaining control of an area taken over by squatters using armed insurrection and violence. During those turbulent times he had been severely wounded, and had been put under arrest and kept in prison for several months. A New England newspaper reported: "The leading spirit of these lawless movements is Charles Robinson. He is the leading spirit also of the Topeka Convention, and the present head of the executive committee of the State of Kansas, and the caller of the election, which proposed to elect a governor, secretary of state, judges etc., in January next. It is said that he had at least five hundred men, armed with Sharps rifles and revolvers, determined to offer a forcible resistance to the execution of the laws. He has threatened to hang Sheriff Jones, Coleman and others, as soon as he can get hold of them."[45] Besides these criminal undertakings Robinson advocated the refusal of the abolitionist settlers to pay taxes to the territorial government. The local newspaper recorded the deed. "Whether the people would fight the U.S authorities, in case an attempt was made to collect the taxes, by force, we cannot say; but we do not desire to see the experiment tried for fear of the consequences."[46]

Abolitionists knew that they had to present a majority opinion when the time came for the territory to petition Congress for statehood. When a new land got beyond the wilderness stage, its territorial government could present a request to Congress for admission into the partnership of the United States of America. Meanwhile the government in Washington, DC, would rule the area with a territorial governor appointed by the president. Chances were Congress would then pass an enabling act, authorizing the citizens of the terri tory to frame the constitution by which they wished to govern themselves. The territorial legislature could then set up a constitutional convention, and if Congress approved the instrument it framed, the territory would become a state. When the territory of Kansas first voted for a proslavery constitution, the free-state settlers refused to

President James Buchanan denounced the people of Kansas as a lawless people "in rebellion against the government, with a military leader [James Lane] at their head of most turbulent and dangerous character." (Library of Congress)

accept its authority and instead set up their own government framework in violation of territorial and Federal laws. Whenever the views of the territorial governor differed from the views of the radical abolitionists they either threatened his life or clamored for his removal.

Thomas H. Gladstone, the Englishman who visited Kansas as a

correspondent for the *Times* of London, wrote, "The Free-State organization gave rise to the double governorship, double judiciary, double legislature, double militia, and in general, double claim to obedience, which has constituted so peculiar a feature in the politics of Kansas." It was tantamount to treason for the free-staters to set up their own government. The actions of the Kansas abolitionists even caused President James Buchanan to state, "The territory of Kansas is said to be in insurrection" to the Federal government. They were told, "You have been offering resistance to the laws of the territorial Legislature, which was no doubt a legal one. The President has declared it legal; Congress has declared it legal; and resistance to those laws is treason." Even Senator Bayard of the abolitionist state of Delaware tagged the conduct of the Kansas Free State Party "incipient treason." In Albany, New York, Garret Smith, fundraiser for the New England Emigrant Aid Society, urged the abolitionists of Kansas Territory into insurrection to the territorial government by saying, "They must resist, even if in so doing, they have to resist both the Congress and the President." At a follow-up meeting at an abolitionist society Smith spoke out, "You are looking to ballots, when you should be looking to bayonets."[47]

The lawlessness of the abolitionist leaders was openly exhibited. Whenever an illegal act was committed by the early Kansas settlers the abolitionists convened a committee and took a vote authorizing their illegal acts to make them appear legally approved by a body of citizens. They would then call a meeting of citizens, vote in favor of their actions, and have it recorded in their books as appearing to be legal. They elected leaders who took on leadership positions without authority of law.

The Military Preparation of Lawrence

In another act of deception Charles Robinson and James Lane signed a treaty on behalf of the citizens of Lawrence to "aid in the execution of the laws, when called upon by proper authority." When the sheriff of Douglas County, Samuel J. Jones, who described himself as "an uncompromising Union man," arrived in Lawrence on April 23, 1856, presenting warrants for wanted men, both Robinson and Lane played fast and loose with semantics in their agreement with the sheriff and refused to help. Jones was acting under the authority of a congressional investigating committee sent out by Congress. He was in town to arrest Samuel N. Wood, one of the strongest antislavery leaders in Kansas, who had stolen some important papers the committee wanted and who had refused to appear before them. Jones came to town accompanied by a party of U.S. dragoons under the command of a Lieutenant McIntosh. When Jones attempted to serve a writ on Wood he was shot in the back by James P. Filer, an emigrant from New York. As a result of this flagrant violation in resisting the laws a posse was organized in Missouri to help Jones carry out his warrants. Kansans were not allowed to raise an organized militia since the territory was protected by Federal troops from Fort Leavenworth. Abolitionists cornered Governor Wilson Shannon, telling him that Lawrence was going to be destroyed by unruly mobs from Missouri and seeking his written proclamation so they could legally raise troops for their defense. Only after the governor gave permission for Robinson and Lane to organize militia troops did he realize that no such threat existed. As a result of Robinson and Lane's duplicity, Shannon lost his credibility in Missouri and became an object of derision in Kansas. Finding himself castigated by both factions and without friends, Shannon resigned his position in a letter to the president stating, "I am unwilling to perform the duties of governor of this Territory any longer," later noting, "You might as well attempt to govern the devil in hell."

With Shannon's written declaration Lawrence was permitted to have a legally armed militia, one which it could use to resist the territorial laws and keep the legal officers from conducting their duties. Following Shannon's removal from the territory, Daniel Woodson became the acting governor. Woodson's views reflected those of his predecessor. He stated: "[The] territory of Kansas was infected with large bodies of armed men, many of whom have just traveled from the states, combined and confederated together, and amply supplied with munitions of war; these armed men had been engaged in murdering the law-abiding citizens of the territory, driving others from their homes, holding others as prisoners of war, plundering property, burning down houses, even robbing United States post offices, and all this for the purpose of subverting by force and violence the government established by the law of congress in the territory." Woodson officially issued a proclamation "declaring the said territory of Kansas to be in an open state of insurrection and rebellion."[48]

After gaining the rights of a militia organization, the citizens of Lawrence quickly began organizing their city for defense. A woman who kept a hotel in town remembered the daily scene. "It looked strange to see the street paraded from morning to night by men in military array; to see them toil day and night throwing up entrenchments, to see them come in to their meals, each with a gun in his hand, sometimes bringing it to the table."[49] Sometime later when U. S. marshal for the Kansas Territory, J. B. Donaldson, came to Lawrence to serve arrest warrants, he was kept from doing so by several hundred armed citizens. Sara Robinson stated that John H. Green, who was good friends with James Redpath, "threatened the life of a deputy U.S. marshal serving under Marshal J. B. Donaldson who was trying to serve a warrant in Lawrence."[50] In reply Marshal Donaldson wrote, "I am well aware that the whole population of Lawrence is armed and drilled, and the town fortified." He recalled "the meetings and resolutions adopted in Lawrence and elsewhere in the territory, openly defying the laws and the officers thereof and threatening to resist the same to a bloody issue."[51]

James Montgomery

Kansas Territory was under the protection of Federal marshals and operated a set of courts with Federal judges that rendered decisions located in the various towns among the settlements. Radicals soon threatened the territorial courts. Federal judges attempting to hold court in Fort Scott were threatened and run off by Jayhawkers under James Montgomery who was becoming one of the chief agitators in Kansas. Emigrating to Kansas, Montgomery first gained notoriety when he organized a gang to chase proslavery settlers back into Missouri. When Missourians returned to reclaim their property, Montgomery considered them claim jumpers, especially after he had already sold the claims, making a handsome profit. When trouble started Montgomery took to the field, causing so much upheaval

James Montgomery and his wife in their wedding photograph. Montgomery became one of the chief agitators in Kansas. He organized a Jawhawking company in Kansas, driving Missourians off their claims, but soon was attacking both free-state and proslavery sympathizers. By 1860 the governor of Kansas had discovered that Montgomery was determined to invade Missouri and Arkansas for the purpose of inciting insurrection among the slaves of those states. (Patrick Marquis Collection)

that Governor Denver found it necessary to order a company of U. S. dragoons to restore order, claiming that men like Lane and Montgomery were "lawless and restless men who are never satisfied except when engaged in some broil or inciting trouble." Trying to justify Montgomery's illegal actions, Lane entered the fray by sending his henchman Major James Abbot to set up a "squatter's court" to settle the matter. Denver accused Lane of "assuming power without the authority of law." When U. S. Marshal Blake Little heard about the illegal court being convened, he deputized a posse and rode in to investigate, but not before Abbot judiciously abandoned his role and disappeared back to Lawrence.

Montgomery took to Jayhawking early. He organized a Jayhawking company in 1857 and attacked both free-state and proslavery sympathizers. An acquaintance remarked, "Montgomery who seems the only active man in the Department, is enormously energetic, and devoted to the cause, but a bush-whacker in his fighting, and a perfect fanatic in other respects. He never drinks, smokes or swears and considers that praying, shooting, burning and hanging are the true means to put down the rebellion." Another of Montgomery's means of putting down "rebellion" was to steal ballot boxes in proslavery settlements in Kansas.[52] From Fort Scott, Kansas, in 1859 Montgomery was threatened by one young woman whose fiancé he had recently murdered. She said that they were to be married in a few days and that her sweetheart was "one of the noblest men ever created, brave and true to his country and to his word" and that he never injured an innocent person. She vowed revenge against Montgomery, saying that even though she was a woman she could fire a pistol and would soon send him to a place where there is "weeping and gnashing of teeth." Another Kansas citizen wrote to Governor Denver complaining about "Montgomery and his murderers, & robbers." He believed "if the officers of the law will arrest Montgomery and his men we will have no trouble keeping the peace among the people in this region."

Montgomery first started robbing proslavery citizens then ordering them to leave the territory or their houses would be burned down around them. The residents of Fort Scott were predominately proslavery, while free-staters and abolitionists dominated the surrounding countryside. Radicals of each faction terrorized the town. In April of 1858 Montgomery's gang attacked a squad of Federal troops, killing two and wounding four. A month later he drove all proslavery settlers from Linn County. The previous month Montgomery's forces clashed with U. S. soldiers and killed one. When proslavery settlers retaliated, Montgomery struck again, going so far as to free convicted murderers from prison simply because they espoused antislavery sentiments. In December 1858 Benjamin Rice, a free-stater and Montgomery's right-hand man, had been convicted by a free-state jury and arrested for murder and imprisoned in the Fort Scott hotel. Montgomery warned, "If any indictment were found against himself, or any of his men, for 'Jayhawking' he would resist to the death any arrest." Montgomery brought his gang of one hundred ruffians to town, freeing Rice, then robbed a local store of $5,000 and murdered the owner in the presence of his family.

Montgomery next turned his attacks on Missouri, openly boasting, "We feed ourselves at proslavery larders and our horses at proslavery corn cribs." In response a Kansas newspaper reported, "One of the most diabolical and hellish plans has been concocted in this county, and perhaps others, for the purpose of robbing and plundering our settlers and murdering our friends. The clans, bowing to leaders such as Montgomery, Brown, Bain and others claiming to be Free State men, but who are the most infamous scoundrels and tyrannical demagogues, have again commenced operations such as stealing horses, arms, clothing, provisions, watches, etc. etc. and driving settlers from their homes." A. J. Hoole, who lived just outside Lawrence, remembered how the abolitionists treated their own neighbors. "Only last week a party of desperadoes went to a man's house, dragged him out of bed, and gave him fifty lashes on his bare back, telling him that, if he did not leave in ten days, they would kill him. They have also threatened others in the same way. . . . The reason they have been treated thus is because they would not join Lane's band, but served on the jury in trying some of his robbers."[53]

In December 1860 the acting governor of Kansas, George M. Beebe, wrote a letter to the president informing him that he had accurate information that Montgomery and Jennison "had received a large amount of arms, ammunition, stores, etc., and had determined to invade Missouri and Arkansas for the purpose of inciting insurrection among the slaves of those states."[54]

Attaching himself to John Brown's gang, Montgomery continued his raids, becoming bolder until he finally joined up with Charles Jennison in "operating a ring of 'desperate Jayhawkers.'" Despite his criminal activities Kansas radicals flocked to Montgomery's company. Using the subterfuge of an itinerant preacher Montgomery crossed the border reconnoitering wealthy Missouri farmers who would afford the best opportunity for a lucrative raid. As early as 1858 Montgomery joined forces with John Brown and began plundering indiscriminately in Missouri. They killed a Missouri citizen named David Cruse, robbing him and two other men of eleven Negroes, seven head of horses, two mules, two wagons, and a yoke of oxen valued at $14,000. Regretfully the government only made a half-hearted attempt to punish Montgomery, instead putting a $3,000 reward out for his arrest. Brown and Montgomery showed themselves to be nothing more than self-righteous abolitionists who considered themselves above the law.

One Kansan summed up Montgomery's tactics. "Montgomery's men enjoyed the opportunities for plundering that the exigencies of the times threw in their way; but Montgomery found at least two obstacles in the way when he attempted to restrain them; first, he was not himself a great commander of men, and second, to forbid them to plunder would have been to deprive himself of their assistance in time of need, and thus to render himself unable to defend the rights of the free-state men." It was reported of the Jayhawkers, "The officers commandeered the most valuable loot from their own men and also set the standard for brutality." One soldier surmised why Jayhawking was not punished. "Montgomery never countenanced plundering, though much of it was done by his men, and he realized that to restrain them would lose to him their services." After Montgomery ordered the destruction and plunder of Butler and Papinsville, Missouri, his regimental surgeon reported that his men were "villains who joined the force for protection in their plundering operations."[55]

Elsewhere along the border continued stories kept pouring in about Jayhawker atrocities. One settler, John Vansickle, writing from Bourbon County, Kansas, on December 28, 1858, complained, "I cannot only give you a faint idea of the brutality that is practiced in the county, it is governed by a set of armed desperados, in the last year there has been not less than 50 families drove off their claims and plundered in this county. The abolitionists have killed and plundered the county until the spoils will not pay any longer in the Territory." A free-state citizen from Fort Scott, William Smith, similarly reported the situation, "Formerly, it was proslavery and free-state, now it is free-state men against a gang of thieves and murderers headed by Jim Lane and Montgomery." The *Herald of Freedom* remarked on Lane's duplicity. "Lane represents himself as the great hero, who at the head of the free-state party vanquished the Border Ruffians. He attempts to show himself its savior. But of course he will not venture on an explanation of the fact that when there was personal danger or great risk he was always among the missing." Governor Robinson of Kansas added that Lane had a bad habit of "falsifying history to sound his own praise."[56]

Author John N. Holloway in his *History of Kansas* wrote:

> Montgomery proposes to retire from the field and attend to the improvement of his claim. He requested that the men be organized under Captain Stewart and Lieutenant [Sam] Walker, who should be

> actively on the watch to keep proslavery men in check. These, after performing a few praiseworthy deeds, began plundering, robbing and stealing, and running off the spoils to the north. They spread terror and ruin wherever they went, threatening proslavery men, many of whom fled the country with their families. They continued this dishonorable course, until they had brought disgrace upon their party, and aroused the whole country against them.[57]

Montgomery had reason to tell his friends that he was giving up Jayhawking. In fact, he was planning a reconnaissance around Martinsburg, Virginia, where he and other radical abolitionists planned on taking John Brown after breaking him out of jail at Charlestown where he had been transferred after his fiasco and arrest for treason at Harper's Ferry. When this venture failed in its intended results, Montgomery soon returned to his former plundering occupations along the border. Finally the Federal government sent a force to put an end to Montgomery's operations. Captain Nathaniel Lyon, an abolitionist himself, with Federal troops from Fort Leavenworth made a faint attempt to arrest Montgomery. Arranging a meeting with Montgomery, Lyon disobeyed orders and instead of arresting him allowed him to escape.

The Removal of Slaves

When Missourians learned of these illegal actions going unpunished, they were naturally filled with anger. Most Jayhawking was perpetrated by early bands of organized Kansas militia. Rather than just guarding their neighborhoods, these early militia units turned to preying on wealthy farms in Missouri. Once the war started, Missourians who had preferred to move to Kansas and those who had been run out of the state due to their radical abolitionism joined Jayhawker units and led their companies against their former neighbors, pointing out which houses to plunder. Plunder was the Jayhawkers' chief concern, but slaves were often compelled from their homes. Investigation following the Jayhawkers' devastating raids usually revealed the names and known places of residence of those who had taken part in them.

With slaves often being the most costly possession of many slave owners, their coerced removal from their homes caused a considerable financial loss to their owners. Lieutenant Henry M. Moore of the Fifth Kansas Jayhawker Regiment stated, "A great many Negroe Slaves are nightly running away from their masters and joining the brigade. I fear wrong means are sometimes used to obtain these slaves by some members of the brigade."[58] It was estimated that there were more than 10,000 slaves who had either run away on their own accord or had been forced from their homes in Missouri during Jayhawker raids. Even the radical Francis P. Blair of St. Louis, who had been responsible for secretly and illegally organizing and equipping a body of 1,000 men for the Union at the start of the war, was himself a slave owner. Like slave owners elsewhere in Missouri, Blair treated his slaves fairly. An apologist reported that his slaves "are doubtless well fed, warmly lodged, comfortably clothed, and adequately cared for in sickness and in health."[59]

The Fugitive Slave Act of 1850 caused many radical Northern abolitionists to thwart the law by establishing a surreptitious system of aiding fugitive slaves to escape into Northern communities or into Canada. The system was known as the Underground Railroad. "These Missourians were noble people, but they believed in slavery, and they were quick to resent anything like encroachment on the rights of slave property."[60] Missourians were offended by Easterners who decoyed their slaves away and disregarded the felonious acts involved in assisting their slaves to make a dash for Kansas. Some of these scoundrels were even known to rescue slaves from officers of the law, besides printing and circulating incendiary documents in their neighborhoods calculated to produce a disorderly, dangerous, or rebellious disaffection among the slaves. The amount in economic loss to their owners was in the millions of dollars. Because it was such a short distance from the Missouri border, Lawrence became the major station on the Underground Railroad. At least 1,000 slaves were said to have passed through Lawrence on their way north.

Escape to Lawrence was considered as good as freedom, according to one account. Escaping slaves were often referred to in railroad jargon as "passengers" or "freight." The Lawrence citizens who aided them were known as "agents" or "conductors," and the homes where they were sheltered were known as "stations." The "railroad" was made up of people's homes and outbuildings. The Federal Fugitive Slave Act that protected the property and rights of all slave owners was thwarted by Kansans at every turn. Lawrence citizens wouldn't openly admit to aiding runaway slaves, because it was illegal to do so, and if the circumstances allowed they still could be arrested and prosecuted. Richard Cordley reported, "There is no doubt that a good many slaves, fleeing from bondage, made their way to Lawrence, and there were aided on their journey towards Canada. Not many of the people knew anything about this, but there were a few whom such fugitives always went and were never betrayed." Cordley himself agitated for slaves to run away, giving speeches back East and vowing to take in any slave who asked for assistance.[61]

Most stolen slaves were tracked back to Lawrence. When Missourians rode across the border seeking their stolen property, they were shot, beaten, or run off. Local law enforcement refused to assist, and in this environment Kansans could practice their illegal activity without constraint. Missourians soon found that Lawrence citizens all believed that "it was their settled purpose to shelter fugitives owning service in southern states, and to kill any who should assist in attempting to enforce the fugitive slave law; stating that they acted upon a settled conviction of duty and obedience to God."

Many citizens in Lawrence housed runaway slaves. Colonel Samuel N. Wood, originally of the Second Kansas Infantry, led his company on the sack of Westport, Missouri, on June 15, 1861. Wood served as a conductor on the Underground Railroad. Wood had been raised a Quaker but renounced his peaceful upbringing as soon as he arrived in Kansas. His house was located next door to the Eldridge Hotel where many Lawrence women gathered to make rifle and pistol cartridges during the border troubles. Sara Robinson recorded, "Yesterday, two of our ladies went out some ten miles, and brought in two kegs of powder," then continued by noting, "Daily and nightly the ladies meet there, in the one room, with its loose, open floor, through which the wind creeps, to make cartridges; their nimble fingers keeping time with each heartbeat for freedom, enthusiastic are they in aiding the defense."[62]

Because many of those who openly assisted in breaking the

Fugitive Slave Law were members of the New England Emigrant Aid Company, they were even more hated by the Missourians. Wood was an outspoken abolitionist and early free-soil politician helping to draft early territorial resolutions besides putting his incendiary rhetoric in writing. He was heard to say that he "did not care how much our resolutions stirred up the enemies of freedom in Missouri or elsewhere, the more the better." On one occasion Wood received a letter from J. B. Woodward stating that he was elated with the idea that Wood might be moving his newspaper to Junction City, because the citizens of that city needed "a press just as rabid and saucy" as Woods'.[63] Participating in an act of lawlessness before the war, Wood joined with an armed mob to seize prisoner Jacob Branson from Sheriff Jones even though the citizens of Lawrence knew that the taking of a prisoner from the hands of the legal authorities would be viewed as an act of insurrection. The rescue was arranged by Major James B. Abbot who helped assist Wood. Later both were arrested for treason, the charge being "acting without authority, and defying the law." During the Wakarusa War, Wood's wife helped carry ammunition to the free-state forces.

Richard Cordley said the Underground Railroad line ran directly through Lawrence and Topeka, then on through Nebraska and Iowa, and on into Canada. On April 4, 1859, Lawrence citizen Colonel John Bowles of the Ninth Kansas Jayhawker Regiment, who was himself actively engaged in the Underground Railroad, wrote a long letter to Franklin S. Sanborn, a leading abolitionist at Concord, Massachusetts. Bowles claimed that during the previous four years he personally knew of "nearly three hundred fugitives having passed through and received assistance from the abolitionists here at Lawrence." One authority claimed, "The Underground Railroad was one of the greatest forces which brought on the Civil War, and thus destroyed slavery."[64]

Since slaves were property, and the ownership of property guaranteed by constitutional law, slave owners had the legal right to cross state lines to retrieve their missing property. When the people of the North were found to be aiding fugitive slaves by way of the Underground Railroad and not reporting them to their rightful owners, Southerners considered this activity a direct disregard for the

Constitution of the United States and a disregard for the legal rights of the individual. The Supreme Court continued to uphold the Fugitive Slave Law in every instance that was brought before it. In Kansas the radically different culture and the self-interest of local demagogues, whose purposes would be furthered by sectional hatred, kept alive and intensified the sectional differences.

Slaves in Western Missouri living north of the Missouri River generally were seized by Jayhawkers and taken to Iowa; those living south of the river were taken to points in Kansas. The two great termini of the Underground Railroad in Kansas were Lawrence for the northern division, and Mound City for the southern division. The prominent officials of the southern terminus of the Underground Railroad were Colonel James Montgomery, well known for his liberating excursions; Colonel Charles Jennison, the "RedLeg" chieftain; and John Brown of Harper's Ferry renown. Another well-known site of the Underground Railroad was established in Osawatomie by agents of the New England Emigrant Aid Society in February 1855. Osawatomie became known as an important station on the Underground Railroad for fugitive slaves from Missouri, a place where the free-state residents provided food, clothing, temporary lodgings, and safe conduct to the stations beyond.

John E. Stewart

As the northern terminus of the Underground Railroad in Kansas, Lawrence attracted fugitive slaves in growing numbers in the years immediately preceding the Civil War. Located in Lawrence were a number of safe houses where runaway slaves could stay and receive food and shelter. Most of the safe houses were located on the outskirts of town away from the prying eyes of any proslavery citizens. The "general traffic manager" of the Lawrence station was John E. Stewart, the same man who had a reward for his capture for burning to death five Missouri citizens in their cabin before the war. Stewart had come to Kansas with the New England Emigrant Aid Company. As a member of a Jayhawker unit in 1861 he burned the entire business portion of Butler, Missouri, to the ground, and later as a captain with the Ninth Kansas Jayhawker Cavalry led many raids into Missouri

Captain John Stewart came to Lawrence with the New England Emigrant Aid Society and lived four miles south of town. He was a conductor on the Underground Railroad. Before the war, Stewart was part of a gang from Lawrence that was responsible for taking a prisoner from Sheriff Samuel J. Jones whom Jones had arrested for murder. Stewart took part with James Montgomery in the complete destruction of Butler and Papinsville, Missouri, in 1861. In the raid on Lawrence, Stewart's house was burned as the guerrillas withdrew back to Missouri. (Kansas State Historical Society)

to bring back slaves and an even greater amount of plunder. Stewart, accompanied by Lawrence citizen John Bowles, was present when Papinsville, Missouri, was completely destroyed, wiping it off the map. The Jayhawkers stole seventy-five head of cattle, five horses, two yoke of oxen, and a quantity of hogs. The courthouse was burned, and the torch was applied, leaving not a single cabin or out building.

The event was recorded by a Kansas newspaper, which proudly

declared, "Our eagles first pounced upon Papinsville, and the town went up in smoke and flame. As we passed through the country, the houses, barns, mills, and other property of Rebels were brought to the altar and full atonement made. Captain Stewart paid his compliments to Butler and the business part of that once thriving and pleasant village was burned to the ground. General Lane's expeditions in comparison with this were visitations of mercy." The following month the *Lawrence Republican* printed an article boasting of the recent raid into Missouri by Stewart's Third Kansas Jayhawker Regiment as part of Lane's Brigade. "The regiment pillaged the towns of Butler and Papinsville in Bates County and stole large numbers of livestock." Many in Kansas were fearful that what the Jayhawkers were doing was eventually going to provoke the Missourians to exact a terrible revenge. As a result Governor Robinson of Kansas replied: "If our towns and settlements are laid waste by fire and sword, in my judgment, we will have General Lane to thank for it."[65]

Actually Stewart did not enjoy a savory reputation even from his own men. After the war started he was the object of a petition calling for his dismissal drafted by sixty soldiers in his command because he collected and sold confiscated Missouri property and was frequently drunk on duty. He was eventually dismissed from the service.[66] Stewart became so wild with robbing and stealing from people for his Underground Railroad cause that even the abolitionists became weary of him.[67]

Stewart built a log fort on his farm in the heavily wooded area along the south bank of the Wakarusa River four miles south of Lawrence near Blanton's Bridge. Along the Wakarusa's heavily wooded banks were hideouts and havens for escaped slaves. There Stewart harbored fugitives who arrived on their own volition, and also slaves brought back from Missouri after raids on plantations in that state. He was probably best known for transporting fugitive slaves to his log fort from the Lawrence ferry landing. Following the Lawrence raid newspaper reports stated that Stewart survived, and "he was last seen going north to Canada with a strumpet," which is a prostitute. "We don't know what happened to his wife and children."[68]

Quantrill knew that he and his men would be passing by many of these safe houses on their route to and from Lawrence. Also included in Quantrill's plans for the raid was to burn the farms of any known enemies on their way back to Missouri. Stewart was one of the main troublemakers that the guerrillas would have liked to get their hands on and was naturally on Quantrill's "Death List" as were many others.

There were other Kansas Jayhawker units besides Stewart's that were just as notorious. On a raid north of the Missouri River the Seventh Kansas Cavalry burned two hundred homes, and in response a Kansas newspaper proudly stated, "Old scores are all settled and with a tolerable fair interest." John Dean, another abolitionist in Lawrence, was also known as an active agent of the Underground Railroad, as was militiaman John Doy, who had gained a great deal of notoriety in January 1859 for attempting to take a group of thirteen Negroes out of Missouri and north into Iowa on the Underground Railroad through Lawrence when he was captured and put in a Missouri jail. Former governor of Kansas Wilson Shannon served as Doy's attorney. In July 1859, ten men, most of them militiamen from Lawrence under the command of Major James Abbot, broke Doy out of jail and took him to safety back in Lawrence. Joshua Pike and John E. Stewart were also in on the recapture. Robert G. Elliott, pioneer Lawrence journalist and politician, tried to rationalize the abolitionists' point of view by writing: "Under the code of the liberators it was considered that the slave held a chattel mortgage for his accumulated earnings, with privilege of instantaneous foreclosure whenever he might choose to quit his master's service." Interestingly, the men who broke Doy out of jail turned in expenses for their action, wanting to get paid for their effort.

Lawrence: A "City of Refuge"

Soon after Lawrence was settled it became recognized as the headquarters of the free-state movement. As a result it was the center of proslavery hatred and at the same time the center of hope to the slaves across the border. The black people of Missouri looked to it as a sort of "city of refuge"; when any of them made a "dash for freedom," they usually made Lawrence their first destination. One citizen recalled the impression the fugitive slaves made on him.

"They came by scores and hundreds, and for a time it seemed as if they would overwhelm us with their numbers and their needs. Union refugees came to us continually by scores and by hundreds; ex-slaves came by thousands."[69]

The editor of the *Lawrence State Journal* stated, "We already see more idle colored men than we ought to about our street corners. . . . Contrabands are becoming one of the institutions of Lawrence. As they break their fetters they very naturally strike out for the center of abolitionism. For some months they have been thickening on our streets, filling and even crowding our few vacant houses and rooms. The question, what shall we do with them? So perplexing in theoretical discussions has become with us a practical one and must be met at once."[70] Once these runaway slaves reached Lawrence they found that they were offered lower pay than white laborers. After Lincoln's Emancipation Proclamation in July of 1863, many of these runaway slaves refused to work, considering that they were also free from labor. Many existed instead on the charity of others. Nearly every household in Lawrence employed a fugitive slave from Missouri. The women had their household "servants" and the men had their own personal "hired hands." Freed Negroes were paid a pittance by their Kansas patrons. They normally received the paltry sum of only one dollar a month. They were used to "saw wood" and "do chores," and many of the females entered families as servants. After being armed and equipped, many of those of military age were forced into the ranks of various militia units.[71]

One remedy to the problem was to put the runaway slaves to work and teach them to read. In Missouri very few slaves were allowed to attend school or to learn to read or write. In Lawrence a night school was established staffed by volunteers to assist in their studies. Such notables as Josiah Trask and Timothy Dwight Thacher of the *State Journal* and John Bowles and Richard Cordley, pastor of the Plymouth Church, offered their services. These men all were involved in the Underground Railroad. Because of this involvement their names would be found on Quantrill's "Death List" when the guerrillas entered Lawrence. Churches in Lawrence were well-known exponents of antislavery rhetoric as well as its schools that became labeled as "laboratories of free institutions." Indoctrination in abolitionism was strictly taught, beginning in the earliest grades. Soon after these runaway slaves were enrolled in school, a church of their own was started separate from the one the rest of Lawrence citizens attended. On March 16, 1862, the Second Congregational Church or the "Freedmen's Church" of Lawrence was established exclusively for runaway slaves out of Missouri. The only member who could read was a black man by the name of Troy Stode. As a result he was chosen deacon and another black man, Anthony Oldham, was selected as pastor.

Besides the citizens of Lawrence who assisted in harboring and protecting runaway slaves from Missouri, many others lived in the Wakarusa bottoms some two miles southwest of town. One was Lieutenant William B. Kennedy, who served not only in Lane's Jayhawker Brigade but was also a conductor on the Underground Railroad. The penalty for assisting runaway slaves under the Federal Fugitive Slave Law was six months in prison and a "$1,000" fine. Richard Cordley found himself taking in escaped slaves even before the war. His first encounter was with a young Negro woman, Lizzie, who didn't complain of cruel treatment but simply didn't want to be returned to her master. Cordley secreted Lizzie in his home and when the U.S. marshal came looking for her, Cordley ushered her on to another house on the Underground Railroad. He claimed most Lawrence citizens would have disobeyed the law and reacted in the same manner. "But when one did escape and came to their door, there were not many who would refuse him a meal or a helping hand. A slave escaping across the line was sure to find friends, and was sure not to be betrayed into the hands of his pursuers. Every slave for a hundred miles knew the way, knew the stations and knew their friends. I have been told by those who ought to know, that not less than one hundred thousand dollars worth of slaves passed through Lawrence on their way to liberty during the territorial period."[72]

3

Damned and Deserved

Terror is a weapon, and war is not popularity-seeking.
—William Tecumseh Sherman

Those in Lawrence who aided the Underground Railroad helping slaves flee from their owners stirred the guerrillas' passions. But they were even more angered by the newspapers that printed such virulent, inflammatory, and incendiary articles provoking Kansans to kill and plunder freely in Missouri. As soon as it began publishing, the *Kansas Free State* run by Josiah Miller and Robert G. Elliott began taunting Missourians to come to Lawrence to "sail on a blaze of glory, such as a couple of kegs of gunpowder, exploded at an opportune occasion would furnish." Elliott was said to have "uncompromisingly opposed the introduction of slavery into Kansas" and to have written articles in his paper encouraging slaves to run away. Elliott was described as being "quiet and still in his manners," always wearing a black suit and stovepipe hat.[1]

The *Kansas City (Missouri) Enterprise* accused the *Kansas Free State* of having "hellish designs of turning the political tranquility of the country with civil discord, national strife and disunion," and charged the paper with "promulgating dangerous, fanatical, traitorous and incendiary ideas." Its editors wrote that the Lawrence paper was a "fomenter of sedition and tumult." Another Lawrence paper, the *Herald of Freedom,* was indicted by a grand jury in Douglas County, Kansas, saying that

> from time to time [it has] issued publications of the most inflammatory and seditious character, denying the legality of the territorial

Major Josiah Miller came to Kansas and started an abolitionist newspaper in Lawrence. He hid runaway slaves in his father's smokehouse as part of the Underground Railroad in violation of the Fugitive Slave Law. Miller was a good friend of James Lane and was the paymaster for Federal troops in 1863, becoming one of the wealthiest citizens in Lawrence. (Kansas State Historical Society)

authorities, advising and demanding forcible resistance to the same, demoralizing the public mind, and rendering life and property unsafe, even to the extent of advising assassination as a last resort. Also that the paper known as the *Free State* has been similarly engaged, and has recently reported the resolutions of a public meeting in Johnson County, in this territory, in which resistance to the territorial laws even unto blood has been agreed upon, and that we respectfully recommend their abatement as a nuisance.[2]

The Newspaper Wars

By 1858 there were twenty newspapers in the Kansas Territory, many spewing out the most violent of antislavery rhetoric. Kansas newspapers were repetitious in their denunciations of Missouri slave owners and in their own justification in opposing slavery. Year after year their editors droned on and on, incessantly making the entire country believe they were the only victims in the border conflict, furtively omitting the mention of early abolitionist atrocities such as those committed by John Brown, James Montgomery, and John E. Stewart. Newspapers in Kansas claimed that its citizens only wanted to build towns, improve their claims, and surround themselves with the refinements of Eastern life, cleverly denying that those same citizens readily crossed the border to raid, pillage, and burn. An early free-state settler, Thomas C. Wells, wrote to his father in Rhode Island explaining the true state of affairs in Kansas Territory. "We do not wonder that you are alarmed for our safety when you read the newspaper accounts from Kansas, they are frequently exaggerated however, and more frequently inaccurate as to names of places and numbers of people engaged in battles etc., but they are more always founded in fact, sometimes do not state the case nearly as bad as the truth would allow." And William Smith, another early Kansas settler, also admitted that getting to the truth was no easy matter. Smith stated, "The Eastern papers are teeming with misstatements."[3]

Compared with newspapers in Kansas, those in Missouri were censored, and many who didn't agree wholeheartedly with the radical abolitionist philosophy were run out of town and their presses destroyed. Reacting to Federal censorship in Missouri the *Marshall (Missouri) Democrat* wrote, "The time has been that we thought and boasted we were a free people. But it appears that belief was a fallacy; or is so now." For expressing such a mild opinion as this the newspaper was soon run out of business by the Federal army in Missouri.[4] Even ordinary citizens in Kansas were afraid to express a contrary opinion in private. John Vansickle living in the Kansas Territory wrote to his father back East about the border troubles caused by roving bands of abolitionists. "You hear a small sketch of this in the public papers. It is only on one side of the question. The people here is afraid to write the facts in the case to their friends for fear it might find its way to the public press as it has often done. Then it finds its way back, then the writer is a victim to be drove off. It is not worthwhile to write any more on the subject."[5]

Abolitionists stepped up their level of hatred and instead of being satisfied to simply liberate Missouri slaves began calling for death to all slave owners and Southern sympathizers. R. T. Van Horn, a staunch Unionist, wrote in his paper, the *Kansas City Journal of Commerce,* "Extermination must be the watchword. The policy of subjugation, even, in Missouri must yield to the sterner one of extermination of all those who are opposed to this government." Van Horn transformed Kansas City into an armed camp. One journalist who visited the city in 1863 said that everyone carried arms and slept with revolvers under their pillows.[6] In the same vein Kansas newspapers expressed such hatred that the most evil of them proved to be the most popular. Their virulent articles gave the citizens incentive and permission to plunder their neighbors across the state line. They printed the speeches of James Lane such as the one in which he told a Kansas audience, "G-d damn Missouri: I want to see her destroyed, her men slain and her women outcasts." Lane's speeches often lasted more than two hours.[7] In one speech Lane vowed, "Missourians are wolves, snakes, devils, and damn their souls, I want to see them cast into a burning hell! We believe in a war of extermination. There is no such thing as Union men in the border of Missouri. I want to see every foot of ground in Jackson, Cass and Bates Counties burned over, everything laid waste."[8] Other Kansas newspapers defended armed incursion using Jayhawker attacks by writing: "In attributing criminal zeal [it was] the least of evils to the winning one."[9] Another prominent Kansas individual, William G. Cutler, also expressed his opinion: "No quarter will be given. Every proslavery man must be exterminated." Lawrence citizen Charles Stearns said that his neighbors hated Missourians so much that they refused to eat ice cream in the town's new ice cream parlor if it was made with Missouri eggs. In another instance abolitionists intended to hang a Kansas man simply because he named his dog Jeff Davis.[10]

Newspaper "Special Correspondents"

Newspapers in Kansas were far different from newspapers today. The first printing presses were brought to Kansas by the New England Emigrant Aid Society to be used as propaganda tools to espouse abolitionist philosophy. The early members of the society were representatives of newspapers in New England. Since newspapers were the most important media during the Civil War, there were three main papers operating out of Lawrence. A peculiarity that sprang up in Kansas was the idea of "special correspondents" representing New England newspapers. They were described as always "[hovering] around certain distinguished personages in Kansas, who write as they are bidden, and whose correspondence is everywhere characterized by personal malice and detraction or who magnify every incident into gigantic importance." Richard J. Hinton said they came to Kansas with "both pen and rifle."[11]

These correspondents not only wrote biased articles from Kansas and sent them back East to be printed in New England papers, they were also paid to sell subscriptions of the New England papers to pay for their antislavery activities. George W. Brown, editor of the *Herald of Freedom* in Lawrence, had a subscription list of 7,000, many of which were sent back East as attested to by Richard Cordley, "The paper was ably conducted, and for a time had a large circulation. . . . The interest in Kansas all over the country gave them [the newspapers] a large eastern constituency." Brown himself was described as "self-willed, strong in his antagonism, and often bitterly personal."[12] Brown regularly placed ads in his paper for 1,000 agents across the country to canvass for subscribers to his paper. Another peculiarity about these "special correspondents" was the fact that their average age was twenty-three years. Southerners bristled that mere boys were giving the world the news of one of the most delicate situations in American history.

Ironically, the *Herald of Freedom* was less "odious" to Missourians than other Kansas newspapers, one reason being that it often reprinted the Southern viewpoint in its columns, even though its editor wrote such incendiary things as "they [Missourians] should be shot down like wild beasts, and their bones allowed to bleach in the sun for centuries."[13] Responding to remarks such as these, the *Kansas City Enterprise* wrote: "We cannot refrain from stating here, that it is painful to see such an incendiary as the *Herald of Freedom* tolerated anywhere. No language is too gross, no falsehood too monstrous for its purpose. It has done more to exasperate public feeling on both sides, than all the men or presses in the Territory combined. It delights in blood, and is appealing to the worst passions of the human heart, in its infernal work. It is the profound conviction that its course is approved by the whole free-state party that has so embittered public sentiment." Responding to false newspaper accounts in Kansas, one settler retorted by writing, "Look at the outrages mentioned in their journals, of babies shot through the sides of houses, etc. There is nothing so low or mean but abolition papers are found to tell it. We, the Union-loving and State-rights party, of Kansas, have kept too still, and allowed the nullifiers to proclaim millions of lies."[14]

What precipitated the Kansas troubles were inflammatory articles that began appearing in Kansas newspapers before the war. Contributing these virulent articles were men like Martin F. Conway who was acting as a "special correspondent" for the *Baltimore Sun*. Conway's editorials were so inflammatory toward inciting an armed insurrection in Kansas that he was brusquely requested to stop. Conway was described as being "one of the more radical stripe," and many after reading his articles in Leavenworth threatened his personal safety. In all probability, this was no mere threat. During the last week of December 1858 there had been five murders in Leavenworth. Everybody carried at least two revolvers.[15] Conway later moved from Leavenworth to Lawrence where he continued to incite the border with his provocative newspaper articles. Conway's neighbor in Leavenworth was Captain Marcus J. Parrott who, before joining Jennison's Seventh Kansas Jayhawker Regiment, assisted him in writing newspaper articles for the Eastern press. When bloodshed did occur in the territory, the facts were often so distorted that for those who knew the truth it became reprehensible. The *Lawrence Tribune* often completely fabricated the facts with falsehoods in attempting to glean sympathy from the Eastern press.

Kansas Papers Defending John Brown

What first struck Missourians as treasonous and criminal was the part Kansas newspapers took in defending John Brown after his infamous raid on innocent settlers along Pottawatomie Creek on May 24, 1856. Timothy Dwight Thacher praised John Brown in the *Lawrence Republican* as a martyr and his followers as brave men in the cause of human freedom. In addition, the Northern press, and many influential Northern clergy and political leaders, proclaimed John Brown a hero comparable to Christ. Brown, his four sons, a son-in-law, and two others of his gang butchered five unarmed settlers in cold blood, hacking them to death with broadswords. The victims of the massacre were described as "some with a gash in their heads and sides, and their throats cut; others with their skulls split open in two places, with holes in their breasts, and hands cut off: and others with their fingers cut off. No man in Kansas has pretended to deny that Old John Brown led that murderous foray which massacred those men. Up to that period not a hair of Old John Brown's head, or that of any of his sons, had been injured by the proslavery party."[16]

Kansan settlers who knew of Brown's intentions were said to have given three cheers to the success of Brown and his men as they left for the massacre. "At the time the blow was struck opinion was divided even among the Free-State men as to its necessity, but as time passed the numbers of those living in the immediate neighborhood who approved of it has increased." Later Brown admitted, "If it was murder, I am not innocent."[17] On February 7, 1857, the *Herald of Freedom* went so far as to say that John Brown was "noble-minded and generous." William G. Cutler in his *History of the State of Kansas* wrote: "The object of the massacre was to protect the free-state settlers, by terrorizing in the most effectual manner the proslavery men, settlers and non-settlers."[18] While Eastern newspapers were decrying the so-called wanton destruction of Lawrence by "border ruffians," they wishfully ignored and failed to print the terrorism of John Brown and his gang at the Pottawatomie Massacre.

Leading free-state advocate Charles Robinson of Lawrence defended Brown, saying his act was justifiable. Commenting on Brown's failed attempt at a slave revolt at Harper's Ferry, an antislavery convention held in Lawrence on December 9, 1959, endorsed Brown's insurrectionary invasion of Virginia.[19] Another Lawrence citizen, Lieutenant Hugh D. Fisher, wrote admiringly about the virtues of Brown's selfless crusade for emancipation. It was only after the war that Brown's true character was noted in articles of the day.

In an 1883 editorial in the *North American Review* a Mr. Eggleston of Solon, Ohio, wrote,

> I knew the old scoundrel long before the war, long before Kansas was known. He [Brown] tried to blow up his mother-in-law with powder; he was guilty of every meanness. He involved his father at one time in ruin. His swindling operation in Franklin, Portage County, Ohio, would make another chapter. The last time I saw him was at Brockaway's Hotel in Cleveland, where he had a large number of Missouri horses selling. Brockaway told me they were stolen and I heard the question put to Brown and he didn't deny it. If New England can't find better material to make heroes of than John Brown, she had better go without them.

Another witness to Brown's criminal and unethical behavior was National Kansas Committee agent E. B. Whitman who wrote to his friend from Lawrence about the John Brown proceedings as a fellow committeeman. Brown had been accused by Democrats during the previous legislative session of "subsisting upon the proceeds of notes given for seeds and clothing" for needy New England settlers. Whitman at first defended Brown against such accusations, but to Whitman's dismay, he later found them to be true.[20]

Unfortunately, most of the country had already been influenced by abolitionist newspapers with the notion that Brown was a noble liberator of slaves and promoted to martyrdom. At his trial for treason for his part in the attack on Harper's Ferry, Brown's family begged for his life, stating that he was insane. It was well known that nine of his relatives on his mother's side were also insane. Six of Brown's cousins were insane, as well as two of his own children. Afterward, John Brown's wife died, also insane. Brown was the first abolitionist to advocate and to practice terrorism as a means to abolish slavery. He has been called "the most controversial of all nineteenth-century

Americans." Today, adherents glorify Brown, giving him significant credit for starting the Civil War, while most scholars identify him as one of the first modern terrorists. One postwar memoir stated that Brown's contemporaries "unhesitatingly declare that this pious fraud established the Freedman's Aid Society, with headquarters in Lawrence, for the purpose of personal gain, and for no other reason. The famous 'Underground Railroad' was a feat of his psychological engineering, the purpose of which was to steal out slaves from the slave states and kite them across the boundary, where they were held for a ransom, and whenever a reward commensurate with his greed was offered for the return of the 'fugitive' he was delivered to his master for a price agreed upon."[21]

Reaction to the criminal actions of Kansans and those of John Brown and his ilk was widespread. Southerners expected their Northern neighbors to renounce abolition fanatics after Harper's Ferry. The *Richmond Enquirer* pointed out, "Armed bands of traitors: in all the panoply of war, are openly invading the State of Missouri, murdering the people, burning the towns, and proclaiming the purpose to 'free every slave in Southwestern Missouri.'"[22] In Congress some of the most condemning voices raised were naturally Southern voices. Said Senator James Henry Hammond of South Carolina, "The whole history of Kansas is a disgusting one from beginning to end." From North Carolina Senator Asa Biggs was quoted as saying, "I have grave misgivings whether the people of Kansas are of that character from which we may hope for enlightened self government." "Why, sir!" cried Senator Alfred Iverson, Sr., of Georgia, "If you could rake the infernal regions from the center to the circumference and from the surface to the bottom, you could not fish up such a mass of corruption as exists in some portions of Kansas." In the House, Representative John D. Atkins of Tennessee branded the free-soil emigrants as "struggling hordes of hired mercenaries carrying murder, rapine, and conflagration in their train." And Representative Thomas L. Anderson of Missouri said he was certain "no part of our Union has been settled by such an ungovernable, reckless people."[23]

The fact ignored by most historians concerning the Pottawatomie Massacre is that John Brown and his sons were trying to intimidate the legal authorities in order to keep them from conducting court in the territory. They threatened Judge Sterling G. Cato of the Territorial Supreme Court, saying that his court had no "right to try anyone under the Territorial laws." When Brown paraded more than a hundred armed men in front of Cato's courtroom, Cato issued warrants for the arrest of the two Browns as well as Henry Thompson, Brown's son-in-law, and another of Brown's cohorts, H. H. Williams. The arrest warrants were given to James P. Doyle to serve along with his two sons, deputy constables William and Drury. In retaliation Brown waited until nightfall on May 23 and proceeded to Doyle's home. The men were called to the door and ordered to come out. When they refused, Brown and his men threw flaming incendiaries through the window. When the senior Doyle came to the door, Brown shot him through the head. When Doyle's sons exited the house, they were seized and marched a short distance from their house and hacked to death with broadswords by Brown's two youngest sons. The murderers then went to the house of Allen Wilkinson, a member of the Kansas Territorial Legislature and called him from his house under false pretenses. They then seized him and took him a short distance down the road where one of Brown's sons hacked him to death in the same manner. The last person murdered by Brown's gang was William Sherman, brother of the owner of the house where Judge Cato held court for the territory. A Kansas newspaper was quoted as saying, "Life is at a discount in Kansas, and crime is at a premium."[24]

James Redpath

Brown's cohort in his Jayhawker raids into Missouri, James Redpath, a newspaper reporter, even went so far as to deny Brown's connection in the Pottawatomie Massacre. Even though Redpath was called a "bright star" in the editorial additions of Kansas, he was described by a fellow journalist as being "always erratic" and a "writer of power, [though] he never pursued a theme logically and to the end."[25] In his newspaper articles Redpath failed to mention John Brown's true motive in the Pottawatomie Massacre. Before arriving in the territory Redpath made a tour through the South in view of learning the possibilities of starting a slave rebellion even if it meant armed insurrection against the Federal government. He was known to admit that he wanted to start a slave revolution that would liberate the slaves, even if it wrecked the Union. Redpath initially went to St. Louis to get a job as Kansas correspondent for the strongly free-state *St. Louis Democrat* so he could endeavor "personally and by my pen, to precipitate a revolution." Redpath was further described as "one of the leading spirits of an organized band of mercenary letter writers, whose business has been that of sending false accounts of events in Kansas during her struggles, to Eastern papers, and basely slandering those who have done and sacrificed most for the cause of freedom."[26]

Once in Kansas, Redpath associated himself with the most violent terrorists of the border: John Brown and James Montgomery. Redpath came to Kansas in 1855, and with the backing of James Lane, founded a free-state newspaper, the *Crusader of Freedom*, in Doniphan. Known as a radical abolitionist he scorned the Fugitive Slave Law by aiding runaway slaves through Lawrence on the Underground Railroad. Redpath became a "special correspondent" of Eastern newspapers in Kansas. He was a "roving editor" for the *New York Tribune* and sent numerous letters back East describing his experiences, which naturally influenced the readership of the paper. One such experience occurred when he attached himself to John Brown days before Brown brutally murdered the five settlers along Pottawatomie Creek. He discovered that he and Brown shared the same violent abolitionist views. Redpath recorded the murder scene as a "sacred spot" in the "great struggle." He afterward defended Brown by denying Brown's role in the killings and shaped Brown's role as a "martyr for freedom" image, which afterward prevailed in public opinion.

Colonel Richard J. Hinton

Another of Brown's cohorts, Colonel Richard J. Hinton, was also a "special correspondent" for Eastern newspapers. "Hinton had gone into Kansas in the autumn of 1856 with an armed company from Massachusetts." He arrived with the New England Emigrant Aid Company carrying 1,500 guns taken from the Iowa State Arsenal. Along with James Redpath he made raids into Missouri before the war with John Brown and James Montgomery. Together Hinton and Redpath wrote the *Life of John Brown*, propelling Brown to national status. William Connelley said that Hinton "yielded allegiance to the resolute old man [Brown], and enrolled himself in his company for future service." After claiming that John Brown did not commit the murders along Pottawatomie Creek, Hinton later justified the massacre by falsely claiming that the murdered men threatened violations of free-soil women. Hinton made a name for himself in Kansas. Known as a radical abolitionist, he was on the staff of General Blunt for a considerable time. Early in 1862, he was mustered as a first lieutenant serving as an adjutant commissioned to recruit and command colored soldiers besides being a conductor on the Underground Railroad.[27]

It was little wonder that with men like these in Kansas printing such deception and lies the feelings of Missourians were turned against Kansans at every turn.[28]

With radicals taking over the U.S. Congress, a subsequent congressional investigation of Jayhawker raids failed to reveal the truth. The only honest facts were uncovered in a congressional minority report, which was overlooked at the time. One Northerner who was interviewed by Congress was C. C. Spalding. Spalding was from Maine and described as a "staunch and loyal citizen." Spalding said he traveled to Kansas in 1859 intending to make his home there. But when he heard what his neighbors were planning, he left in disgust. He said the farmers around him boasted of the fine opportunities they would have when hostilities were well under way to go over the border and take what they desired or needed from the rich Missouri planters.[29]

Kansans had one thing to their credit. They knew that the battle in Kansas was to be fought not just with weapons but also with ideology, and for this they needed newspapers. They understood the importance of being able to disseminate ideas through print in order to mold an ideological perspective based on their political views. Therefore their editorial writings were not "conservative" but were transparently recognized as being vindictive and advocating armed conflict. Lawrence's newspaper, the *Herald of Freedom,* was a well-known organ of the New England Emigrant Aid Society.

"It invariably supported the company against all detractors, while the company office in Boston acted as general subscription agency for the *Herald* for all New England. Many people, both at the time and since, have believed that the *Herald*, because of its radical tendencies and the tactlessness of its editor, did more harm than good to the free-state cause." Besides the *Herald,* the New England Emigrant Aid Company also owned other newspapers in Kansas, notably the *Atchison Freedom's Champion* and the *Quindaro Chindowan,* along with others.[30]

Besides writing for the *Herald of Freedom,* Richard J. Hinton also served as a "special correspondent" for the *Boston Traveler*. The *New York Tribune* opined, "The pen proved to be earlier as a weapon than the Sharp's rifle or Colt's revolver. It was always as necessary, and perhaps proved the more dangerous of the three, against the proslavery spirit and action." In this tradition the *New York Tribune* started publishing its diatribes as early as 1854 when it wrote, "The contest already takes the form of the People against Tyranny and Slavery. The whole crowd of slave-drivers and traitors, backed by a party organization, a corrupt majority in Congress, a soulless partisan press, an administration with its law officers armed with revolvers, and sustained by the bayonets of a mercenary soldiery, will altogether prove totally insufficient to cope with an aroused people."[31]

John C. Hutchinson

Lawrence citizen John C. Hutchinson wrote for New England newspapers as did his brother William who also wrote for the *New York Times*. The truthfulness of their stories was criticized by Henry Raymond, editor of the *Times,* when he requested William Hutchinson to report his correspondence in a more balanced unbiased manner. It was John Hutchinson who helped Charles Robinson jump John Baldwin's land claim and helped free Jacob Branson from the arrest of Sheriff Jones. Even Branson's wife openly defied the law. When Sheriff Jones came to her house with a warrant for her husband's arrest, she threatened to shoot the sheriff with loaded pistols in her hands. The sheriff politely withdrew, deciding instead to seize Branson at another opportunity. William Hutchison became the adjutant general of the Kansas State Militia, fighting against the reprisals of Quantrill's men. William Hutchinson served as a private early in the war under James Lane in Washington, DC, where they planned to kidnap Robert E. Lee. Later Hutchinson served in Lane's Brigade during the destruction of Osceola, Missouri. Hutchison's house was also used for a polling place for free–state elections.

John Kagi

John Brown's cohort John Kagi, who had assisted Brown on his raids into Missouri and was killed at Harper's Ferry, had been a "special correspondent" for the *New York Evening Post*. Kagi had been run out of Virginia for assisting fugitive slaves when he was only seventeen years old. Besides the *Post,* Kagi was also a "special correspondent" for the *National Era* in Washington. Several of John Brown's men were said to help runaway slaves, but Kagi was described as "an adept threat." Colonel Richard J. Hinton, who had made raids in Missouri before the war, further described him as being "the best educated" of Brown's gang "but coarse in appearance and an agnostic."[32] Riding with Brown, Kagi made numerous raids into Missouri, stealing slaves and murdering their owners. With so many noted Lawrence abolitionists known to be murderers and thieves, Kagi's writings for New England newspapers about what Lawrence was like, and his sensationalized descriptions of Missourians gave an improper image to those back East.[33]

The Purpose of "Special Correspondents"

Special correspondents had a twofold purpose. First, they were chosen to represent New England newspapers by selling annual subscriptions to readers in Kansas. Second, they were chosen to describe the conditions in Kansas to those back East. In order to get settlers to come to Kansas, elaborate stories and vivid descriptions were composed about the temperate climate and the little effort it took to grow crops or to make a living. When writing about the conflicts occurring in Kansas, the "special correspondents" usually portrayed them as being between low-class border ruffians who were precipitating fights against uprighteous God-fearing New Englanders who were upholding freedom and fighting against the evils of the slave power from neighboring Missouri. One Missouri citizen, Mrs. W. L. Webb, wrote, "The border ruffian was the direct antecedent of the Guerrilla, but the border ruffian was no ruffian except in Abolition journals."[34]

In proposing armed criminal action these newspapers tried to sway their readers with an inaccurate description of those from Missouri. In January 1862, a Republican-backed newspaper published an article that portrayed a group of captured Missouri volunteers as "shabby, with villainous countenances." One Missouri citizen was angered by this deception. Elvira Scott from Saline County personally knew the men held as prisoners to be among the wealthiest and most dignified men in the county. In her diary she vehemently argued that the men had been compelled to take up arms against the Union when the government could no longer protect their homes and families from plundering Jayhawkers who stole or destroyed all they could lay hands on. She believed it was natural for people to want revenge. "It is human nature. Their once happy homes are smoldering ruins; their families destitute and suffering."[35]

Every skirmish, every contest, had to be described as a bitter struggle between proslavery and free-state men. In order to champion their cause the "special correspondents" sensationalized their accounts. Besides using special correspondents, the New England Emigrant Aid Society proposed to send lecturers into every part of New England. The motives of the territory's first governor, Andrew Horatio Reeder, appointed on June 29, 1854, were exposed in the papers. "Since his recall from Kansas [Reeder] has been in the east making inflammatory speeches, exciting the people, and thus obtaining hundreds of them to be in Kansas on the day of election."[36] Meanwhile back in Lawrence, election day saw barrels of whiskey being dealt out from the backs of wagons in return for votes, and Lawrence citizens were not above buying votes, if desperately needed. Carmi W. Babcock, city administrator and owner of the Babcock and Lykens bank in Lawrence, bribed legislators with city lots in return for votes in favor of making Lawrence the capital of Kansas.[37]

The "special correspondents" couldn't expect the backing of wealthy New England financiers unless they made them believe the battle for Kansas was worth fighting and winning. Not everyone who came to Kansas was a radical abolitionist, but once they arrived most newcomers were forced to become such by those who were already there. No one in Kansas was allowed to have neutral feelings. If there had been "special correspondents" in the Southern army writing for Southern newspapers in Missouri, the propaganda war between Kansas and Missouri might have had different results. But Missouri was an occupied state filled with foreign troops enforcing martial law. Rarely did Southern newspapers make it into the state, and very little describing Missouri's Southern victories leaked out. It wasn't until after the war that Southern memoirs reflected the truth, but by then the North had already won the military war, which gave it the right to claim victory in the propaganda war as well.

When Southern papers did write articles about the guerrillas and their battlefield victories, they were usually very informative, such as the following account written during the war concerning Quantrill's men.

> The sketches we have published of Quantrell's men, another of which we give today, have given our readers a vast amount of information regarding the life they lead, and the service to the cause they render. They went into the war for the love they bore their country. From that day to this they have never faltered and never will falter till our independence is achieved. They are brave, they are full of spirit. They are game to the very bottom. Look at the feats of John Morgan. He can count in killed, wounded and captured, not less than five men for every man he has ever commanded. Quantrill can boast of putting out of combat nearly twenty for one of his followers.[38]

Samuel F. Tappan

Lawrence citizen James W. Winchell shared the limelight with Samuel F. Tappan as a "special correspondent" for the *New York Tribune*. It was one of the nation's foremost newspapers with Horace Greeley as its editor. At the time Greeley was one of the most sought after speakers, and his word carried great weight, whatever the subject he spoke about. Tappan arrived in Kansas with the first party of the New England Emigrant Aid Company. Known as a fanatical abolitionist, he was also a "special correspondent" for the *Boston Journal* and the *Boston Atlas* and a regular correspondent for the *New York Times*. He was an avowed lawbreaker of the Fugitive Slave Law and eagerly aided runaway slaves on the Underground Railroad, passing them through Lawrence. Through his efforts he precipitated the beginning of the Wakarusa War by freeing Jacob Branson from Sheriff Jones. When the sheriff was in town to arrest Tappan for his part in freeing Branson, Tappan struck him in the face and escaped.

Richard Realf

Not even a murder charge kept foreign anarchist Richard Realf from becoming a "special correspondent" for the *New York Tribune*. As soon as he came to Kansas in 1856 Realf made a raid along the Neosho River where he murdered a Mrs. Chris Carver, sister of John C. Van Gundy. Realf wrote a number of articles for the *New York Tribune* as well as the *Springfield (Illinois) Journal* and a paper in Concord, New Hampshire. He also wrote for the *Chicago Tribune*. Realf, as well as foreign revolutionaries John Henry and John E. Cook, John Brown's coconspirators in the 1859 attack on the U.S. arsenal at Harper's Ferry, wrote for Eastern newspapers.

Lieutenant Colonel Samuel F. Tappan came to Lawrence with the New England Emigrant Aid Society. Once in Kansas he joined the radical abolitionists in thrwarting the territorial laws. (Colorado Historical Society)

General Samuel C. Pomeroy

Another agitator, General Samuel C. Pomeroy, helped carry articles out of Lawrence during the Wakarusa War to newspapers back East. The *Leavenworth Herald* reported, "On Wednesday night last, General Pomeroy was arrested on the Wakarusa, by one of the piquet guard of the law-and-order party, and taken into camp. He had documents in his possession containing all the plans, movements, etc. of the revolutionary party of Kansas Territory. Pomeroy was on his way to Kansas City to mail said documents to the Massachusetts Emigrant Aid Society."[39]

Antislavery Free-State Newspapers and Writers

Even though Kansas' newspapers backed different political leaders who oftentimes opposed each other, they were still united in their basic political principal of supporting anything antislavery. Every Kansas newspaper was a molding force aimed at making Kansas a free state. Not only did their biased perspectives make startling reading back East, but Eastern abolitionist poets and scholars who also wrote for Eastern papers that were eventually sold in Kansas were eagerly read and talked about. Poets like John Greenleaf Whittier and writers Ralph Waldo Emerson and Henry David Thoreau and religious men like Henry Ward Beecher were prime examples of the kind of writers whose perspectives graced the pages of New England papers. Beecher was known to donate funds for weapons to be put into the hands of the insurrectionists in Kansas, and the crates used to ship them were marked "Bibles." The *St. Louis Republican* remarked, "We are credibly informed that these holy instruments of the Beecher school for evangelizing Kansas are daily arriving in our city. Yesterday several suspicious boxes, consigned to a house in this city, were observed on the levee and spotted. The Emigrant Aid Society, the pet of the Abolitionists, instead of the plow and the peaceful implements of agriculture, it seems are using all their efforts to stock Kansas with the tools of death, to be used by their emissaries in the region."[40]

What was known as the Kansas Free State Committee in New England was made up of influential men, abolitionist in their beliefs and newspapermen in their professions. These men wrote with "pens of fire" and helped spread the message that the Kansas Territory was in a state of war against Southern domination and interests. With the Eastern papers inciting the Kansas settlers, and the Kansas newspaper correspondents inciting the Eastern press, the level of sensationalism nationwide was raised to a fever pitch. Lawrence citizens like

Robert Gaston Elliott, partner with Major Josiah Miller as coeditors of the *Kansas Free State*, wrote articles encouraging slaves to run away from their masters. Articles such as these pleased their wealthy benefactors back East who supplied funds flowing with regularity to further aid their criminal designs. Elliott provoked the Missourians' ire by letting the Lawrence militia quarter in his newspaper office, giving them aid and comfort in their fight against Missouri citizens. As a matter of practice in Lawrence, "All the public buildings are turned into barracks, the preaching hall with the rest."[41]

Other Lawrence citizens also made a mark in their editorial essays. Men like Timothy Dwight Thacher, as editor of the *Lawrence Republican,* and Lieutenant Colonel Norman Allen, who commanded an artillery battery in the Kansas militia during the war, also made significant editorial contributions. Thacher was frequently called upon to speak at mass meetings held by the young Republican Party. He was invited in 1857 to come to Lawrence by his old schoolmates Lyman and Norman Allen to take over the *Lawrence Republican.* He plunged into the venture without reserve. It was described as "not only a free-state paper but a Republican paper, and not only a Republican paper but a radical antislavery paper." As a writer, Thacher was described as "condensed, argumentative, brief and pungent." His incendiary articles inflamed those in Missouri who all belonged to the Democratic Party, as when he wrote,

> Never did there exist a party so entirely demoralized and bereft of all virtue and all sympathy for virtue, as is now the so called Democratic Party. It has given itself up to the management and upholding of every crime, national, social or political, that has chosen to seek its protection. It has declared war against religion, liberty, temperance, and every movement seeking to improve and elevate man. It is the recognized ark of refuge into which filibusters, land pirates and all promoters of mischief flee for aid and protection. It is the party relied on in the perpetration of every national crime, and the protection of every national evil. It is the fomenters of war abroad and discords at home.

In April of 1863 Thacher left the *Lawrence Republican* in charge of his brother and went to Kansas City where he bought the *Kansas*

Captain Norman Allen was a businessman in Lawrence and a militia officer before the war. Allen commanded an artillery battery in Lane's Brigade at the destruction of Osceola, Missouri, where more than three hundred houses were destroyed. (Douglas County Historical Society)

City Journal of Commerce and continued writing and publishing his incendiary articles.[42]

Not only did Kansas newspapers heap praise on the Jayhawkers' raids into Missouri, but their contemporary editorials boasted of the vigilance of their local militias. Hovey Lowman, editor of the *Lawrence State Journal,* in the August 6, 1863, issue commented, "The martial spirit of the people is fully aroused. All around, the eye meets the gleam of the freshly burnished Sharps rifle, and the ear catches the significant click of the newly oiled revolver." He taunted the guerrillas: "We invite any number of Border Ruffians to visit any part of our State. The nearer they come to Lawrence the better. Mr. Quantrill is not invited to do bloody and infamous deeds upon unarmed men in any part of this State; but we venture to say that his chances for escaping punishment after trying on Lawrence just once are indeed slim, perhaps more so than in any other town in the State. Lawrence has ready for any emergency over five hundred fighting men, every one of whom would like to see Quantrill." In other articles Lowman boasted that if Quantrill's gang came into their state, the guerrillas would be "welcomed with bloody hands to hospitable graves." Lowman verified, "At the time appointed, Lawrence was in a condition to have defended itself against twice the number that he [Quantrill] could have brought against it."[43]

George Washington Brown and the *Herald of Freedom*

George Washington Brown operated the *Herald of Freedom* in Lawrence. He was indicted for treason for bearing arms against the government in 1856 and for writing inflammatory articles. Brown was partially responsible for starting the Wakarusa War. Even his wife joined the fray by carrying ammunition to the free-state forces. Though united as radical abolitionists the free-soilers were known to be divided into cliques and factions. Brown was criticized by the more radical anti-slavery crowd for being more conservative than some of his contemporaries. Brown's neighbor in Lawrence, Joseph Savage, described him as having "an oily tongue but . . . [being] very mercenary in his make-up and on the whole unreliable in times of trouble and discord." His fellow townsman, Richard Cordley, said he was "self-willed, and strong in his antagonism, and often bitterly personal."[44] Brown even used his inflammatory articles against those he didn't consider as radical as he was. In one newspaper article he attacked fellow newspaperman, T. Dwight Thacher, editor of the *Lawrence Republican,* by saying, "He stands the impersonation of a cringing sycophant, ready to kiss the foot that would tread upon his own and other people's necks." When Brown's *Herald of Freedom* was suffering financially, his wife traveled back East to help raise money. A scandal developed when she returned and found her husband involved with one of his clerks, who soon became Mrs. G. W. Brown the second. Another account described a war of words between Brown and Charles Robinson. The governor spread the story of Brown's wife being an adulteress, though when the proof made it into print "Mrs. Brown hurriedly packed up and went back East. What did not help the matter was that her husband immediately moved one of his young female employees into his bed."[45]

Daniel Webb Wilder

Besides the newspapers in Lawrence there were many more in the surrounding towns that printed in the same vein. There was the *Atchison Champion*, the *Kickapoo Pioneer*, the *Doniphan Constitutionalist*, the *Wyandotte Citizen*, the *Elwood Gazette*, the *Squatter Sovereign*, the *Topeka Tribune*, the *Leavenworth Times*, the *Centropolis Leader*, the *Quindaro Chindowan*, the *Emporia News*, and the *White Cloud Kansas Chief*. Also the *Leavenworth Daily Conservative* was delivered three times a week by a stage driven by Lawrence citizen Samuel Reynolds. Its editor, Daniel Webb Wilder, was one of Jayhawker Marshall Cleveland's strongest supporters. Author Thomas Goodrich wrote a scathing description of Cleveland in his book *Black Flag—Guerrilla Warfare on the Western Border*. "Many who joined Jayhawker bands were nothing more than common criminals. Marshall Cleveland and his gang of thinly-veiled patriots brazenly worked both sides of the border, robbing and murdering Unionist and rebel alike. A former follower of Jennison, Cleveland soon broadened his range to include bank robbery and counterfeiting, as well as the wholesale plundering of emigrant wagon trains."[46]

Wilder mocked anyone who opposed the Jayhawkers. In the September 19, 1862, issue of his paper Wilder wrote: "We stated some time ago that Dr. Gray, whose horse was taken by the Jayhawkers was supposed to be a Union man. We learn that we were sadly mistaken. The Doctor packed up his dentist tools and went to Platte City, where he has ever since been venting his traitorous feelings in the most violent manner. The doctor wanted to wipe out Leavenworth, but unluckily while Platte City was in possession of the Union forces they confiscated his stock in trade. Secession don't pay, does it doctor?" In the Jayhawker town of Atchison, John A. Martin, a journalist and member of the Kansas infantry, joined with Webb Wilder and his paper at Elwood, Kansas, keeping their pens in constant service. Even religious men like Bishop John Morgan Walden of the Methodist Episcopal Church at Quindaro joined in the editorial confrontation. The letters of Lieutenant Colonel Daniel Anthony, stationed in Leavenworth with the Seventh Kansas Jayhawker Regiment, were often printed in his hometown newspaper in Rochester, New York.

Colonel William A. Phillips

A relative unknown writer for the free-state cause early in the history of Kansas was Colonel William A. Phillips. He was known to be a free-state editor in Southern Illinois before settling in Kansas.

Horace Greeley selected Phillips as a "special correspondent" for the *New York Tribune*. Colonel R. J. Hinton said that Phillips had a "caustic pen, was egotistic, a little bitter, and somewhat apt to take unwarranted personal prejudices; not especially a kindly comrade" and "could be relied upon to help those who helped a fugitive slave." Phillips' pen may have been slightly too caustic for those living around Leavenworth on May 17, 1855. He was arrested, taken to Weston, shaved on one side of his head and face, tarred and feathered, carried astride a rail, and sold as a vagrant by a Negro on the charge of expressing sentiments so as "to disturb the domestic relations of the people." Using his title as a journalist to travel freely, he actually became a spy for the Lawrence mob, relaying information from Missourians whom he had interviewed.[47]

It was known that Kansans had been making raids over the Missouri border for more than two years before the war started. Both economic and weather conditions helped precipitate the start of the Jayhawker raids. Guerrilla Lee C. Miller said, "Before hostilities opened Kansas men began raiding the western border of Missouri. As soon as the Southern men started to the Southern part of Missouri to organize, Kansas men came in by the thousand. They drove off all the stock they could find, and hauled off all the furniture from the houses."[48]

One newly arrived settler wrote, "When I came to Kansas in 1857, it was little more than an extended camp. There was but little law and little authority. There were a great many claims, but not many farms. There were a great many farmers, but not much farming. There had been a great deal of money spent but not much money made." A. J. Hoole observed, "Everyone seems bent on the Almighty Dollar, and as a general thing that seems to be their only thought. . . . Money is scarce; a great many people want work done, but they have no money to pay with. Everyone seems to be resting on his oars, as the saying is. Nothing going on, except among some of the Abolitionists who are doing a good business stealing horses from Proslavery men."[49]

Economic Downturn and Political Corruption

The downturn in economics seriously affected tax collections, and the general economic atmosphere was not conducive to a quick recovery. In the aftermath of the Panic of 1857, during which many banks in the nearby states had closed their doors, paper currency was no longer acceptable as a circulating medium. With politics playing the major role, the business depression combined with drought during the summers of 1857 to 1860 made up the minds of many a shiftless Kansan. The ground was as dry as ashes. Seeds sown in the garden did not even come up in many cases. Over the country generally there were thousands of acres of corn from which not an ear was gathered. The prairie grass that produced good hay was dried to a crisp. The Wakarusa River, which always contained pools of water along its course, had no water whatever in its channel. One Kansan reported, "During the summer the sun poured down its burning rays day after day, and the hot winds seemed like the breath of a hot furnace." Others noted, "The hot wind parched the soil and no harvest followed the seed time." The drought lasted for thirteen months, forcing an estimated 30,000 people, or one-third of the population, to leave Kansas Territory. Many of those who remained gave up farming and resorted to Jayhawking becoming a majority among the Kansas settlers. Richard Cordley remembered, "They clung to a hope of a return of the former days, but those days never came back."[50]

Articles in the *Herald of Freedom* attested to the serious conditions of dust storms, scorching winds, and no rains. "The weather continues cold and cheerless. Vegetation has not yet made its appearance. Cattle are suffering. The winds continue to blow, the dust flies, and the prospect is quite cheerless." The season of 1858 promised well, but a frost on May 18 and a wet season in early summer cut the wheat crops, and a dry summer cut the corn crop to about one half or less.[51] One noted Kansan, John J. Ingalls, wrote to his father that "the actual exports from the country, corn, pork, and hides, had not been enough before 1860 to pay for the whiskey that was drunk every month, and men lived on what they brought with them or on the charity of their friends." "A great many people left the territory, some going back East, and still more going West to the new gold and silver fields of Colorado." The original settlers were no more than opportunists. J. Sterling Morton quotes a speculator of the time as truthfully portraying the state of affairs when he said,

"The inhabitants were only amateur farmers 'merely aggravating the soil a little.' They who remained could do little more than hold on and wait till the tide should turn."[52]

Those in need sought relief from funds channeled to Lawrence to the emissaries of the New England Emigrant Aid Society. Distribution of the funds was supposed to be done equitably, but unfortunately there was graft and greed involved. "Goods are constantly arriving from the east for our unfortunate settlers. They are placed in charge of our Kansas Committees. [Shalor and Joseph] Eldridge are charged with the duty of distributing them. There are loud complaints against our committees and especially against the Eldridges. The brothers were described as 'possessing more of pride, than intelligence, overbearing and haughty in their demeanor, I fear they are as guilty as charged.'"[53] Part of their arrogance was derived years earlier when the brothers were in charge of bringing armed emigrants into Kansas by way of Nebraska, and later when Shalor became the quartermaster for the Second Kansas Jayhawker Regiment. They assumed that this responsibility gave them a special position among the abolitionists. "This party was regularly formed in military order, and was under the command of Gen. Pomeroy, Cols. Eldridge, Perry, and others. They had with them twenty wagons, in which were a supply of new arms, mostly muskets, with bayonets and sabers, and a lot of saddles, etc., sufficient to equip a battalion, consisting of one-fourth cavalry and the remainder infantry." Officials stated that "they had with them neither oxen, household furniture, mechanic's tools, agriculture implements, nor any of the necessary appurtenances of peaceful settlers."[54]

When new emigrants first arrived in Kansas Territory they were met by greedy land speculators. In 1857 town lots, which only the surveyor could find, rated as high as lots in cities of ten thousand people. To supply the demand for town lots, "cities" were laid out in all directions. There were beautifully lithographed maps of towns which showed no visible sign on the prairie. These fictitious documents enabled many a land dealer to double his money in a month. Everybody ran wild with the "craze" for land and speculation. Money was loaned at rates as high as 3, 5, and even 10 percent a month. It was said, "Money was loaned at unheard of rates, to be used in unheard of bargains. Everybody was getting rich trading back and forth in property that produced no income, and had no intrinsic value."

Early Kansas settler Watson Stewart admitted, "Speculation in claims became quite a business; persons leaving the country would sell their claims for such price as they could get, and the purchaser would hold and sell to the newcomer for, sometimes, two or three times the amount paid."[55] In 1857 Cordley said he witnessed a lull in affairs. "Business was dull, and money was scarce, and everything moved heavily. The three years that followed were very dull years. All growth had ceased, all business was depressed, and times were quiet enough for a hermit."[56]

Kansas Jayhawker Attacks on Missouri

Thus the time was ripe for Jayhawker attacks into Missouri. Those who led the first forays for plunder across the Missouri border were known not to have visible means of support. While Quantrill was living in Lawrence before the war, he was an eyewitness to the corruption of the politicians and civic leaders in Territorial Kansas. Much of the corruption centered on acquiring land grants to construct railroads. Martin F. Conway said he opposed a plan to have land grants secured. He knew that men like "Charles Robinson, Thomas Ewing and Marcus J. Parrott, were endeavoring to secure land grants last winter, were plotting a scheme to get them into their own hands, and swindle the people of Kansas out of any benefits from them." During the summer of 1860 Quantrill had a job as a surveyor north of the Kansas River on the Delaware Indian lands. At the time he was living with an Indian named John Sarcoxie, said to be a "superior Indian," son of the chief of the Delaware Nation. Quantrill's association with Sarcoxie gave him insight into the fraud and corruption running rampant on the frontier. His disenchantment with the men and society of Territorial Kansas was no doubt influenced by the harsh treatment accorded the Native Americans and the greed for their land by white settlers and town and railroad speculators. For many years New England emigrants, speculators, and railroad promoters and politicians had been agitating for the Indians' removal from their tribal lands.

The L. P. & W. Railroad, which later became the Union Pacific, negotiated a treaty with the Delawares, then set out to get the treaty ratified by the United States Senate of which James Lane was the leading character. To achieve these goals it was considered necessary to bribe opposition leaders, pay the sums demanded by rapacious lobbyists, and offer attractive inducements to senators, congressmen, and Kansas officeholders and politicians to support necessary legislative measures. While the L. P. & W. had no cash, it could pay its lobbyists and political and capitalist supporters in land or stock. Accordingly, some were paid in land to the total amount of 10,560 acres initially worth $1.28 an acre and others with 83,180 shares of the company's stock with a face value of more than four million dollars. One year later the land was selling for $6.50 an acre. The following Kansas politicians and businessmen received land or stock from the L. P. & W.: Charles Robinson, James H. Lane, Samuel C. Pomeroy, Martin F. Conway, Thomas Ewing, Jr., James M. Winchell, Carmi W. Babcock, Josiah Miller, F. P. Stanton, Mark Delahay, Robert S. Stevens, and Benjamin Simpson, most of them cronies of James Lane. Is it any wonder how these formerly impoverished settlers came to own the most opulent homes in Lawrence?

Lane himself was only beginning to be associated with the corruption in connection with Indian contracts, which would surface to ruin him in a few short years. Quantrill's association with the Indians and his observation of Lane and his hirelings heightened his already existing disillusionment and cynical attitude toward the territorial government and its leaders. In a letter to his mother on February 8, 1860, he expressed his feelings on the subject: "The devil has got unlimited sway over this territory, and will hold it until we have a better set of men and society generally. The only cry is 'what is best for ourselves and our dear friends?'" The *Lawrence Daily Republican* editorialized against corrupt officials like James Lane by saying, "Politics soon become a mere game of plunder, in which the biggest blackleg carries off the heaviest prize. Sound Republicanism and thorough Democracy must not atone for drunkenness, debauchery and dishonesty."

James Lane: Jayhawker Leader

So during this period of economic downturn and political corruption came the Jayhawkers attacking farms across the border to satisfy their thirst for plunder. Jayhawkers, as everyone knew, stood for undisciplined, unprincipled, murderous, and thieving Kansas soldiers. The principal leader of all Jayhawkers was James Lane. His initial views on the Negro question were no different from those of Missourians. Lane was quoted as saying, "I know of no difference between a mule and a Negro for labor."[57] Even so, he eventually became the leader of the antislavery forces that ultimately made Kansas free-soil. Although he arrived as a Democrat, Lane stood at the forefront of the free-soil faction in Kansas, and was a founder of the Free State Party. He put his military training to use by organizing free-state militia units throughout the territory. Known as an unscrupulous opportunist in both his personal relations and political associations, he nevertheless became the hero of Kansas radicals. He was often called a consummate politician, espousing a different belief for each new crowd of voters. He was also a notorious womanizer, violent, paranoid, and highly unbalanced. However, this kind of personality was just what the Kansas radicals supported and rallied behind.

Lane suffered a brief hiatus in his political career following the dispute over a land claim in 1858 that ended with Lane killing his neighbor, Gaius Jenkins. Regardless of his despicably immoral character and his being charged in the murder of his neighbor, Kansans voted for him anyway. When Kansas entered the Union as a free state in 1861, Lane, by this time a Republican, had won election as a U. S. Senator from Kansas. Kansans accused Missourians of voting irregularities, but their own irregularities were overlooked. Lane "had voters present from other townships, thus perpetrating an invasion of the polls as vile as that of the Border Ruffians, and probably gained his majority by such fraudulent voting. By dint of money, promise of office, liquor, and fraud, he triumphs, and then claims that it is due to the gratitude of the people." After Kansas gained statehood, ballot box stuffing by abolitionists continued even without the accusations of Missourians voting fraudulently. In Lawrence during the state elections in December 1861 there were 1,118 votes cast and only 463 male residents.[58]

Lane arrived in Washington just as the Civil War broke out, and soon became a staunch ally of Abraham Lincoln. Not content to support the Union cause from the floor of the Senate, Lane helped form two Kansas volunteer regiments that fought against Confederate forces in Western Missouri, and while in Washington he formed a "Frontier Guard" to protect the White House. During the war, Lane was specially targeted by Confederate forces operating in Missouri and Kansas, who still hated him for his leadership in the free-soil cause. Lane was for a time a leader of the so-called radical Republicans, who not only opposed slavery but also supported civil rights and political equality for the Negro. During the Civil War, Lane's Brigade aided numerous Negroes fleeing Missouri and Arkansas, and as a recruiter for the Union army in Kansas, he personally assembled one of the first black regiments.

During the early stages of the war Lane led his undisciplined mob of Jayhawkers toward Osceola, Missouri, on September 23, 1861, for plunder rather than aid Colonel James A. Mulligan and his command who were under siege by General Sterling Price's forces at Lexington. His command consisted of the Third, Fourth, and Fifth Kansas Jayhawker Regiments. Lane was thoroughly chastised in the papers when they commented by asking, "If he is so brave and such a great General, why did he not relieve Colonel Mulligan, at Lexington when repeatedly urged to do so?"[59] Lane remarked in his own style, saying simply that Osceola had been "cleaned out." Before entering the town Lane had the city shelled into destruction. The population of Osceola on September 22 was 2,500. On September 24, it was 183. Anything that could be carried away comfortably was taken: horses, cows, fowl, furniture, clothing, jewelry, and slaves. No family was spared, the homes of men serving with Union forces being robbed with all others. Teams and wagons were first stolen and then loaded with the movable goods of the community. Lieutenant Hugh Dunn Fisher came back laden down with a Communion service for his unfinished church in Lawrence and several silk dresses for his wife. According to Fisher, Lane had made him the commissary officer prior to the destruction of Osceola after Governor Robinson refused him a commission because of his association with Lane. Professor Burton J. Williams of the University of Kansas wrote that Fisher "became as efficient at 'liberating' enemy property as his commanding officer."[60]

Before leaving Osceola, the Kansans shot nine citizens, and set on fire all but four of the three hundred buildings in town, including the courthouse, which burned to the ground with all the county records. The Kansans raced out of Osceola with three hundred of their force so drunk they had to be carried back in wagons. A million dollars' worth of property had been stolen or destroyed, and Osceola, one of the most beautiful towns in Western Missouri, had ceased to exist. Lane brought government wagons with him, anticipating the plunder he would be acquiring. The Jayhawkers took 350 horses and mules, 400 head of cattle, and a long line of wagons loaded with flour, sugar, molasses, and other plunder. Part of Lane's personal share was a fine carriage, a piano, and a quantity of silk dresses. Afterward Lane led his force as rapidly as he could toward the Kansas line and Lawrence, where the loot was to be divided, burning houses as he went. His raid was condemned in the strongest terms by Governor Charles Robinson of Kansas, and by Major W. E. Prince, who commanded Federal troops at Fort Leavenworth. Osceola never recovered after the war.[61]

Lane's raid was more notorious for the laudatory dispatches sent to the press of the North, designed to prove him a hero, than anything else. Explaining the sack of Osceola to Union General Samuel Sturgis, Lane tried to say that his forces met stiff resistance when in fact only a token force of local men happened to fire on his advance guard. When Sturgis queried Lane as to the murder of an Osceola banker and the theft of between $8,000 and $10,000 from his widow, Lane apparently responded, "I grant you my fellows have done some wrongs," followed with a laugh of infinite gusto. Frank Wilkie, an Iowa newspaper reporter, wrote that Lane described the sacking of Osceola "with a twinkle in his eye and a pleasant laugh at the fun of the thing to reminiscences of Negroes and prisoners shot after being compelled to dig their own graves." All in all General Lane struck Wilkie as "Nero fiddling and laughing over the burning of a Missouri Rome."[62]

One Missouri resident described Lane's Brigade at Osceola as being "nearly naked, and minus shoes and hats in many cases. They were not armed, but a number of them had hams of meat on their backs, which they no doubt had stolen from some man's meat house on the road. These are the kind of men that Lane's brigade is to be composed of, thieves, cut-throats, and midnight robbers."[63] Even many Kansas citizens disapproved of Lane's tactics across the border because what they had practiced in Missouri they were now using to prey on their own Kansas neighbors. A Kansas citizen commented, "There never has been a time in Kansas when robbery, theft and murder ran riot, as since the big General playing of Lane. Until Lane took the field, property was respected in all the counties except a few immediately on the border; now it is unsafe everywhere. The thieves are protected in, and are a part and parcel of, the Lane army. Civil war will inevitably result in Kansas, not between Unionists and Secessionists, but between thieves and their victims."[64]

Robinson vs. Lane

During the war, raising state troops had always been the prerogative of the state executive in the office of governor. James Lane by his political machinations obtained authority through the War Department and President Lincoln in Washington to raise troops with him as their head. Lincoln's interference usurped the sovereignty of the state of Kansas, pitting Governor Robinson against Senator Lane. With most officeholders beholden to Lane for their positions the different factions in Lawrence did not get along. It was no secret that Robinson and Lane were personal and political enemies. Robinson wrote, "The world never will know nor believe the insanity, or deep depravity of some of our politicians, especially of one James H. Lane." And the *Lawrence Journal* remarked, "The election of Lane to the Senate of the United States, we shall proclaim hereafter, as we have heretofore, in strenuous efforts to prevent it, as a deep, ineffaceable disgrace upon the state of Kansas."[65]

Robinson was not a particularly popular man in Lawrence at the time of the raid. Charges of impeachment had been brought against him for corruption. Lane coveted all power and graft that came with political position, and anyone not willing to share it with him became his sworn enemy. Robinson was proven innocent, but the accusations ruined his career. Robinson was acquitted of speculating with state funds, but his state auditor and secretary of state were found guilty. Those who voted for his acquittal were immediately given lucrative political and military offices. There were those both envious and suspicious when they learned that Robinson acquired 2,160 acres of prime bottomland in Kansas as a gift to his wife from the Kansas Pacific Railroad, which it sold to Mrs. Robinson for the unheard of sum of one dollar. Robinson initially built a residence on a commanding site south of town on the high ground of Mount Oread. Later he built a more luxurious home known as one of the most opulent in town. It was built entirely of black walnut, with a high finish on doors, window casings, and mantels.

Charles Ransford Jennison

Lane's chief Jayhawking subordinate was Charles Ransford Jennison. Jennison was born on June 6, 1834, at Antwerp, Jefferson County, New York. There he attended primary school until the family moved to Albany, Wisconsin, in 1846. While at Albany he finished secondary school, studied medicine, and after finishing the latter course of study, practiced for a short time in Wisconsin and later in Minnesota. In the fall of 1857 he decided to continue his migration westward and removed to Kansas Territory, settling first at Osawatomie and then Mound City. Osawatomie, already identified with abolitionist John Brown, was known for its strong free-state convictions. Jennison quickly became a staunch supporter of Brown, and his personal temperament toward the proslavery faction soon proved radical and strident. While living in Mound City before the war Jennison associated himself with James Montgomery, another ardent abolitionist, and from his new home base Jennison led many a raid against the proslavery settlers on both sides of the Missouri-Kansas border.

All too often, indiscriminate plundering characterized these forays. And on at least two different occasions, proslavery men were hanged under Jennison's direct leadership. In the case of Russell Hinds, who was "tried" and lynched by Jennison's gang on November 12, 1860, for capturing and returning escaped slaves to Missouri for the reward, the Kansas Jayhawker chief made no apology. The county, according to Jennison, had "been infested by a band of desperadoes known as kidnapers for the past year, and it had become necessary for us as anti-slavery men to take a stand against these increasingly frequent offences." Thus, they publicly announced "that any man found guilty of that crime should pay with his life and accordingly as we had the proof we arrested one Rus Hinds and tried him publicly and hung him for being engaged in that unholy business." Convinced his position was "honorable and just," Jennison further directed his attacks against the court of Federal Judge Joseph Williams in the southern judicial district of Kansas Territory at Fort Scott. After several free-state men received harsh treatment from that court, Jennison raised a posse to disperse the court and forced the judge and his supporters to flee the area. Thus the Jayhawkers were setting the stage for the type of warfare to be expected along the border and undoubtedly the type of retaliation that would follow.

4

Lawlessness Abounds

The angel of destruction has dipped her wings in blood and driven the angel of mercy from the land.

—Colonel Jacob Hall

The outbreak of the Civil War merely helped legitimize Jennison's conduct, for a short time at least, and caused him to focus his efforts on the prosecessionist elements of Missouri. Kansas Governor Charles Robinson commissioned him captain of the Mound City Guards on February 19, 1861, and by September 4, 1861, he was commissioned lieutenant colonel of the Seventh Kansas Cavalry Regiment, soon widely known as "Jennison's Jayhawkers."

Jennison's Jayhawkers

Headquartered at Kansas City, Jennison was assigned to command the western border of Missouri and quickly adopted a "scorched earth" strategy of warfare against his Confederate enemy. He seized from the guerrilla-infested territory of Western Missouri the materials needed to wage war and destroyed property he could not use.

Mrs. Judge Graves was living in the Missouri countryside, but because of the Jayhawker raids it was advisable for her to move to Kansas City. She recalled, "Daily wagons were seen loaded with pianos and other furniture, carpets, etc., for the purpose of furnishing Union homes and camps. Kansas settlers were well supplied from Missouri homes." Jennison's favorite quote was one he told his fellow Kansans, "I have grown stoop-shouldered carrying plunder out of Missouri in the name of Liberty." Jennison's plunder was described by fellow Jayhawker Captain Henry Palmer of the Eleventh Kansas Regiment. He said that when Jennison and his command returned to Kansas from his first raid into Missouri, "They marched through Kansas City, nearly all dressed in women's clothes; old bonnets and outlandish hats on their heads, spinning wheels and even grave stones lashed to their saddles. Through the country strewn with worthless household goods, their road lighted by burning homes, this regiment was little less than an armed mob until Jennison was forced to resign, May 1, 1862."[1] The Kansas adjutant general remarked, "Colonel Jennison performed some acts worthy of commendation, conspicuous among which was his resignation."[2]

One of Jennison's early exploits was the capture of a wagon train that belonged to Upton Hays and Henry C. Chiles, which was hauling government freight out of Westport, Missouri, to Santa Fe, New Mexico. Much of the stolen property found its way into the stores of Kansas merchants. On October 21, 1861, a company of Jackson County men under Upton Hays rode to Gardner, Johnson County, Kansas, and took back their stolen goods from two stores, one owned by I. W. Sponable and the other by Sanford B. Sponable and L. H. Church

After Hays returned to Missouri the merchants asked Jennison to retaliate. Soon after this incident, Jennison burned Hays' house and stole seventy head of sheep, forty-five or fifty of the finest stock in the country, and carried off his carriages and Negroes. Hays organized a company to resist these predatory raids. Upton's wife Margaret recalled, "Our property is all taken from us and I am left without a home for our four little children to take care of. I cared not for this or whether I had a second dress, but now what will become of us, God only knows." Jennison destroyed the farm and outbuildings, even pulling up the fences and taking them back into Kansas. At one time sixteen burning farmhouses could be seen from the Hays homestead two miles south of Westport. Jennison's Jayhawkers also burned the home of Samuel Hays, Upton's brother.[3]

The Day the Jayhawkers Attacked

Upton Hays was the son of Boone Hays and grandson of Daniel Boone, the famed pioneer. Hays became a brilliant military officer once the war commenced. It was said of him that "perhaps no finer horseman ever rode herd over the prairies. He was brave, generous, true, devoted and noble, a patriot. No man had more friends than he had." Margaret Hays recalled the day the Jayhawkers attacked.

> We have been overrun with Jayhawkers and they have robbed and harassed us, and our neighbors have suffered a great deal from them. Uncle Jimmie [Judge James B. Yeager] has lost upwards of ten thousand dollars worth [of goods]; they came to his house one night and took eight negroes, a fine carriage, a two-horse wagon, some horses and mules, and robbed his house of all bed clothing and everything valuable. In a few days they came to the same house, took about seventy head of sheep and 45 or 50 head of the finest stock there was in the county. In a few days after they went to another neighbor some two miles off, took the negroes, went to the beds and rolled them up saying they would take them to their wives. The same day they took some thirty head of stock from Uncle Lemme's [Linville Hays, Upton Hays' brother].
>
> The next day twenty Jayhawkers came to our nearest neighbors with ten wagons and said they came to take everything the old man had. Some went into the house packing up, some in the orchard, some fixing to load up wheat; some had all the stock driven up. In the evening fifty-three of them came to our house and surrounded it. They said they came to take everything we had and burn us out. They took two wagons loaded full from here, my carriage, and every negro on the place.

Mrs. Hays described the conditions in her neighborhood. "Times are very hard: robbing, murdering, burning and every other kind of measure on every side. Every man has to join the Federal army or hide out in the country and have his property taken away from him. And if they are not shot on the spot they are banished from this country."[4]

Another citizen attacked in Westport by Jennison was Judge James B. Yeager. Yeager had settled in Jackson County in 1837, becoming a judge of the county court. He was also in the freighting business. His son Richard was in charge of one of his father's wagon trains on a trip out West. When he returned he found that Jennison's men had paid a visit to his father's home and stripped it of everything they could carry off. He immediately quit the freighting

Margaret Watts Hays was the wife of Colonel Upton Hays, who earned the Kansas Jayhawkers' ire for trying to defend his home and property. Early in the war, Charles Jennison confiscated one of Upton Hays' wagon trains. On a return raid Jennison burned Hays' home along with the homes of sixteen of his neighbors. He also stole Hays' livestock and all his possessions, taking them back into Kansas. After her husband's death in 1862, Margaret Hays and her children lived in a small house on the Hays farm until she was exiled from Jackson County, Missouri, and lived there supported by relatives and friends until the end of the Civil War. The day after she left Jackson County, her last home was burned. One of her treasures saved from the Jayhawker raids was a wooden yardstick with the initials N H carved at the end, which had been a gift to her mother from Nancy Hawks, the mother of Abraham Lincoln. (Franklin Family Collection)

business, joined Quantrill's company, and became one of its noted leaders. Because of his son's actions, Richard's father was arrested and taken to Kansas City, where he was thrown in jail. Later he was sent to the Gratiot Street Prison in St. Louis.[5]

In Southern Jackson County, Jayhawkers struck the farm of Jim Chiles' father-in-law, Solomon Young. Young was one of the wealthiest men in Jackson County, owning more than 5,000 acres. Even though Young was a freighter whose wealth in 1860 was listed as $50,000 and had a contract selling goods to the government, he was branded a Southerner because he owned slaves. Only a few days after the firing on Fort Sumter in South Carolina, beginning the Civil War, James Lane rode out from Lawrence, Kansas, seeking an opportunity for plunder. While Young was on a freighting trip, his wife observed a dirty man with wild hair come riding into the farmyard in front of a mean-looking crew wearing morocco leggings. He was Jim Lane. Harriet Young, Solomon's wife, and her children were ordered to cook and make biscuits for these ruthless raiders. Harriet fired up the kitchen stove, fried meat, and baked biscuits until her hands were a mass of blisters. Outside the home, shots rang out, and hogs squealed as the Redlegs slaughtered more than four hundred valuable Hampshire hogs. The marauders hung hams and shoulders over their horses, leaving the rest of the meat to rot. The Jayhawkers stole fifteen mules and thirteen horses, then killed the hens and set the hay and stock barns ablaze. Solomon's young daughter Laura remembered that the Jayhawkers took the family's good handmade quilts out and laid them in the mud so that they could play cards on them, and used the family's hens for target practice. Next they threatened to kill the Negro servants to make them tell where any hidden silverware was kept.

The following September, Federal soldiers returned and stole another 150 head of cattle, and a year later Jayhawkers attacked again, stealing sixty-five tons of hay, five hundred bushels of corn, forty-four hogs, two horses, a bridle and saddle, and the family's feather beds. A month later, Jayhawkers again returned and stole thirty thousand nails, seven wagons, twelve hundred pounds of bacon, and took possession of the house. They hanged Solomon's fifteen-year-old son Harrison to try to make him tell where his father was. The Federals rode off leaving him hanging, but his mother and her servant cut him down in time to save his life.

Again in the summer of 1863, Colonel Andrew G. Nugent, whose men had murdered Cole Younger's father the year before, stole

$20,000 in gold from Solomon that he was bringing home with him from a California and Salt Lake City freighting expedition. Later in the war, Captain Jacob Axline paid a visit to Young's farm and stole thirteen thousand nails, six thousand rations, and one thousand bushels of corn.[6]

On an 1861 raid in Jackson County, Missouri, the Seventh Kansas Jayhawkers attacked near Pitcher's Mill, destroying 3,000 bushels of wheat and destroying the homes of the Pitchers, Porters, and Nolands, besides stealing seventy horses, twenty wagons, and fifty Negroes. They had just been issued Sharps carbines, Colt Navy revolvers, sabers, and uniforms prior to the raid. Thomas Pitcher had gone south to join Price when the Kansans struck his neighborhood. His daughter Nancy related what happened. The homes of several of her relatives were burned, and their Negroes, horses, and everything they owned were taken from them. She said the Jayhawkers killed boys as young as ten years of age. "They went to the house of David Porter. His daughter was sick in bed. They stripped the clothes off the bed, stole what they wanted and set fire to the house."

After returning from Price's army, Porter joined Quantrill. Continuing into Independence, Jennison had his troops surround it before the town was awake. Independence was an object of especial hatred from the Kansans. It was the first Missouri town to raise the Confederate flag and to raise the first Confederate company. The surprised citizens quickly sought hiding places. The soldiers pulled them out of cellars, barns, and garrets. Unionists and Confederates alike, totaling about four hundred, were corralled on the courthouse square. Other troops were busy gathering up plunder—horses, carriages, guns, and furniture—and bringing it to the public square. Author Roberta Bonnewitz wrote in her book *Raytown Remembers*: "The desperados would systematically strip a community. Negroes were rounded up, and willing or not, hauled to Kansas. Merchandise from stores and valuables from homes were loaded into wagons for the return trip."[7]

Mrs. Nanny Cogswell was born in Virginia, but her husband was a strong Unionist. He ran a general store on the square in Independence. Simply because of where she was born Jayhawkers stole thousands of dollars' worth of Brussels carpeting, which they used for saddle blankets. After stealing several thousands of dollars' worth of stock, they proceeded to smash everything else in Cogswell's store, even pouring a barrel of molasses over it and then trampling it into hopeless ruin. While in Independence a squad of Jennison's men broke into the store of F. D. Coburn, a local shoemaker. Inside he had 120 sheepskins that had been dyed a bright red. The Jayhawkers helped themselves to his stock and made leggings for themselves. Coburn stated that afterward when people saw Jennison's men riding throughout the countryside they referred to them as the "Redlegs." On one occasion Jennison shot a woman for attempting to shield her husband, helpless from illness. She was crippled for life, never to walk without crutches.[8]

Union officer George Caleb Bingham wrote of Jennison's Independence raid. His "self sustaining regiment, as it was locally known, robbed the private homes of the place. Watches, jewelry, shawls, scarfs, comforts, blankets, and counterpanes were packed up and carried off." Bingham claimed that the real bandits were not Quantrill's bushwhackers but the Kansas Redlegs and Jayhawkers who were under the protection and patronage of General Ewing.

> The carriages, buggies, and wagons were strung out around the streets, and the furniture was piled on the sidewalk around the courthouse fence. Colonel Jennison, sitting upon his horse, read a list of Union men who could go home. Then he directed Marshal Miles to pick out the remaining Union men. These were directed to the south side of the square. To the remaining group he lectured for nearly half an hour, denouncing them as traitors, rebels, and secessionists, and threatening all who did not take up arms for the Union. He also warned the secessionists that for every Union soldier killed ten of the most noted secessionists would suffer death. About fifteen conveyances, including wagons, carriages and buggies were loaded with confiscated property of all descriptions including colored women and children. The long train went down West Lexington Street to Kansas City and afterward to Kansas and freedom.[9]

A few months later, a short distance south of Independence during February of 1862, Martha F. Horne living on a large farm in Cass County recalled a Jayhawker raid. The men were all gone in the army.

> In February the Jayhawkers came, and hitching up our wagons with the few remaining horses that had not already been taken by the Redlegs or the Federal militia, loaded in supplies that we had hauled out from Kansas City for our winter's use, and took negroes, provision stores and all out to Lawrence. We heard that on arriving at Lawrence the redleg thieves robbed the negroes, taking horses, wagons, supplies and all, and left the deluded creatures to root hog or die. Following that, the Kansas thieves stole everything that was movable. About the only things they left were the wells, the cellars and the post holes, after they had taken up the plank fencing. It is known that they dug up young orchards close to the line and reset them in Kansas. They also mounted houses on wheels and hauled them over into Kansas.[10]

Because of such acts, Jayhawker raids caused great anxiety and fear in the citizens along the border. Mrs. S. E. Ustick remembered how the Jayhawkers would

> swoop down on us day and night, searching our homes for money or contraband goods. They usually appropriated whatever they desired on their raids that was obtainable. They came to search our houses. They frequently ran their bayonets through all the clothing in the wardrobe or through the mattress to see if there was anything concealed there. When making a dash into Missouri towns they would order the men in the town to erect the Union flag and command the women not to give food to Southern soldiers or Bushwhackers under penalty of death, telling us if we failed to comply with this command they would return and sack and burn the town, shoot the men, and take the women and children prisoners.

She told of her personal experiences. "My house, occupied by myself and four daughters, my husband having died before the war, was searched seven times by drunken Jayhawkers, six times being at night, which greatly frightened and unnerved us when we heard the clank of sabers as they surrounded the house and pounded upon the doors with their heavy guns, demanded admittance. With pistols cocked they asked questions, blowing their drunken breath in my face, cursing the most bitter oaths until I was so frightened I could not tell my name."[11]

Jayhawkers Lived Off the People

Back in Independence, where the war was the bitterest between Kansas and Missouri, J. A. B. Adcock recalled that the Federal soldiers stationed in Independence lived off the people. "They would go out with those large government wagons, and were particular to go to the homes of southern men and fill them with corn from the barn, then kill hogs and chickens and put on top of the corn. Then they would drive all cattle and horses and take all household goods that they could use, and some things they had no use for."[12] One resident of Independence said that the houses in town were used for stables. "A number of good business houses on the square are now occupied as horse-stables by the Kansas Eleventh." After Richard Leach of Independence was arrested as a Southern sympathizer he was given permission to leave the state. "I was glad to get away," he said, "and leave a people who had now become thieves and robbers, which constituted the loyalty of Union men."[13]

Major Preston Plumb of the Eleventh Kansas Regiment was General Thomas Ewing's chief-of-staff. While stationed in Independence Plumb acted as the provost marshal and practiced another wily method of robbery on Missouri's peaceful citizens. As provost marshal Plumb had enormous discretionary power over civilians around Independence. He could force labor from the citizens and seize any property he deemed needed for the military or for his own personal use.

Plumb once had four Redlegs seize a noted and wealthy Unionist and livestock dealer, A. S. H. Crenshaw. Plumb had his regimental quartermaster seize all of Crenshaw's corn and hay, then burn down his house. Plumb's Redlegs drew their pistols and roughed up Crenshaw, making him believe he was going to be hanged. They offered to buy Crenshaw's stock for a dollar a head. Fearing for his life, Crenshaw signed a bill of sale for $650 for one hundred cattle and thirty hogs. The Redlegs said they would give him $150. Again they offered Crenshaw $1,200 for thirty-one mules and horses. This travesty was followed by another so-called sale that took fifty-eight mules, the last of his stock. Crenshaw was kept in jail for more than a year where he was mistreated, as a result becoming ill and going blind and never receiving a dime for his property from Major Plumb.

Ewing finally released Crenshaw after forcing him to promise to keep his treatment a secret. A board of Federal officers met to investigate the case and acknowledged that General Ewing and his subordinate officers were all guilty of a conspiracy to rob and murder Crenshaw. Ewing was eventually reassigned to another department.[14]

Other citizens also had sad tales to tell. Mrs. Maggie English said that Jennison's men quartered themselves in the homes of prosperous farmers, collecting silver plate, burning family portraits, loading Negroes into their masters' carriages and sending them over into Kansas, and finally burning their homes. "Our home was raided and robbed, as others were; a box of old family silver was unearthed and taken, keepsakes were appropriated, even to a locket containing a dead child's hair, amid the piteous entreaties of the mother to spare her that one small treasure. The house was burned and the plantation devastated."[15] On August 12, 1863, one Jayhawker recalled what he saw of the area around Independence. "Most of the buildings on the road to Independence from the south were burned. There were some smoky brick walls still standing, mournful relics of domestic happiness. Most of the buildings were destroyed by Jennison a year or more ago."[16]

Lieutenant Colonel Preston Plumb was General Thomas Ewing's chief-of-staff and commander of the Eleventh Kansas Jayhawker Regiment. He also served as the provost marshal when his troops occupied Missouri, a position that enabled him to confiscate civilian property at will. (Greg Walter Collection)

In fact, the Jayhawkers had indeed been devastating the Missouri border for years. After Jayhawkers attacked Independence on October 29, 1861, they moved south to Brooking Township. They burned John Flanery's home and twenty-five others along with the High Grove Baptist Church. All that was spared was the Bible a soldier had placed on a tree stump. Though Flanery was a Southern sympathizer he had protection papers from the Union command but was continually shot at and almost killed. He was finally persuaded by his wife to join the guerrillas. In addition, Jayhawkers burned the Big Cedar Missionary Church in Brooking Township started by Robert Samuels, Henry Younger, and William Hagan. One of Cole Younger's relatives recalled, "Our homes were invaded and ransacked by the Federal soldiers and women and children were dragged off to prison. It was noted by all that during the winter of 1863 houses were burned by the hundreds and whole neighborhoods devastated and laid waste."[17]

Southern churches suffered a particular malignity from Federal troops. Since most of the guerrillas were members of these pioneer churches, they were the first to receive special attention. A letter from the Federal commander in Independence to a local pastor compelled the clergyman to offer supplications in behalf of Lincoln's government.

> You will breathe a little more loyalty in your prayers and sermons, you will pray for the President of the United States, his Cabinet and all Federal officers in favor, for the perpetuation of the Federal Government; for the success of the union army, and the final overthrow of the rebellion. In short, you will admonish your hearers to be loyal to the Government under which they live and have lived, to love the country and serve it as they do or should their God. In case the above cannot be conscientiously complied with by you, it will be my painful duty as a Federal officer, and commanding officer of this Station, to either close your church or put another pastor in your place.[18]

Rather than be compelled to act against their conscience, most Southern pastors decided to voluntarily close their church doors. Jayhawkers then either used the vacant buildings as stables for their horses or simply burned them to the ground.

Nannie Harris, who survived the Kansas City jail collapse but saw her sister-in-law crushed to death in it, recounted the depredations of Jennison and his men:

> He [Jennison] ordered the execution of wounded Confederate soldiers on parole; he murdered men in the presence of their families. The silver-plate and jewelry Jennison and his men stole and carried into Kansas would have stocked many jewelry stores; the bedding, wearing apparel and furniture they carted over into their beloved commonwealth was ample to supply the homes of the whole horde; the cattle, horses and mules these thrifty thieves drove to their State from Missouri were enough to stock the farms of any of the "Emigrant Aiders" in Kansas. Jennison's command hauled from the graveyard near Harrisonville a number of tombstones, this was a gruesome kind of highway robbery, but they doubtless reasoned that the smooth side of the marble slabs would make substantial doorsteps. They took the patchwork quilts from the negro cabins as eagerly as they pulled from the beds of the invalid among the aristocrats the downy silken comforts and costly counterpanes. They tore up the hearths to seek hidden treasure; they took family carriages and drove as their occupants; they packed in wagons all wearing apparel, household articles, harness, plows or whatever they wanted and could make room for. They left not a horse, mule or any cattle they could manage to drive away; they robbed hen roosts, took children's toys, even compelling one gentleman to take off his coat, pants and shoes and give them; they broke dishes they could not carry away; handsome party finery that did not appeal to their pilfering proclivities they wiped their muddy boots on; one Sunday afternoon I counted in the Sni Hills seven dwellings burning at once, two homes of poor widows.[19]

On or about November 27, 1861, Lieutenant Francis H. Ray of the Seventh Kansas Jayhawker Regiment led fifteen men to the area of Cracker Neck just south of Independence, Missouri, and burned twelve homes. Kansas Redlegs and Union soldiers often came to the Samuel Luttrell farm in the neighborhood, taking horses, food, and about everything they wanted. Luttrell was the uncle of John W. Koger of Quantrill's company. Luttrell hid his horses and his slave girl, Julie, in the hazel brush on the south end of his farm. These areas were known as "timber stables" and some farmers even kept their livestock in their homes to keep them from being stolen. The soldiers found the horses and Julie and took them to their headquarters at Fort Leavenworth. Luttrell felt he could abandon his horses, but not little Julie. He rushed to the soldiers' headquarters and managed to get her released and brought home.

On one raid into Missouri, Jennison's command carried off all the silverware in sight in the neighborhood of the Masons, Stonestreets, Cowards, Fields, Thorntons, and others of the well-to-do residents of that section. The Jayhawkers' unwarranted attacks riled many officers in the regular Federal army. General Egbert B. Brown, commanding the Southwestern District of Missouri, said that "all freebooters and thieves, come from what source they may, and parties pretending to act by authority of Government, but using their positions to lay waste the country," would be put down.

Effects of Jayhawker raids were felt by almost every family along the border. During one raid through the Blue Township just south of Independence Jayhawkers rode up to the Michael Casey farm and demanded food. After eating they started carrying off everything of value. Casey's newborn baby was lying in the bed wrapped in a blanket. One of the Jayhawkers grabbed the blanket, baby and all, and started off with it. Casey shouted at him, "Hey, hold on there, there's a baby in the blanket." The Redleg thereupon unceremoniously dumped the baby out on the bed and made off with the blanket.[20]

In the early spring of 1863 Jayhawkers stationed in Kansas City burned all the stores and destroyed forty dwellings in the Six Mile Township of Jackson County near Sibley, Missouri. One citizen, George A. Steel, wrote to a relative, saying: "Sibley was burned a few days ago. Pa had eight tons of hemp burned in one of the warehouses. Several of the neighbors houses were burned."[21] Those who didn't join the guerrillas but stayed at home had to hide whenever the Jayhawkers or Redlegs were in the vicinity. Following a Jayhawker raid through Jackson County the father of guerrilla John Brown was killed by Kansans who were still in the neighborhood and came upon him as he was hunting for his cattle. The Jayhawkers also burned down his house. The Brown family had an almost inaccessible hiding place called the Tennessee Gulch, where they took their horses and hid for days at a time without being found. This was a wild place, grown over with tangled underbrush and trees, and was the finest kind of hiding place. While the men were in hiding the women would bring them food and keep them posted on the movements of invaders.[22]

Jayhawkers Take No Prisoners . . . But Do Take Everything Else

During the summer of 1863 John Hagan, a cousin of the Flanerys and a well-known and respected citizen living in the Valley of the Little Blue a few miles south of Independence, was driving with this wife and three children to visit his brother William. On the way they met a band of Federal soldiers, who were much exasperated because the telegraph wires had been cut. Hagan was ordered by the soldiers to leave his family and go into the woods with them. His wife later searched for him, finding his body shot through the head.[23] Such murders were not uncommon. In another senseless murder Federal soldiers killed the father of William and Louis Hulse. Hulse's children ran to their neighbors the Barretts to ask for help. They cried, "They shot down Father in the barn lot and Mama can't carry him!" When Bob Barrett asked the Union officer in Kansas City why they had killed Hulse, he replied, "Because he had given food to some of Quantrill's men." After the murder of Hulse, Mrs. Barrett saw an immense herd of cattle being driven past her fence. It was collected from the farms of neighbors to be driven to Kansas. Because of these acts William and Louis Hulse joined Quantrill.[24]

In another raid, Jennison's Seventh Kansas Cavalry with Lieutenant Colonel Daniel Anthony in command stuck Morristown in Cass County, Missouri, in January of 1862. Morristown was home to two hundred citizens. Jayhawker Fletcher Pomeroy witnessed Anthony and part of his command returning to camp on Sunday, January 12, "having met no enemy but bringing in lots of confiscated property. Before leaving the regiment pillaged the countryside in all directions."

Writing from Camp Johnson in Morristown on January 6, 1862, Archibald Carnaghan serving in the Seventh Kansas Jayhawker Regiment proudly wrote home to his parents describing his predatory exploits.

> I sold a good Jay-hawked horse for ten dollars, I think if times are good

> I can send a good deal home against spring. We kill and strip as we go. Where we go Secesh weaken and what we take, the greater portion is turned into the government. I dare say this regiment more than pays for itself. We live on the top of the heap. We have the best regiment in the west. We have splendid horses to ride and pockets full of money. We have and take money, watches, jewelry, horses, mules, sheep, hogs, cattle and bed-clothes, burn their houses and kill all who have ever taken up arms against the government. We take no prisoners.

As an afterthought Carnaghan scribbled in the margin of his letter, "We free all the negroes we come to."[25]

In a subsequent Jayhawker raid the Seventh Kansas Cavalry with Jennison commanding struck again at Morristown in July of 1862, this time completely destroying the town and murdering four prisoners before leaving. After citizens tried to rebuild their town and shattered lives, James Montgomery struck Morristown again the following September, burning to the ground what had been rebuilt.[26]

As a matter of fact, "freeing the negroes" had a different meaning to the Jayhawkers. Negroes were compelled and oftentimes forced to leave their homes. The Jayhawkers ordered the Negroes to take their owners' horses and mules along with saddles and harnesses to help drive the remaining stolen stock of cattle, sheep, and hogs back into Kansas. The Negro women and children were ordered to seize carriages, wagons, and whatever other conveyances they could find and load them up with household goods. Belongings such as furniture, bedclothes, farming implements, tools, and even personal items were loaded up for the trip back into Kansas. The majority of the goods were kept by the Jayhawkers' themselves. The Negroes were allowed to keep a small portion of the plundered property, which they usually sold immediately, most of it winding up at local street auctions.

What was well known is that Jayhawkers plundered and killed both Southerners and Unionists alike regardless of their political affiliations. Letters of complaint written to the political and military leaders in the district gave witness to the Jayhawkers' criminal proclivities. General Henry Halleck, commander of the Department of the West, wrote to his superiors concerning the Jayhawkers: "They are no better than a band of robbers; they cross the line, rob, steal, plunder, and burn whatever they can lay their hands upon. They disgrace the name and uniform of American soldiers. The course pursued by those under Lane and Jennison, has turned against us many thousands who were formerly Union men. A few more such raids will make Missouri as unanimous against us as is Eastern Virginia." In further contact with Secretary of War Edwin Stanton, Halleck wrote, "Sir: Since the Kansas troops entered this department their march has been marked by robbery, theft, pillage and outrages upon the peaceful inhabitants, making enemies to our cause wherever they went."[27]

General Henry Halleck was the commander of the Department of Missouri before serving as general-in-chief of all U.S. armies. He wrote to his superiors about the depredations of the Kansas Jayhawkers, but to no avail. President Abraham Lincoln once described him as "little more than a first rate clerk." He was a pallbearer at Lincoln's funeral. He lost his friendship with William Tecumseh Sherman when he quarreled with him over Sherman's tendency to be lenient toward former Confederates. (Patrick Marquis Collection)

Besides the theft of slaves in Missouri, Jayhawker raids resulted in so much stolen property taken out of the state that for a while it was a problem to dispose of it all. It soon became apparent that a ready-made market for the stolen goods was to be found in the lucrative trade with settlers and frontier military posts farther west. These military posts, usually located far away from settled areas, were most dependent upon supplies brought from a great distance. Military stores were usually purchased from the large markets back East, but with the war in progress it was difficult to obtain supplies. Many unscrupulous merchants near the military posts desired Indian wars because the military authorities would need supplies in abundance, which would create a market for their products.[28]

The military needed large quantities of clothing, blankets, grain, hay, lumber, wood, and commissary supplies. There was also a great demand for horses, mules, and cattle. As a result, during the early part of the war cattle, horses, and mules were taken from many of the border counties of Missouri during Jayhawker raids. It was estimated that at least four-fifths of the cattle in Vernon County, Missouri, were stolen by Jayhawkers during the war. During the same period it was stated that in Webster County, Missouri, the cattle there were nearly all stolen. Unfortunately, cattle not stolen were killed. In Henry County it was reported, "Beef cattle in immense numbers were driven from our county during the first years of the war, and seemingly, horses and mules enough have been stolen and driven away to outfit an army."[29]

From one single raid a Kansas Jayhawker readily admitted,

> Between the 2nd and 12th of May, 1863, five companies of the Ninth [Kansas Jayhawker Regiment] were scouting in Bates and adjoining counties, and when we came out brought fifty-four horses, mules and jacks, two hundred and seventy-five cattle and five hundred head of sheep, all swept up regardless of ownership, as I believe, from the farms along our lines of march. . . . Possibly the quartermaster's returns in Washington will show that all this stock was properly accounted for, and even that it was paid for at a good round figure; but it is certain that it was never used for a public purpose and that, except as stated, it all went to enrich a few men who would have resented the designation of thieves with a show of righteous indignation. Now such acts as this, and they were not infrequent along the border, naturally aroused fighting blood.[30]

When Jayhawkers came to the neighborhood of R. E. Selden in Bates County, a neighbor, Mrs. Mariah Cogswell, upbraided them for stripping women and children of their clothing. One of the Jayhawkers replied, "Slaveholders ought not to have anything to wear or anything to eat. They ought to die."[31] "As a result, few residents were to be found in Bates County. The county became a tenantless wilderness. Fires raged unchecked, through prairie, wood and overgrown field. Fences, buildings, improvements of all kind had been swept away. Where only three years previously had been a flourishing commonwealth, composed of 6,000 people now roamed the savage wolf, half starved dog, and perchance the hunted outlaw, who sought refuge in the forbidden territory." As late as 1869 one Bates County resident, Theodrick C. Boulware, commented, "One could ride for a distance of ten miles on the prairie without seeing a single house. They had all been burned."[32]

The lucrative market for any type of stolen goods resulted in their being shipped directly from Kansas to the settlers and gold seekers who were still flooding west to escape the uncertainties of war. These supplies were shipped on wagon trains that had been established before the hostilities began. The freight sent westward before April 1861 was composed of new commercial products manufactured especially for new settlers. When the war began, manufacture soon turned to production of war materials, but the need for commercial items remained great. The only way to satisfy the demand was to send good used items that were still functional. These were furnished from Jayhawker raids into Missouri. Every male individual had need of a slouch hat, woolen shirts, buckskin pantaloons, moccasins, knives, a good rifle, and a revolver.

The type of horses needed for the heavy work of campaigning on the frontier was hard to obtain. Purebred horses stolen from Missouri farms were much sought after. These imported animals were found to be better acclimated than the native stock. Leavenworth was the great supply depot for the posts on the plains and along the Missouri River Valley. With the Seventh Kansas Jayhawker Regiment stationed there, it was an easy process to carry stolen plunder back to their base and ship it west on ox-drawn wagon trains.

A citizen of Westport south of Kansas City recalled the Jayhawkers' mode of illegal operation. "The first Union troops stationed in Kansas City were well disciplined, and no irregularities were permitted. Later a body of militia was posted here who indulged in excesses, confiscating property and permitting Jayhawkers and Redlegs from Kansas to commit whatever depredations they pleased. Wagons would be brought in from Leavenworth and loaded with furniture

Each week wagon trains such as this one from Leavenworth hauled more than $20,000 worth of stolen goods taken in Jayhawker raids in Missouri to be sold to the military posts and gold fields farther west. (Denver Public Library)

and valuables of every kind belonging to southern sympathizers."[33]

One report stated,

> The vast majority of the army stores were transported by contractors to the various depots established on the great routes of overland travel. These contractors or freighting companies were the merchants of the overland trade. The freighting companies carried on a great amount of business not only by carrying government freight, but also private freight. The company of Russell, Majors and Waddell at one time had 6,250 wagons and 75,000 oxen engaged in freighting. The height of the freighting business on the plains was from 1863 to 1866. Between May and November 1864, 63,000,000 pounds of freight were carried over the plains and in 1865 about 224,000,000 pounds.[34]

To the Marauders Go the Spoils

The District of the Border was part of the Department of Missouri with headquarters in St. Louis, under the command of General John

M. Schofield. When General Ewing took over as the commander of the District of the Border he initially tried to put down Jennison's plundering operations. He made the charge that there were "very many men in Kansas who are stealing themselves rich in the name of Liberty," playing on Jennison's own admission and promising "to stop with a rough hand all forays for plunder from Kansas into Missouri." Jennison's plunder trains were so large that his commercial operations selling stolen merchandise to the gold fields out West were staggering.

Research shows that cities like Lawrence and Leavenworth were shipping $20,000 worth of goods west every week. By today's standards that would amount to roughly two million dollars every month. Jennison was aided in his nefarious efforts when his second-in-command Lieutenant Colonel Daniel Anthony was elected mayor of Leavenworth. Anthony had a dry goods store in Leavenworth that undoubtedly did a brisk trade in plundered goods. There were two thousand militiamen located in Leavenworth, and many of them had made raids into Missouri. Commenting about Leavenworth, General Ewing wrote that the plunder "taken by the marauders that infest all this region are concentrated, sold and distributed; here they accumulate it, and what is not parceled out here is forwarded as from a central depot, to various marts, or rendezvous, east, west and north."[35]

A good deal of money was made in the resale of stolen goods. From just one small raid in 1861, the Seventh Kansas Jayhawker Regiment took back into Kansas 150 mules, 40 horses, and wagon loads of furniture and clothing. As the commander of the expedition, Anthony took the lion's share. Anthony proudly boasted of the ill-gotten gains he had accumulated from plundering in Missouri. He wrote to his brother-in-law back East: "Don't you want a captaincy or a majorship in the army, or don't you want to come out here and speculate in cattle, horses and mules, there is a good chance to buy cheap, and stock a large farm here at little expense. There is money in it to anyone who will attend to it. I would advise you to come out and try it."[36]

In May of 1862 after Jennison was forced to resign from the army and give up his lucrative position in the Seventh Kansas Cavalry, he turned his attention full time to the overland trade. Now "citizen"

Jennison hurriedly established a partnership with a Redleg accomplice and Leavenworth businessman, J. G. Losee, freighting goods to the gold fields of Denver, Colorado, and other locations in the West. Anticipating an increase in trade, the two men quickly constructed a new building to hold their merchandise. Although there are no historical freighting records left in existence, it is reasonable to assume that with the ban on unauthorized livestock sales in Leavenworth the Jennison-Losee warehouse and livery stable was used to store goods and house livestock collected by the Redlegs until the pilfered merchandise could be hauled west for sale. It was well known that Jennison used many of the horses and property stolen by his regiment in his business. Losee's common practice as a Redleg was to circumvent the legal process and accuse any unfriendly person of possessing stolen horses as a pretext for seizing the animals and retaining them for his own use or profit. The magnitude of the operation was astonishing. One Jennison-Losee wagon train bound for Denver reportedly contained goods valued at seventy thousand dollars.[37]

Indeed, Jennison's own brother, a "detective" working for the provost marshal, was implicated in a scheme in which he confiscated horses, mules, and property from escaped Missouri slaves who could not prove ownership. General Ewing wrote to Lieutenant Colonel Daniel Anthony on July 20, 1863, advising that he was declaring martial law in Leavenworth and adding, "I will not abate or surrender my military jurisdiction, which extends to both arrest and punishments, in favor of a civil jurisdiction extending only to arrests, nor allow any town in my district to become a city of refuge within whose precincts the pirates of the border may escape the swift process of martial law."

Corruption, Graft, and Greed

Corruption, graft and inefficiency were common in the army. Along with the responsibility of command came the ability to assign friends and cronies to lucrative positions. As commander of the Lane Brigade, General James Lane originally assigned James Blunt as his quartermaster. The Quartermaster Department made all contracts for transportation as well as purchasing military supplies. These supplies included clothing, camp and garrison equipment, fuel, horses,

General James G. Blunt helped organize the hated Kansas Redlegs who preyed on Union and Confederate alike. The Redlegs soon acquired an evil reputation. Their organization with headquarters in Lawrence became one of professional thieves, robbers, murderers, and arsonists, attacking anyone who had sympathy for the South or who had any type of wealth or possessions they coveted. Blunt later spoke against them but found himself powerless to quell their criminal operations. (Greg Walter Collection)

forage, wagons, harness, tools, and all other articles needed in the army. In other words, the quartermaster furnished the supplies from the clothing on the enlisted soldier to the flag on the flagstaff, or from the kettles in the mess kitchen to the mowing machines used for cutting hay at the frontier posts. The quartermaster received government funds to purchase supplies for the army.

Lane openly admitted what he did with plundered Missouri property. "The property is turned over to the commissioners who confiscate it and appraise it and then it goes into the hands of a quartermaster, who sells it to soldiers and others for the benefit of the government."[38]

In actuality, corrupt quartermasters purchased stolen goods from their friends with government money and sent them westward, receiving a percentage of the graft in return. During the years 1864 and 1865 the quartermaster department spent $28,374,228 purchasing supplies. One Kansas newspaper, the *Olathe Mirror,* described some of the corruption going on. "There are a large number of men following this army, who appear to occupy a position between the civil and military. They steal all the supplies as soon as a State is occupied by our forces and then sell them to the Government at enormous prices." A Philadelphia newspaper expressed its opinion about those in Kansas. "A state where New England hypocrites and humbugs rule one end of the state and highwaymen and horse thieves the other."[39]

The other lucrative position was the Commissary Department responsible for the subsistence of the army. It was the duty of this department to purchase the subsistence stores. The principal articles of a soldier's ration were pork, bacon, beef, flour, beans, and other articles of farm produce.[40]

It will be remembered that from one solitary raid on the Jackson County farm of Solomon Young, Jayhawkers stole more than 1,500 bushels of corn, 150 head of cattle, 15 mules, 15 horses, and hams from 400 Hampshire hogs. In some instances, unscrupulous suppliers for the army shipped substandard rations to the frontier posts. One officer's wife wrote: "None of the posts at that time were provided with decent food. The bacon issued to the soldiers was not only rancid, but was supplied by dishonest contractors, who shipped in any foreign substance they could, to make the weight come up to the required amount; and thus the soldiers were cheated out of the quantity due them, as well as imposed upon in the quality of rations. I saw a flat stone, the size of the slices of bacon as they were packed together, sandwiched between the layers. The supplies provided for the consumption of those troops operating in the field or stationed at the posts had been sent out during the war [Civil War]."[41]

Despite the start of the war, individuals were still infected by "gold fever." Thousands of young men from all parts of the nation were still trying to dig their way to riches in the gold fields in Colorado. The migration had started as early as 1849 when gold was discovered in California, precipitating other finds in other Western states. Even the early prospectors of 1849 were anxious to return to the gold fields, thinking their mining experience would be helpful, and hurried to other regions as soon as a new gold discovery occurred. Richard Cordley saw many men from Lawrence leave for the gold fields. "In the spring of 1859, quite a number of the enterprising young men of Lawrence, growing weary of waiting for the tardy emigrant, concluded to turn emigrants themselves. They started over the plains for 'Pike's Peak,' and were the inaugurators of the movement which brought Colorado in such prominence."

Charles Robinson, governor of Kansas under the Topeka constitution, wrote to Amos Lawrence in Boston, "Large numbers are going to Pike's Peak but no gold is seen in our streets."[42] Some eager miners like Quantrill had already been disillusioned and returned to their former surroundings, but many others stuck it out in hopes of discovering fortune. In Colorado, Utah, and even as far away as California there was a growing need for anything that could be used to set up housekeeping in the mining camps. Household furniture, cooking utensils, spinning wheels, clothes, farming implements, harness and tack were the most sought-after commodities. Jayhawking raids on the old established farms of Missouri readily furnished coveted items. Because the living quarters in the mining camps were primitive at best, any type of building supplies were eagerly sought. Sod huts were windowless and damp. Wood, lumber, nails, windowpanes, and tools of every description were needed for building more substantial and comfortable dwellings. As a result, such items were the most desired during Jayhawker raids. In 1861 Jayhawkers stole 60,000 pounds of nails from Jackson County resident Solomon Young. Prospectors needed horses, mules, cows, luggage, sawmills, blankets, and any type of conveyance that could be had, items easily confiscated from Missouri farms.

Anything that provided the settlers the necessities of life was greatly needed and readily available in Missouri. Once acquired by whatever means necessary, such goods were sold mainly at wholesale, chiefly to retailers in Denver, Aurora, and elsewhere. Trade in these goods made a soldier's occupation a lucrative proposition, and many a young Kansas lad eagerly joined up in a Kansas unit to do a little "Jayhawking" on his own hook. As an example, Kansas farmer Watson Stewart spoke about the results from the plunder his brother Samuel, an officer in the Tenth Kansas Jayhawker Regiment, had been contributing to the family. "Samuel had been promoted to the Captaincy of his company, and from him we received substantial aid towards living expenses and the improvements on, and the stocking of the farm."[43] As some of this stolen plunder made its way to the

Western settlements, discovery of stolen goods was evident when Western settlers found household furniture with personal belongings still inside. A wedding dress found in one bureau was proof that goods being shipped west were items of plunder. Wagon trains loaded with stolen goods from Missouri made regular trips from the more important Jayhawking frontier outposts in Kansas, most notably from Leavenworth, Atchison, and Lawrence. Once the war started, the usual regularly scheduled wagon trains once commanded by men like Solomon Young, Richard Yeager, and Dick Chiles were now commanded by enterprising Kansas entrepreneurs taking their ill-gotten trade for a profit farther west.

5

A Gallant and Perfectly Fair Blow

The expedition to Lawrence was a gallant and perfectly fair blow at the enemy, one, which served the malignant and scoundrelly people of Kansas right.

—General Sterling Price

On August 19, 1863, as Quantrill's officers were busy discussing the upcoming raid, their men looked to their horses and equipment while talking among themselves. These guerrillas were the kind of men who were difficult for civilians to understand. They were men who laughed at death. They had been in so many tight situations and perilous places so many times that they had become oblivious to the danger. They may have argued among themselves, but heaven help any outsider who sided against one of their own. Theirs was a comradeship born of adversity. Oftentimes they would endanger their own lives in an attempt to save a fellow guerrilla. They were forged together by common experiences. They shared a blanket with each other on many a cold night and willingly shared what little food they had between them. They would stand guard over each other at night, making sure their companions could get a few hours' sleep in relative safety. And because of these actions they were bound to each other often closer than brothers.

The friendships that endured the dangers of war lasted a lifetime. Harrison Trow described his fellow guerrillas. "Many whose lives were blighted; who in a night were made orphans and paupers; who saw the labor and accumulation of years swept away in an hour of wanton destruction; who for no reason on earth save that they were

Missourians, were hunted from hiding place to hiding place; who were preyed upon while not a single cow remained or a single shock of grain; who were shot at, bedeviled and proscribed, and who, no matter whether Union or disunion, were permitted to have neither flag nor country." John Newman Edwards further wrote, "The guerrilla had his virtues, his chivalry and his romances. He was brave and dashing, and he believed in the righteousness of his cause."[1]

After observing a group of guerrillas, one citizen described their appearance.

> They were generally dressed in rich Federal uniforms, rode good horses and wore an air of jaunty nonchalance, peculiar to the life they lead, all of which with a knowledge of their prowess, their unsatiated hate of the male Yankee race and their high respectability as gentlemen, inclined me to huzzah for Quantrell's men. If it be said that their career has been marked by acts of desperation, let it be answered that they have been driven to them by untold, unutterable wrongs; and that they marched to the destruction of Lawrence over a route whose only landmarks were the burnt, blackened and desolated homes once occupied by Southern men, while the bones of murdered father, mother or sister often lay glistening upon the heap of ruins.[2]

The Guerrillas Talk of the Target

The rank and file of Quantrill's men soon realized that there had never been this many guerrillas brought together before and so heavily armed. Each guerrilla besides having at least two revolvers was also carrying either a carbine or a shotgun. It was evident that something big must be up. After the murder of their female relatives, revenge hung heavily in the air. As they sat in camp making ammunition their talk turned to where they were heading and what the target was going to be. Frank Smith knew that only Quantrill's closest lieutenants knew what was being planned. "A few guessed a raid on Lawrence, but most thought it would be Kansas City."[3] There could be only a few places that would satisfy their thirst for revenge.

Leavenworth was a leading city in Kansas. The most notorious Jayhawkers, Charles Jennison and Daniel Anthony of the Seventh Kansas Jayhawker Regiment, operated from there, and a large percentage of stolen plunder from Missouri was taken there to be sold. Jennison was famous for the number and quality of horses he had stolen out of Missouri. Whenever Jennison rode along on Jayhawking expeditions, much of the plunder was usually taken to his home in Squiresville a few miles southwest of Lawrence. It was well known in Kansas that "Colonel Jennison was nominally in command part of the time, but he was too busy playing poker over at Squiresville, or elsewhere, to find time to take the field in person." When his second-in-command Colonel Daniel Anthony was in charge, the plunder was normally transferred back to Leavenworth.[4]

As an example, Anthony wrote his father a letter bragging about the amount of plunder he had recently taken, summing up by adding, "The negroe's train into Kansas was over a mile long."[5] Leavenworth as a target would pose hazardous risks. There were 12,000 citizens and 2,000 militia living there, and to reach it required a journey of more than sixty miles through enemy territory and crossing the Missouri River twice coming and going. Also the ride would put the raiders within striking distance of more than one Union command post.

Atchison, Kansas, was another hotbed of Jayhawker activity. Besides gathering in its share of plunder, the town made regular overland freighting trips, carrying stolen loot to the settlements out West. The town was also a known headquarters for the Underground Railroad. But Atchison was much too far for a simple raid. It was more than eighty miles away from Missouri, and all the Federal forces located on the western border were between the guerrillas and the town. Most of the guerrillas thought that Quantrill was planning a raid on Kansas City since that was where the provost guards made up of several units of soldiers from the Ninth Kansas Jayhawker Regiment and the women's prison guards comprising several companies of the Eleventh Kansas Jayhawker Regiment were still garrisoned in town. But an attack on Kansas City would only result in getting at a small number of soldiers. Another problem with Kansas City was that there were 5,000 people living there, and it had too many good roads leading in from every direction, increasing the opportunity for quick enemy reinforcement.

If there was going to be a big target, everyone guessed that it had to be Lawrence. Lawrence had always been known as the headquarters of the Jayhawkers and Redlegs. The whole town was an abolitionist stronghold, and nearly every citizen was a viable target. Lawrence suffered an unsavory reputation. It was commonly referred as the "Citadel of Stolen Goods." Most of the plunder stolen from Missouri was taken back to Lawrence and sold at public auction on the main street, while much of the wealth of Western Missouri was loaded up on wagon trains and taken to the gold fields still operating in Colorado and points farther west. Even those citizens not actively participating in the Jayhawkers' raids readily condoned them.

One settler commented about the support Lawrence gave the Jayhawkers. "No punishment could have been too severe for a community whose sympathies these rapacious renegades enjoyed or whose cowardice prevented a vigorous protest against their infamous machinations."[6] The added wealth brought with it prosperity even if it was not honestly earned. With the Federals becoming more emboldened in their depredations and brutality, the guerrillas knew they had to take an audaciously daring step in their retaliatory measures. Many of them had seen the wealth that they had spent a lifetime accumulating swept away in a single Jayhawker raid.

One Southerner reported:

> Originally, the Jayhawkers in Kansas had been very poor. They coveted the goods of their Missouri neighbors, made wealthy or well-to-do by prosperous years of peace and African slavery. Before they became soldiers they had been brigands, and before they destroyed houses in the name of retaliation they had plundered them at the instance of individual greed. The first Federal officers operating in Kansas, that is to say, those who belonged to the State, were land pirates or pilferers. Stocks in herds, flocks, droves, and multitudes were driven from Missouri into Kansas. Houses gave up their furniture; women their jewelry; children their wearing apparel; storerooms their contents; the land its crops; the banks their deposits. To robbery was added murder, to murder arson, and to arson depopulation.[7]

Banded in Purpose, United in Design

The men of Quantrill's command reminisced how the war had affected each of them and how they had arrived at this point in time. They were there banded together for one purpose and united in one design. As they spoke to one another, every man seated himself on the ground with a clean white cloth placed in front of him to clean his pistols. Each man carefully placed each piece in order, like a doctor arranging his instruments. Then each piece was cleaned and oiled. Knowing that their officers would insist on clean weapons, the men took great pains in seeing who would have the cleanest weapon at inspection. Next the horses were attended to. Saddles and blankets were removed, and the guerillas' mounts were curried and combed. Burrs were picked out of manes and tails. Each guerrilla would run his hands lovingly and carefully over his horse's legs and flanks, feeling for any injuries, splints, swelling, or heat that would signal any internal or external injuries that might be a hindrance on a long arduous expedition. The guerrillas also checked their horses' mouths for any discoloring of the gums, making sure they were healthy and pink. Teeth were also examined carefully, making sure there were no sharp edges that would prevent them from eating. Horses' hooves were carefully checked. If needed, they were trimmed and shod. For economy and out of necessity guerrillas shod their horses using only three nails in each shoe. In comparison government troops would use four nails in each shoe. The difference made a definite impression, making the identification of either Federal troops or guerrillas in the area easily recognizable.

As evening set on August 18, 1863, the men gathered around their campfires. In contrast to other campsites this was a quiet gathering. It was said that they massed themselves in silent companies or spoke low to one another and briefly as if they naturally expected something big was about to happen. Never before had they seen so many doctors in camp, and it was noted that the physicians had brought their medical bags with them. There was Dr. John W. Benson, who had belonged to other various military units before assigning himself to Quantrill's company. Seen with him was Dr. M. C. Jacobs, who was married to Amanda Hudspeth. Amanda's two brothers, Joel and William Hudspeth, were also in camp. Dr. P. H. Henry was also there. Dr. Henry had previously been captured by the Federals for assisting Southern wounded, but he was released in time to render aid to Quantrill's men during their victory over Colonel

James T. Buel's forces at Independence on August 11, 1862. Henry was a Southern man who would do anything to help the Cause. He had aided Andy Blunt to escape from the Federals when he was a prisoner in Independence following the Lowe house fight. There was Dr. J. M. Angel, who had formerly served as a surgeon in the regular Confederate army before joining Todd's company in Jackson County. Already in camp was Dr. W. M. Doores, who had been listed on Quantrill's muster role as early as July 6, 1862. Assisting him was a doctor named Herndon. It was obvious that what was being anticipated was a sustained operation that would definitely include caring for wounded men.

As the guerrillas continued arriving in camp, old faces were recognized that had not been seen in many long months. In the intervening wait the men talked among themselves, exchanging information about their families and the events they had experienced since their last meeting. John Newman Edwards stated, "The rendezvous night was an August night, a blessed, balmy, mid-summer night, just such a night as would be chosen to give force to reflections and permit the secrets of the soul to escape."[8]

Quantrill's Men: Young, Intelligent, Fearless, and Desperate

It became generally understood among "the outfit" that Lawrence was to be their destination, and the spirits of the men rose as the time approached for the order to mount. Thomas Cobb who was acquainted with Quantrill remembered,

> His [Quantrill's] men were all young and from the best families in the State, they were intelligent, fearless and desperate. They had seen their homes burned, their families turned out doors and many of their kindred and friends murdered in cold blood. So they went forth to a war of extermination, Quantrell was their leader. He was quiet, modest, gentlemanly and cultivated but jaunty and desperate. He never drank, gambled or dissipated in any way. His men were for the most part like himself, strictly temperate and quiet.[9]

The men who gathered that August night came responding to the Jayhawkers' policy of total extermination. One newspaper reported why they were there.

> The wanton cruel destruction of houses, furniture, horses, stock, and every species of property, belonging to Southern men, their wives and daughters insulted, punished with imprisonment and often corporeal sufferings unheard of among civilized troops, crippled for life, stripped of their clothes in the dead of winter and forced to seek shelter over the frozen ground in a perfectly nude condition, often having their persons violated, mocked and jeered at by a brutal soldiery, forced to work as slaves and to suffer with hunger and every privation that the most refined cruelty could suggest, husbands, fathers, and brothers hunted by these slot hounds of the huckstering politician who sits in his den like a gorilla prototype, grinning and jesting over the agonies and throes of his victims.[10]

Perry Hoy was captured at the Tate house fight and hanged in Leavenworth on July 28, 1862. Quantrill earnestly sought an exchange of prisoners for Hoy; instead, General James G. Blunt refused the exchange. Quantrill then raided Olathe, Kansas, on September 6, capturing twenty-nine Union troops. By the time the raid was over the Rebels had killed fourteen men in response to Hoy's death. This image is encased in a mourning pin that was worn by a family member after Hoy's death. The back of the case contains a section of his hair. (Emory Cantey Collection)

It seemed as if every Southern man in Western Missouri who was old enough to carry a gun was present. Many an old face was recognized, but also scattered among the crowd were guerrillas not old enough to be called men except for the weapons they carried and the experiences they had recently endured from the wanton attacks on their homes and families. Allen Parmer's neighborhood, like that of most of his friends, had been ruined and completely destroyed by the Jayhawkers. Parmer from Clay County described his own experiences when he joined the guerrillas, which were similar to many others. Parmer went on to say, "I was only sixteen years old when I joined up. There were very few at that first muster roll that was over twenty."

Though they came from almost every county along the border most of "Quantrill's recruits came from Jackson County, young farm boys, wild, reckless; dare devil fellows, all of them aching for adventure. Those from eighteen years old and up were described as old men."[11] Many of Quantrill's men were called "boys" because the majority of them were under twenty years of age. One of the youngest was James Shaw Milliken who had his own fascinating story to tell. Milliken was born in Milliken, Louisiana, near the Arkansas line. The town was named after his father Richard M. Milliken who owned 10,000 acres and was one of the largest slave owners at the time. James was twelve years old when the war began and weighed only seventy-five pounds. At thirteen he enlisted in a unit known as the Missouri Minute Men, Confederate Dare-Devils. Milliken recalled, "Oh, I joined four or five Confederate companies. But they just used me as bait to enlist older boys, and when they started away to the front I got the can, as you fellows say. I got tired of being used as a tool to shame the older boys into going to war, and finally ran away and got into one of Quantrell's companies commanded by Capt. Joe Lee."[12]

Another youngster was Riley Crawford. It was Riley's two sisters who had just been murdered in the Union jail collapse. Riley's father Jeptha was forty-nine years old. The previous winter he was murdered by Federals on his own doorstep in the presence of his family. His wife and nine children were thrust out into the cold during one of the most severe winters on record, and then the Federals burned the house down around them. As Mrs. Crawford tried to save some of her possessions from the flames the soldiers tore the bonnet from her head and threw it back into the fire. Without the kindness of Southern neighbors the entire family would have perished. Upon Quantrill's return from Texas in the spring Mrs. Crawford took her four sons, William, Marshall, Marion, and Riley to the guerrilla chieftain's camp, telling him to make soldiers of her boys in order to avenge their father's death. Riley was only fourteen when he joined Quantrill.

William Gregg remembered the episode by saying,

> It would be too tedious for me in this brief history to mention all the atrocious acts of the Kansan, combined with federal troops stationed in Missouri, though many of the troops stationed in Missouri were Kansans, hence I will give you one circumstance in illustration of a hundred other similar ones. About the 18th of February 1863, Col. Bill Penick stationed at Independence, whose men were part

> Missourians and part Kansans sent a scout of about seventy five men sixteen miles south east of Independence to the houses of Col. Jim Saunders and Uncle Jeptha Crawford. The scout arriving at the house of Saunders first, divided. One half going to Crawfords, Mrs. Saunders and her daughter prepared dinner for the half stopping there. The Colonel furnished feed for their horses. All went well until dinner was over, mind you the snow was fourteen inches deep with the mercury 10 degrees below zero, when Col. Saunders was placed under guard. The house burned. The women not allowed a bonnet or shawl. On leaving Saunders place, they told the wife they were going to take her husband to Independence and make him take the oath [of allegiance to the Union].

In front of the Federal commander Saunders was mercilessly shot down.[13]

There were others barely older than Riley Crawford riding in Captain Bill Anderson's company. James Andrew "Dick" Liddel was probably the youngest. He was only twelve when he rode in to join Quantrill after Federals killed two of his relatives. There were four Kimberlin brothers from Blue Springs who rode with Quantrill: William, eighteen; Richard, sixteen; Robert, fourteen; and Julian, twelve. Like Riley Crawford they joined after Federal soldiers killed their fifty-one-year-old father Samuel on November 28, 1862, hanging him from the rafters of his own barn then burning it down around him. Bill Ridings was only sixteen when he joined the guerrillas, as was Dock Rupe, who joined his older brothers Harvey and John with the guerrillas. Hobbs Kerry was seventeen when he joined up. Nineteen-year-old William McWaters joined Sterling Price for a six-month enlistment at the start of the war. When he returned to his home in Platte County he found his parents' home burned, his father and brother killed by the militia, and the rest of his family banished. The next thing he did was join Quantrill where he eventually came riding into camp with Bill Anderson's company. The oldest man was called "Daddy" Estes. Estes joined the band because his wife and daughters had been cruelly abused and his home destroyed.

Riding at Bill Anderson's side was noted guerrilla Hiram Guess. All of Anderson's men were known to be formidable fighters. Guess

By the time of the raid on Lawrence, Kansas, Hiram Guess had already gained a reputation as one of the bravest and fiercest fighters in Quantrill's company. (Rick Mack Collection)

had already made a name for himself as one of the bravest in the company. At one time surrounded by the enemy Guess and a companion charged through the Federal cordon with pistols blazing and rejoined their comrades in time to make another attack. There was no doubt that almost all the guerrillas in Bill Anderson's company carried the most horrendous memories of individual Federal atrocities. They placed tokens of loved ones tucked inside their shirts or a small item of remembrance from their homes that were no more. As Anderson's men dismounted and prepared to make camp, those observing them and who knew them personally were well acquainted with each of their histories. One of those riding in Anderson's ranks was sixteen-year-old Newton "Plunk" Murray. Murray was physically small, standing only five feet tall with light complexion, blue eyes, and light red hair. When Missourians captured the Federal arsenal in Liberty on April 20, 1861, Plunk's father Thomas helped hide the supplies on his farm in Clay County. Murray joined Anderson after Federal soldiers attempted to hang his mother. The soldiers also killed all their livestock. He tried to join General Price but was turned down because he was too young.

Also accompanying Anderson was William Grindstaff. His sister Mollie had been in the jail collapse and had escaped serious injury, but just the image of his sister's attempted murder drove him to seek revenge on anyone wearing a blue uniform. Brothers Louis and Thomas Vandever had more reason to seek revenge than Grindstaff. Louis's wife Susan and her sister Armenia had died in the jail collapse. Both men had been with Anderson for quite some time, ever since Jayhawkers swept through their neighborhood early in the war, looting everything there was to carry and taking it back to Kansas. James Mundy was already riding with Quantrill when his sisters Susan and Mattie were arrested along with the other guerrillas' female relatives and put in prison. They survived the jail collapse, but James Mundy remained with Quantrill bent on revenge.

Jayhawker Victims

As the men gathered in small groups, they not only recounted the murder of the young girls but also the inhuman treatment that had touched many of them individually. Guerrilla George T. Maddox remarked that the Federals' "main forte [was] to kill old men and make war on women and children." In the previous three months the Federals had murdered more than two hundred old men and young boys along the border for their Southern sympathies. Cole Younger attested to the fact, stating, "The Eldridge house in Lawrence, Kansas, from which place had gone out the Jayhawkers who in three months just previous had slain 200 men and boys, taken many women prisoners, and stolen no one knows how many horses." Gregg said, "Quantrill and his men were in Lawrence not only to avenge the death of many citizens of Missouri, but the death of four innocent girls, loved wives and sisters of Quantrill's men."[14]

While patrolling in Jackson County with his Sixth Kansas Jayhawker Regiment, Major Willis C. Ransom ordered the death of forty-seven-year-old Alfred Laws, who lived near the Blue River, for feeding a squad of Federals disguised as guerrillas. In another instance, a company of Redlegs from Lawrence commanded by Captain George Hoyt rode into Westport, Missouri, one day, took Philip Bucher from his wife and children, marched him out on the commons, made him kneel down, and shot him. Another quiet citizen, Henry C. Rout, twenty-five years old, was hanged without provocation. In late January 1862, Jennison's men burned two hundred homes in Lexington, Missouri. The following October 4, also at Lexington, a Union death squad of six men pulled John McPhadon out of bed. His two daughters clung to him, begging him not to go. After he was forced a few yards from his house, each of the Federals fired a round into his body. Although he claimed to be a Southern man he was never known to be under arms and had stayed at home all the time. Another unoffending citizen, John Phillips, was also hanged.[15]

Guerrilla Jim Cummins remembered that Federal raiding parties began to patrol extensively through Jackson County. "They would throw old men into prison because they could give no information as to the whereabouts of any of Quantrell's men. Young men were murdered outright and women were insulted and abused. The people therefore were in great fear. When they went to bed at night they went with the fear that the morrow would bring forth a terrible awakening. All traveling was dangerous."

One Kansas officer, while out on a scouting expedition in Missouri, wounded and captured an old man who was out hunting his lost stock. Lest he should suffer some from his wounds, this considerate officer finished him with a pistol bullet. Henry Morris lived five miles north of Lone Jack. In 1862, his son, eleven-year-old John W. Morris, was killed by Penick's troops from Independence. Federal troops went to the home of Jeremiah Blythe on the Harrisonville and Independence road, looking for Cole Younger who had been wounded following the fight at John Flanery's house. When they arrived, no one was home except twelve-year-old Theodore Blythe.

> They took him to the barn and ordered him to tell all he knew of Quantrell's men and Younger and their whereabouts. He was to be killed if he failed to tell the truth. The boy was not the least bit frightened and kept them for a time in conversation, all the while looking for an opportunity to escape. Seeing at last what he thought to be a chance he dashed away from his captors and ran to the house, entering amid a perfect shower of bullets. He was not hit however and, seizing a pistol, he dashed out of the back door and ran towards some timber. He reached the garden fence and started to climb over it when a ball struck him in the spine and he fell back dying but game to the last. Turning over on his face as the Jayhawkers rushed up to finish him, he shot one dead, mortally wounded another and severely wounded a third but before he could fire a fourth shot, seventeen bullets were put into his body.[16]

Also in Jackson County, thirteen-year-old John Fox, who had a brother with Quantrill, was shot and killed by Federals while his sister and mother had hold of him begging for his life. He was charged with feeding his brother.[17] Federals also killed fourteen-year-old James Nicholson because he had two brothers with Price.[18]

Whether their victims were young or old, the Jayhawkers had no mercy as even elderly citizens were not exempt from Federal cruelty. Howell Lewis was eighty-one years old when he was killed by Federals in Jackson County. One of Penick's men, calling himself Jim Lane, killed a Dr. Triggs for his money. A Mrs. J. M. Thatcher living in Westport, Missouri, recalled the incident concerning her husband's death. "Colonel Penick, who was in command of 400 bloodthirsty men who had been taken from jails, penitentiaries and what-not, was stationed among us. Our houses were raided and ourselves subjected to indignities." Even though her husband had taken the oath of allegiance he was taken out and shot because the Federals knew he was trying to take his family to another county for safety. Federals hanged fifty-nine-year-old Sam H. Jones simply because he was from Virginia. They also shot George Tyler as well as Hedrick Farwell and forty-five-year-old Henry Lowers of Buchanan County. Lowers left a wife and seven small children. Union soldiers also murdered other citizens by the name of Givens, Manchester, Beamish, Parker, S. S. Bollings, James Newton, and Samuel L. Ralls, all of Jackson County.[19]

Why Quantrill's Men Became Guerrillas

As night fell and the guerrillas gathered together to eat their supper, their talk naturally turned to what had compelled each of them to be there with Quantrill. They all realized they had something in common. Besides all being young men, some were too young to join the regular Confederate army under General Price but were too determined to stay at home. And, even if they did, they knew that the Federals would come back to question them or torture them if necessary. In fact, most had no homes to return to. They had been burned to the ground by Federal forces in retaliation for their Southern sympathies.

George Hudspeth, a wealthy farmer from Blue Springs, had four sons in camp: William Napoleon Hudspeth, also known as "Babe,"

Joel R., Robert, and James. They had come to Blue Springs from Kentucky and were engaged in the freighting business. In explaining their plight, John Newman Edwards said,

> Lane robbed them, Jennison robbed them, Anthony robbed them, militiaman and Jayhawker alike robbed them; they were burnt out and plundered; shot at and waylaid; hunted here, driven there, and persecuted everywhere, but they could not be reduced in either purse or spirit. Patriotism was the standard they judged every man, and those who were not patriotic were untrue. No matter how all the highways were guarded and all the garrisoned places overgrown with soldiers, the Hudspeths kept the faith and fought the good fight to the end.[20]

Babe Hudspeth's home was first burned in the spring of 1862. Jayhawkers returned in July of 1863 and burned the family out of a log cabin they were staying in and also burned their corncrib and smokehouse. Morgan Mattox said he saw Jennison's men go to the home of George Hudspeth. "They robbed his place of Negroes and everything else that was worth taking." Because the menfolk had joined Quantrill, the Hudspeth women were banished from the state. The Hudspeths had a litany of reasons for joining Quantrill. When Jayhawkers set fire to their uncle's home, the mother and her Negro slave tried to save some things from the fire, but the Negro was seized by the Redlegs and carried back to Kansas with the rest of the loot. Their remaining relatives, including cousin Ben Morrow, also saw their homes burned and looted by the Kansas Redlegs.

Morgan T. Mattox was only fifteen when he turned against the Federals. On one of Jennison's raids near his home he was taken prisoner and so observed firsthand as the Jayhawkers looted Missouri homesteads. Mattox saw the Jayhawkers steal thousands of dollars' worth of goods from the families in the Six-Mile Township of Jackson County, besides watching the Jayhawkers steal his own horse, saddle, and bridle. As they were plundering, he witnessed three of Jennison's drunken soldiers kill a prisoner, Sel Stark, in cold blood. Escaping his captors, Mattox quickly found Quantrill and became a guerrilla on August 11, 1862. He was questioned by Quantrill when he asked to join up. He remembered that Quantrill didn't accept anyone in his command who was not "moved by injury

Lieutenant Ben Morrow. Morrow's property was stolen and his home was burned by Kansas Jayhawkers. Morrow was an officer in General Joseph Shelby's brigade, but was home in Blue Springs when he heard about the murdered girls in Kansas City and decided to ride to Lawrence with Quantrill. (Patrick Marquis Collection)

to selves or family, imbued with malice and bent on revenge." Quantrill used Mattox on occasion to slip into Kansas City to buy ammunition caps and powder for his men.[21]

Levi Potts and his seventeen-year-old brother Martin were also from the Blue Springs area of Jackson County. They along with many of their neighbors suffered from Jayhawker raids in the vicinity of the Morgan Walker farm. The Potts had come to Missouri from Simpson County, Kentucky. Their grandfather had fought in the Revolutionary War. Daniel DeWitt, one of Morgan Walker's neighbors, was a special target of the Jayhawkers. It was on his farm that the Kansas abolitionists who first intended to rob Walker were killed. During the war DeWitt was plundered by Jayhawkers at least seven times in two years, leaving his farm stripped of everything and his house and buildings burned to the ground.[22]

James Little, who always rode at Quantrill's side, was naturally present when the guerillas gathered for the raid on Lawrence. When he was only seventeen he joined Quantrill along with his older brother John. The brothers apparently joined when Jayhawkers started plundering through the Sni-A-Bar Township following the Morgan Walker raid. John was killed in ambush at the Little Blue ford in August of 1862 by a Federal patrol from Independence led

Andrew J. Walker was one of Quantrill's first recruits. He rode in the advance on the Lawrence raid, seeking retaliation for the burning of his home and the theft of all his possessions by the Jayhawkers who carried them back to Kansas. (Emory Cantey Collection)

by Sheriff James Knowles. With the constant number of Federal patrols running through their neighborhood it was unsafe to return home, so Jim had been with Quantrill from the beginning. He became Quantrill's closest follower and never let Quantrill go into battle alone, often protecting him by shielding him with his own body. As he sat around the campfire he kept a watchful eye on his trusted leader, observing him as he was busily directing operations and issuing orders.

Andrew Jack Liddil, one of Quantrill's first recruits, was also there. Liddil said that Jim Lane and Lieutenant Hugh Dunn Fisher were the two men they were mostly after. Liddil remarked that the reason the guerrillas were planning vengeance upon Lawrence was because of the Redlegs' burning and robbing at one time twenty-five farmhouses and barns and carrying off the stock and taking away all the Negroes who would go. Liddil said he recalled once seeing the Redlegs returning to Lawrence with their plunder and captured slaves.[23]

As Andy Walker finished caring for his horse and prepared to sit down to supper, he confided to those around him how he came to be a guerrilla. Walker was twenty-six when he joined Quantrill. It was out of necessity. Following the Jayhawker raid on his father's farm before the war in December 1860, in which two of the Kansas criminals were killed, further raids in retaliation for their killing forced him from his home. In later raids four hundred Jayhawkers swarmed across the border, robbing Walker of his stock and equipment and burning his home to the ground. When Walker returned he found everything he owned destroyed. Only one slave cabin was standing on the farm; everything else had been burned, and all of the family possessions had been taken back to Kansas. Andy's mother counted five of her neighbors' homes burning at the same time. The raid turned Walker against anyone in a Federal uniform.[24]

The Jayhawkers' atrocities in Missouri added a long resumé to those who rode into Quantrill's camp. Thirty-two-year-old H. C. Cogswell from Bates County joined Quantrill after Jennison plundered his home and destroyed the property of his relatives. Howard Bragg's house was burned and all of his stock stolen. Federals burned down the home of William McCoy's mother. In Johnson County, Missouri, guerrilla Captain John D. Brinker's sister and younger brother were imprisoned for aiding their brother. Before being sent to prison Mattie Brinker was seized in the spring of 1862 and along with four other Southern girls used by the Federals for over a week as human shields during their patrols through the county in violation of the laws of war. John Brinker managed an earlier well-known escape in Johnson County from the Federals under Major Emory Foster. Brinker and fellow guerrilla Frank Burgess were surrounded in a house by a Federal patrol when both men made a sudden dash from the house, killing and wounding two of Foster's men before making their escape. Foster burned the house and killed the owner for harboring guerrillas.[25]

Sidney Scott also lived in Johnson County. His house was burned and his livestock driven off by Kansas Jayhawkers. Also living in Johnson County was Charles A. Longacre, originally from Tennessee. As the Jayhawkers raided through the county they raped Longacre's family slaves while his mother was forced to watch. Longacre said that after killing two elderly relatives the Federals also raped his sister. The rest of the women and children in the neighborhood were then driven from their homes. His mother and sister were arrested and imprisoned in St. Louis. All this happened because the Federals found Longacre's name on Quantrill's muster roll, listing him as a Confederate soldier.[26] Like Quantrill, Longacre had first joined the Missouri State Guard and fought under Colonel Jeremiah Vardaman Cockrell. One of his brothers was married to Mary H.

Cockrell, the sister of General Francis Marion Cockrell, the brother of Colonel Cockrell. Another brother enlisted at the same time and served under General Jo Shelby. In January of 1863 Longacre left the regular army to join Quantrill. Historians have noted that Longacre was a distant relative of Kate King, Quantrill's wife.

All of Tom and Preston Webb's relatives and neighbors had suffered from Federal atrocities. Kansas Jayhawkers forced their brother-in-law to chop up his front porch steps for kindling wood in order to set fire to his own house during the winter of 1862. Preston and Tom had a younger brother John who had stayed home during the war. Federals raided their home and shot their younger brother in cold blood, then set fire to the house. When his mother took a pillow and placed it tenderly under the head of her dying boy, it was torn away and thrown in the flames, with the threat that if she did it again they would throw the body in. After joining the guerrillas Preston Webb became one of Quantrill's best scouts. It was said of him, "He had the eye of an eagle and the endurance of the red deer. He first taught himself coolness, and then he taught it to others. In traveling he did not travel the same road twice." His brother Tom joined Quantrill just prior to the Lawrence raid.[27]

William "Buck" Fields was raised to be patriotic. Both of his grandfathers had fought in the War of 1812. He was only seventeen years old when Redlegs killed his father near Independence in 1861, precipitating him and his two brothers to join the Southern army. Buck first joined General Shelby then joined Quantrill the following year after hearing that the Federals had raped two of his cousins. He was now there with Quantrill for revenge.

William Halley was from Frankfort, Kentucky, and was nineteen years old in 1861 when he was jailed in Independence for killing two of Jennison's men who had plundered his mother's home. Quantrill's band raided the jail, scattering the Union soldiers, and freeing Halley who immediately threw in his lot with Quantrill. Halley's sweetheart in Independence feared for him because he rode with the guerrillas, but it was the safest place to be for a wanted man. After his rescue the other members of his family were compelled to leave the county. They removed to Weston, Missouri, a town of five hundred persons, and remained there throughout the war.

Three unidentified Kansas soldiers were photographed sitting on horses that had been taken during a Jayhawker expedition in Weston, Missouri. (Rick Mack Collection)

Frank Smith from Blue Springs was only fifteen years old when he became acquainted with Quantrill following the Morgan Walker affair. Jayhawkers struck his neighborhood early in the war, stealing his horse, saddle, and bridle. Because of constant Federal harassment he rode to Wyandotte, Kansas, to find a job because it was impossible for him to plant a crop at home. While he was in Kansas, Jayhawkers seized him and tried to coerce him to join them, threatening to kill him if he refused. After being threatened to have his head cut off by the Federal commander at Independence, he managed to run away and was only seventeen years old when he joined Quantrill.[28]

John T. House was sitting around the campfire with other young men from the Brooking Township of Jackson County. He had his own story to tell. Early on during the war Jennison rampaged through his neighborhood. His father Ephriam House lived on a farm close by. When Jennison asked the elder House where his sympathies lay and he replied with the South, Jennison mercilessly shot him down in cold blood. The Jayhawkers then burned his house and drove away his livestock. John was away from home serving with the Missouri State Guard at the time. He returned home when his enlistment expired and after finding that his father had been murdered and his house destroyed and his possessions carried back to Kansas, he joined Quantrill.

Twenty-four-year-old Randolph Venable was House's neighbor. Along with other Brooking youths he joined the guerrillas after the October 27, 1861, Jayhawker raid through their neighborhood when twenty-seven of their homes were put to the torch. Those of Mary "Polly" Fristoe and her neighbor Mrs. Rucker, both of Brooking Township, were those left burning in the Jayhawkers' wake. The house of guerrilla Jeremiah Dave Hylton, a neighbor of Mrs. Rucker, was also burned, causing him to seek out Quantrill's camp. Describing the raid, the justice of the peace in Brooking Township, Leander M. Dehoney, said he stood in his yard and looked toward Blue Springs and counted twenty-four houses burning.[29] Two days later on October 29, Jayhawkers torched the home of Martin V. B. Flanery, who then left to join Quantrill. Flanery initially fought under Price. When his term of enlistment was over, he returned home and began farming, but was constantly shot at and almost killed. It was in March 1863 when Martin decided to join the guerrillas. His wife told him, "If it were me, I would go, as you cannot live in peace here, and I would sell my life as dearly as possible." Riding with Quantrill was the way Martin decided to strike back.

John McCorkle was still inconsolable days after he buried his sister and cousins. Tears and anger accompanied his reply when asked about their murders.

> Imagine, if you can, my feelings. A loved sister foully murdered and the widow of a dead brother seriously hurt by a set of men to whom the name assassins, murderers and cutthroats would be a compliment. People abuse us, but, by God, did we not have enough to make us desperate and thirst for revenge? We tried to fight like soldiers, but were declared outlaws, hunted under a "Black Flag" and murdered like beasts. The homes of our friends burned, our aged sires, who dared sympathize with us had been either hung or shot in the presence of their families and all their furniture and provisions loaded in wagons and with our livestock taken to the State of Kansas. The beautiful farming country of Jackson County, Cass County and Johnson County were worse than desert, and on every hillside stood lone blackened chimneys, sad sentinels and monuments to the memory of our once happy homes. And these outrages had been done by Kansas troops, calling themselves soldiers, but a disgrace to the name soldier. And now our innocent and beautiful girls had been murdered in a most foul, brutal, savage and damnable manner.[30]

Even before joining Quantrill, McCorkle suffered the malice of Union soldiers. His father was a successful businessman but was forced to leave the state because of his Southern sympathies. McCorkle was born near Savannah, Missouri, but later moved to a farm in the Valley of the Little Blue in southern Jackson County. When the war started McCorkle rushed south and joined Sterling Price. When Price left Lexington, McCorkle took sick and was left at the home of a Southern sympathizer. He recounted that as he lay ill with a fever Jim Lane discovered him and "told us he would be back and kill us and would give us that night to prepare to die, but for some unknown reason he did not return and I suppose the reason he did not return was that he was too busy in burning the town of

Osceola and robbing and murdering its citizens."[31] When his enlistment expired, McCorkle returned home and again attempted to take up farming. Union officials from Independence demanded he put up a $1,000 bond as a guarantee he would not take up arms again against the government. Not satisfied with that demand, they threatened to put his female cousin, Molly Wigginton, in prison if he did not join the pro-Union Enrolled Missouri Militia. He finally made up his mind to join Quantrill when Federal soldiers took him from his fields to use him as a human shield as they escorted the mail from Independence to Harrisonville.

McCorkle still remembered the night Jayhawkers attacked his home with only his mother and sisters present.

> One night during his absence, in the autumn of 1861, while the family was asleep, the door of Mrs. McCorkle's room on the first floor was broken open and a squad of noisy soldiers rushed into the apartment. The alarmed lady entreated them to retire until she could put on her clothes, but they cursed her and told her to get up pretty damn quick or they would prod her with their sabers. A bright fire was burning in the open hearth; the wretches took blazing brands and carried them about as they ransacked the closets, dresser drawers and trunks.
>
> The young girls who were asleep upstairs were aroused by the disturbance below, hastily dressed and ran to their mother's room. The outlaws then turned their attention to the girls, using insulting terms, searched their persons for valuables, all the while singing ribald songs or telling obscene jokes. They took from a pocket in the housemaid's petticoat forty dollars, tearing her apparel from her person. The creatures made the girls go before them as they searched every apartment in the house, from which they purloined every article of value they could carry. Then returning downstairs three of the wretches took by force three of the girls into the yard and made them march back and forth in the moonlight in their thin nightgowns making most vicious threats and insinuations. The fellows demanded to know where a negro man, faithful servant of the family, was hiding, saying they intended to shoot him on sight because he remained with the damned rebels when he could go with them and be free. After several hours of this atrocious conduct the creatures started away, but just when the family began to breathe freer they burst in again and demanded breakfast. Not waiting for someone to get food for them,

> they were too frightened to refuse; they went in the kitchen and pantry and helped themselves to every edible in sight.
>
> Finally the Jayhawkers, with threats and curses, went their way. Later during the early summer of 1863 Federals returned again to loot McCorkle's parent's home then burned down the house.[32]

Nathan Kerr, McCorkle's brother-in-law, became a guerrilla after Federal troops hanged his father who chose to die rather than abandon his devotion to the Cause. Kerr married Charity McCorkle on January 26, 1860. Because of her relation to one of Quantrill's men, Ewing had her arrested then murdered by his soldiers. Her cousin, Nannie Harris, arrested along with her, was seriously injured in the jail collapse. Nannie was the sister of Thomas Harris, one of Quantrill's closest followers. Thomas experienced similar incidents as his sister when Jayhawkers early in the war attacked his family in their home. They cursed his mother and sisters, tearing their clothes from their bodies, looking for money. They ransacked the closets, dresser drawers, and trunks. Tom's little sister began to cry when a Jayhawker held a sword against her face threatening to cut her head off. The poor little thing was so frightened and subdued that she did not speak a word for days. Similar to other raids, as Jayhawkers plundered Harris's property they sang obscene songs to the women and young girls. Jayhawkers burned down the Harris home on February 22, 1863.

George W. "Bud" Wigginton was a cousin of Thomas Harris and John McCorkle. He too had reason to join Quantrill. In February 1862 Jayhawkers rode through Lafayette County, Missouri, destroying everything in their path. Any home with a piano found the Jayhawkers gleefully breaking it to pieces. One Lafayette County resident, E. A. Christie, an old man who had but one arm to defend himself, was strung up by the Jayhawkers twice and his son seven times until they told where their valuables were hidden.[33]

Federals rode to the farm of Bud Wigginton's sixty-eight-year-old father, also in Lafayette County, mercilessly shooting him in the presence of his family. His personal property was all taken and his house burned down, leaving only the land. The soldiers also killed Bud's brother Wallace then threatened to throw Bud's sister Mollie in prison if he did not join the local Union militia. After burning

Wigginton's home the Kansas colonel in charge of Independence reported to General John Schofield, Federal commander of the Department of Missouri in St. Louis, that he had killed thirty guerrillas during a recent sweep of Lafayette County. Congressman Austin A. King replied to the report by saying, "'Truthful and loyal' Union men of that county all knew that only unarmed civilians had been killed. One hundred and fifty horses reported confiscated from secessionists were in fact stolen from peaceful, law-abiding citizens. The pernicious effects of such raids were augmented by provost marshals who had been planted in each county and 'who seem to think it absolutely necessary to commit a certain amount of oppression in order to render their authority respectable.'" Schofield responded by asserting that the activities of Missouri guerrillas were largely a reaction to aggressions from Kansas.[34]

The Youngers and Their Kin

Coleman and James Younger were early targets of Federal brutality. Their uncle John Fristoe lost his home and his livestock in a Jayhawker raid through Brooking Township. Their brothers-in-law, George Clayton, John Jarrette, Kit Rose, and Richard Hall, also rode in to join Quantrill. Jim Younger was seventeen years old when he enlisted under George Todd. After only a few skirmishes Jim was described as "cool and brave in battle."[35] Federal reprisals against Cole and Jim for being with Quantrill resulted in Federal militia from Harrisonville, Missouri, murdering their father Henry Washington Younger, who was a staunch pro-Union man completely opposed to secession. Early Jayhawker raids had already stolen four thousand dollars in carriages and wagons and forty saddle horses. The total loss was estimated at $20,000.

Henry Younger owned two large farms in Jackson County and one in Cass County and operated a livery stable and two stores in Harrisonville. Federals burned all three of the Youngers' homes. Jayhawkers looted their property in Harrisonville, forcing the Younger family to live at their farm in Jackson County. On February 9, 1863, twenty-two Federals appeared suddenly at midnight and commanded Mrs. Younger to reveal the hiding place of her son Coleman. Threats accomplished nothing, so with cocked and pointed carbines the Jayhawkers

Guerillas Thomas (left) and George Wallace Talley (right) took part in a skirmish at Cole Younger's winter camp in February 1863. George Wallace was killed, but Tom managed to escape with the help of his cousin Cole Younger who came to his rescue and saved his life. (Emory Cantey Collection)

compelled Mrs. Younger to set fire to her own house after the soldiers had poured oil over the floor. She was held captive until the last timber was consumed. There was a deep snow on the ground at the time, through which the poor woman trudged three miles to a neighbor's house for shelter. Contracting consumption, Mrs. Younger fell into poor health, precipitating her premature death. Cole remarked to those around him, "The knowledge that my father had been killed in cold blood filled my heart with the lust for vengeance." It only added to his hard feelings when sometime later a Federal officer raped his sister. Cole remarked concerning Lawrence that it was the place from which the Jayhawkers had gone out and "in three months previous [had] stolen no one knows how many horses." Looking back, Jim Cummins described Cole as being "cool and desperate, and headed the advance in that memorial raid."[36]

Brothers Tom, George, and Wallace Talley were cousins of the Youngers. They lived six miles south of Independence, Missouri. While they were away fighting with General Price, Jennison killed their sixty-eight-year-old father John. When their enlistments ended and they returned home, George and Wallace joined Quantrill. Linking up with their cousins Cole and James Younger, they established winter quarters in a remote area of their farm, deciding to stay and care for their families during the winter rather than ride to Texas with the other guerrillas. Wallace was killed when surrounded by Federals in a skirmish on February 10, 1863.

William Gaugh, the Hills, and the Bishops

William Gaugh was only sixteen when he joined Quantrill. He had tried to join Price's army, but the old general told him, "As badly as I need men, I cannot take a boy of sixteen from his parents." He became a second lieutenant and was considered one of the best shots in Quantrill's company. Gaugh carried four pistols all the time and when riding on the charge carried one in each hand, guiding the horse by holding the reins in his teeth. In personal appearance he was small of stature, but well-built with curly black hair and blue eyes. In spite of his youth he was looked upon as one of the most valuable men in the command and was often entrusted by Quantrill with missions of importance. On one expedition north of the Missouri River, Gaugh and three other guerrillas killed thirty-six Federals. Gaugh and another guerrilla were the only two who survived the skirmish. They were captured by a Federal officer on the banks of the river while trying to make their escape. The officer held a revolver to Gaugh's chest with an order to put up his hands. Remembering Quantrill's order never to surrender, Gaugh made a quick move, raising his own revolver and shooting the Union officer dead. Then just as quickly, Gaugh dived into the water and swam across to safety amid a hail of bullets.

Gaugh sat around the fire listening to his fellow guerrilla John A. Workman tell how he came to join Quantrill. Workman reminisced by saying, "Those Kansas Redlegs came over here and laid waste our homes. What would you think of a man or party of men who would come to your home and take your wife and young baby out and lay them on a mattress in snow a foot deep and then burn down your house? Those things were done here. In some of our counties we didn't have seven houses left standing. Naturally the men in our families were enraged. We couldn't stay at home; we would have been shot." After the war Workman commented, "Quantrill was actuated by the same motives that actuated us. He was not naturally a man of blood, but the border strife changed him."[37]

Tuck, Woot, Tom, and John Hill were cousins of Frank and Jesse James. They were born in Logan County, Kentucky. In 1846 the family moved to Pleasant Hill, Missouri. No family in Missouri was held in higher esteem than the Hill family. The family consisted of a widowed mother and thirteen children. Union soldiers attacked their home and chased fifteen-year-old Tom through a cornfield. He ran to Quantrill's camp, found his brothers, and got permission to join up. Tom's older brother gave him a pistol, and thus he became a guerrilla. Being Southerners they were marked by the Jayhawkers. Later, twenty-five Kansas marauders went to the Hill home and after stealing all they could carry away set fire to the house, telling Mrs. Hill she could put out the fire if she wished to. Tuck, whose full name was Francis Marion Hill, was born in 1843 and became a captain under Quantrill. His brother, James Wootson "Woot" Hill, and Thomas served under him as lieutenants. Besides being stalwart soldiers the Hill brothers were "ladies men," and on one occasion when they were visiting their girls the Federal soldiers surrounded the premises. The Hill brothers got rid of the Federal soldiers with little trouble, killing every one that had surrounded the house.[38]

Tuck was an expert horseman and an unerring marksman. It was said that with his bridle reins between his teeth and a pistol in each hand he could shoot a ring around a tree. During his first enlistment in the Missouri State Guard, Tuck carried important dispatches through the Union lines from one general to another, and he led his own company, which he recruited, into many successful battles. After only three months he was given an honorable discharge so he could join with Quantrill.[39] Tuck was captured several times during the war, but each time managed to escape. He was wounded twelve times and had seven horses shot out from under him. One record states that Tuck Hill owned the only known photograph of Quantrill, the reason being that Quantrill had a $50,000 reward on his head so all photographs of him were destroyed to make recognition of him more difficult.[40]

One of Quantrill's best scouts, twenty-three-year-old Jackson Bishop, was described as "a cool, desperate, dauntless, iron man." Because of his Southern sympathies the Federals hunted for him constantly. His brother Henry, another daring guerrilla, was waylaid and killed at a creek crossing south of Westport by soldiers from the Sixth Kansas Jayhawker Regiment commanded by Major Willis C. Ransom. Jack determined to avenge his brother's murder. With this object in view he rode boldly into Kansas City where Major Ransom had his headquarters and opened fire upon him as coolly as if he were saddling and bridling a horse. Ransom was a notorious Jayhawker and was only surpassed in cruelty by Lane, Jennison, Anthony, and Stewart.[41]

Gibson, Reynolds, Kerry, Houx, and the Berry Brothers

In the counties adjoining Kansas at the start of the Civil War there lived 80,000 white citizens. Due to Jayhawker raids 90 percent of the citizens had either been killed or driven from their homes before Quantrill gathered his men for the Lawrence raid. Joseph "Pink" Gibson rode up from Bates County to join Quantrill after Kansas Jayhawkers burned down his house. He became one of the best fighters in the group and soon earned the admiration of Quantrill. One of Gibson's neighbors, Dr. T. C. Boulware, said that he "noticed on his trips through the country that one could ride for a distance of ten miles on the prairie without seeing a single house. They had all been burned." The men living in Bates County all joined the Southern army because they considered they would be in less danger than staying at home where the families of Southern soldiers would be marked for revenge. One Southern lady, Mrs. R. K. Johnson, said her uncle, who was blind in one eye, was forced at pistol point to serve as a guide for a squad of Union soldiers. When they were finished with him, they put out his good eye, shot him, and left him for dead. Her neighbor had a son who returned from Price's army and was found at home by the Federals. They took him into the yard and hanged him before his mother's eyes, and then turned the hogs in to devour his body.[42]

Jayhawkers killed the father of sixteen-year-old guerrilla William

Reynolds. After burying his father, Reynolds rode off to join Quantrill. Jayhawkers returned frequently to his mother's home, demanding whatever they desired and telling the inhabitants it was due them. Another teenager joining Quantrill was seventeen-year-old Hobbs Kerry, as was Matthew Houx. In November 1861, Houx with a hundred men ambushed a Federal wagon train near his home in Johnson County. Houx's home had earlier been plundered by Jayhawkers and everything of value stolen and carried back into Kansas. Like many others in Quantrill's company Houx first joined Sterling Price in the Missouri State Guard where he served under Jeremiah Vardaman Cockrell, who was a preacher in Johnson County before the war. After fighting in the battles of Wilson's Creek, Lexington, and Pea Ridge, Houx returned home and joined Quantrill and was on the guerrilla chieftain's muster roll dated July 6, 1862.

Running away to join Quantrill's company was a dream of many a young boy in the border counties of Missouri. Some of the guerrillas rode for miles, coming in from distant counties just to join up. They knew they could get more revenge with Quantrill than anywhere else, and besides Quantrill was the most successful guerrilla leader in Missouri. Ike, Dick, and James Berry were all from Callaway County, Missouri. Their fifty-nine-year-old father remained at home to look after his daughters. After Federals from neighboring Montgomery County raped their sisters, the Berry brothers looked for a place to serve, finally joining up with Captain Bill Anderson, who they thought would afford them the best opportunity for revenge. They had previously ridden with Colonel Upton Hays and had performed gallant service with General Jo Shelby and his Iron Brigade.

The brothers were described as the "most daring and reckless adventurers of those famous 'rough riders' of the border." One exciting story tells how

> Isaac, home on sick leave and knowing that there was a price on his head, boldly came into Westport one evening apparently without arms, and went into a saloon where Union soldiers were drinking and gambling. He quietly approached a table where Major Harvey, commander of the garrison, and other officers were at cards. He was asked to take a hand in the game and was openly received. Everyone present felt that he had walked to his own destruction, but they meant to play cards

Jim Berry (shown here) and his brothers Isaac and Richard were from Callaway County, Missouri. They enlisted at the start of the war, serving under Colonel Upton Hays, then joined Quantrill looking for revenge after their sisters were raped by Federal soldiers. (Emory Cantey Collection)

with him, and then take him at their pleasure. The stakes were high, and luck was with Ike Berry. E'er long he had all the money. At the first move of the Federals, however, Ike whipped a long dirk from out of his boot and warned all present that if any man moved, those nearest him would suffer. He then calmly stored the money in his long trouser pocket, being careful to close this with the button. Then with his eyes on everyone present he backed out of the place quietly, mounting his horse and rode back to his command by paths which none knew better than he. Major Harvey in relating this incident later said that it was the most coolly daring thing he had ever witnessed.[43]

Lee Miller, William Bassham, and John Barnhill

During the first year of the war, Lee C. Miller started out as a captain of ninety men in Price's army, gaining fighting experience at Rock Creek, Carthage, Lexington, Fort Scott, Springfield, and Pea Ridge. His family had a long history of patriotic service. His grandfather fought in the American Revolution in Henry "Light-Horse Harry" Lee's command. His father fought in the War of 1812. His oldest brother was in the Indian Wars in Florida, and his second brother was in the recent Mormon War, while his third brother served in the Mexican War. Miller recalled, "We had two objects in going to Lawrence, one was to seek revenge and the other to let Kansas know that fire would also burn on the west side of the state line." Jayhawkers had plundered so freely for years in Missouri that the guerrillas felt it was time for them to pay back in return. Miller commented, "It will be remembered that Kansas men were laying waste our border and that hundreds of homes were being ruined."[44]

William Bassham had been a stage driver on the Old Santa Fe Trail, but had quit and come home to Independence in August 1862. He had not been connected with the war in any way at that time, but someone preferred the charge that he was a Quantrill man, and he was locked up in jail. Quantrill's men broke into the jail and released Bassham, who decided to join the guerrillas for his own safety.[45]

John Barnhill joined Quantrill early on during the war. He participated in the first known skirmish in Jackson County between the guerrillas and Jennison's gang of cutthroats. On January 27, 1862, at the home of Noah McAlexander in the Sni-A-Bar area of Blue Springs, three of Quantrill's men, William Gregg, William Haller, and another guerrilla, were inside eating when they were surrounded by seventeen of Jennison's Jayhawkers. There were three unarmed men inside, Barnhill, Crockett Ralston, and John Frisby. The armed men determined not to be taken alive. As the unarmed men were allowed to leave before the firing began, Ralston and Frisby made a run for it and were captured and shot. Gregg, Haller, and Barnhill managed to escape. Barnhill immediately joined up with Quantrill for his own safety.

Kinney, Prewitt, Ross, Evans, Hockensmiths, Lea, Johnson, and Offutt

There were many men assembled in camp who had a wealth of experience with Federal Jayhawkers. Richard "Dick" Kinney was recruited by John Jarrette in the winter of 1862 in Lafayette County. He fought alongside Cole Younger at the skirmish in Wellington, Missouri, on September 18, 1862. Kinney had seen many of his neighbors wantonly killed and robbed of all they owned. Also present was Allen Prewitt, who was born near Waverly in Lafayette County. He entered the Confederate army, serving under General Shelby at the beginning of the war, then joined the guerrillas on the Lawrence raid under Bill Anderson. John Ross fought with Quantrill at Independence on August 11, 1862. He was with William Gregg and ten other guerrillas when they captured the steamer *Sam Gaty,* destroying a half-million dollars' worth of supplies slated for the Federal army. At the start of the war James Evans lived with Samuel Hays, Upton Hays' brother, and witnessed firsthand Jennison's raid on November 12, 1861, when the Jayhawkers stripped the Hays' home of all valuable goods and murdered Samuel for trying to protect his property.

Clark L. Hockensmith was eighteen when the war started. He joined Quantrill along with his sixteen-year-old brother Henry. The brothers lived in the Big Cedar Township where the battle of White Oak Creek took place in August 1862 and were present as the Jayhawkers raided through their neighborhood. In the same neighborhood lived Captain Joseph C. Lea. Lea was described as "a fearless young man who had experienced many close calls in the Border Wars. He was powerful, over six feet tall, with a 'wild dashing air that always distinguished him in any company.'" His fifty-five-year-old father, Dr. Pleasant Lea, had moved to Jackson County in 1852 and built a large colonial home on eight hundred acres, said to be the finest home in the neighborhood. When the Federals discovered that Joseph was one of Quantrill's most noted and respected officers, they rode out from Independence to his father's house looking for him. One source claimed that Jennison's Jayhawkers killed the elder Lea and that his sons witnessed the murder of their father. Another version says that Kansas Redlegs shot Pleasant Lea and his only remaining slave then stole the furniture from his house before setting it on fire.[46]

In yet another version a neighbor recalled: "One day Dr. Lea went to the nearby home of Josiah N. Hargis to obtain a newspaper. Some Federal soldiers stationed in Independence under the command of Colonel William Penick stopped him along the road. After breaking both his arms trying to get information about his son they shot him. Before returning to their garrison the soldiers burned the Lea house, killed another elderly farmer and burned fourteen others that same day."[47]

Oliver Johnson was twenty-two when the war started. He had the distinction of being the largest of the guerrillas, standing six feet six inches tall. The next largest guerrilla was Otho Offutt, who was one of the ten original members of Quantrill's first company. Offutt was one of the most powerful men among the guerrillas, being six feet five inches tall and weighing 210 pounds. His name was on the July 6, 1862, roster of Quantrill's company. Offutt joined Quantrill prior to the Tate house fight in March 1862. He, like most of his comrades, had many hairbreadth escapes, and was shot to pieces more than once. On one occasion when rushing from a house, a revolver in each hand, fighting his way through a line of Federal soldiers by whom the house had been surrounded, he was shot through the breast, but he succeeded in getting to his horse, on which he made his escape.[48]

Hodges, Carter, Koger, Poisals, Whitsett, and Muir

Nicholas Cunningham Hodges served under Dave Poole. He was born on April 10, 1849, and lived in Lone Jack, Missouri. He joined the guerrillas when he was thirteen years old and was so short that he had to lead his horse to a stump in order to mount it. Another young boy who joined at an early age was Isaac M. Carter. He enlisted with Quantrill when he was fourteen years old. Commenting on his time with the guerrillas Carter stated that he often passed through some of the most exciting and thrilling scenes and experiences in which hairbreadth escapes were made. "Each man in the command fully knew what our mode of warfare in all of its horrors meant. To us it was victory or death. But let no injustice be done Quantrell or his faithful men by believing that they adopted the guerrilla tactics from choice or as an occupation of sport and pleasure. It was to avenge and to retaliate great wrongs and cruelties that had been perpetrated upon Southern men and their families and properties that we entered into this line of service." When the war was over, Carter became the pastor of the Methodist Church at Edna, Texas.[49]

Ed Koger was one of Quantrill's first recruits. He was shot and killed from ambush on July 31, 1862, by a party of Federals stationed in Independence and led by Sheriff James Knowles. His younger brother John took his place in the ranks of the guerrillas. The home of Koger's uncle was plundered, and everything was taken from him, including his horses, food, and anything the Jayhawkers wanted. John was a farmer, strong built and sunburned, and became known as one of the most fearless and daring men in the band. The other guerrillas looked up to Koger with awe and respect. There sprung up a superstition that the bullet or knife hadn't been molded or whetted that could kill John Koger. And still there hardly ever was a fight in which he didn't get hit. So much so that it got to be a byword after a fight: "Where was John Koger hit this time?" Koger was wounded in twelve different engagements during the war, and at the time of his death he still carried five bullets in his body. When the war was over, Koger took a census of his wounds one day and found twenty-two.[50]

Mack and James Hamilton Poisal felt they needed to join Quantrill for the wrongs done to their family after three Union Jayhawkers murdered their father Thomas Sebastian Poisal. Thomas was simply driving a team of oxen near Waverly when he was mercilessly set upon and shot. A young boy, who saw the killing, ran to the Poisal home and told the sons what he had seen. Mack, James, and their best friend Simeon Whitsett found the three men, killed them, and threw them into a hog lot. Afterward Simeon Whitsett and James Poisal were arrested in retaliation for a Federal defeat near their home in Odessa, Missouri. After several weeks of being brutalized in jail they were released then recruited by Upton Hays before joining Quantrill.

Boone Muir, cousin to brothers George T. and Daniel Boone Scholl, who was recently killed in the Westport skirmish on June 17, 1863, shared common Jayhawker depredations with many of the guerrillas as the Kansans swept through their neighborhoods killing and plundering everything in their path, including stealing religious articles from the Pleasant Grove Baptist Church where the Muirs attended. One day a large group of Yankee soldiers were eating dinner at the Muir home when one asked, "Why don't you tell the bushwhackers to come out and fight us like men?" Mrs. Muir, knowing Quantrill to be close by, replied, "You tell them; you will see them before I do." Before the meal was finished the bugler called the men to their saddles. The soldiers hurried away, making for Westport and chased by the guerrillas "bareheaded, whooping and yelling, shooting as they came." On July 21, 1862, Federals arrested Muir's entire family and sent them to prison at Fort Leavenworth. Muir's home suffered the same fate as many of his neighbors', simply because he was a Southern sympathizer.[51]

Harrison Trow, the George Brothers, and Ezra Moore

Harrison Trow was from Blue Springs. He was only sixteen when he was captured by Jayhawkers during one of their raids through Jackson County. Trow recalled: "They took my old mule from me, my clothes and everything else I had and then set me loose." It angered him so much he sought out Quantrill to seek his revenge. After the Southern victory at Independence in August 1862, Trow was captured and imprisoned, chained on his back. He was sentenced to be shot but managed to escape and rejoin Quantrill.

Immediately following the battle Jayhawkers rode in and plundered the town, knowing that Quantrill's men had left. A resident of Independence, Mrs. R. T. Bass, recalled: "The next morning a squad of soldiers were sent into town to carry out the invariable custom of searching the premises, and judging from the booty secured, silverware, jewelry and clothing were the most contraband articles." She remembered the soldiers

> thoroughly overhauling every drawer, closet, trunk and every nook and corner of the house. They set fire to the houses that sheltered helpless women and children. We counted from our front door eight burning at one time. They cut the parlor carpet and portraits with their sabers until they were completely ruined; found where the silver was concealed and declared it contraband, persuaded the old family negroes to leave, as well as family horses, cows and everything worth having, leaving the only thing ever left in their wake, desolation and broken homes.[52]

David C. George from Oak Grove wrote a letter describing the Jayhawker's actions. "Stealing horses is quite a common occurrence here, but by reason of the close proximity of the state of Kansas which furnishes them a place of retreat, as well as a market for such stolen stock their arrest and detection is exceedingly difficult." The George family made an early sacrifice to the Southern Cause when their eighteen-year-old son Gabriel was killed while riding with Quantrill during the February 22, 1862, assault on Independence. Gabriel's brothers were all in the Southern service. After his brother Hiram George was hanged by the Federals in January 1862 to get him to tell where Quantrill was, another brother named Hix George joined Quantrill the following June, becoming one of the best fighters in the command. Hix stated his reason for joining Quantrill: "They [the Federals] burned and took everything I had. Killed my father, hung my brother." The home of their mother was burned three times, each of them had been wounded, and they lived solely to fight and to take revenge.[53]

The George brothers both rose to the rank of corporal. Hix's fellow guerrillas said that he "never fired a shot at the enemy without cursing them, either in a biting whisper or out loud, and that he was an excellent shot." Their older brother Nathan George had been the postmaster in Oak Grove before leaving to become an officer in Price's army. Nathan was married to the daughter of Jeremiah Farmer, the Baptist pastor in Brooking Township who married many of the guerrillas before and during the war. Because the members of the George family were all Southerners, their home was burned seven times during the war, the first time being on June 12, 1862. After the women's jail collapse Hiram knew Quantrill would exact a terrible revenge. Being one of Quantrill's earliest recruits he knew Quantrill well. He told those around him, "He [Quantrill] was a very mild-mannered person and as kind and gentle as a woman but when aroused, however, he had the spirit and vindictiveness of a tiger and would fight a buzz saw."[54]

The house of guerrilla Ezra Moore was burned down the same day as that of his neighbors, the Georges. Ezra was married to one of David George's daughters and lived on land given to him by his father-in-law. Another daughter, Amanda, was a sweetheart of Captain Andy Blunt. Ezra was killed while fighting with Quantrill at the battle of the Ravines on July 10, 1862. During the battle Ezra was shot while trying to climb up a bluff and was taken prisoner. As he lay wounded and bleeding the Federals shot him again over his left ear, killing him, and leaving powder burns on his face.

Quantrill's Rendezvous in Oak Grove

Quantrill's order to rendezvous at Captain Perdee's in Oak Grove was a wise strategic decision. The entire area was a Southern enclave. Perdee's nine-hundred-acre farm was adjacent to David C. George's nine-hundred-acre farm. Two of Captain Perdee's sons rode with Quantrill, and many men in Quantrill's company were well acquainted with the area. Hiram George married Mary White, one of the neighbor girls. The Oak Grove Baptist Church was in the neighborhood. This is the church where Quantrill was a regular attendee and where he met and started a brief courtship with eighteen-year-old Miss Albarita W. Hudson. He gave her, so it is said, the first photograph he ever had made of himself in Jackson County. The pastor of the Baptist church in Oak Grove, Hiram Bowman, was a cousin of the Georges. Also, guerrilla John Koger was the son-in-law of Reverend Bowman.

The guerrillas who gathered in Oak Grove recalled the harsh treatment the Jayhawkers had given their neighbor Warren Welch. At the start of the war Welch enlisted in the Missouri State Guard, was wounded in Arkansas, then returned to his home in Oak Grove to find that the Federals had looted and burned down his mother's house, leaving her and her five children with nothing but the clothes on their backs. He told his fellow guerrillas that the Jayhawkers wouldn't let him live in peace.

The Daltons and Frank and Jesse James

Frank Dalton was fifteen when he rode in with some neighbor boys on March 8, 1863, to join Quantrill. Dalton said that his "father had been assassinated by a company of Jim Lane's 'Kansas Jayhawkers.'" Besides losing his father, Dalton said he joined to avenge the "inhuman treatment of our mothers and sisters," who had been beaten and whipped by the Kansas soldiers.[55]

Dalton's neighbors were Frank and Jesse James. The James family were said to be outspoken about their sympathy for the Southern Cause. Frank James was eighteen years old when he joined Price's army on May 4, 1861. After taking part in the battle of Wilson's Creek, Frank came down with measles and was hospitalized in Springfield. He was captured and forced to take an oath of allegiance to the Federal government. When he returned home and spoke out for the South, he was thrown in jail in Liberty. As soon as he was released, Frank stated, "I heard that Quantrill was in Jackson County, so I decided to enlist under his flag. I met Bill Gregg, Quantrill's first lieutenant in Clay County, and with him rowed across the Missouri River to Jackson County and joined Quantrill at the Webb place on Blackwater ford of the Sni." Gregg and William Gaugh were on a recruiting mission north of the Missouri River when they first met Frank James. Gaugh armed him and along with Gregg encouraged him to join Quantrill. Frank gained an immediate reputation with Quantrill as fellow guerrilla Jim Cummins remarked, "I don't think Frank James ever had an equal in a running fight."[56]

In May of 1863 Federal militia rode to the James farm looking for Frank. Preston Colvert, a cousin of Jesse's mother, remembered the story she told how Frank's younger brother Jesse came to become a guerrilla.

> Jesse joined Quantrell in the spring of 1863 to avenge the treatment of his stepfather and himself. My son Frank had already joined the guerrillas. One day a band of Home Guards came to our house and tried to force my husband to tell them where Quantrell was then operating, thinking he knew because Frank was with him. Dr. Samuels and Jesse were plowing when the militiamen reached the farm. They took the doctor to a tree and with a rope around his neck demanded to know where Quantrell was. He did not know, but the soldiers believed he did. So they strung him up three or four times. He was almost dead and as they half dragged him to the house the captain of the militia said to me: "Now we[']re going to take him out and shoot him, and let the hogs eat him."
>
> They rode over the hill and I heard several shots fired. I did not know for three or four days that the doctor had not been killed. The home guards had simply fired into the air to make me believe they had shot my husband and had taken him to the county jail at Liberty. The soldiers pointed guns at my head and threatened to kill me too if I didn't tell them where Quantrell was, but I didn't tell. After the Home Guards had gone, Jesse said to me: "Ma, look how these soldiers have beaten me." I took off his shirt and his back was striped from the rawhides the soldiers had used on him because he would and could not tell where Frank was. But Jesse did not whimper. He saw me crying and said: "Never mind, ma. I am going to join Quantrell." He was then only 16 yrs. old but was a good rider and marksman. I did not see him for a year but heard Jesse was one of the most daring men in Quantrell's command.

Federal militia returned time and time again to the James farm looking for Frank and Jesse and looting the property. When Mrs. Samuels recognized one as having previously plundered her property and was now trying to come into the house, she said, "I got a shovelful of hot coals and told him if he tried to come in I would throw them in his face."[57]

In another account Frank Dalton said that when Jesse first told Allen Parmer he wanted to enlist, Parmer told him he thought he had better talk to his brother Frank first. Frank tried to talk Jesse out of enlisting, but when Jesse told him that their mother had been whipped and beaten and that their father had been hanged until his attackers thought he was dead, Frank weakened. Only when Jesse opened his shirt and showed the big welts from a beating given him by the Jayhawkers did Frank acquiesce. Frank motioned toward Quantrill and said, "Come and talk to the Colonel." Quantrill told Frank he had all the "yearlings" he could look after, but when Frank told him what had happened to Jesse and the family back home, and assured the colonel Jesse could even beat him shooting, Quantrill agreed to let Jesse enlist. William Gaugh was reported to have handed Jesse a revolver when he joined. It had a large wheel from which the cartridges were fired. "What do you call that?" asked Jesse. "That's a lawnmower," replied Gaugh. "Learn to mow 'em down with that."[58]

John Newman Edwards wrote that Jesse had been in on the ambush with Todd and Anderson at Westport on June 17 where Daniel Boone Scholl, Alson Wyatt, and Ferdinand Scott were killed. Because of the remarkable fighting he did that day, Bill Anderson invited Jesse to join his company. Anderson remarked, "Not to have any beard, he is the keenest and cleanest fighter in the command." William Gaugh described Jesse as being mild and a gentleman, while "Frank was bold, reckless and a regular dare-devil. Frank was the jolliest companion of the two, full of fun and always cutting up in camp while Jess rarely ever said anything." Gaugh continued by saying, "Jesse was about his age and was a quiet pleasant fellow, brave and fearless, but very quiet in camp. He was a good man too, never swore or raised hell around camp, and didn't get drunk; the fact is I don't know that I ever saw Jesse drink anything."[59]

Many historians believe that Jesse James was not at the Lawrence raid. If this is true, then there was only a short window of opportunity for Jesse to join Quantrill's company between the date of the raid on August 21 and September 10 when Quantrill started south to Texas and Jesse was known to be riding with the guerrillas. In support of this argument, it was during May of 1863 that Federal militia rode to the James farm looking for Frank and not finding him they beat Jesse mercilessly and abused the rest of the family. Contemporary historians say that Jesse ran away and joined Quantrill shortly afterward. This more logical account gives Jesse three months to have joined Quantrill. John Newman Edwards wrote that Jesse was in a June 17, 1863, skirmish which took place a month before the Lawrence raid. The February 5, 1899, issue of the *Philadelphia Inquirer* mentions that in July of 1863 "Frank and Jesse James, with Captain George Todd's company of Quantrell's guerrillas, met Major Ransom's Federal cavalry on the Pleasant Hill and Blue Springs road and several Federals are killed." The article went on to mention "Frank and Jesse James in the sack of Lawrence, Kansas."

Jesse's neighbor Jim Cummins, in remarking about the Lawrence raid, stated, "Jesse James, Quantrill and Cole Younger fought like devils and more than one Red Leg paid for his crimes then and there. The houses were fired and the Kansas soldiers were killed as they left." And in his book *Noted Guerrillas,* Edwards mentioned Frank and Jesse James fighting bravely on the retreat from Lawrence.

There are numerous other eyewitness accounts mentioning Jesse at Lawrence during the raid. An account in the *Lawrence Gazette* of July 5, 1907, by Lawrence citizen H. B. Leonard in conversation with Andrew Jack Liddil, described the guerrillas who were in his father's house during the raid. Liddil confirmed that they were Todd, Bill Anderson, and the James boys. Another account by Lawrence citizen Mrs. Gurdon Grovenor stated that it may have been Jesse and Frank who attempted to burn her house, "both of whom were present that day in Quantrill's command." And Jesse's own mother admitted in a story reprinted in the September 3, 1922, issue of the *Lexington Herald* that her son Jesse took part in the Lawrence raid.[60]

James Hines, William James, and Jim Cummins

Jesse's inseparable companion in camp was seventeen-year-old James Hines, who had only recently joined the guerrilla command.[61] William Wyeth James, a cousin of Frank and Jesse, was also in camp. He was born in lower Mississippi on July 6, 1848, remaining at home with his parents, having no companion except an old Indian. Suffering from malaria, he was sent to recover with relatives in Missouri and attend school near Independence. In July 1862 when he was fourteen years old, Federal soldiers came to the house and attacked the family. William grabbed a gun and shot several of them, forcing him to run away and join Quantrill. The Federals issued an order saying he should be shot or hanged when captured. William was wounded three times during the war.[62]

Jim Cummins was a neighbor of the James family in Clay County. He was credited with teaching Frank and Jesse James how to ride and shoot. His fellow guerrillas described him as not knowing the word fear, and was said to have been the best rider in Quantrill's company. Cummins was a wonderful shot with either a six-shooter or a Winchester. He said that he joined Bill Anderson in the spring of 1862 and that he met Quantrill in Jackson County in 1863. He described Quantrill as "a handsome man, looking more like a minister. He was refined in manner and quite well educated, always cool, quick, and determined."[63]

When friends asked him how he came to be riding with Quantrill, Cummins replied with a story.

> There were five of Captain Bigelow's men in militia uniform, cursing and abusing my mother because she had nothing left for them to steal, because she had two sons in the Confederate army and for being a Rebel herself. One of them, whose name I have never learned, drew back his fist to hit mother, cursing and abusing her all the time. I think I first began to carry a gun when I was about thirteen years old. Anyway, I carried it for many years. I loved it, practiced with it and was a good shot. After the border troubles started I carried it always with me. I had it when I turned the corner that evening, and I am thankful to God that I did have it, because it enabled me to send that fellow to hell in a hurry who was threatening to strike my mother. That was one

Jim Cummins (left) and Plunk Murray (right) were early recruits to the Confederate Cause. Cummins joined Quantrill after Federal militia murdered his uncle. He rode with Quantrill almost the entire length of the war. Murray joined Quantrill when he was sixteen years old after Federals hanged his mother in an attempt to gain information from her. After the war he became a Texas Ranger. (Emory Cantey Collection)

> of the good acts of my life. When he fell to the ground the others with him reached for their revolvers. I killed three of them altogether and broke the arm of the fourth. I found an order on one of the three I had killed, signed by Bigelow, directing them to go to the home of a Samuel R. Cummins, my father, and commandeer livestock and provisions.

Cummins was mustered into the Confederate service at the house of his uncle. When the Federals learned of it, they rode to his uncle's house. They took him from his threshing machine and shot him and then jumped their horses over him and left the prints of the horses' shoes on his body. The soldiers would not allow his body to be buried. Jim recounted, "So my mother and some other women had to bury him. Then the men who had done the killing gave my mother fifteen days to get ready to leave the state. The reason of this was because she would feed her boys when they came home to visit her and her friends." Jim's mother sent his younger brother to a friend in another state to keep the Redlegs from killing him.

Jim remembered other atrocities committed by Federals in his neighborhood.

> Today I can imagine I can hear the cries of old man Ferrill, seventy years old, who was taken out of his bed by these men and a rope put around his neck and tied up in the top of a thorn tree and left to die that way. Then the killing of Mr. John Harris. He was a southern man and had come home on parole when these men came to his house to kill him. They entered his house at night and silently went to his bed where he lay asleep. Then they killed him as he lay there by the side of his dear wife. I can imagine now that I can hear those cries and groans of the men who were killed by these Red Legs.

It was soon afterward as Lieutenant Fletcher Taylor of Bill Anderson's company rode into the county recruiting that Cummins joined up. Cummins was sixteen when he enlisted under Quantrill but later claimed like many other guerrillas that he did not take part in the raid although in later accounts Cummins made statements explaining his eyewitness experiences at Lawrence.

Cummins portrayed Quantrill in extraordinary terms:

> With conquest he was a living, breathing, aggressive, all powerful reality riding through the midnight, laying ambuscades by lonesome roadsides[,] catching marching columns by the throat, breaking in upon the flanks and tearing suddenly a surprised patrol to pieces mercilessly. By day he was a terror and a superhuman if not a supernatural thing when there was blackness and darkness upon the earth. . . . Quantrill was, to the guerrillas, their voice in tumult, their beacon in a crisis and their hand in action.

Cummins' reason for riding with Quantrill was similar to others'.

> Every man of them had a grievance. Every man of them through his relatives had been a sufferer in the sorest and severest sense of the term. Their fathers, and even mothers of some of them, had been robbed and brutally murdered. Their wives, their sisters and little children had been illy [*sic*] treated and insulted; the houses of their relatives and friends had been sacked and burned, insult upon insult, murder after murder, robbery after robbery, fire after fire, all these indignities had been heaped upon these inoffensive people by this Lawrence gang.[64]

Querrillas from Surrounding Counties

There were many families from counties surrounding Jackson County that had likewise suffered Jayhawker attacks. Young men rode into Jackson County seeking Quantrill as the best opportunity to seek revenge. Many came from Clay County north of the Missouri River. They were there because of what the Jayhawkers had done to their neighborhoods. One Kansas Jayhawker, Private J. Freeman, wrote about what he saw of Clay County while on one of his company's plunder expeditions. "This once beautiful and peaceful land is forsaken and desolated, ruined, and only fit for bats, owls, and cockralls [*sic*] to inhabit."[65]

Peyton Long, like Jim Cummins and the James brothers, was also from Clay County. He had fought in all the major battles with the Confederacy since the war started. His combat experience included fighting in the battles of Carthage, Wilson's Creek, Dry Wood Creek, and Lexington in Missouri; Pea Ridge in Arkansas; and Iuka and Corinth in Mississippi. It wasn't until the summer of 1863 that he joined Quantrill's command. Long was an excellent fighter and showed no quarter to his enemies. Jim Cummins said, "Peyton Long of Clay County was an exceptional man. When any particular man, or officer, engaged with the enemy would make himself especially conspicuous, Long was the man selected to put a quietus on him, and he always did a good job."[66]

Thomas Edward "Bud" Pence from Clay County joined Quantrill in 1862. His younger brother Alexander Doniphan "Donnie" Pence followed him six months later. Federals had come to their home and put a rope around their father's neck and threatened to hang him if he did not tell where Bud was. They broke a fiddle over his head and also a stock of a gun in their persuasions before hanging him. These had no effect, and he was pulled up off his feet two or three times, but no information was gained. When the Federals rode off, he tried to keep his youngest son Donnie from joining Quantrill, but to no avail. Like Jesse James he joined his older brother with Quantrill soon afterward.[67]

A large percentage of Quantrill's men were from the Brooking Township south of Independence. John and Martin Kritser were brothers from this area of Jackson County. Their family were strong Unionists, but when war broke out a troop of Union cavalry rode up to the farm demanding to be fed and have their horses taken care of. As the brothers were leading the soldiers' horses from the barn the soldiers fell on them with heavy leather straps, cursing them for being "damned Secesh" until they were tired of beating them. John stated that after this incident he wanted no part of a blue uniform. Gathering up a brace of double-barreled shotguns, the brothers rode off to join the Confederate army.

After witnessing Jayhawkers kill his brother and steal his livestock then burn down his house, eighteen-year-old George Barnett rode south to join the Southern forces but soon returned and joined Quantrill. Those around him asked him why he had chosen guerrilla warfare with Quantrill rather than remaining with the regular army. Barnett told them, "It was certain, I thought, that I should go into battle and fight until I was killed. It all seemed hopeless, the odds were great, but there was no choice. I saw my brother killed. I saw our farm home in ashes and my mother left desolate, robbed of all the livestock and provisions we had gotten together to keep her." He continued by saying, "Redlegs had come into Missouri a short time before and swept a wide swath for miles, clean of livestock, slaves, food, wagons and horses. They even had loaded their wagons and those they had stolen, with furniture and harvest crops. They took the small amount of Federal money they found." For this reason Barnett was in camp with Quantrill ready to ride on the biggest operation of his career.[68]

There were four Hall brothers: John, Isaac, Joseph, and Bob. Isaac

Guerrilla George Barnett joined the regular Confederate army when only seventeen years old, then returned home and joined Quantrill. Barnett gave his reasons for going to Lawrence, Kansas, as the atrocities committed against his family by the cruel Federals who killed his brother, burned his farm home, and left his mother desolate and destitute after being robbed of all her possessions. (Emory Cantey Collection)

"Ike" Hall joined Quantrill's band in the spring of 1862 after his brother Joseph had joined the year before. Their eighteen-year-old brother Bob joined Ike later that same year, along with his older brother John. During the winter of 1862 Jennison's Jayhawkers forced the Halls' mother to set fire to her own home then watch it burn. "When she cried and put up her hands to wipe away the tears they jerked her hands down and cursed her." They allowed her to try to save some things, but then they made her throw some of it back into the fire. The Jayhawkers stole their slaves and cattle and burned the houses of four neighbors the same day. It was alleged that Jayhawkers raped their sixteen-year-old sister Margaret and twenty-year-old sister Ann. Joseph Hall was with a Captain Parker and a group of guerrillas that attacked a band of Jayhawkers at Wellington, Missouri, as they were in the act of robbing a store. The citizens of Wellington thanked the guerrillas and fed them. It was said that the brothers fought like demons in battle with Ike becoming a captain under Quantrill.[69]

Sergeant Levi "Lee" McMurtry and his brother George were in camp and anxious to ride to Lawrence. McMurtry was the nephew of Upton Hays. Levi's father James married Hays' sister.

On November 12, 1861, Jayhawkers stripped the Hays' home of all valuable goods and their team and carriages were driven off with their eleven slaves inside. Upton's wife Margaret said that all her neighbors either had to join the Federal army or had to hide out in the country. And if they were not shot on sight, they were banished from the country.[70] Lee McMurtry was twenty years old at the start of the war and became one of Quantrill's orderly sergeants.

The rendezvous at Captain Perdee's farm was less than a mile to the west of the destroyed town of Columbus, Missouri. Gooley Robinson's widowed aunt lived near the town. Her house was burned and her livestock driven into Kansas by Jayhawkers. Guerrillas Horace Davenport, J. Stogden, and R. Cockrell were from Columbus. Their homes were destroyed by Jayhawkers as well as many others on January 8, 1862. Four days earlier, the Seventh Kansas Cavalry burned forty-two homes around Rose Hill in Johnson County. Besides this atrocity, the Jayhawkers stole many slaves from the surrounding farms. At one place two little children were set out in the snow while their house went up in flames. In an irony peculiar to the Border Wars, these Johnson County guerrillas received a partial retribution for the Jayhawker's wanton attacks when Quantrill's guerrillas gathered for the Lawrence raid near the spot where their destroyed town and homes once stood.

Fifteen-year-old George M. Noland's father and older brother were away with Price fighting in the Southern army when Jayhawkers made a raid on their home. During the attack George described his escape:

> I was in a little four room frame and brick house surrounded by Lane's band, waiting for me to come out. They knew I was in there, and they all had their guns pointed in my direction, so as to get me when I appeared. I was in the brick portion of the house, listening to the rafters crackle and fall. I knew I had to get out some time soon. There was a lot of dense smoke drifting in one direction. It came down to the ground and was about as high as the house. There was hardly anyone over there. Seeing that it was my only chance, I climbed through a window and risked it. It was like diving and I had to hold my breath, but I got away, and not one of them saw me.

Noland's older brother Morgan returned home and joined Quantrill. When he was killed fighting, George took his place in the ranks. Noland told those around him that his reason for joining Quantrill was that "Lane had spoiled his home, killed the men and he wanted him to get what was coming to him."[71]

Sylvester Akers and his brother Henry were members of the Christian Church in Buckner. The sanctity of their home and quiet neighborhood was disturbed by Jayhawker attacks early in 1862. Sylvester left his wife and three children to ride with Quantrill. Henry was listed as an early member of Quantrill's company, having his name on Quantrill's July 6, 1862, muster roll. Another Buckner resident included on the July 16, 1862, muster roll was Richard "Dick" Burnes, who had risen to the rank of corporal at the time of the raid.

Jayhawker Atrocities Recalled

After sharing their own personal stories the guerrillas recalled their comrades recently killed. A lot had happened in the previous three months in Jackson County. Dan Vaughn had been an early member of the guerrillas. He was riding with Quantrill, seeking revenge for the murder of his younger brother James, who was captured by the Federals and hanged in Kansas City on May 29, 1863, at Fort Union. To the crowd that gathered to see his execution James stood on the gallows and declared, "You may kill me, but you'll never conquer me, and taking my life today will cost you a hundred lives and this debt my friends will pay in a short time."[72] At the time of Vaughn's death his sisters were imprisoned at Fort Leavenworth. Later his mother and other female relatives were sent to the Gratiot Street Prison in St. Louis. His older brother Dan had ridden with Quantrill for over a year before joining the regular Confederate army where he was killed at the battle of Pea Ridge, Arkansas.[73]

Besides the personal loss of life in the guerrilla band, vast amounts of property and homes were destroyed by Kansas Jayhawkers. In late January 1862 the Seventh Kansas Jayhawker Regiment burned 150 homes in Chapel Hill. After the destruction of the town Lizzie Brannock wrote a relative explaining the horrors that had transpired in her neighborhood.

> Jennison and his gang came upon us[,] stripped us of nearly everything and would have burned us out but for proving that we were Union and had never done anything against the government. The Kansas troops would give us no rest, anything that was in Missouri was to be destroyed and taken. Our country is desolate, indeed almost entirely a wilderness, robbery was an every day affair so long as there was anything to take[;] our farms are all burned up, fences gone, crops destroyed[;] no one escapes the ravages of one party or the other. I had nothing much to lose and what I had is gone. They burned 150 houses; helpless women and young children sick were taken out and left standing in the snow while all they owned on earth save the land was destroyed before their eyes.

Later Redlegs returned and burned the Brannock home, sending Lizzie's husband and brother to the Gratiot Street Prison in St. Louis.[74]

It was at dawn on January 1, 1862, when the Seventh Kansas Jayhawker Regiment fell upon the defenseless town of Dayton in Cass County. Of the forty-seven homes in the place, all were burned but one. Major Thomas P. Herrick of the Seventh Kansas Cavalry led his troops into nearby Holden, in Johnson County, and burned forty to fifty homes, stealing what they did not burn. Two days later Herrick and his men destroyed the village of Columbus, also in Johnson County, looting and burning it to the ground, and on January 8, the Jayhawkers swept back into nearby Pleasant Hill in Cass County.

One citizen vividly recalled that the leader of the Jayhawkers "took away ten thousand dollars worth of stock and fifty-five negroes. This is the third time the Kansas troops have been in our town and carried away not less than $150,000 worth of property. The country is being ruined." On or about the same day, Jayhawkers swept into Kingsville, Cass County. One citizen recalled: "I counted one evening, while standing on Brushy Knob, 160 houses on fire" while eight helpless prisoners were mowed down in cold blood; a ninth escaped with only his ears cropped. A few months later on September 19, 1862, the Tenth Kansas Cavalry swept through Pleasant Hill again and burned twelve homes.[75] A month later, on October 16, Lane's Brigade sacked Kingsville a second time and killed eight citizens, stole a large quantity of horses and other property, and burned several houses.

Most of the men who rode with Quantrill were there by necessity because most had no homes to go home to. Towns like Dayton, Morristown, Butler, Papinsville, Pleasant Hill, West Point, Chapel Hill, Columbus, and Kingsville were burned off the map, and many ceased to exist. The ones that managed to survive took years before they regained their former prominence. After completely destroying Morristown, leaving only five houses standing, a Jayhawker of the Seventh Kansas Regiment wrote home: "A wilderness of solitude reigns supreme. It is my first view of war's terrors, and even my worst pictures of imagination are more than realized. Those who have never seen such desolation need never wish to."

While the Seventh Kansas Jayhawker Regiment was pillaging in Lone Jack, Missouri, Sergeant Webster Moses of Company D wrote to his girlfriend back in Illinois, bragging about his criminal activities:

> When we were at Lone Jack about ten of us went out Jayhawking. We went out before breakfast and stopped at a rich secesh, and told them we wanted some breakfast. While they were getting breakfast we caught their horses and took the best ones. When we came to breakfast they did not have dishes enough. The negroes said they had hid them. We asked the gentleman where they were and he told us. We found some silverware among the rest. I got the cups, two silver ladles and two sets of spoons. I gave Downing one ladle and the other to Captain Merriman. Some of the boys got in some places about $100 worth of silver and some got considerable money.[76]

Moses' comrade-in-arms Sergeant Daniel Holmes wrote a letter in the same manner to his sister.

> We live quite well, not from what we draw from the commissary but what we jayhawked. I don't suppose you know the meaning of that word that means when we are traveling through Secesh country we come to the home of some leading Secesh, or of some man in the Secesh army, then we take his horses and property, burn his house, etc, or as we say, clean them out, well in the operation we generally get a young hog, some turkeys, chickens, etc. once in a while a crock of honey, then don't we live."[77]

Guerillas on the Move

As the guerrillas relayed their personal experiences to each other, accounts of Jayhawker atrocities could have gone on for days. All gathered, there were 294 men, rank and file. Following his discussion with his officers, Quantrill finally gave the order to break camp. They left their rendezvous soon after breakfast on the morning of August 19. They had some fifty miles to ride from the Perdee farm to the Kansas border. They rode two abreast with their column trailing over a mile across the prairie. Quantrill kept numerous vedettes posted around his column with orders to ride back and report to him any signs that didn't look normal. He anticipated that spies might alert nearby Federal commands, so the vedettes told those along the way that they were Union soldiers going to reinforce General Blunt in the Indian Territory.

Toward sundown they rode past Walnut Grove in Johnson County. Colonel John T. Holt had already left for the north side of the river to collect the recruits who were waiting for his arrival. He would later link up with Quantrill in the heavy timber along the Grand River bottoms near the Kansas border. Only half of the guerrillas present had full Federal uniforms. These Quantrill had riding at the front of his column under Captain William Gregg. Captain Todd was in charge of the rear guard. Quantrill sent men ahead into Lone Jack, west of Perdee's, requesting dinner for a number of his officers and men.

After fifteen miles the column reached Lone Jack and took dinner at the Potter farm at five o'clock in the evening. This year there had been heavy crops and plenty to feed passing travelers. The slow process accomplished more than one purpose. Going slow allowed them to use caution, and it definitely attracted little attention from those living along their path. If they were discovered by a Union patrol this early in the operation, the raid would have to be called off and the element of surprise would be lost.

At their first stop the men purchased meat and flour from Potter and his neighbors and cooked their meals on open fires. Their horses were fed from Potter's own supply of oats. Neighbors brought food as soon as they heard the guerrillas needed to be fed. There they waited until dark. Quantrill hoped that if any spies observed his column they would lose them in the dark and that just possibly hearing of a large guerrilla force gathered in the area the Yankees would think Quantrill was taking his men back south for their winter sojourn in Texas. Union spies had in fact been alerted, and as Quantrill surmised mistakenly assumed that the guerrillas were gathering for an early return to Texas. Unfortunately for those in Lawrence they were given the same false information. From a telegram received from the commander at Fort Leavenworth saying that the guerrillas had headed back to Texas, members of the Lawrence militia were told to stack their rifles and go home and "sleep the sleep of the rest."

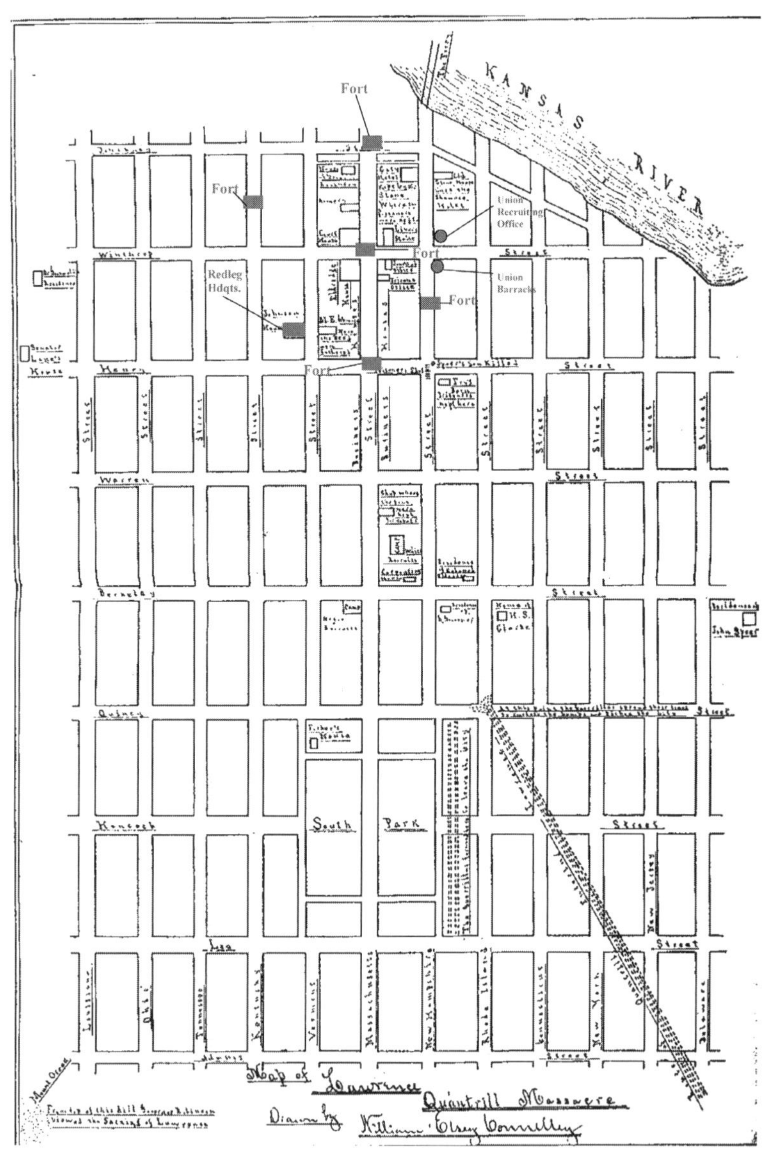

Map of Lawrence: Quantrill Massacre
(William E. Connelley, *Quantrill and the Border Wars.*
Cedar Rapids, IA: Torch Press, 1909, 1978.)

6

Damned Yankee Town

And Lawrence thus perished, with its long list of thieves,
Withered and scattered, like dead autumn leaves;
The few that are left the true tale may tell,
How their deeds and their souls are recorded in Hell.
—*Houston Daily Telegraph,* March 11, 1864

The journey toward the Kansas line commenced again at eight o'clock that evening. It was dark as the guerrillas rode away from the Potter farm, heading straight for the Grand River bottoms. Scout John McCorkle recalled that his entire march until he reached the Kansas line was "through smoking ruins and blackened fields."[1] Sensing no danger, Quantrill had Todd take over the lead column. Todd chose Fletcher Taylor and sixteen men to ride with him two hundred yards ahead of the main body so that if they should approach any enemy soldiers they could give notice of their presence without the main column being discovered. They reached the headwaters of the Grand River in Cass County at five o'clock in the morning of August 20. Sometime during the night Colonel Holt rode in with his one hundred new Clay County recruits from north of the Missouri River. Also there by prearrangement, they were joined by fifty guerrillas from Cass and Bates County. With Holt's recruits and the additional fifty guerrillas Quantrill commanded more than four hundred men; the largest guerrilla organization ever gathered during the war.

The Destination Revealed

They remained concealed in the timber for most of the morning, relaxing and letting their horses graze. After they finished eating breakfast Quantrill's officers gathered the enlisted men into formation. It was there that Quantrill officially told his men what was to be their destination and telling any of those not wishing to take part that they were free to go. With their heartbreaking memories having recently been recalled so vividly, they were all anxious to strike a blow in retaliation. Quantrill strode to the center of the group and formally revealed their intended target. He told "them of the great hazard of the trip, that the entire command stood a chance of being annihilated and all that felt they were not equal to the Herculean task not to undertake it, and, that any man who refused to go, would not be censured." Not a man stirred. Lee C. Miller's reflections about Quantrill were akin to those of the rest of the guerrillas. "Never was a fearless fighter more careful of his men. And while he would often lead us into places that scarcely any other man would dare go, no man in the command ever flinched or refused to follow him."[2]

The guerrillas were given time to think over whether to make the dangerous journey or not. The men were ready, their horses were ready, and all were eager to get started. Frank Smith recalled, "I doubt if there was ever in the history of this country or have been at any time since a like number of horsemen who were as good riders and pistol shots and mounted on as good horseflesh as Quantrill's command when it rode across the Kansas line on its way to Lawrence to sack and burn the town. Many of the guerrillas' horses were thoroughbreds, pure Kentucky strain." They had remained hidden in the thick timber for most of the day. At 3:30 p.m. Quantrill shouted out the order to "saddle up." They were on their way to Lawrence.[3]

The Entrance into Kansas

It was fifty miles to their destination, and they still had to get past the Federal outposts stationed along the border. At between five and six o'clock on the evening of August 20 Quantrill led his column into Kansas ten miles south of Little Santa Fe where he turned directly west toward their destination. Quantrill kept

Captain Joshua A. Pike from Lawrence was in charge of two cavalry companies from the Ninth Kansas Regiment stationed at Aubry, Kansas. He watched as the guerrillas rode past his post toward Lawrence, but failed to notify the town. (Kansas State Historical Society)

those with Federal uniforms riding in the front and rear of the column. It was dusk as Quantrill led his men past Aubry, Kansas. They were spotted by Captain Joshua A. Pike commanding two hundred soldiers of Company K of the Ninth Kansas Jayhawker Regiment. Pike assembled his men on line and from a quarter of a mile away simply watched the guerrilla column ride past. Quantrill had given orders not to fire unless fired upon. Lieutenant Gregg recalled, "On and on we marched over the Kansas plains and through the villages, most of them patrolled by soldiers with whom we avoided a collision; Lawrence was our goal, and we were dubious that if we did collide with the Yanks, our greatest hope might be foiled; besides we were then too far advanced to engage any thing short of Lawrence."[4]

After the guerrillas silently slipped away, Pike rode back to Aubry and telegraphed Captain Coleman, then at Little Santa Fe, Missouri. A short time later Pike sent Coleman a second message, saying that Quantrill had entered Kansas with eight hundred men. Coleman forwarded this dispatch to troops to his south and also to Kansas City to General Ewing's headquarters along with a messenger to notify the surrounding towns that the guerrillas were present. At that time of day the telegraph office in Kansas City was closed, and it wasn't until ten forty-five the next morning that Ewing received the message. Coleman and one hundred men then hurried to Aubry where he assumed command of the two hundred men there. By midnight they were organized and following the trail of the guerrillas. Pike's one failure was not to wire any Union posts in the direction that he saw Quantrill's column heading.

Ten miles inside of Kansas, Quantrill halted his column to let the horses graze and give his men time to eat. "Some of them even went to the farm houses near by and procured milk and other things they wanted, and some of them ordered supper. After a good rest they mounted and rode on."[5] Included on their "Death Lists" were names of Jayhawkers who happened to live on the route they were taking. Kansan George Martin recalled, "That as early as May, 1861, Union men began to move out of Missouri. The 'refugees,' as they were called, were then an important element of newcomers. It was ironical that many refugees, who were robbed and their families driven out, enlisted in Kansas regiments and returned to Missouri as Union soldiers for revenge."[6]

The first target the guerrillas encountered was the home of a Captain Sims who had formerly lived in Missouri but had moved to Kansas at the start of hostilities. Sims often led Jayhawker patrols back into Missouri, pointing out former neighbors with orders to kill and plunder. Fortunately for Sims he was not at home when the guerrillas stopped to inquire for him. This part of Kansas was sparsely settled, and there were few who would have seen the column riding past.

A short while later, the guerrillas passed through Spring Hill a little after ten o'clock at night. Quantrill knew that Federal soldiers were stationed in town, and he reminded his men of the order, "Make no attack unless fired upon." The citizens in town were not yet in bed, and even at that late hour there were still soldiers milling about the main street; but the guerrillas did not make any attempt to stop. Quantrill ordered his men not to talk to anyone. Deception and silence were two measures that Quantrill insisted upon.

They did not attract any undue attention, and as they rode past an inquiring soldier asked who they were and where they were going. An officer answered back that they were a scout on their way to Lawrence to get their horses shod. After passing through town they turned northwest toward Gardner, which they passed shortly after 11:00 p.m. Gardner had been an early fence house for stolen Missouri goods. There were a number of Federal soldiers in town, but they did not seem to suspect anything as the guerrilla column rode past.

The land then became unfamiliar in the dark. In the strange surroundings the guerrillas were compelled to procure a guide among the farmers along their route. One was recognized as a Jayhawker by Quantrill and Todd. He was killed when he was no longer familiar with the area. Lieutenant Coleman Younger said several farmers were called from their beds to serve as guides. When the farmers' directions would get hazy, Quantrill would ask, "Is this as far as you know the country?" When they replied that it was, Younger said that Quantrill would send them back home. Frank Smith recalled that he was not aware of any guides being shot. He said he did not hear a shot between Gardner and Lawrence.[7]

The Search for "Wanted Men"

Captain Todd was still leading the column. With him were nine of Quantrill's best men. They were Cole Younger, John Ross, Warren Welch, Jack Liddil, James Lilly, John Koger, Fletcher Taylor, and Lee C. Miller and his brother. They were known as "Todd's Bloody Nine." Quantrill was riding in the rear, making sure no one straggled or fell out. Some of the guerrillas tied themselves in their saddles to keep from falling off in case they fell asleep during the long night march. It was a typical August night described as "intensely warm and still." Many of the men removed their hats, letting the night breeze blow through their hair. A slight cloud rose from the horses' hooves and covered the men in the rear of the column with a layer of dust.

As they rode nearer to their destination Quantrill passed the word again that no one was to fire their weapons for fear it would spread an alarm. As the column passed a farmhouse within fifteen miles from Lawrence, Todd heard two pistol shots ring out. When he rode up to the place where he had heard the shots, he saw Lieutenant Fletcher Taylor standing over a dead Federal. It was the home of Private William Bentley of the Twelfth Kansas Jayhawker Regiment. Bentley was not at home, but two other Jayhawkers were there. One had immediately sensed the danger and escaped into the darkness with a wound to his wrist. Taylor had shot the remaining soldier. Todd was furious that Taylor had fired his pistol, but he insisted it had been self-defense. Taylor was heard telling Todd, "George, I had to, I had to!"[8]

At three o'clock in the morning the column passed through the small hamlet of Hesper. The moon had disappeared, and the night was extremely dark except for the stars, which made the way doubtful. The guerrillas stopped at the house of a wanted man, Private Samuel Hunt Davis of the Eleventh Kansas Jayhawker Regiment. A sudden rapping at the window awakened Mrs. Davis. A voice called to those inside, "Where is the man of the house?" "There is no man here," was her reply. Several times more the raiders inquired and received the same reply. Finally, after consulting among themselves they left.

At the crossroads one mile west of the Davis farm lived Captain Andrew J. Jennings of Company E, Twelfth Kansas Jayhawker Regiment. Quantrill inquired of Mrs. Jennings, demanding to know where her husband was. Mrs. Jennings replied, "He is in the war fighting the rebels." A man who appeared to be an officer and was probably aware that Mrs. Jennings' statement was true, ordered the men away, telling them, "Let the woman alone." Luckily for Jennings, he was not at home.[9] The guerrillas vowed vengeance on anyone associated with the Twelfth Kansas. The regiment was commanded by Charles W. Adams, James Lane's son-in-law. Newspapers in Lawrence admitted that Adams was "particularly unfit" for his position and were it not for the influence of his father-in-law he would have been ousted a long time ago. With Lane's influence, Adams acquired 1,280 acres of land in support of the prospective railroads. In December 1862 the Twelfth Regiment was ordered from Olathe to Kansas City. As soon as they entered Missouri their mission turned into a plunder expedition. One of Adams' men remarked: "The boys were in the most profound ignorance of their destination, but by the time they began to suspect it to be Missouri, and the object, confiscation, sometimes called jayhawking."[10]

The home of Joseph W. Stone of the Eleventh Kansas Jayhawker Regiment was just opposite the highway from Jennings' home, and both houses were searched simultaneously. As one squad of guerrillas were inquiring for Jennings, another squad was searching for Stone. When Mrs. Stone refused to open the door so the guerrillas could search the house, they began kicking down the front door. Before

At age twenty-eight Colonel Charles W. Adams, with the patronage of his father-in-law, Senator James H. Lane, became the commander of the Twelfth Kansas Jayhawker Regiment. At every opportunity, Adams led expeditions to plunder the Missouri countryside. (Douglas County Historical Society)

the war Stone had lived in Missouri and was wanted for crimes before he fled across the border. At one time a posse from Missouri entered Kansas looking for him, but Stone's neighbors came to his assistance, and the Missourians returned to their homes without accomplishing their mission.

After gaining entrance to Stone's house, a detail of guerrillas began searching the rooms and finally found their quarry. Stone's younger son Elijah, also a private in the Eleventh Kansas Jayhawker Regiment, slipped out the back door and escaped in the confusion, but the elder Stone was captured by George Todd. Stone was responsible for having Todd's father arrested and thrown in jail in Independence early in the war where he was kept in a cold cell and almost starved to death. For this one unjustified cruelty Stone put his life in danger.

A light was held up to make sure it was the man they were looking for. One of the guerrillas said, "We've got you old man, this time sure." Stone was still in his nightclothes. He was told, "Get on your clothes; you've got to go with us." Gunfire would have attracted too much attention this close to Lawrence. After the column had proceeded about a half-mile to a quiet spot, a halt was made. Stone was told he was to die and ordered to dismount from his horse. When he refused, he was struck in the arm with a rifle by guerrilla Sam Clifton with such force it broke his arm. He was made to kneel and given time to pray. Then he was shot. The nearby house of O. G. Richards was entered next, but luckily for Richards he was across the Kansas River and was not at home. Richards was responsible for aiding Stone to escape the clutches of the Missouri posse sent to arrest him earlier in the war.

A boy named Jacob Rote, who was found living with Stone, was forced to accompany them as a guide as far as the Wakarusa River. There were still several more "wanted" men the guerrillas sought who lived just outside Lawrence. The guerrillas turned west for a short way before turning back north, heading for the small town of Franklin, which lay four miles southeast of Lawrence.[11]

Before arriving in Franklin, the guerrilla column stopped and entered several more homes of wanted men along the way. One was the house of William Bromelsick. He was at home with his wife, small son, and a hired hand. The only light in the house was a candle held by Mrs. Bromelsick. The guerrillas insisted that Bromelsick come with them. He asked permission to first tie his shoes, which was granted. When he bent down, he blew out the candle in his wife's hand, throwing the house in darkness. In the confusion both Bromelsick and his hired man escaped out the back door and hid in the nearby timber.

When the guerrillas remounted, Quantrill ordered them into a long trot as they passed through Franklin without stopping. A doctor living along the route observed the marching column and counted them as they passed, placing the number in the band at 450. When they reached the Wakarusa River bottoms, they forded at Blue-Jacket Crossing just outside Franklin. They were then just four miles from Lawrence. Quantrill recognized the country and so rode to the front to lead the column himself. The cocks were starting to crow, and it was beginning to dawn. It was a beautiful morning with not a speck of a cloud in the sky. The air was so still that the guerrillas were covered with sweat and dust from their all-night ride. The lighter it got, the faster they traveled. Realizing that they were behind schedule, Quantrill cried out, "Lie forward on your horses so you don't attract attention. Push on boys; it will be daylight before we get there!"

The Approach to Lawrence

The column was still riding two abreast. To keep from being discovered out on the open prairie and raising an alarm for the militia companies, Quantrill passed the order, "Form fours!" The guerrillas maneuvered their horses into a column of fours and put their mounts into a gallop. Both men and beasts sensed the change as the guerrillas' hearts beat faster. Lawrence was just over the next rise. The night sky was beginning to lighten. Between Franklin and Lawrence the guerrillas rode to a small hill from which the town of Lawrence could barely be seen in the distance.

Sallie Young was out riding with friends on the day of the Lawrence raid. She was captured by Frank James, escorted back to Lawrence, and compelled to point out houses of noted troublemakers. (Kansas State Historical Society)

The only slight distraction was the mayor's son Hoffman Collamore who was out hunting on horseback a mile from town. Seeing him armed and apparently thinking he was a picket, the guerrillas shot him from his horse. Thinking him dead, they rode on until converging on a party consisting of Private John Donnelley of the Eleventh Kansas Jayhawker Regiment in uniform accompanied by Steven Horton, Miss Sallie Young, and Miss Nin Beck out riding in the early morning coolness. They saw the guerrillas riding toward the town, but thought they were Union troops, as one of their party suggested that a company of one of the Kansas regiments was expected in that day.[12] When Donnelley sensed they were not Union troops, the women urged him to spread the alarm, but instead Donnelley ran away.

Though pursued by two guerrillas through field after field, he managed to escape.

Donnelley was the escort of Miss Sallie Young. She had just come from Lecompton and was staying with the family of ex-governor Wilson Shannon. She was described as a beautifully buxom lady. After being separated from her escort, she attempted to flee back toward town and give a warning but was soon caught by Frank James and politely required to report to Colonel Quantrill. Quantrill said to keep her as a prisoner and use her to point out the houses of wanted men on their lists, thus proving that the raiders had decided their victims in advance. After the raid some accused her of having ridden southward on her pony at the very grey of day, and having shown the leader the way in and pointed out free-state, Yankee houses. All this betrayal was supposed to have been in remembrance of a friendship between her and Quantrill in the days of their youth in Ohio, but this claim was simply not true. A Lawrence citizen noted, "There was a woman who rode around giving orders and doing the bossing. She was a sort of captain." But the story was not credited by the more levelheaded.

During the raid Miss Young tried to save lives and houses by giving false information to the guerrillas, saying that wanted men were not in town or that houses slated to be destroyed belonged to others. Some say she saved several lives by her earnest intercession in their behalf, or as claiming them as friends of her own, when in fact they were strangers. Lawrence resident Mrs. Harriet M. Jones remembered Sallie saying, "She was out horseback riding and met the gang. They forced her to be their pilot." Judge Lawrence Bailey said that "she had used her influence to save the lives of a number of citizens, with ready invention and great presence of mind, giving such accounts of them as to induce her captors to spare them."[13]

The column was halted. Quantrill took this time to issue last-minute instructions. Before the war when Quantrill was living in Lawrence, he had wanted to go to Leavenworth and had asked the owner of the Kansas Stage Company, P. A. Hawkes, for a ride on one of his stagecoaches, saying he didn't have any money but would make it right at some future time. Quantrill told his men that the Kansas Stage Company had a large stable in town and gave them its location.

Said he, "The company once did me a favor and I don't want you to do anything against them. Don't fire the barn or take any of its horses." Its company office was on the street a little north of the Eldridge House Hotel. The stable with about twenty horses, harness, and feed stood about three hundred feet behind the street in front. During the raid the stable was searched by Quantrill's men but left entirely undisturbed despite the work of carnage that was going on all around it. The guerrillas obeyed Quantrill's order implicitly.[14]

Quantrill ordered Lieutenant William Gregg to "take five men and go ahead and check out the town." While they were waiting for Gregg to return, Quantrill stopped by an old farmer's house on the right side of the road to ask questions regarding the military situation in Lawrence. Quantrill approached the farmer as he was in his hog lot feeding his pigs. As the farmer stood before the guerrilla chieftain, Quantrill told him. "If you tell us the truth we'll spare you, if not you will die." The farmer stated "that there were 300 regular Federal troops in Lawrence and 300 militiamen." Harrison Trow heard the farmer say that "across the Kansas River there were probably four hundred soldiers in camp, and on the Lawrence side about seventy-five." When Quantrill heard the farmer's statement he just laughed and said, "They outnumber us two to one, but we will whip them and as for those Redlegs we will exterminate them. Not a man of them is to escape."

The Search for Jayhawker Leaders

The farmer reported that one military company was camped on the road into town. Quantrill inquired about Jim Lane and what time the farmer had left town. He replied he had left at four o'clock, and Lane was not seen when he was there. Lieutenant Gregg recounted later, "It was well understood that the purpose of the raid was to attack Lawrence. But the first intention was to capture Gen. Jim Lane. Quantrill was often heard to say that, 'I [want] to kill Jim Lane, the chief of all the Jayhawkers, and the worst man that was ever born into the world.' It was Lane that had put a $50,000 reward on Quantrill's head."[15] The fact of the matter was that James Lane had returned during the previous evening to attend a railroad meeting at the Eldridge House Hotel that lasted until ten o'clock that night. Afterward, Lane was invited to the Harris and Simons Confectionery Shop at 149 Massachusetts Street by Captain Sidney Clarke, the assistant adjutant-general of the Lawrence militia, where they sat eating ice cream until midnight accompanied by John Speer and about a dozen others.

Quantrill then asked the farmer where Colonel Samuel Walker lived. Walker was a radical abolitionist, a Jayhawker, a politician, and despised as much as James Lane and John Brown. He was responsible for numerous Jayhawker raids into Missouri and had a five-hundred dollar reward on his head for his capture from the governor of Missouri. Before the war Walker tried to have Quantrill arrested on spurious charges in order to capture him and thus have him killed while "trying to escape." It was in 1855 when Walker came to Kansas, bringing a large colony of immigrants from Ohio, and was instrumental in inducing others to come. He settled on a claim seven miles west of Lawrence where he lived until he moved into Lawrence at 1112 Tennessee Street.

After arriving in Kansas, Walker organized a military company of eighty-six men called the "Bloomington Guards" to fight the proslavery settlers and drive them off their claims. During the Wakarusa War, Walker attacked Fort Saunders and Fort Titus, taking the type from the *Herald of Freedom* newspaper office and using it as grapeshot for the cannon. Every time the cannon fired into the fort, the soldiers would shout, "Another issue of the *Herald of Freedom*." Though at one time serving as sheriff, Walker suffered arrest himself for assault and battery. Walker was currently serving as a captain in one of the companies of Lane's Brigade. After the farmer answered all of his questions, Quantrill ordered one of his men to take charge of him until he could determine whether the man was telling the truth.[16]

While waiting for Gregg to return, Quantrill next moved to the nearby farm of Robert H. Miller. The family were close personal friends of James Lane, and with Lane's patronage Miller was made postmaster of Lawrence. Miller lived in a brick farmhouse with his family and those of his two sons Josiah and William and a daughter Margaret. The family was originally from South Carolina. In the summer of 1856 Robert was seized in his native state and tried for treason for his radical antislavery beliefs. His life was said to be in peril until he was released from prison. After being tarred and feathered he fled to Kansas. In Lawrence he became a conductor on the Underground Railroad and hid runaway slaves in his smokehouse and barn. His son Josiah served in the Lawrence militia and was the paymaster for the Eleventh Kansas Jayhawker Regiment, the same regiment that served as the prison guards for the murdered girls in Kansas City. He found being the paymaster a lucrative position and soon was able to build a new house just outside town. Josiah was elected probate judge of Douglas County in 1857 and helped start the *Kansas Free State,* the first newspaper in Lawrence, along with his friend Robert Gaston Elliott.

Josiah was in the process of building his own farm not yet completed next to his father's. He became wealthy from his association with Lane and owned a number of buildings in town known as the Miller Addition in the 700 block of Massachusetts Street. In one of the buildings was the headquarters of the Free State Abolitionist Organization. While some of the guerrillas watered their horses in Miller's yard, Quantrill woke the family and began asking questions. Robert and Josiah were both on Quantrill's "Death List." The occupants initially thought the guerrillas were Union soldiers until Margaret blurted out, "You are not soldiers, you are Quantrill's." Quantrill leaned forward over his saddle and replied, "You have guessed right. I am Quantrill, and these are my men." The only man the guerrillas found inside was William Miller. Quantrill threatened to take him prisoner, but the entreaties from the women made him change his mind. He ordered them all to stay in the house, but after the guerrillas rode away William mounted a horse and tried to warn the citizens in town. He was chased two miles by the guerrillas and shot at.[17]

Close by was the house of Captain Samuel S. Snyder who lived two miles east of Lawrence. Snyder was a marked man when the guerrillas came to Lawrence. They knew where he lived, and his house was one of the first they passed on their way to the business district. Two guerrillas were detailed to Snyder's house. Snyder was already up and in his farmyard sitting on a stool milking his cow when he was discovered and shot. His Jayhawking days were over as he toppled from his milking stool dead. His name was one of those that could be found at the top of Quantrill's list of wanted men. Snyder had been with Lane during the destruction of Osceola, Missouri, and on his return to Kansas had stripped Missouri churches of their furnishings for the churches back in Lawrence. Snyder took Bibles, hymnbooks, stained-glass windows, pews, altar furniture, and even the steeples from the roofs. He was presently serving as an officer in the Second Kansas Colored Regiment. Snyder was most influential in recruiting runaway Negroes for his Kansas regiment and arming them to fight against their former Missouri owners. Aiding Snyder was another Lawrence citizen, Richard Josiah Hinton, who was commissioned as a Union officer to recruit and drill black troops. As a matter of fact, it was Snyder who was in charge of the camp of colored recruits located on the southwest corner of Berkeley and Massachusetts Streets as the guerrillas entered the town.[18] There were two soldiers living with Snyder, brothers Samuel and Solomon Bowers. Samuel was a new recruit and was killed. Solomon, who was in the town militia, though shot nine times managed to get away. The guerrillas did not pursue him in their hurry to get downtown with the rest of the command.[19]

The Entrance into Lawrence

When the two guerrillas split off from the main group and rode toward Snyder's house, Quantrill looked toward Lawrence and made the final decision to go in. What the raiders saw as they approached Lawrence was not a town built by the sweat and toil of its own citizens, but rather a town that was in effect made up of many parts of Missouri towns transplanted for Lawrence's benefit. The skyline reflected in the churches of Lawrence was the skyline that used to shadow many a community of Missouri's Christians. As the darkness slowly lifted, the guerrillas could see the spires and steeples that Captain Snyder and Lieutenant Hugh Dunn Fisher and their fellow Jayhawkers had stolen from churches in Missouri in order to adorn their own church buildings in Lawrence. To complete the holy accoutrements, even pews and Bibles had been appropriated for use by Lawrence's pious church-going citizens. A former Jayhawker raid on Harrisonville, Missouri, resulted in the looting of the depository of the American Bible Society, leaving behind only a supply of Bibles. Following in their wake, another Jayhawker unit led by Colonel Jennison took the Bibles, transporting them back to Kansas.

Two more guerrillas turned off from the main party and began riding to the farm of Joseph Savage. Savage heard the knock at the door but took his time washing his face before answering. Savage had come to Lawrence with the New England Emigrant Aid Company and was a conductor on the Underground Railroad; thus his name was on the guerrillas' "Death List." Savage escaped death by his slow response in answering the knock at the door. Thinking that no one was home, the two guerrillas hurried on to catch up with their comrades.

In the first faint glimmer of dawn Quantrill took a final muster of his men. At this time guerrillas who were wearing Federal uniforms took this brief pause to discard them, revealing their elaborately colored guerrilla shirts underneath. They were described as having "plumed hats with low crowns and slightly rolled brims and wore shirts of red flannel or butternut homespun." In the fog of war that was coming they all wanted to be easily recognized. It was a clear, warm, still morning. Quantrill turned to his men and said, "Boys, this [Lawrence] is the home of Jim Lane and Jennison; remember that in hunting us they gave no-quarter. Pursue and kill every man that runs. Shoot every soldier you see, but in no way harm a woman or child." Frank Smith recalled Quantrill saying, "Kill every man in Federal uniform." When Quantrill looked up, he could see Gregg and his reconnoitering party returning from spying out the town. As they rejoined Quantrill they pulled their horses alongside, reporting that there was no sign that the citizens were expecting them. Lawrence's streets were 80 feet wide and the city blocks were 250 feet wide by 600 feet long divided into 24 lots with 50-foot fronts that were 125 feet deep with large open spaces between houses.

Quantrill's organization was known for the discipline he maintained over his men. This discipline was necessary to keep an effective guerrilla force fighting under the conditions that they were forced to bear. Hiram George remarked that Quantrill "was a man of few words but those few were law." Fletcher Taylor remembered that Quantrill had given an order saying, "If I find any man insulting a woman, I'll hang him to the first limb I come to." Quantrill stressed to his men, "No matter how much a woman may abuse you, take her abuse. Let her talk and scold, but say nothing to her in resentment. We are fighting men, not women. No provocation will excuse an insult of back talk to a woman."[20]

Many of the guerrillas knew the time had finally come for action, and the thought of the overwhelming obstacles ahead of them caused some of them to waiver. A few expressed their reservations, knowing that the town was full of soldiers, by saying they would be cut to pieces and it was madness to go on. But Quantrill's determination never faltered. Recalling the brutality that his friends had suffered along the border, he turned to his men and shouted, "You may do as you please. I'm going to Lawrence." And with that challenge he spurred his horse toward town. In an instant his men joined him, pistols at the ready.

The Attack on the Recruit Camps

Andy Walker riding next to Quantrill reported that he didn't see any pickets posted in town and that therefore they rode up the main street of town unnoticed until they got to the camp of the recruits. In a matter of days these new recruits would have joined their comrades in Jayhawker raids into Missouri. Therefore the first obstacle of resistance encountered was the two camps of soldiers housed in tents on either side of Massachusetts Street approximately three hundred yards apart. One guerrilla described the scene. "Two rows of tents stretched their white walls along the main highway leading to the village, each tent containing four soldiers. Six pickets were stationed about two hundred yards down the road to sound the alarm of approaching danger."[21]

As the raiders spurred their horses into a run, Quantrill simply pointed to the tents and silently a squad of guerrillas turned off and swept toward the unsuspecting soldiers. Gregg recalled, "As soon as Quantrell reached me, he was riding at the head of the column; I pointed to the forty tents arranged in the open space. Without a word of command being given, and without a halt being made, the command divided and charged through that camp."

The first camp was that of the twenty colored recruits bivouacked on the west side of Massachusetts Street just south of Quincy Street. They offered no resistance. Most tried to run across the guerrillas' path and make it to safety on the other side of the Kansas River, yelling as they ran, "The Secesh are here! The Secesh are here!" John McCorkle said, "Immediately the negroes and white men rushed out of their tents, the majority of them starting in the direction of the river and some going in the direction of town. The command was given to break ranks, scatter and follow them. A few of the negroes reached the river, plunging into it, but none succeeded in reaching the opposite shore."[22]

Some historians believe that none of the black soldiers were killed and that they all escaped, but this was impossible since the raiders had already broken into separate columns and were racing down Vermont, Massachusetts, and New Hampshire Streets, completely surrounding both camps and successfully sealing off any avenue of escape. It would have been with difficulty if any had indeed made it safely away. From their camp it was more than two blocks to the wooded ravine that ran through town. The ravine was two blocks west of Massachusetts Street, and its banks were covered in a thick growth of elder and smaller bushes. The cornfield behind Senator Lane's house was more than three blocks away, and it was more than seven blocks to the river and the guaranteed safety on the other side. Lawrence citizen Samuel Reynolds said that "all but four of the two unfilled companies" managed to survive. Another Lawrence citizen, William L. Bullene, son of Lathrop Bullene, saw the recruits' camp attacked and recalled that the guerrillas' firing was "very rapid, and, as the men were taken by surprise, few escaped." John Speer added, "The guerrillas were unerring shots with revolvers, and excellent horsemen."[23] The Negro soldiers were afterward laid out, awaiting burial in the Second Congregational Church of Lawrence.

Negro soldiers were considered contrabands by those in Lawrence. Many of them had been compelled to join the army after being forced from their homes in Missouri. Most accounts list the Negro soldiers as volunteering, but the word "volunteer" had a very loose meaning to the officers of Lane's Brigade. Lieutenant Henry Miles Moore of the Fifth Kansas Jayhawker Regiment admitted that slaves were sometimes taken by questionable means on the part of some members of the brigade.[24]

After equipping and arming them, Lane used them in his military operations, plundering the counties of Missouri. The *Lawrence Daily Republican* on July 21, 1862, wrote, "A company of colored men has been organized, to join Lane's Black Brigade. Yesterday morning, seventy-five names were enrolled, and the number will soon be raised to a hundred." Josiah Trask, editor of the *Lawrence Kansas State Journal,* gleefully bragged in his paper in January 1862, "Contrabands are becoming one of the institutions of Lawrence. As they break their fetters they very naturally strike out for the center of abolitionism."[25] The reason Lane advocated recruiting black troops during the Civil War was that he had early on sensed that the first man to enlist black troops would become a hero of the radicals and abolitionists, whose support might well carry him to the White House.

When Negroes were compelled by Jayhawkers to leave their homes in Missouri, they took as much of their masters' belongings with them as they could carry. Slaves who didn't wish to leave their homes were beaten and the women raped in the presence of their owners. These atrocities were reported in the July 22, 1862, *St. Louis Republican,* which commented: "Vagabond Union troops entering Missouri were creating secessionists everywhere." One Union general wrote to Secretary of War Edwin M. Stanton, adding, "When there is added to this the irregularities of the soldiery, such as taking poultry, pigs, milk, butter, preserves, potatoes, horses, and in fact everything they want; entering and searching houses, and stealing in many cases; committing rapes on the negroes and such like things."[26]

Southern families along the Missouri border knew full well the effect of Negro soldiers. Many had already been visited by Lane's Black Brigade and had discovered they didn't behave any differently than their Jayhawker counterparts. Missourians got one of their first tastes of Kansas Jayhawkers using black soldiers in November of 1861 when Colonel Charles Jennison raided through Jackson County, centering his plunder expedition on Independence. The most shocking aspect of Jennison's retinue to the people was an entire company of Negroes, armed, mounted, and uniformed as soldiers of the Union. They were led by a slave who had been enticed away from a master who was widely known for unwavering loyalty to the Union. Throughout December Jennison's Jayhawkers stayed in Jackson County, continuing to plunder wagonloads of dry goods, groceries, furniture, and every horse, mule, and conveyance they could steal and sending them back to Kansas.

One black man who willingly ran away was Jack Mann. After getting to Kansas, Mann joined the Jayhawkers then guided them back to his old neighborhood. John McCorkle remembered Mann as "exceedingly insulting to Southerners and especially old men and women." On one Jayhawker raid Mann led a squad of Redlegs to the home of Dick Maddox. Finding only Dick's wife Martha at home, he cursed and abused her. As he was tearing through the house searching for valuables, Mann found Dick's wedding suit. He undressed in front of Mrs. Maddox and put on her husband's clothes. Then he strode before her, exclaiming, "How do you like my looks with this wedding suit on?" Mann was soon to pay with his life for his thievery and abuse of peaceful Southern families.[27]

Three hundred yards farther along the guerrillas came to the camp of the white recruits located in a vacant lot on the east side of Massachusetts Street. The horses, which had been worked into a frenzy by the all-night ride and the sudden charge, didn't make any attempt to avoid the tents but instead charged right through them. Canvas was thrown into the air by the sudden impact. Men scrambling from inside the tents frantically tried to get out of the way to avoid being trampled to death or shot in the attempt. Without a chance to defend themselves, they were suddenly seized by fear. Flight was their only savior. In the human desire to band together during times of danger, four or five recruits tried to huddle together and take flight as a group. In scenes such as this one several would be cut down at one time with only one managing to get away.

The twenty-two white recruits had all been recruited into the Fourteenth Regiment but had not yet been assigned to their companies. They were expecting to be sent to the front any day. Some accounts list them as being recruited for a new regiment under the command of Colonel Jennison.[28]

The time waiting before joining their respective units was spent in target practice and learning military drill and discipline. Other than this minimum training the recruits were given various responsibilities such as doing guard duty at different picket posts in and around the city. The white recruits had already been issued uniforms and rifles equipped with bayonets. Lawrence citizen Hovey Lowman asserted that the recruits had been given uniforms and that they had a camp guard, but it was called in moments prior to the attack. Because of the hot August night, not all were sleeping inside their tents. Some were asleep on the porches of nearby residences. Lieutenant Gregg mentioned that as he rode into town the guerrillas "saw soldiers sleeping on the porches of the nearest houses, and opened fire on them with their revolvers." Only four out of the twenty-two white recruits survived the charge. Not until they heard the brisk staccato of pistol fire that didn't seem to cease did anyone raise an alarm among the citizens of the town.

The sentry on duty for the white recruits was Private James Cooper. As he saw the charging horsemen coming toward him, he discharged his rifle, shouting, "Corporal of the Guard! Post 6!" Cooper was from Pennsylvania. He was a former military officer and West Point graduate but was dismissed from the army back East for drunkenness. Cooper started to run before the charging guerrillas when he suddenly wheeled about, brought his gun to "Charge-Bayonet" and was heard to say before he was shot down, "Damned if I run another inch." The other recruits quickly exited their tents "swarming out like bees and tried to rally and form a square with their rifles and bayonets." Guerrilla Andy Walker said that after the recruits were aroused from their tents they grabbed their rifles, and "the bullets came at us from every direction." Harrison Trow remembered, "Scarcely any resistance was made, as every time they stuck their heads out of a tent it was met with a bullet." Lawrence citizens recalled that it was "strange to a great many that no resistance was made, especially when the people of the city had expected an attack previously, and had made preparation to meet the rebels when they came. The papers, even, had said they were ready for them."[29]

"Quantrill is here!"

The *Lawrence State Journal* printed an article stating that recruit Cosma T. Colman joined the army to escape payment of a debt owed to a John C. Treat. On this particular morning Colman was one of the recruits assigned mess duty during the week of the raid. He had been up before dawn, and when he heard the first shots tried to holler a warning to his friends, "Quantrill is here!" Along with four other soldiers he tore off his uniform and ran to save his life. He made it as far as the home of Joseph Rawlins. Rawlins had boarders staying with him, including a young minister. Several times guerrillas rode to the house and ordered the men to come out. Colman begged Rawlins not to do it, but one group of guerrillas were more persistent so Rawlins opened the door upon the guerrillas' demand. Colman recalled, "They did not attempt to shoot, but told us to unload our wealth, which we proceeded to without a second invitation. The guerrillas then went inside[,] ripped up a straw mattress and set it on fire. The dozen people inside were forced into the street but the patrols did not offer to molest them." Colman said that "not a person was shot at or killed on our street after the first rush. . . . At least a dozen could have been shot down had the Patrol so desired." Colman noticed that the guerrillas were only shooting men in uniform. Fortunately, Colman was not harmed since his father Ezekiel had arrived in Lawrence from Boston in 1854 and was described as "an outspoken abolitionist."[30]

Colman had come to Lawrence with his family as a part of the New England Emigrant Aid Company from Boston. The family first lived on a farm six miles west of Lawrence where Cosma's brother Charles Jackson Colman was a lieutenant in the Ninth Kansas Jayhawker Regiment before enlisting as an officer in command of colored troops in the First Kansas Colored Regiment in May 1863. It was just before this time that the Ninth Regiment raided through Bates County, driving Southern families into Arkansas, murdering seven men, and burning eleven homes. The Colman family served as conductors on the Underground Railroad. Their house was a large one known as "Colman's Retreat." In the floor of the kitchen was a trap door or loose board that could be lifted up, and slaves who had escaped from their masters could be hidden beneath. The Colmans were early agitators in the border troubles and had been good friends with John Brown. A relative wrote, "One fugitive named Neeley was brought to Kansas by John Brown who was a frequent visitor to the Colman home."[31]

Armed Recruits as Special Targets

Other recruits were also special targets for Quantrill's men. Private Milton A. Parker's family had also been closely associated with John Brown. Parker was an apprentice in the *Lawrence State Journal* newspaper office. Privates Charles R. Allen and Isaac J. Parker had prior military experience in other Jayhawker units before enlisting in the Fourteenth Kansas Regiment. Parker had been with Lane during the destruction of Osceola, Missouri. Three recruits, all brothers, Privates Lewis, Samuel, and David Markle, had at one time enlisted in the Southern army but had deserted then fled to Kansas and enlisted in the Union army.[32]

Two other recruits, instead of being with their comrades, were still spending time at their civilian jobs in town. Recruit Robert Speer, eighteen years old, continued working in the *Lawrence Republican* printing office and was sleeping there the morning of the raid. Private Addison Waugh continued putting in hours as a clerk in Griswold's Drug Store. It was there he died, and his body was burned when the building was destroyed.

Captain Leroy J. Beam and Lieutenant John K. Rankin were the recruiting officers at the time for the Fourteenth Kansas Jayhawker Regiment and were in charge of the white recruits. Rather than staying with his men, Beam was living in town at the Union recruiting office just across the street from the home of William Bullene at 736 New Hampshire Street. The building was on the list of structures to be destroyed. Beam knew he could not stay in his office and to show himself in uniform meant instant death. He was a wanted man because of his agitation in the early border troubles when he accompanied John Brown on the attack on Fort Saunders and when he served under Captain Sam Walker at the fight at Fort Titus. Beam and his three brothers fought in all the early battles during the territorial period. Beam managed to slip out the back door and crawl under the building unobserved. When the building was set on fire he pulled off his uniform and ran naked through the streets trying to find a place of safety. Every guerrilla who saw him took a shot at him. The bullets flew past him, but none found their mark. Finally he ran to the rear of Bullene's house and was able to hide inside. Lawrence citizen Richard Cordley commented, "There was a large

Second Lieutenant John Knox Rankin lived in Lawrence and was the recruiting officer for the Fourteenth Kansas Regiment. (Kansas State Historical Society)

number of military men in town, but scarcely one of them were killed. Soldiers knew they could expect no quarter, and so took care of themselves. The men 'specially marked' fared the best, for they knew what to expect and took themselves out of the way."[33]

Lieutenant John Rankin and his cousin Captain William A. Rankin lived only a short distance from the camp. They had both been soldiers in the Second Kansas Jayhawker Regiment before John Rankin began recruiting for the Fourteenth Kansas. William Rankin became quite prosperous serving as assistant-quartermaster, division quartermaster, purchasing quartermaster, and chief quartermaster with Lane's patronage. William Rankin was best known for being Lane's agent in hiring runaway slaves to work on his farm. The cousins lived close enough to the camp that they heard some of the frightened recruits running through their yard screaming, "Quantrill is here! Quantrill is here!" When the alarm was sounded, the cousins ran into the street, making for their militia rendezvous. Both were heavily armed. One guerrilla holding the reins for his two companions who were searching a nearby house saw them running through the street. He fired at them as they rushed by, and they returned fire, but no one was hit.[34]

Another recruiting officer in town was Lieutenant Charles H. Holt. Holt lived at 745 Indiana Street. When the guerrillas came to his house Holt's sister told them that there were no men in the house. Holt decided not to defend himself or his home but instead ran out his back door heading west with the guerrillas firing at him all the time. He was fortunate enough to escape with his life to the wooded ravine running through town.

In the histories written after the raid a great amount of effort was spent trying to portray the recruits as too young to be in the service and defenseless and without arms. The "camp of the unarmed recruits" was a misnomer. For years following the raid the enemies of Quantrill tried to make believe that the recruits were unarmed boys not yet mustered into the service. This is pure fabrication when the facts are researched. Recruit Cosma T. Colman testified that the recruits were armed with muskets complete with bayonets.[35] Official records show that the oldest recruit was thirty-six with the youngest two recruits being sixteen. Their average age was twenty-one. In comparison their ages were slightly older than the raiders they came in contact with that day.

Several eyewitnesses reported that the recruits opened fire on the advancing guerrillas. Near the soldiers' camp was the home of William H. R. Lykins. His stepmother, Mrs. Mattie Lykins, said that she had not paid him and his family a visit for more than three years. Mrs. Lykins continued: "The day before the falling of the [Kansas City female] prison I had chanced to write his wife that I would be in Lawrence on the following Monday." It was late in the afternoon on August 17 before she reached her stepson's home. She later recalled the events of that day:

> After bathing my face and hands and resting awhile, I joined the family on the front porch. I asked my step-son, as I took my seat, what was the news in Lawrence. "We have the best of news," he replied. "The commander of Fort Leavenworth notified us last week that Quantrell and his band had left the border of Missouri and had gone South. On the strength of this authentic information," he added, "we were ordered to stack our arms in the arsenal and to go home and sleep the sleep of peace and security. We have had a hard time of it this summer" he added. "We have stood our guard every night for months and we were beginning to feel pretty well used up for want of rest from drill and guard duties." That evening before retiring for the night, I heard continuous firing for several minutes. As my [relative] had just informed me that citizens had been ordered to stack their guns in the arsenal, I did not know what the firing meant, so I asked the cause of it. He said, "Col. Jennison is raising a new regiment called the Kansas 17th and a few recruits of this regiment are encamped near the town, to avoid the heat of the day they usually drill early in the morning and late in the evening and are in the habit of firing off their guns after the drill."

So it was commonly known that it wasn't an unusual event to hear firing from the direction of the recruits' camp.

On August 21, the morning of Quantrill's raid, Mattie Lykins had just risen to lower the window shades in her room when she heard the firing on the soldiers' camp and looked out her window. She hurried to her daughter-in-law, telling her to get up, that the town was full of armed men riding in every direction. Her daughter-in-law slowly got up and, rubbing her eyes, looked out and said, "Oh! Those fellows belong to Jennison's regiment. They are just riding about in the cool of the morning for fun." William Lykins thought otherwise and threw on his clothes and started for the door with the hope of making his escape to a cornfield nearby. But by that time the guerrillas had surrounded his house and were guarding every avenue of escape. Mattie Lykins remarked later, "It was my misfortune to be in Lawrence on that eventful morning, never for one moment suspecting danger."[36]

Another account proving that the recruits were armed was given by Kate Riggs and her husband Samuel. When they heard shots they naturally thought the camp of the recruits were firing their weapons. They were awakened just at dawn by shots being fired very rapidly. Mrs. Riggs recalled, "I sprang up, exclaiming 'why, what can the boys [recruits] be doing?' Samuel ran to the window to see a large body of men riding into town, and exclaimed, 'Quantrill's band as sure as you live!'"[37]

An additional Lawrence citizen who believed that the sound of gunfire was coming from the camp of recruits was Charles Prentiss. Prentiss was awakened by his fellow clerk William Speer who woke to the sound of gunshots as they were sleeping in the rear of Albert Winchell's liquor store. "The bushwhackers are here!" Speer said. Prentiss replied, "No, it was only the recruits firing off their guns."[38]

Prentiss's father, Sylvester B. Prentiss, was known to have aided fugitive slaves. He lived one mile from Lawrence and served in the early Lawrence militia under James Lane. Prentiss raced into town to join his militia company but escaped injury by returning home and keeping inside. Both Prentiss and his wife presented guns through their windows and threatened anyone who attempted to enter. It was not the first occasion Mrs. Prentiss had handled firearms. During the border violence of 1856 Mrs. Prentiss rode through enemy lines taking ammunition to the free-state forces in Lawrence. Once she sewed gunpowder in her riding skirt, and another time she concealed a keg of powder under the seat of her buggy.

Hiram Towne of the Lawrence militia also lived close to the camp of the recruits at 840 New York Street about three hundred feet from Lane's residence. It was one of the finest dwellings in Lawrence. Before rising, Towne said, "I heard shooting and thought it was some recruits who were camped in the south part of the city." When he finally realized that the city was being attacked, Towne grabbed his gun and started for the rendezvous but immediately saw that no resistance was being made. He hid his gun then made for a cornfield before he could be discovered. The guerrillas declined to burn his house because living in it was an elderly widow, Emily Hoyt.[39]

Another house close by the camp of recruits was the home of Edward P. Fitch. His wife Sarah heard the firing in the camp and inquired of her husband the reason for it. Fitch knew the shots were coming from the direction of the recruit camp and was not alarmed.

He simply replied, "Oh, it's the boys having some fun," so it was naturally assumed by those in Lawrence that the recruits were armed and had been issued ammunition.

In describing the guerrillas' initial attack, author Carl Breihan wrote, "However, this diversion did not check the speed of the general advance. A few of the guerrillas turned aside in pursuit of some fleeing soldiers, but the main body swept on down Rhode Island Street." It was now slightly before five o'clock. As the head of the column reached Henry Street one group deflected to the left into Vermont Street, and as many more to the right into New Hampshire Street. Their objective was to cut off those who might attempt to escape from Massachusetts Street from the rear of the buildings, effectively sealing off any escape. Richard Cordley noticed, "The attack was perfectly planned. Every man knew his place. Detachments scattered to every section of the town, and it was done with such promptness and speed that before people could gather the meaning of their first yell, every part of town was full of them. They flowed into every street and lane like water dashed upon a rock."[40]

"On to the town!"

After the brief skirmish at the camp of the recruits, Quantrill yelled out to those riding behind him, "Rush on to the town. On to the hotel, quick!" Lee C. Miller said that Quantrill had a soft voice except in times of danger, when in giving commands his troops could hear him above the din of battle at any reasonable distance. With Gregg and a handful of men at his side Quantrill rode down Massachusetts Street toward town while his separate companies deflected down the side streets. They were riding six abreast and were described as "desperate looking men, clad in the traditional butternut, and belted about with revolvers, some carrying as many as six. Most of them also carried carbines. Miller stated, "We were armed with six-shooting pistols, and short six-shooting rifles, that we carried slung over our shoulders. Now every one of us had from twenty-four to thirty-six shots without stopping to reload."[41]

A view of Massachusetts Street, Lawrence, Kansas, circa 1864. (Kansas State Historical Society)

A view of Massachusetts Street in Lawrence, Kansas, looking north. (Kansas State Historical Society)

They fired their pistols to the right and to the left to keep the militia from rallying and offering any resistance. As they approached the Eldridge House Hotel, they saw a Union officer coming out of the building. It was a Federal major on his way to Fort Leavenworth thirty miles away. Gregg hollered out, "Get that major!" and gave chase. The officer ran into a nearby livery stable and escaped through the loft chased by Gregg. Quantrill and Andy Walker continued as far as the riverbank to the ferry landing. When they came to the end of the street they found themselves entirely alone. A shower of bullets greeted them. Walker shouted to Quantrill, "Good God, Quantrill! Let's get away from here, or they'll kill us!" Both men then turned back toward the hotel. It was just as Gregg had always said: "The town was full of soldiers, but the sudden and unexpected appearance of Quantrill and his men completely paralyzed them. At the time of the Lawrence raid, the entire male populace of Kansas were soldiers, minute men, organized and equipped by the government." Resident Robert G. Elliott remembered: "The people were awakened from their slumber by the crackling of pistols and the tramping of horses, and as they ran out to form companies or to find a place of security, they were shot down in cold blood."[42]

Quantrill's officers guided their companies to their assigned places. Guerrillas charged down the streets, yelling the words "Osceola!" and "Remember the murdered girls!" Sergeant Cave Wyatt rode next to Bill Anderson. After disposing of his blue uniform Anderson was described by an eyewitness, "Dressed in homespun butternuts; he is coatless and hatless and sits upon a horse which is almost a counterpart of himself. The horse goes without guidance, and the man rides without support. The horse is dashing after men as they run, just as a hunter would follow a fox. His rider sits erect with a revolver in each hand, and fires with either with unerring accuracy at any poor fellow that comes in sight." The other riders were observed in a similar manner. "The horsemanship of the guerrillas was perfect. They rode with the ease and abandon of men who had spent their lives in the saddle amid rough and desperate scenes. Their horses seemed to be in the secret of the hour, and their feet scarcely seemed to touch the ground. Their riders sat upon them with bodies erect, and arms free, some with a revolver in each hand, shooting at each house or person they passed and yelling at every bound."[43]

As the guerrillas raced into town, they passed marked houses of the most notorious wanted men on their lists. One was Colonel James Blood. Blood had come to Lawrence with the New England Emigrant Aid Company. He soon became the first mayor of Lawrence and an officer in the local militia, besides owning a business in town. Upon passing Blood's house guerrillas fired at it, sending bullets through the windows and pelting the wood siding. Blood gathered his family in the front room, awaiting a knock at the door, but the guerrillas were busy elsewhere. Mrs. Robert Morrow, a neighbor, came rushing in, urging Blood to escape. He too thought it best and left his house until stopped by guerrilla Captain Noland who robbed him then permitted him to pass unharmed.[44]

Major Edmond G. Ross commanded two military companies in Lawrence at the time of Quantrill's raid. (Greg Walter Collection)

Colonel John Holt's recruits were ordered to seal off the ferry landing on the east side of town where Major Edmund G. Ross in command of Company E, Eleventh Kansas Jayhawker Regiment, and a portion of the Ninth Jayhawker Regiment were camped on their way to Fort Leavenworth. Another group of Kansas militia led by Colonel Frank B. Swift was also camped on the north side of the river. On the west side of Lawrence a guerrilla group under Captain Andy Blunt and Lieutenant James Wilkerson rode to the top of Mount Oread to act as lookouts and to cordon off the west side of town. The abolitionists named the heights after the Massachusetts Oread Institute. The hill rose to several hundred feet and was lined with seven-foot-high defensive earthworks connected with long lines of entrenchments and rifle pits surrounding a stone fort, but no defenders were present during the raid. Since the hill was the highest ground in sight, a flagpole had been erected to give warning during times of invasion and danger, but Blunt kept the signal from being used.

Holt's recruits, following close upon Quantrill's heels, soon arrived and began taking up positions behind the buildings along the river. Robert Woolridge lived on the north side of the river and operated the rope ferry for the Baldwin brothers. On the evening before the raid he had brought the ferry over to the north side of the river. The Southern recruits were assigned to keep the soldiers on the other side from using the ferry and offering assistance. But the soldiers were so afraid the guerrillas were going to cross the river and annihilate them that they crept down to the ferry and cut the cable, thus saving the guerrillas the trouble.

Private John D. Baldwin of the Fifth Kansas Jayhawker Regiment owned the ferry and was home on furlough. Baldwin had been with Lane during the destruction of Osceola, Missouri. He observed the raid taking place but made no effort to aid his neighbors across the river, simply shooting at any guerrillas that came into view. Harrison Trow remarked, "The Federals on the opposite side of the river made scarcely any attempt to come to the rescue of their butchered comrades. A few skirmishes held them in check."[45]

In the ensuing exchange of gunfire two of Holt's men and one of Quantrill's, Lieutenant James L. Bledsoe, were wounded. Some reports claimed Bledsoe was shot by Archibald Cameron, a sergeant in the First Kansas Regiment. Under intense fire from across the river brothers John Hicks George and Hiram James "Hi" George carried Bledsoe to safety. Another guerrilla, Tom Hamilton, was also wounded. Gregg ordered the George brothers to secure a carriage for use as an ambulance. Guerrilla Lee C. Miller stated, "We made it a rule never to leave a wounded comrade behind." Following the raid Captain Dick Yeager forced Samuel Boise, a Lawrence resident, to drive the horse-drawn ambulance with the wounded guerrillas and follow them out of town. It was covered with feather beds and placed in the advance guard.

The potshots by the soldiers north of the river actually saved many lives. Their firing kept the guerrillas from venturing too close to the river where they attempted to avoid unnecessary casualties. Two or three tiers of houses all around the "bend of the river" were thus saved, as well as those who were fortunate enough to take refuge in them. Also the rifle fire from the north side of the river prevented the guerrillas from getting some good horses out of a livery stable situated on the south bank.[46]

Quantrill at the Eldridge House Hotel

As Quantrill turned away from the riverbank he joined the main body of guerrillas milling in front of the Eldridge House Hotel. The Eldridge that morning was filled with guests— travelers, officers and soldiers on furlough, besides many women. Lieutenant Gregg and several other guerrillas circled the hotel, swearing at the top of their voices that they were going to kill every man in town in order to frighten anyone listening into submission. Inside a gong was rung to awaken the guests, which the guerrillas expected was some sort of alarm. The guerrillas backed away from the building in order to get a better shot at the windows. Inside, the soldiers and guests were in a panic. Many of the occupants were Federal officers enjoying the luxuries of the surroundings. One citizen remembered that in the hotel's most famous room (No. 7), "buckets of whiskey, freely circulated lent inspiration."[47]

Robert Gaston Elliott, an eyewitness staying at the Eldridge House, analyzed the raid by noting:

> It had been held that only an organized army of considerable strength would dare bring its forces within striking distance of Lawrence. The rapidity of their [the guerrillas'] movements and the extent of their occupancy within so short a time multiplied every estimate of their numbers; and the boldness of the invasion, the confident manner of the leaders, with the abandon of recklessness that everywhere marked their followers, impressed everyone with a sense of a force impossible to resist. The calamity had burst upon all with such sudden and unconceived force and flashed with such terror that the will was subdued and the emotions paralyzed.[48]

Major Edwin P. Bancroft was an officer with the Eighth Kansas Regiment and later with the Ninth Kansas Regiment. He took sick during the battle of Vicksburg, Mississippi, and returned to Lawrence and was staying in the Eldridge House Hotel. Quantrill guaranteed his safety during the raid. (Kansas State Historical Society)

Major Edwin P. Bancroft of the Eighth Kansas Jayhawker Regiment home on sick furlough was also staying at the hotel. His brother that very morning had planned on getting a carriage to take him back to his own house. He was discovered along the way, shot several times, and robbed of his money. James W. Winchell, a correspondent for the *New York Tribune,* was also staying at the hotel. Winchell said that Quantrill first came to the Eldridge House seeking out James Lane. Winchell eventually managed to escape to the house of Charles Reynolds and became an eyewitness to the raid.

Reynolds himself was on the guerrillas' "Death List." Reynolds had come to Lawrence with the New England Emigrant Aid Company and had helped get funds from Amos Lawrence in Massachusetts to build the town. By naming the town after Amos Lawrence the abolitionists thought that it would be gratifying to him and would be the means of obtaining funds whenever needed. Reynolds also served as a chaplain in the Second Kansas Jayhawker Regiment, which began its military career by plundering the towns of Western Missouri. He was also in the town's militia. His brother Samuel operated the stage line and held the mail contract between Lawrence and Leavenworth. His stables would accommodate seventy-five head of horses and cattle. At the time Reynolds had twenty to thirty horses, several stagecoaches, and a large amount of equipment. As with those of most Lawrence citizens, his horses were of dubious origin. After removing the horses, the guerrillas burned the house, stables, and a hundred tons of hay. Reynolds had been forewarned and was able to save himself by hiding in a cornfield.[49]

Major James B. Abbot was also staying in the hotel, but his safety would not have been guaranteed. Before the war Abbot had traveled back East to buy Sharps rifles and a brass howitzer for the militia of Lawrence. Besides having come to Lawrence with the New England Emigrant Aid Company, he was an agent of the *Herald of Freedom.* During the Wakarusa War he was a second lieutenant with the Liberty Guards. He had earlier been promoted to the rank of brigadier general in a Kansas brigade by James Lane in 1856. He helped liberate free-staters like Jacob Branson from arrest, and his home was used as a station on the Underground Railroad. Abbot knew what his fate would be if he were captured. Abbot ran downstairs, through the back yard, and across an open space, fortunately without being observed, into a wagon shop belonging to Stephen H. Dix. There he sat for two hours, in trembling dread of discovery.[50]

Carmi W. Babcock and James C. Horton were also staying at the Eldridge House. Babcock owned a one-half interest in the Lawrence ferry with the Baldwin brothers. He became the first postmaster in Lawrence but was later ignored by the Lawrence Association who made Erastus D. Ladd postmaster in his place. This was probably due to Babcock's charge that "the Emigrant Aid Company of Boston is a swindle on the public, the principal object of those concerned being that of making a grand land speculation under the guise of making Kansas a free state." Horton had come to Lawrence from New York and was soon made the register of deeds. Fellow townsman Joseph Savage said of him, "He was good at getting others to do his work and he was never known to stand up to an open fight," and he was not prepared to offer resistance in this confrontation either. After the hotel was seized, Horton was captured and taken by a guard to point out the location of the businesses and homes to be destroyed. Despite being local politicians, both Babcock and Horton were protected by Quantrill when the hotel surrendered.

One resident of the hotel, a Mrs. Tisdale, was quickly awakened by the noise outside. She was in possession of some of her husband's important papers and was concerned about being able to save them. She rushed into the hallway to speak with someone about the condition of affairs. She met a Mr. Thompson who was also fearful for his valuables. Mrs. Tisdale offered to hide Mr. Thompson's money by tying it to the steel rounds of her hoopskirt. Mr. Thompson then fled, telling Mrs. Tisdale to escape the best she could by getting to the river and taking the ferry or by swimming if she had to. She sallied forth carefully and necessarily slowly, down the stairs to the "Ladies Entrance," which led to Winthrop Street, around the corner from the opposite side of the hotel where Quantrill was arranging with Captain Banks for the hotel's surrender. Once on the street she turned for the river. One guerrilla started toward her but was turned back by an officer who said that they could offer no discourtesy to a lady.[51]

The guerrillas quickly stationed guards at every door of the Eldridge House, and anyone trying to escape was shot. The only means of defense for those inside the hotel were a few sidearms and rifles. Realizing that resistance was futile, Captain Alexander R. Banks, the provost marshal of Kansas who was staying in the hotel, fastened a white pillowcase to a ramrod and waved it from a window. Banks called out for Quantrill. Soon he saw a tall, slender rider with blue eyes, sandy brown hair, and an imperial mustache approach. It was Quantrill. He was riding a beautiful brown gelding. On his head he wore a black slouch hat with a gold neck cord and gold tassels along the brim. He had on gray pants and black high-topped cavalry boots. He wore a highly decorated brown guerrilla shirt and had four .36-caliber Colt Navy revolvers in his belt and two more in saddle holsters. He also carried a large dirk in his belt. A rifle and other weapons hung from his saddlebow. Seeing the guerrilla leader approach, Banks yelled out, "We are defenseless and at your mercy, the house is surrendered, but we demand protection for the inmates." To these terms Quantrill readily agreed. A cheer of "Hurrah for Quantrill" went up from the guerrillas when they found that the main center of resistance was won without firing a shot.

Captain Banks was not the only person credited with ensuring the safety of the Eldridge House boarders. Robert S. Stevens was one of the most notable and respected personages in Lawrence that day. Stevens, a Democratic attorney, had a variety of financial interests in Kansas during this time. He was primarily working on getting grants to build a railroad through Kansas and had just arrived in Lawrence the previous evening at nine o'clock. He was staying at the Eldridge House to attend a railroad meeting relating to the affairs of the Kansas Pacific Railway held the night of Thursday, August 20.

Observing Major Bancroft and his wife nervously pacing the hallway, Stevens quickly gave his valuables to Mrs. Bancroft, who was not searched since the guerrillas respected the privacy of all women. Stevens pointed out that Quantrill's men took pains to avoid harming women, children, and the elderly. Most of those in the hotel were milling about in the hallways, not knowing what to do. Military officers housed in the hotel quickly discarded their uniforms before stepping from their rooms. James Winchell, a resident of the hotel, recalled, "Although we had with us some officers in the military service, none had the ill-fortune to be in uniform."[52]

Sensing the danger to the occupants, Stevens approached one of the older guerrillas and revealed a Masonic sign. When the secret sign was returned Stevens requested that the man summon Quantrill. In about five minutes Quantrill returned, dismounted, and entered the hotel. Quantrill demanded to know who had sent for him. As Quantrill approached Stevens he immediately recognized him. The two men were delighted to see each other. Stevens "took him by the hand, led him aside, and finally got from him a promise of protection for the whole crowd." Before the war Stevens had defended Quantrill in Douglas County against spurious charges brought by Quantrill's enemies in the Jayhawker gangs and was able to get Quantrill set free of the false charges. In their brief conversation Quantrill told Stevens that his force comprised 453 men.[53]

George Todd was the first to mount the staircase of the hotel and arouse the sleepers. "He marshaled them out, armed only with his six-shooter; while scores of U. S. officers of all ranks, were rushing to and fro in their flight, forgetting or fearing to use their weapons." Stevens recalled, "Four bandits came up [stairs] and demanded watches, money, etc., which generally were given up." Todd noticed Captain Banks's splendid new uniform and ordered him to take it off and exchange clothes with him. Accompanying Todd was John Jarrette and a squad of other guerrillas who had already begun ushering the prisoners downstairs into the lobby. Guerrillas then started searching individual rooms and robbing those guests found milling around. One occupant observed, "While Quantrill thus guarded the stairs to prevent any from passing down, his men were passing through the crowded hall, and taking all the cash and valuables they could lay hands on. No violence was used and no loud or boisterous talk was indulged in." Todd and Jarrette found one room locked. They called out to those inside to save themselves as the hotel was set on fire. Voices were heard from within, cursing the guerrillas. Jarrette broke down the door. Three soldiers were found hiding inside. In the melee that followed all three were shot. The soldiers would have been saved if they had not offered any resistance. They were the first of the seventeen Yankees killed by Todd during the raid.[54]

Quantrill then ascended to the first floor landing overlooking the sixty-five prisoners being gathered together in the hotel lobby. Once the rooms were cleared, all occupants were led downstairs to the main hall. James M. Winchell tried to hide in his room but was forced out by several guerrillas who presented their revolvers and demanded his surrender. One of the assembled individuals asserted, "No absolute violence, however, so far as I am aware, was offered in the hotel."

As Winchell was waiting with the group of prisoners he soon realized that it was Quantrill who had ascended the landing and was gazing over the lobby. Winchell remembered, "Presently a bushwhacker came up the stairs, paused upon the landing, and looked us over. It was Quantrill, the terror of the border, and a former citizen of the town. To some old acquaintances he spoke civilly enough, and with two or three shook hands, assuring us that we were entirely safe, and should receive complete protection from personal violence. This promise, I think, he did all in his power to redeem."

Winchell went on to describe Quantrill further.

> Quantrill would pass anywhere for a well-looking man, and exhibits in his countenance no traces of native ferocity. He is of medium height, well built, and very quiet, and even deliberate in speech and motion. His hair is brown, his complexion fresh, and his cunning, but pleasant blue eyes and aquiline nose, give to his countenance its chief expression. During the few moments which he spent with us at this time he conversed freely about himself and the present expedition, receiving with marked complacency some compliments on the completeness of his present success, and not hesitating to express his consciousness that it was by far the greatest of his exploits.[55]

Thirty-year-old Arthur H. Spicer, who knew Quantrill from his time in Lawrence before the war, tried to start up a conversation. He had worked with Quantrill surveying new lands on the north side of the Kansas River but now worked as a saloonkeeper and was often in trouble for violating the liquor laws. Spicer spoke out, saying, "Hello Charley, We called you Charley Hart then, you know." Quantrill replied, "It makes no difference what they called me." Quantrill was well acquainted with Spicer's brother and asked if he was in town, to which Spicer replied that he was away with his company. His brother, Colonel Newell W. Spicer, was a tempting target. He had come to Kansas with the New England Emigrant Aid Company and had immediately joined in the early border troubles, being an officer in the early militia organization. When the war started, Spicer fought at Wilson's Creek and other battles along the border.

Turning away, Quantrill instructed one of his men to take charge of Spicer and compel him to act as a guide to find Lane's new residence into which he had just moved. Quantrill told his men that he had an account to settle with Spicer and that if he did not serve them well to shoot him. Other occupants also tried to strike up a friendly

Lieutenant Colonel Newell Spicer (sitting) came to Kansas with the New England Emigrant Aid Company and became an officer in the early town militia. Spicer led attacks against proslavery men in Kansas before the war. He also fought against Quantrill at Wilson's Creek in 1861. Quantrill specifically sought for him during the raid. (Kansas State Historical Society)

banter with the guerrilla leader. One asked why he had not come before at the full moon when he said he would. Quantrill coyly replied, "You were expecting me then, but I have caught you napping now."[56]

Since the hotel was slated to be burned, Quantrill ordered the occupants to be taken to a safer place down the street. Within an hour the hotel was engulfed in flames and completely destroyed, only the walls remaining. As a result the entire draft enrollment and papers of the provost marshal were destroyed. Quantrill assigned Todd to escort the prisoners away and guard them amid the deadly fury that was taking place around them. The prisoners were initially taken down the block to a defensive embrasure built in the middle of the street. It was dug out of the ground with the earth thrown up and used as a parapet.

As the prisoners were being led away under guard, one guerrilla recognized one of the prisoners as a Redleg and rode up and fired two shots at him. The guard, Henry Porter, ordered the man to stop, saying that the prisoners were guaranteed protection by Quantrill, and he would shoot to kill if he was not obeyed. One prisoner heard the man reply, "Damn you, I won't obey you, and I will shoot Quantrill himself." Porter countered by saying, "I am placed here to protect these prisoners, and I will do it. If you shoot any of them, I will kill you," and in so saying Porter presented his revolver in a menacing manner. Quantrill, who had gone on ahead to the Whitney House Hotel, was talking with his old friend Nathan Stone. When informed that the Eldridge House prisoners were in danger, he rode back and ordered Todd to bring the prisoners to Stone's hotel where they would not be exposed in the street.

Quantrill at the Whitney House Hotel

The prisoners were marched away by twos. Quantrill rode up and reassured them by saying, "One man, Stone was kind to me years ago and I lived here, and I have promised to protect him and his family and house. All of you go over to the City Hotel, and go into it, and stay in it, and you will be safe. But don't attempt to go into the street." The hotel was originally called the Whitney House because it was built by a Mr. Whitney. It was also known as the Durfee House, then afterward the City Hotel, and now was kept by a Mr. Stone. It was a two-story wooden structure painted brown, standing opposite the ferry landing in plain view of the soldiers on the other side. Whenever the soldiers saw any unwary guerrillas, they would fire their rifles at them, narrowly missing the citizens. Lydia Stone, the proprietor's daughter, made her way to the riverbank waving a white handkerchief at the soldiers until they understood that they were putting their own comrades' lives in danger.

When Quantrill lived in Lawrence before the war he boarded at the Whitney House Hotel. Lydia Stone was a beautiful blue-eyed young woman known for her oil paintings of Kansas. She became a favorite of Quantrill and to her he gave a photograph of himself besides a ring that she always wore. Once when he came down with typhoid fever he was nursed back to health by the Stones, and he felt indebted to them and so ensured their safety during the raid. Quantrill continued to ride beside the prisoners as they were being escorted to the hotel. When a general outcry went up by the guerrillas outside the Whitney House to kill the prisoners, Quantrill "swore he would protect the prisoners if he had to kill every man that interfered." His personal guard was then stationed around the building, protecting it and the prisoners inside.[57]

Lydia Stone was the daughter of Nathan Stone, proprietor of the Whitney House Hotel in Lawrence. Before the war she nursed Quantrill during an illness and in return he gave her a ring and a photograph of himself. During the raid Quantrill extended protection for her and her family. (Kansas State Historical Society)

Francis E. Smith lived in Lawrence where he became an officer in Lane's Brigade and took part in the destruction of Osceola, Missouri. He later belonged to Jennison's Fifteenth Kansas Jayhawker Regiment. (Greg Walter Collection)

One of the prisoners recalled that when they reached the safety of the hotel Quantrill asked for something to eat. Someone brought him a tin cup full of coffee and a loaf of baker's bread. He sat upon his horse, drank his coffee, ate a part of the loaf of bread and threw the rest away. Some of the prisoners who had known him before the war ventured to risk a conversation. Among them were Anson Storm, Captain F. B. Smith, and Thomas J. Sternberg. One of them asked Quantrill, "Charlie, how could you do such a thing to a town where you have so many acquaintances and some friends?" His reply was: "My men came here for revenge and I can't stop them from what they are doing."

Quantrill's Methods of Warfare

Historians fail to take into consideration important revealing written reports by eyewitnesses. One stated, "Investigation has shown that Quantrill's methods of warfare were not looked upon with favor by some. He was too humane, and generally shrank from the needless taking of human life." One of Quantrill's officers, Lieutenant Fletcher Taylor, remarked, "Quantrill was humane and kind, as some can testify at Lawrence, where he saved a great many." One author remarked: "Quantrill was more considerate than Lane had been, as he told one of his prisoners taken at the Eldridge House that he would spare the women from outrage, which Lane, in his raids in Missouri, did not do." Mrs. Gurdon Grovenor remembered, "They killed a passel of men but Charlie Hart didn't molest women or children."

It was a matter of fact that "the universal testimony of all the ladies and others who talked with the butchers of the 21st . . . is that these demons claimed they were here to revenge the wrongs done their families by our men under Lane, Jennison, Anthony and Co. They said they would be more merciful than were these men when they went into Missouri." Even Richard Cordley readily admitted, "That some of the raiders had suffered personal wrongs and were inspired with feelings of revenge, we can well believe."[58]

The Actions of the Town Militia

When firing was first heard on the west side of town, militia members grabbed what weapons they could and tried to make it to their assigned rallying points. Cordley admitted, "A large number did actually start with what arms they had toward the street." Militia member Levi Gates lived a mile from town. He had come to Lawrence with the first party of the New England Emigrant Aid Company and was instrumental in organizing and supporting the town's militia. His wife was a proprietress of a boarding house in town. As soon as he heard the firing, he picked up his gun and made his way to join his company. Seeing all the roads well guarded, Gates stopped and fired at one of the guerrillas, possibly hitting him. Gates managed to get off one more round before making a run for the ravine. He was spotted by a lone guerrilla who rode up on him and shot him. Like Gates, Private E. B. Guild seized his musket and started out for the militia rendezvous but saw the futility of the effort and instead ran to save himself.

When militiamen Privates John and Thomas McFarland and Levi Sperry heard the firing, they gathered up their weapons, mounted their horses, and rode toward Lawrence. Other militiamen met them on the way and told them what was transpiring, causing them to reconsider riding further and defending the town. Other militiamen, Sergeants Jacob McFadden, Nathan McFarland, and Michael Martin, who had been with Lane during the destruction of Osceola, Missouri, continued on and met their fates before being able to escape.[59]

Private Octavius W. McAllaster of the Lawrence militia lived on the east side of Rhode Island Street in the 700 block. Since it was a very warm morning, he was up at five o'clock and saw the guerrillas riding into town. At first he thought they were United States troops, as it was a very common thing for them to be passing through the city. City marshal William Soule and E. W. Wood boarded with McAllaster. McAllaster was wearing his uniform, which he quickly hid before attempting to hide himself in his well. Wood hollered for him to come out, then all three men hid themselves in the basement under the kitchen. McAllaster later said that it was fortunate for him that he did not stay in the well for when the guerrillas starting discovering men hiding in such places they began throwing large boulders down the wells to discover whether anyone was hiding there.

McAllaster had been influenced by James Lane to come to Kansas and fight. His musket and ammunition were kept downtown at the *State Journal* office where he worked. Soule had his revolver and at first decided to fight if the guerrillas tried to enter the house. But when they started pounding on the front door, demanding those inside to come out, fear gripped the men inside, and instead of fighting they thought it best to make their escape. Seeing only one guerrilla outside, they ran out the back to a nearby cornfield. Before they could get away they were accosted by a group of guerrillas who simply robbed them. Prior to permitting them to go on their way, the guerrillas ordered them to go to the stable of David Evans and bring out all the horses. Evans was a member of Lane's Brigade and had

Captain George W. Bell was a member of the Twelfth Kansas Jayhawker Regiment stationed in Lawrence. He also served as the county clerk. On the day of the raid, Bell donned his uniform, grabbed his rifle, and headed toward town only to be chased down and killed by the guerillas. (Greg Walter Collection)

taken part in the destruction of Osceola, Missouri, thus guaranteeing that his property would be destroyed. Evans escaped, but Louis H. Swan, who had also been at Osceola, was discovered and killed.[60]

Captain George W. Bell of the Twelfth Kansas Jayhawker Regiment lived on the side of Mount Oread overlooking Lawrence. He too grabbed his gun and cartridge box and headed toward town. His family desperately tried to dissuade him, but Bell bravely replied to their entreaties: "They may kill me, but they cannot kill the principles I fight for. If they take Lawrence, they must do it over my dead body." Bell's brave words were soon forgotten when he saw that resistance was futile. He threw away his rifle and tried to seek shelter at the Miller home where the guerrillas had earlier stopped before entering town. Peter Ridenour said he first saw Bell running toward town with his musket on his shoulder, then later saw Bell being chased about two blocks from where he stood. He said Bell ran to a fence and jumping over it ran into a stable. The guerrillas followed him, firing their revolvers until they killed him in the stable. Bell's house was on the list to be burned, but his family managed to save it.[61]

7

A Just Retaliation

The Confederacy and the world may learn of the murderous and uncivilized warfare inaugurated by the Federals and thus be able to appreciate their cowardly shrieks and howls when with a just retaliation the same measure is meted out to them.

—General Sterling Price

Quantrill kept his personal company with him, the only original members left being George Todd, William Gregg, and Jim Little, giving orders for the other companies to spread through town and find the men on their "Death Lists." Citizens recalled, "In the residential parts of town, especially to the west of the ravine, squads of Bushwhackers were seen going from door to door and carrying lists of names of prominent citizens who were targeted to be killed, hunting their victims in the streets, houses and gardens, and plundering and burning houses and barns." One citizen hiding near the hotel remembered hearing that Quantrill ordered his men "not to go into any part of the town where people were firing guns, as they had to hurry away and had no time to engage with the scattered persons at their houses." Another citizen remembered that one of the leaders took from his pocket a paper and read over a list of houses his men were to burn. "Many citizens heard these lists read off and saw them consulted when the guerrillas were inquiring for certain parties." This was the first order of business.[1]

"Death Lists" and "Buildings to Be Destroyed"

After the "Death Lists" were gone through, buildings marked to be destroyed were sought out with orders to set fire to the houses by applying matches to window curtains or bedclothes. Quantrill's band divided into groups of six or eight and were directed where they were to go about their assigned tasks of searching for wanted men house by house. Frank Smith said: "Men were shot down in the streets, in their yards and wherever they were encountered if they had on a Federal uniform or were known to have worn a Federal uniform or openly advocated the abolitionist cause. They were given no chance. No mercy was shown them."[2]

Quantrill procured a buggy and a team of white horses from a nearby stable. Alone and unafraid he passed through town, riding as far as the top of Mount Oread, observing the empty rifle pits and defensive redoubts. After checking on his men guarding the western side of town he returned to the Whitney House soon afterward and went inside and asked for breakfast. While their leader was thus engaged, Quantrill's men were busy searching for the names on their lists. This scene was remembered by Lieutenant Gregg, who recalled, "During all this time, his command was busy hunting men with blue clothes and setting fire to the town."[3]

Rather than making for the militia rendezvous, James G. Sands, Alonzo Fuller, and Lieutenant Brinton W. Woodward were hiding for fear inside their houses. All three lived near Sand's Saddle, Hardware and Livery Stable. Fuller's brother had been mayor of Lawrence in 1861, and Brinton W. Woodward who owned Woodward's Drug Store was the first druggist in town. Woodward had been an officer in Company F of the Kansas Guards under the command of James Lane and had been cited by Lane for defending Lawrence during the Wakarusa War. As a result, his business on Massachusetts Street was destroyed by the raiders. A peculiar happenstance saved the lives of all three men. Sands had a stable behind his store where he kept his pet pony named "Freddie." As a squad of guerrillas rode up the street, one of their officers asked. "Why are not these houses burnt?" As they dismounted to carry out their orders, they were met by "Freddie" who ran past them. Other guerrillas yelled at them to help them capture the animal, and so they were distracted in

Lieutenant Brinton W. Woodward was an early agitator living in Lawrence. He served as an officer under James H. Lane and took part in the border troubles between Kansas and Missouri. He was a valuable target during the raid on Lawrence. (Douglas County Historical Society)

their mission so that not only the houses but the lives of the three men inside were saved.[4]

In the Eldridge House Hotel a large quantity of arms were stored in the northwest room on the first floor. Besides the hotel, the city armory two doors down had been chosen as the rallying point for Lawrence's independent company of militia. Sixty muskets and a cannon had been requested from General Thomas Ewing, commander of the District of the Border, just a few months before the raid. The rifles were issued to individual militia members, but General Collamore had them collected and stored in the armory where they were in a central location for immediate use. Most citizens had their own personal weapons at their homes. A Kansas City newspaper earlier reported on the transfer of weapons: "The people who are here have put themselves upon a war footing. The militia companies drill every day. The government will fully supply them arms in a few days. The citizens have also all supplied themselves with arms at their own expense. Every house is an arsenal, and many of them could be defended against fifty bushwhackers."[5] Instead of armed militia members running to defend the town, many of the militia members were shot down without arms as they tried to reach the weapons in the armory. Lieutenant Cole Younger affirmed it by saying, "We shot the soldiers down as they ran out of the houses on the way to the rendezvous their officers had given them."[6]

The Search for Redlegs

The next most important target on the guerrillas' list was the Johnson House Hotel, also called the Eastern House, just a block southwest of the Eldridge House Hotel. The headquarters of the hated Redlegs, it was the second largest hotel in town, being three stories tall and made of native stone. Author John C. Shea pointed out that the Redlegs "were cordially hated by the Quantrell party, and individual members were hunted on the morning of the raid with unusual care and perseverance."[7]

The mock courage that accompanied the Redlegs as they burned and plundered the homes of innocent citizens in Missouri during their Jayhawking raids now escaped them. Many ran away seeking safety, leaving their wives and children to fend for themselves. William Gregg was quoted as saying, "I couldn't understand why armed men did not bravely exercise their ability to defend their wives and families and property with their last breath." The guerrillas naturally expected these trapped men to fight to the death, but it simply didn't happen. Gregg remarked, "No Kansan seemed to have a burning desire to take as many Missourians with him as he could in death." Quantrill also offered a comment on the subject, "The women of Lawrence were the bravest lot I ever encountered but the men were a damn set of cowards."[8]

Colonel George Hoyt, the leader of the Redlegs, was not to be found, but many of his men were. Hoyt and his Redlegs often defied legal authority and at one time even attempted to assassinate Governor Robinson when he tried to put an end to their stealing. It was well known that the Lawrence livery stables were full of their stolen horses and cattle. Most citizens in town either supported or condoned their activities. Sara Robinson, the governor's wife, claimed, "I visited a room filled with harness and saddles, part of the stolen property which Hoyt and his gang had brought in."[9]

One of the stables that cared for stolen horses was Fry's Livery Stable located at 804 New Hampshire Street. The stable was made of brick and stood at the corner of New Hampshire and Henry Streets. It was owned by Samuel Fry, who also owned a bakery in town. Fry advertised his stable in the *Herald of Freedom,* "On hand, buggies, carriages and saddle horses and horses sold on commission." Working in the stable was Samuel S. Jones, a blacksmith and a private in Company B, Twelfth Kansas Jayhawker Regiment. Jones was called an "extremist in the cause of slavery" and was a radical abolitionist. He was shot down over his anvil, one of the first Jayhawkers killed during the raid.[10]

First Lieutenant George Ellis in charge of troops guarding railroad property north of the Kansas River was staying at the Johnson House Hotel. As soon as Ellis heard firing he ran into the barn behind the building. With his uniform blouse flapping in the breeze he was chased into the loft by guerrillas and feared to come out. One bullet grazed his head and shot holes were later found in his blouse and sleeves. Ellis managed to crawl away and escape as the building burned.

Once the hotel was surrounded, the guerrillas called out to the occupants to throw down their arms and come out. There were fifteen men trapped inside. When they refused to immediately surrender the guerrillas began shooting at the windows while continuing to yell for the men to give themselves up. Seven of the occupants decided not to be taken prisoner and started climbing out the windows but were immediately shot down in the attempt. A Southern account stated, "A number of U.S. officers were called out of the hotels and as they made their appearance an unceremonious bullet took them off without benefit of clergy or court martial." Another Southern newspaper reported, "Many officers of high rank among the Kansas Jayhawkers [were] shot down and suffered to stiffen in the cool morning air."[11]

Two doors down at his carriage factory, Ralph C. Dix, along with his brothers Steven, Frank, and Chaucey and several of his employees, decided to make for the Redlegs' headquarters despite watching it being pelted by pistol fire. His wife urged him to save himself, but he only replied, "No, I want to await developments, and aid the citizens. Our arms are across the street in the arsenal and surely some resistance will be made." They assumed that the ablest resistance would be put up by the Redlegs. Despite her protests, her husband and his small militia group started for the Redlegs' headquarters. They reached a rear room of the Johnson House by climbing over the barbershop roof next door. After her husband had been gone only a few moments, Getta left her children in charge of her Negro maid and ran to the rear of the hotel. As she was running toward the hotel Getta said she saw Redlegs "jumping from windows and fleeing for their lives. Several were killed as they ran." As she arrived at the hotel, she saw Steven Dix being shot, his body tumbling down the back steps. She ran to his side, but found he was already dead. As she ran to the front of the building she discovered that the remaining occupants had just surrendered and saw her husband being led out with a group of seven other men.[12]

Joe Finley, a notorious Redleg, was immediately recognized and shot after handing his pistol over to his captors. The other prisoners panicked with fear. Falling on their knees with arms raised pleading for mercy, the prisoners screamed and cried not to be killed. Lee C. Miller stated, "The officers in the hotel begged to be taken prisoners, but Quantrell reminded them of General Halleck's order and of the hundreds of old men they had killed in Missouri." The leader in charge of the guerrilla group spoke out harshly, "I have killed seven Redlegs and I'll kill eight more." One guerrilla recounted, "We did expect the resistance of soldiers, and men, instead of which we met with cowards, renegades and Kansas Red Legs, all pleading instead of shooting; begging instead of fighting."[13]

Getta Dix reached her husband and clung to his arm begging for the guerrillas to release him. His guard replied, "No, I won't let you take your husband away. I'm going to kill every damn one of them." The men were then led about two hundred feet down a nearby alley and shot. Frank Dix managed to escape by crawling through a rear window. Besides Ralph Dix and Joe Finley, the other victims were Asa White, George Kallmer, John A. Cornell, another man by the name of Goldman, and the proprietor Benjamin Johnson. White had been a member of the New England Emigrant Aid Company and had fought against the Missourians during the border troubles. Cole Younger stated, "Not a 'redleg' so far as I have ever heard escaped. We exterminated them." A Lawrence citizen agreed by adding, "They pursued the Redlegs with particular earnestness and showed them no mercy when captured."[14]

Another Redleg, Jacob Pike, saved himself by jumping into the hotel's cistern. Two other Redlegs, brothers Henry and Oliver Paul, were living in town. Private Henry Paul, a former member of the Eleventh Kansas Jayhawker Regiment, was living at the Johnson House with the other Redlegs but managed to escape. His brother Oliver, a member of the local militia, was living at home when he grabbed his rifle and headed toward town, but when he was met by Dr. Richard Huson he was told that no resistance was being made and that all the citizens were being killed. Rather than fight, Oliver threw his rifle away and escaped with others into a nearby cornfield. A large number, however, did actually start toward the street with what arms they had. Most saw at once that the street could not be reached and turned back. Some went forward and perished. Whenever militia members came together they would ask each other, "Where shall we meet?" They assured each other that it was too late to rendezvous anywhere, so they then sought to save themselves. Two militiamen not as fortunate as the others were brothers, Privates John and William Laurie. While running away after deciding not to defend the town, they were recognized and shot. Both had been in the early border troubles, and William Laurie had been recognized by the guerrillas as a Jayhawker during the Shawneetown, Kansas, raid on October 17, 1862.[15]

The Search for Abolitionists and Militiamen

After cleaning out the nest of Redlegs from the Johnson House Hotel, the guerrillas moved next door to the residence of George E. Holt. John L. Crane and his family occupied the upper part of Holt's house at 731 Connecticut Street. Holt and Crane were partners in the boot and shoe business with a store located downtown on Massachusetts Street. Both men had come to Lawrence with the New England Emigrant Aid Company, both were widely known as radical abolitionists, and both were in the Lawrence militia. Crane kept his musket handy for just such an emergency, but unfortunately it was kept in his store.

As the two men discussed what was their best option for action a squad of guerrillas rode up to the house demanding that the men come out or the house would be torched. The men kept their silence until a lone horseman rode up and made an individual request for

First Lieutenant Charles Drake served in Company E of the Eleventh Kansas Jayhawker Regiment, the regiment that served as the prison guards for the murdered girls in the August 1863 Kansas City jail collapse. While in Lawrence, Drake was described as a "radical Union man." (Greg Walter Collection)

their surrender. When they finally obeyed, they were questioned about having any weapons then robbed. A guerrilla officer soon rode up. He was told that the men had surrendered and inquired what should be done with them. The officer discovered their names on his list then notified their guards, "They had been in Missouri killing our people." He then ordered the guerrilla not to waste any more time and to shoot the two men. Crane and Holt began to protest, but a pistol report silenced them both. Crane was killed instantly. Holt was shot below the right eye and left for dead but miraculously survived.[16] Besides the two men's names being on Quantrill's "Death List," Holt's house was also slated to be burned.

One of the first houses the guerrillas came to, being on the southeast verge of the city near the point where the raiders entered, was the residence of Henry S. Clarke. Clarke owned a furniture store in Lawrence and had been a former sheriff of Douglas County. Redleg Colonel George Hoyt stayed in Clarke's home. Clarke was in the militia, and his house was slated to be burned. Clarke said, "I had the impression that they could not get into town without letting the home military company, of which I was a member, know it. I had a gun and nine rounds of cartridges. While they were shooting I got my gun with the intention of joining my company." As Clarke peered out his window he prepared himself for the inevitable. "As I looked towards the southeast I saw horsemen coming, four abreast, which was not an uncommon sight during the war, and a lone horseman, a boy, riding east, going towards them. While I was still watching they separated by twos, taking the boy right in between them. As soon as he was fairly within their lines they commenced shooting at him and charged toward town, yelling like demons."

Clarke later stated that he witnessed the shooting of two recruits in army clothes. When two guerrillas came to his door, he handed them his money as a way of saving his life. Before riding away the raiders told him if he had some things he wanted to save for his wife and baby to get them out as they were going to fire the house. When they returned and he was forced outside, Clarke spied one guerrilla sitting on a horse in his front yard. He was described as a fine-looking man who appeared to be an officer and was holding a cigar box in his hand. Clarke saw two guerrillas ride by and salute the young man as colonel. The officer turned out to be Colonel John Holt, in charge of the hundred recruits from north of the Missouri River who had joined prior to the raid. One of Holt's men rode up and asked, "What orders?" Holt replied, "Continue your way west and stop at the point of the hill," indicating Mount Oread. "You go to the top of the hill beyond, picket that line, and don't allow a man to escape."[17]

Thinking to strike up a friendly conversation in order to help save himself, Clarke approached the Rebel officer hesitatingly, saying, "Good morning, Colonel. Your boys have got us this time." "Yes," said the colonel. "That is what we aimed to do. You have made the spoon, and we are making you eat with it today." "But," said Clarke, "I did not think your men ever killed defenseless citizens. I supposed they never went beyond robbing and plundering." Clarke bristled at the question and angrily replied, "Union men have not only robbed and burned houses, and killed defenseless men, but they have shot down women and burned the houses of widows over their heads." Fearing even more for his life than before, Clarke panicked. He thought he would change the subject by inviting Holt inside for breakfast. Holt replied. "Well, I shall not refuse, as the feds will give me but little rest for two or three days."

Feeling secure as long as Holt was present, Clarke offered to feed other guerrillas as they rode up. Holt continued standing in Clarke's front yard until the guerrillas started to depart. Before leaving Captain George Todd rode by. Clarke recalled, "He was something over six feet tall, straight and handsome, and rode a spirited, prancing steed. His dress was a beautiful, new Federal uniform. I remarked to Col. Holt that I supposed that man must be a Federal officer[,] a prisoner, but he did not act as if he cared much about it. 'Federal nothing,' retorted Col. Holt, 'that is Captain George Todd. He took that suit from some Union officer.' I learned afterwards that it was a new uniform just received by Capt. A. R. Banks, Provost Marshal at the time, and who was captured at the Eldridge House."

Finally Holt told Clarke he must be leaving and directed him to stay out of sight. He informed Mrs. Clarke that if any guerrillas attempted to burn their house to say that Colonel Holt made his headquarters there and had left orders for the house to be spared. After Holt rode away, several riders rode up and proceeded to burn the house. They ordered Clarke to remove his furniture. Clarke said that the house did not belong to him; that it was owned by a widow lady, and they could burn it if they wished. The leader of the guerrillas replied, "We do not want to injure widows, as the Union men did with us," and so the house was left undisturbed.[18]

Peter D. Ridenour, who lived in the 900 block of New York Street at the foot of Mount Oread, was a member of the town's militia. Ridenour owned a grocery store and warehouse downtown. He had a Negro boy working for him, and before heading toward the armory he turned his horse loose so the guerrillas couldn't recognize it if it had been stolen from Missouri. Besides the arsenal where the sixty newly arrived muskets for the city's defense were kept, a great deal of gunpowder was stored in Ridenour's warehouse. When Ridenour first heard the firing he assumed his militia company was making a stand. He only lived one block from the militia rendezvous and was running in that direction when he witnessed several other militia members shot down in the street. Ridenour quickly reasoned, "They had fired on armed men in the streets to prevent them from rallying a force for defense of the town."[19]

Ridenour was on the guerrillas' "Death List," and his house was one of those slated to be destroyed. One source wrote that Ridenour sold stolen property in his store, one item being some 43,000 nails stolen from Solomon Young, guerrilla Jim Chiles' father-in-law. Ridenour panicked when he saw two guerrillas riding toward him. He ran back into his house, chased by the two men. He locked the doors and watched his pursuers ride past, shooting at the house as they rode by. Luckily, Ridenour and his colored boy managed to escape by running out the back door and hiding in the garden. Jim Noland returned with two other guerrillas and carried out a box of family pictures and placed them for safety in the yard before burning the house. Before the house was set on fire, Mrs. Elmore Allen arrived at Ridenour's house. She said that guerrillas had already come to her house looking for her husband. Elmore Allen was in the Ninth Kansas Cavalry Regiment. During the border troubles he had helped Jacob Branson escape arrest from Sheriff Jones, and his company during the past spring had been plundering the Missouri border. His criminal activities now made him a wanted man.

Downtown at Ridenour's place of business Henry Richards and a young man by the name of Place worked in Ridenour's warehouse and slept upstairs. They found themselves completely surrounded by guerrillas with no place to run. Guerrillas crashed through the front doors and found the men hiding inside. They escorted the men from the store, saving their lives. Richards immediately headed for the river and hid in the tall weeds along the riverbank. Place swam the river and ran for Leavenworth where he knew he would find Governor Carney who owned a business in town.

Another soldier identified and captured in Lawrence was Louis Wise. Wise had served in the Eighth Kansas Jayhawker Regiment and had ridden on punitive expeditions in Cass, Johnson, and Lafayette Counties in Missouri before returning home in February 1863. Besides owning a farm outside town Wise and his family lived above his bakery shop along the main street. His stock of goods included most anything that could be sold. Listed in his inventory books were notations of sales to the military and militia units around town. An early description of Wise given by his neighbor Edward Fitch included an accusation that Wise had illegally jumped claims of early setters. While out Jayhawking as members of the Eighth

Colonel Horace L. Moore was an officer in the Second Kansas Jayhawker Regiment before becoming a militia officer in Lawrence. (Kansas State Historical Society)

Kansas, Wise's company had been engaged in a skirmish with Colonel Silas Gordon's guerrillas near Hickory Grove, Missouri, where in retaliation the town was completely destroyed. When the raiders seized Wise, he vainly grabbed his child up in his arms, hoping to save himself. The guerrillas separated him from his family then led him from the building where he was shot. Nearby, Wise's neighbor and fellow comrade in the Eighth Kansas, Private Christopher Leonard, was also killed.

Robert Morrow's house was slated to be burned but was saved by an unusual turn of events. Morrow had been an early politician in the first free-state legislature in violation of the territorial government. He had already made his escape when guerrillas came to his house inquiring for him. Desperately trying to save her house Mrs. Morrow told the guerrillas that she was a Southern woman and had two brothers in the Southern army. Out of compassion one of the guerrillas took a piece of charcoal and wrote on the side of the house in large letters, "This is a Southern house," thus saving it from ruin.

Several individual militia members continued running into the street to join their companies. John L. Read whose house was in town had initially been in the First Kansas Regiment and was now an officer in the town militia. Read managed to escape detection, making his way to the river and safety. The guerrillas remembered Quantrill's order, "Shoot any soldiers seen running in the streets." A soldier named Bradley lived in James Lane's neighborhood. He grabbed his gun and started in the direction of the armory. Three guerrillas spied him running and rode toward him

Lieutenant John J. Lindsay first enlisted in the Second Kansas Regiment before joining the Eleventh Kansas Jayhawker Regiment, the regiment that served as the prison guards for the murdered girls in the Kansas City jail collapse. Lindsay's name was on the guerrillas' "Death List" as they entered Lawrence. (Greg Walter Collection)

firing as they came. Although wounded, Bradley managed to make it back to his house.

Another militiaman, Captain Daniel W. Wilder, lived in a large stone house near the intersection of Winthrop and Kentucky Streets. Wilder knew the guerrillas would soon be coming for him so he hid in the cellar of his house. He was a militia officer who in 1860 had been a Kansas delegate to the Republican convention for Abraham Lincoln. Even though he lived in a stone house, the guerrillas approached and tried to set fire to the window curtains, but the blaze from inside was easily extinguished.

Sophia Bissell recalled: "Five men rode into our yard, and the leader rode his horse right up on the piazza [porch]: each one seemed to have a position assigned them, one set fire to the stable, one set fire to the house up stairs setting fire to the husk mattresses on the bed and to things in the bureau drawers, one of them stayed sometime in the dining room arranging quantities of money he had tucked away all over him, and the fifth was opening the trunks in the house that we hadn't carried out." Her brother-in-law Henry C. Lawrence was living with them at that time. Sophia's sister begged the leader of the group not to harm her husband. As soon as he was released he immediately ran through the house and out into a cornfield to hide. Sophia said, "I had run down the stairs to ask the leader not to burn the house. 'Won't you spare the house?' I asked. 'We are just plain quiet people and have never done any harm.' He took off his hat and made a flourishing bow and said, 'For your sake I will spare it.'" But Sophia was unable to put out the fire. The husk mattress fell to pieces. Sophia recounted: "We burned our hands and had to give it up and go down stairs. Then the leader told them to get onto their horses and be off; they all took off their hats and made us bows and said. 'Now you know what we have been suffering down in Missouri.'"[20]

The Search for James Lane and Other Leaders

With the raid so far going according to plan, Quantrill and a group of his men headed for Senator Lane's residence. Quantrill had previously given orders that if anyone captured Lane not to harm him as he wanted the pleasure of personally taking him back to Jackson County and trying him for war crimes. They had already visited the houses of every prominent abolitionist in town. Cole Younger stated, "Meanwhile Quantrill had ridden on with the main body to the house where the map we carried stated that General Jim Lane was living." Lane's son had risen early and was outside drawing water for the animals. In the dim early morning light the guerrillas fired at the young man. He ran back through the house and out the back door toward the ravine that ran through town toward the river. He was followed by the guerrillas. As he neared the ravine he stumbled and fell across a large tree, appearing to have been shot. In the midst of the fusillade the guerrillas shouted, "I guess the devil is dead." When the guerrillas turned away he ran to the home of John H. Shimmons, Lane's business partner and fellow Jayhawker, where he put on a woman's dress and sunbonnet. He was not recognized as a boy and was able to escape.

In the meantime Lane had heard the initial report of pistol shots and had known instinctively what it meant. The farmer Quantrill had questioned as he entered Lawrence reported that Senator Lane was not in town at the time. What was not known was that Lane had returned to Lawrence late in the evening of August 20 to attend a meeting at the Eldridge House Hotel which wasn't over until slightly before midnight, so very few citizens knew of his presence. Therefore there was no perceived hurry to carry out one of the main objectives of the raid. Lane first knew his life was in danger when a Negro recruit ran past his house yelling that the guerrillas were attacking. Completely panicking, Lane quickly tore the nameplate from his front door and escaped in his nightshirt through the cornfield behind his house.

Lane owned considerable property in Lawrence besides the hundred-acre cornfield into which he escaped. The corn was of the tallest type in Kansas and reached above the head of the tallest man, so that within its borders one was safe from the enemy. Worried that he might be discovered, Lane had wild thoughts running through his head. Later telling his friend John Speer how he feared for his life, Lane said that several of the raiders had come very close to where he had been hiding. Lane showed Speer a small penknife he had at the time and explained that if his capture had been imminent he "intended to thrust that little blade up into my brain to escape torture."[21]

Arriving at Lane's residence, Quantrill, followed by John McCorkle and several other guerrillas, proceeded to the front door. Mrs. Lane opened the door to hear Quantrill say with gentlemanly politeness, "Give your husband my compliments, Madam, and tell him I should be most happy to meet him." Mrs. Lane replied, "That I will do, sir. I am sorry that it is not convenient for him to meet you this morning." Quantrill then gave orders for his men to search the house. One guerrilla went to the bedroom and found the bed still warm. Among the loot found inside were three pianos that were recognized as being stolen from Southern families in Jackson County. One was a beautiful Steinway that Lane had given his daughter from a previous looting expedition in Missouri.

Besides the pianos, the guerrillas were amazed at the large amount of additional plunder adorning Lane's residence. In the cellar the guerrillas found vast amounts of stolen goods, including barrels of sugar, molasses, and coffee. While going about the business of searching the house, Quantrill's men confiscated the rings worn by Mrs. Lane and her daughter. Quantrill did allow Lane's family to remove some of their valuables.

The only other items the guerrillas confiscated were Lane's gold-embroidered silk military flag, which Quantrill tore in two. Another flag found was Lane's "Black Flag" that carried the words "Presented to General James H. Lane by the women of Leavenworth." Later Quantrill sent it to Sterling Price to prove the treatment of guerrillas by Kansas soldiers in giving "no quarter." Jim Little took Lane's sword and gold-plated scabbard with silver mountings that had been presented to him by the Fifth Indiana Regiment. Both the sword and the scabbard bore an engraved inscription to Lane for his service during the Mexican War. Little carried it back to Missouri where he broke it in half, burying it beneath the water of a local spring. Younger said that the guerrillas searched a second house for Lane but "failed to find him there."[22]

Also living in Lane's neighborhood was Lieutenant Lucius S. Shaw. Shaw was an officer in the Lawrence militia. Living with him was Captain Hugh Cameron. Both men had served together in the Second Kansas Jayhawker Regiment. Cameron had come to Lawrence with the first party of the New England Emigrant Aid Company. He gained an unsavory reputation for being a cruel officer to his men and at one time had been placed under arrest on charges of brutality brought by one of his junior officers. Frequently, he ordered that men be cruelly punished for minor offences. He seemed to delight in ordering men to be hung up by their thumbs until their toes partly rested on the floor, or to be bucked and gagged. Cameron was eventually relieved of command for misappropriating soldiers' rations and selling them for his own enrichment. Unfortunately, two others in Cameron's regiment, Privates Richard R. Loomis and James S. O'Neil, were killed by the guerrillas.[23]

Lieutenant Shaw, armed with a pistol, managed to fire a few shots at a guerrilla who was chasing a Negro down the street. Cameron had a pistol and a musket, which he rested on a fence and managed to fire at the guerrilla, wounding him in the hip. Before other guerrillas came to his aid, Cameron and Shaw ran back inside the house. Guerrillas surrounded the house and demanded that the two surrender. Cameron didn't want to give up his gun but was persuaded by Shaw to do so because the guerrillas threatened to kill everyone inside if they did not. Cameron finally gave in to the guerrillas' entreaties and gave himself up. Finding themselves in possession of two such highly prized targets, the guerrillas hurried off with their prisoners. In the confusion Shaw managed to make his escape. Miraculously, Cameron too was somehow able to get away.

Another Federal officer living nearby was Captain Charles P. Twiss. Twiss's company was attached to General George Deitzler's brigade and had fought at Dug Springs and Wilson's Creek. Twiss was armed but managed to keep from being discovered.[24]

A block from Lane's house was the expensive home of Jerome F. Griswold. There were three families living with him. Besides Griswold there were the families of Josiah C. Trask, Harlow W. Baker, and Simeon M. Thorp. All without exception were wanted men. Griswold was known as a radical abolitionist. In politics he resisted anything that aided a conservative compromise between Kansans and Missourians. Josiah Trask was a newspaperman and owner of the *Kansas State Journal.* Though never having served in the regular military, Trask was promoted to major and organized the Lawrence militia. He became their drillmaster and frequently turned out to help defend the town when needed. He also helped Samuel N. Simpson with the Negro school in Lawrence. In the early morning darkness as Trask was standing at his second-story window overlooking the front porch, he yelled at the horsemen riding past, not knowing they were guerrillas but thinking they were militia members making their way to the armory. By mistake Trask yelled at the guerrillas, "You want to go up town and take measures for the safety of the city."[25]

Harlow Baker was co-owner of a store in town with Peter Ridenour and was married to Mrs. Ridenour's sister. In politics he violently opposed anything proslavery. Simeon Thorp was a lawyer and a member of the Kansas legislature. All four men were armed with pistols and hesitated when the guerrillas called on them to surrender. At first they were prepared to sell their lives as dearly as possible, but soon fear gripped them all. At last they agreed to come out. When they did so, they were quickly surrounded. The guerrillas asked them their names, and finding them on their "Death List" lined them up and started walking them toward town with a mounted guerrilla riding next to each one. Baker was bringing up the rear

Captain George Earle was an officer in the Ninth Kansas Jayhawker Regiment. He came to Lawrence with the New England Emigrant Aid Society before the war. He organized a militia company and was known for running Missourians off their claims around Lawrence. Earle was with James Lane when they destroyed the town of Osceola, Missouri, in 1861. (Douglas County Historical Society)

when a guerrilla suddenly shot him, the bullet ripping through Baker's neck. A second shot tore through his lungs. As he fell, another bullet tore through his wrist. Immediately the rest of the guerrillas fired. Thorp, shot in the side, fell near Baker, while Trask started running but only made it a short distance before he was finally cut down. Although wounded, Griswold turned and ran back toward his house and was in the act of scrambling over a pile of firewood when he too was shot and killed. Though badly wounded, Baker and Thorp miraculously were still alive and lay motionless for the rest of the day, feigning death.

Two military men living on the same street as Griswold but closer to downtown were Private Charles Anderson and a Private McClellan. McClellan was spotted a hundred yards from his house running to join his militia company when he was discovered and shot down. Anderson when discovered tried to hide in a cellar but was found by a group of guerrillas and forced to run, seeking shelter in the ravine running through town. He was followed by his pursuers where he fell mortally wounded, dying within hours after the guerrillas had ridden away.

Another name near the top of the guerrillas' "Death List" was that of Captain George F. Earle. Earle had a lengthy history in Lawrence.

Emigrating from Massachusetts with an armed company of the New England Emigrant Aid Society, he started the first militia company in town named "The Stubbs." They were sixty-five men armed with Sharps rifles and Colt pistols. The Stubbs were later mustered into Company D of the First Kansas Jayhawker Regiment. Earle was infamously known for using his militia company in ejecting squatters off early Lawrence town lots so they could be given to Eastern abolitionists. In one instance Earle tore down the house of a Missourian named Short so his claim could be seized. Earle served as sheriff in Lawrence during 1860 and during this capacity Colonel Sam Walker tried to get Earle to arrest Quantrill on spurious charges. Earle was especially hated for accompanying Lane during the destruction of Osceola, Missouri. After serving in the Second Kansas, Earle became the captain of Company K, Ninth Kansas Jayhawker Regiment. The guerrillas searched his house and finding no one home demanded of the neighbors where he was. When they replied that they didn't know because they were strangers in the neighborhood the guerrillas rode on, sparing the house.

The Search for Breakfast

After capturing the Eldridge House Hotel, securing the town, and wiping out the chief points of resistance, some of the guerrilla leaders took time to find something to eat. Captain Todd along with Cole Younger, William Gregg, Andy Blunt, Jesse and Frank James, John Koger, and George Maddox rode to Lathrop Bullene's residence, inquiring for food. Bullene's home was situated in the middle of town at 732 New Hampshire Street. Besides owning a dry goods store in town, Bullene owned three valuable horses of unknown origin, which were seized by the guerrillas. Bullene came from New York and in 1858 was elected to the Lawrence City Council. He was not home at the time of the raid, being in New York buying store goods, but his wife and children were home. Bullene's house was slated to be destroyed, but after Mrs. Bullene served breakfast for Captain Todd and his men, Todd promised that her home would be spared and that it would be protected. She handed the men the results of the previous day's baking: pies, bread, and cake accompanied with pans of milk for the thirsty guerrillas. Sixteen-year-old William S. Bullene kept a pistol in his boot, which his mother took away from him several times, fearing that he might get caught with it on his person and be injured. Mrs. Bullene recounted, "Imagine my terror until the others assured me these were men who would not harm women or children."[26]

Captain Bill Anderson and some of his men obtained breakfast at the home of Private George M. Bromley of the Thirteenth Kansas Jayhawker Regiment. Bromley had been personally recruited by James Lane. Another group of guerrillas stopped by the house of William T. Faxon on Rhode Island Street. They ordered Mrs. Faxon to make coffee, then ordered her to taste it first. After they had eaten and arisen from the table, they attempted to burn the house, but Mrs. Faxon was able to extinguish the flames. Earlier in the day James Faxon had escaped after being shot at by the raiders. He had run to the Bullene home, seeking safety. Faxon was a first lieutenant in the town militia besides being a clerk in Bullene's store. Before leaving town another group of guerrillas stopped at the Bullene home, inquiring for weapons. Mrs. Bullene hid Faxon behind an open door while she invited the guerrillas to help themselves to a large supply of guns and ammunition her husband kept in the closet.[27]

The Search for General Collamore and Other Jayhawkers

While the officers were getting something to eat, a small group of guerrillas rode to the home of General Collamore. Fifty-year-old George W. Collamore from Massachusetts had been the quartermaster general of Kansas under Governor Robinson and was a brigadier general of the state militia. Collamore had left his guns in his office rather than his home during the raid. The guerrillas knew where he lived and wished to prevent any resistance he might naturally initiate. As soon as Collamore looked out his window, he saw that his house was surrounded. He slipped out the back door with his hired man Patrick Keefe and both lowered themselves down a well that was covered by the back ell of his house. The guerrillas entered the house searching for him. Failing to find him, they set the house ablaze and stayed to watch it burn. The guerrillas reasoned that no one could have escaped the flames and lived. Mrs. Collamore stood beside the well talking with her husband until the smoke from the house drove her away. The same smoke that drove away Mrs. Collamore filled the well with deadly fumes and suffocated both men inside.

As soon as he heard pistol shots, Captain Joseph G. Lowe jumped out of bed and ran to turn his horses loose, not wanting the guerrillas to recognize them. Lowe had been an early agitator in the border troubles of 1856 and was a member of the Lawrence militia. When he was captured he gave the Masonic sign of distress and was fortunate enough to be captured by a guerrilla of like persuasion and was allowed to escape.

After the raid Lowe and Colonel Joel Grover came out from their hiding places and assisted in retrieving Collamore's and Keefe's bodies from the well. Lowe insisted on going down the well to help in getting the two men out. Colonel Grover said, "Let us put this rope around your body." Lowe objected and instead took it in his hand. To one question Lowe made reply; to the next he made no answer, and when Grover drew upon the rope it was useless in his hand.[28]

When the guerrillas broke into squads of six or eight, seeking out their selected targets, remembrances of brutal Jayhawker atrocities were brought to mind. George H. Sargent was on the guerrillas' "Death List," and his home was slated to be destroyed. Sargent was in the grocery business with Edwin Smith on the west side of Massachusetts Street near Sixth Street. He had come to Lawrence from Massachusetts with the New England Emigrant Aid Company. Sargent and Smith were downstairs together when the raiders attacked. When they first heard gunshots Smith took refuge in the basement, pulling the trap door shut over his head. Boarding with Sargent were two other wanted men who were upstairs at the time. Among them were Charles A. Palmer and Private Samuel Young. Palmer had come to Lawrence from Massachusetts with his two brothers, Barnabas and Nathan, and his father, Daniel W. Palmer.

When he wasn't engaged as a Jayhawker, Charles Palmer held a job as a printer in one of Lawrence's newspaper offices. As Palmer attempted to run from Sargent's house, he was fired at by several guerrillas. When they saw him fall, they presumed he was dead. He was never hit but was badly burned from attempting to lie motionless as

Major John A. Halderman was from Lawrence and fought against Quantrill early in the war at the battle of Wilson's Creek, Missouri. (Kansas State Historical Society)

the flames destroyed the structure close by. Samuel Young was a private in Company K, Eleventh Kansas Jayhawker Regiment, the regiment that served as prison guards over the slain girls in Kansas City.

The guerrillas entered Sargent's house confronted by the men's wives. The male occupants were upstairs and were afraid to come down. The guerrillas did not venture to go up and look for them. Instead they entreated the women to have the men come down, saying the house was slated to be burned. They promised that the men would not be harmed. When the men did comply, they were ushered out the back of the house into the rear lot and were not harmed. After this incident, the guerrillas readied the house for destruction, assisting the women in removing their valuables, furniture, and a heavy piano. While the men were being guarded in the rear lot, another group of guerrillas rode up and began shooting. Sargent was shot first while his wife was begging for his life. The guerrillas next turned and shot Samuel Young. Though only wounded, Young feigned death, and while the house was burning the women dragged his body away from the flames. Smith came out from hiding and helped Mrs. Sargent drag her husband's body through the weeds to the shelter of the brush on the riverbank, where they remained until the guerrillas departed. Sargent lived for eleven days before succumbing to his wounds.

Daniel Palmer owned a gun shop just south of town. He was often in trouble with the law, having recently been arrested for assault and battery. His son Barnabas was a first sergeant in Lane's Brigade and had been with Lane during the destruction of Osceola, Missouri. Daniel Palmer and his hired man fired on the guerrillas from the store as they rode past. Both men were wounded in the exchange. Their shop was set on fire, and the two wounded men, unable to escape, were burned up inside the building. No wounded men were thrown back into burning buildings as some claimed, but some victims attempted to crawl away from the flames and were shot a second time and as a result were burned beyond recognition. One eyewitness stated, "The noise and confusion were horrible; a crossfire was kept up from windows and doors, until the falling roofs buried the miserable wretches in a fiery grave."[29]

The Continued Search for "Wanted Men"

The guerrillas continued moving systematically from house to house, checking for names on their "Death Lists." Those caught running through the streets were considered militia members hurrying to arm themselves and form companies. The smell of powder smoke pervaded the air mingled with the smoke from burning stores and houses. The scene was horrible to every eye but those of the guerrillas. "Their own homes had been sacked and burned, their own wives and children turned out, homeless wanderers, and often times insulted, abused and killed outright. But now a sudden vengeance is visited upon the guilty thieves of Lawrence, its Red Legs are made to feel the smart of their own work."[30]

As squads of raiders were dividing up and searching houses for wanted men, some of those they were seeking miraculously managed to escape. James F. Legate took his pistol and succeeded in making it to the river and swimming to safety on the other side, but not before being shot at numerous times by the guerrillas. Legate had taken an early part in free-state politics and owed his job as the United States assessor to the patronage of James Lane. Legate eventually made his way into Leavenworth and headed straight for Charles Jennison with the news of the raid. It was Legate who started the rumor that the guerrillas were killing everyone and burning everything in sight, when in fact they were

Captain Sidney F. Clarke was a member of James Lane's inner circle, being his political secretary while also serving as the adjutant general of the Lawrence militia. Under Clarke's tutelage the Kansas Redlegs came into being. Noted for indiscriminately robbing and killing both Southern and Northern sympathizers, the Redlegs' numerous murdering and thieving expeditions became impossible to control. (Armand DeGregoris Collection)

being very discriminatory by using their "Death Lists" and their lists of "Buildings to be Destroyed."

Captain Sidney F. Clarke, the assistant provost marshal general, was at home at the house of his father-in-law Major Edmund Gibson Ross. Clarke was Lane's political secretary and was another one of the most wanted men on Quantrill's list. At the start of the war he was with Lane in Washington, DC, planning to capture Robert E. Lee. Clarke was Lane's closest confidant and due to Lane's patronage was appointed to his position as assistant provost marshal of Kansas in June 1863.

Upon arriving in Lawrence he immediately joined the radical wing of the Free State Party and was elected to the Kansas legislature. With Lane's blessing Clarke had a free hand in hiring "detectives" for the military departments of Kansas, Nebraska, and Colorado. He soon appointed George Hoyt, the Redleg chieftain, as a "detective," giving him extra legal authority. In turn Hoyt appointed the most vicious Redlegs, Jack Bridges and John W. Blatchly, as his deputies. Able C. Wilder, another Lane crony, encouraged Clarke to appoint only men who would be "true to us," a veiled referral that they would share the profits of their stolen merchandise with them. Evidence showed up in a letter to Clarke requesting that Bridges be given "detective papers" and assuring Clarke that if he did as requested, Bridges would "share liberally with his friends."

Clarke lived in the 1,000 block of Tennessee Street with his wife, Henrietta, and two small sons. After hearing gunfire, Clarke tore off his uniform and tried to make for Lane's house to warn him, but when pursued and fired at he managed to get over the brow of a hill before he could be captured. His house was destroyed, burning up his military uniform and government papers. Clarke's congressional career soon ended in controversy. He was suspected of corruption and lost his bid for reelection.[31]

Clarke's father-in-law, Major Ross of Company E, Eleventh Kansas Jayhawker Regiment, was in charge of two military companies stationed in Lawrence. Ross assisted in raising the Eleventh Kansas Infantry in 1862, and at the organization of the regiment was elected captain of one of the companies. Subsequently, Governor Carney appointed him major of the regiment when it was changed from infantry to cavalry. Ross was present with his command in all the battles in which it was engaged. His men were bivouacked in tents across the Kansas River, while Ross enjoyed the comfort of his own home on the south side of the river. When Ross first heard firing in town he was able to load his gun but soon realized the futility of resistance. As he was running away, a young man running beside him was killed on the road. Ross's comrade-in-arms was Private John G. Anderson from Sweden who belonged to Company M, in the Eleventh Kansas Jayhawker Regiment.

Lawrence citizen Lillian Leis commented about Ross and his military unit. She expressed her disdain for the wanton use of alcohol by the soldiers in town. "Sometime since, Captain Ross the commandant of Lawrence closed the liquor shops. On the pledge of the owners not to sell to soldiers, he permitted them to resume business. Instead of fulfilling their promises, they sold to soldiers that were passing through town and allowed them to get drunk on the premises. He would do the State a greater service if he would destroy all the liquor within its limits than he could possibly do with his Kansas company fighting rebels." Richard Cordley also commented about the unruly environment in Lawrence. "As the town grew, wild and restless spirits came in, and several saloons were kept in full blast."

Arthur Spicer had earlier been arrested for keeping his saloon open after hours. Matilda Wiedemann said, "It was no uncommon sight in those times to see men lying about in a drunken stupor." Erastus Ladd, an attorney in Lawrence, made a statement following the raid that criminal activity ceased after the guerrillas' raid due to the fact that the raiders had destroyed all the liquor shops, thus eliminating violations of law and order, and that when the raiders took the money from the stores and banks, there were no robberies.[32]

Dr. L. Kellogg, who had come to Lawrence with the New England Emigrant Aid Company, was seized during the raid by the guerrillas and ordered to identify houses on their lists. After several hours of being in the company of the raiders he was released unharmed. As the guerrillas continued searching individual houses for wanted men, one of the first they sought out was that of Edward P. Fitch, who was living at 929 Connecticut Street. Fitch had come to Lawrence with an armed company of the New England Emigrant Aid Society. He was a member of Lawrence's home guard and had been in the Kansas militia during the Wakarusa War, becoming one of the more well-known troublemakers. Before the war he was responsible for pushing proslavery men off their claims and had also served as a conductor on the Underground Railroad. Guerrillas entered his parlor prepared to burn the house. One guerrilla who appeared to be an officer yelled a command at the others, "Let the women and children go." Fitch was hiding upstairs but appeared when the house started to burn. As soon as a guerrilla spied him, Fitch was shot. With the house in flames Sarah Fitch begged to retrieve her husband's body, but because of the danger she was refused. Mrs. Fitch remarked afterward, "The guerrillas marked their victims especially the members of the Independent Company and had a list of the company."[33]

Special Targets on the "Death Lists"

A special target on the raiders' "Death List" was Judge Samuel A. Riggs. Riggs had been prosecuting attorney of Douglas County from 1859 through 1860. Before the war he had issued spurious warrants against Quantrill for horse stealing and kidnapping. The warrants were put into the hands of Sheriff Samuel Walker, who attempted to arrest Quantrill. Riggs was in the town's militia and kept a musket in his dining room. He also owned a large quantity of gunpowder at the edge of town used by the military. When he realized that Quantrill had control of the town, he hid the musket in his basement.

Guerrilla James Noland encountered Riggs in front of his house and, after questioning him and finding his name on his "Death List," drew his revolver and attempted to shoot him. Riggs knocked the gun aside and started to run. Mrs. Riggs standing next to her husband seized the reins of Noland's horse, causing it to flare up, deflecting his aim. Noland tried to ignore Mrs. Riggs while attempting to follow her husband. As Riggs ran around the corner of his house, Noland followed him with Mrs. Riggs still clinging to his horse's bridle. Because Quantrill had issued orders not to harm any women in town, Mrs. Riggs was able to save her husband's life, giving him time to escape. Riggs' house at 937 Rhode Island Street was later burned.[34]

Another judge on the guerrillas' list was Judge Louis Carpenter of Douglas County. He lived in the 900 block of New Hampshire Street. It was a probability that Carpenter was a collaborator in Quantrill's unwarranted arrest in 1860 on trumped-up charges brought by his enemies. At noon the day before the raid, Carpenter came home and said, incidentally, "There is a story on the street that Quantrill is coming to Lawrence to destroy it, as he has so long threatened to do. But," he added, "we have had so many reports of that kind no one believes them." He confidentially asserted, "It would be impossible for him to get here with his band without our being reliably notified." Carpenter was an active member of the militia but was unable to join his company as the guerrillas quickly surrounded his house. Raiders halted Carpenter while consulting their "Death List." While they were checking for his name, Carpenter attempted to run and was killed as he tried to escape.

The raid almost spelled ruin for John Speer. He had first arrived in Lawrence on September 27, 1854. Speer was editor of the *Lawrence Republican* newspaper on the opposite corner from the Eldridge House Hotel, and it was no coincidence that this was the first building to be destroyed. His three sons slept downtown. Besides the material loss, two of his sons were killed during the raid. Speer lived on the outskirts of town where his house was used as a station on the Underground Railroad. While the raiders were pillaging the business portion of the town first, Speer was able to escape to a cornfield, where despite being in the town militia he remained concealed until the raid was over. Speer became Lane's hireling after being set up in the newspaper business in order to engage the paper to promote Lane politically. Speer also became the collector of internal revenue for the state of Kansas due to Lane's patronage. A colleague of Speer's wrote, "He was brave and forceful and always willing to submerge his own interests in furthering those of his friend Jim Lane."[35]

As a matter of fact, Speer printed such inflammatory articles that it made him one of the most wanted men on the guerrillas' list. An example is the piece in the June 19, 1861, *Lawrence Republican* in which he wrote: "Is it not time that some stringent measures were adopted in the treatment of our 'misguided brethren' of Missouri? A few cases of hanging, judiciously administered would do much toward curing the secession disease in that quarter. Let them be treated as outlaws in all cases and hanged or shot immediately when captured." The raiders confiscated Speer's horses and set fire to his house after helping the family drag a heavy sofa from the flames. Mrs. Speer and her children were able to put out the fire and save the building. A few years earlier, Mrs. Speer had exhibited her contempt for the law when U.S. Deputy Marshal Samuel Salters came to her house searching for Samuel N. Wood to serve a warrant for his arrest. She threw a dipperful of water in his face, screaming at him for entering her house. When the sheriff finally found Wood he was in the company of John Speer and James Abbot. Speer wrestled Salters to the ground while Wood grabbed the officer's revolver and Abbot beat the lawman into unconsciousness.

The next newspaper office to be destroyed was the *Lawrence Tribune*. Sleeping inside was Colonel Marcellus M. Murdock, an officer in the local militia, along with two other printers, one of them nineteen-year-old John Speer, Jr. Before the building was engulfed in flames, the first two men hid in the drain well in the cellar of an adjoining building and escaped. A passing guerrilla spied John Speer, Jr., running out the back door. He was stopped and his money demanded. After he handed over his pocketbook his identity was checked against the guerrillas' list. When his name was found, he was immediately shot down. While the *Lawrence Republican* newspaper office was being engulfed in flames, eighteen-year-old Private Robert Speer and David Purington were sleeping in the rear. The building was completely destroyed, and no trace of the bodies of the two men was ever found.

William Speer slept with fellow clerk Charles Prentiss in the liquor store owned by Corporal Albert Winchell. When they realized the guerrillas were upon them, they loaded a rifle kept in the store by Winchell as his part in the Lawrence militia, but soon abandoned the weapon and ran out the back door and hid under the building. They were forced to seek another place of refuge when the guerrillas poured out the whiskey, which was running through the floor over them as the building was set on fire. William Speer was accosted but gave a fictitious name when the guerrillas checked their "Death List." His name was undoubtedly included because of his father's reputation as a Lane supporter. He was told to hold a horse for one of the guerrillas. As the buildings around them were being set on fire a bystander yelled to those nearby, "There are bombs in one of those buildings!" The citizens scattered, and Speer managed to escape to the ravine west of town.[36]

Citizens later wrote that many guerrillas were drunk during the raid when in fact it was only their fighting blood that was up and in their anger they appeared less rational. While in town the guerrillas destroyed all the liquor shops, including the one owned by brothers James and Joseph Brechtlesbauer. One squad of guerrillas paid a visit to the home of Private John W. Thornton. Thornton heard the guerrillas enter town firing their weapons and decided to stay indoors. Only when his house was set on fire did he attempt to run outside. Guerrillas fired at him, hitting him several times in the hips, but still he attempted to flee. Another ball struck him in the back, exiting through his side where he fell unable to move. His wife ran to him, covering his body with her own. Another guerrilla managed to fire another shot, the ball grazing Thornton's cheek. When Mrs. Thornton cried and held up her hands for mercy, the guerrillas finally left, believing that Thornton was as good as dead. Fortunately, he recovered from his wounds and lived for many years afterward.

Thornton's neighbor Private James Murphy had been in Lane's Brigade during the destruction of Osceola, Missouri. He was shot as he ran out of his house. When Private Dan Thornton of the Fourteenth Kansas Jayhawker Regiment saw the carnage taking place around him, he crawled underneath his barn and escaped being seen by the guerrillas. Thornton said he saw the features of the two James boys, and they were indelibly photographed upon his mind.[37]

Another citizen who recognized Jesse James as being in the raid was Mrs. Ana Boettler. Mrs. Boettler remembered that "Jesse James, then a beardless boy of 16, was with the gang. I was living with a woman named Stephens, whose husband was a federal soldier. Jesse James and three or four others of the gang invaded the house with the avowed purpose of killing Stephens." Another eyewitness stated that Jesse at Lawrence "was but a boy of sixteen, but he boasted of having killed thirteen men in Lawrence."[38]

As the actual assault slowed to a house-to-house search, many quick-minded individuals managed to duck out of town unobserved. Although many "wanted men" managed to hide or escape, the guerrillas were still able to kill a score of militiamen and Jayhawkers. Richard Cordley, an outspoken abolitionist preacher, lived in a stone house just south of the city limits at 812 New York Street. He had been warned as soon as the guerrillas appeared and made his escape to the river where he hid along the banks. Cordley was wanted because he had held religious services for the Negroes and for being one of the conductors on the Underground Railroad and harboring runaway slaves on his property.[39] The guerrillas searched for Cordley, repeatedly asking for that "negro harborer." For his actions in violating the Fugitive Slave Law, Cordley's house was burned.

Two of the most radical abolitionists stayed with Cordley while they were in Lawrence. Lewis and Sherman Bodwell had traveled from Connecticut in 1856, attaching themselves to an early emigrant aid company to come to Kansas and fight for the cause of abolitionism. They were arrested by the United States marshal on their way to Kansas for inciting rebellion but were later released. Lewis Bodwell, a preacher like Cordley, was from Topeka. He was described as "retaining all the force and firmness of his Puritan ancestry."[40]

Lewis was responsible for escorting John Brown out of Kansas as he made his escape toward Virginia and Harper's Ferry infamy. Both brothers had taken part in the early border troubles. Lewis first enlisted in the First Kansas Regiment, and his brother Sherman enlisted with the Second Kansas, fighting at Wilson's Creek before setting his sights on the more enterprising Jayhawker unit of the Eleventh Kansas Regiment, eventually becoming a sergeant. Sherman's most disreputable experience was riding in a punitive Jayhawking expedition in Jackson County.

A little over a month before, on July 13, 1863, an elderly widow by the name of Holly, who was living around Independence, was discovered warning her neighbors of the approach of the Jayhawkers, giving them time to hide their valuables. For her audacity the Jayhawkers burned down her home, leaving her destitute. While in the neighborhood Bodwell's platoon questioned thirty-three-year-old Charles B. Alderman, the sole provider for three small children. Sensing that Alderman was not a Northern sympathizer, the marauders reported that he was shot "trying to escape," the usual explanation for executed prisoners. It was Bodwell's regiment that served as the prison guards for the murdered Southern girls in Kansas City. Neither Lewis Bodwell nor Richard Cordley was harmed during the raid on Lawrence. Both escaped into the timber along the riverbank after running for over a half-mile. A boat was hailed and came over, taking them across the river to safety.

One of Lewis Bodwell's acquaintances was Corporal Charles Schmidt of the Eleventh Kansas Regiment. Schmidt was an anarchist in Germany when he was forced to flee the country after taking part in the 1848 revolution. Bodwell remembered him as an atheist. Schmidt was discovered during the raid and killed.

Jayhawker Plunder in "Innocent" Lawrence

Stolen Missouri property that had not yet been auctioned off was kept in makeshift warehouses located in the southern portion of the main town. The structures were more like shanties with walls built of hay and a rough board roof to keep the items safe from the weather until sold. Runaway slaves from Missouri were given the job of guarding the stolen loot until a sale could be arranged. Cole

Younger recalled: "The camp contained thousands and thousands of dollars worth of pianos and carpets and old mahogany furniture and silver-plate that had been stripped from the homes of Southern sympathizers. We set fire to the tents and burned the camp from end to end with all its contents." As he rode past these crude structures, Lieutenant William Gregg recognized much of the stolen goods. He commented that the amount of plunder was staggering. Gregg estimated that there was more Missouri property in Lawrence than Kansas property. Gregg recounted:

> When the order was given to burn, I repaired to the southern portion of the main town, where I found about forty shanties, built, three sides board, the fourth a hay stack and covered with hay. All of these shacks were filled with household effects stolen from Missouri. Many we recognized, many of these had feather beds, quilts, blankets etc. stacked in there higher than I could reach. Five bedsteads, bureaus, sideboards, bookcases and pianos that cost thousands of dollars, many of these shacks were in charge of negro women, many of whom we recognized that had been run off from their owners in Missouri. We went among the shacks touching matches to hay. It is stated that we destroyed property in Lawrence worth $1,500,000. I don't know about that. I have always contended that the fires we started that morning destroyed as much property that had belonged to Jackson County people as that belonging to the citizens of Lawrence.[41]

There had always been a sizable criminal element in Lawrence. With the large amount of plunder that made its way into the city, every citizen was in possession of some purloined item from their Missouri neighbors, from the bedding they slept on, to the furniture in their parlors, to the farm implements they used in their fields, to women's silk dresses that were worn by Lawrence ladies and later recognized by the raiders. All of these items were bought for a bargain at weekly auctions on the street corners of the town.

Early in the war the *Lawrence State Journal* commented on its citizen's thievery. "Can anyone tell how it is that virtuous young women, who have poor ancestors on the male side, poor brothers, and are definitely poor themselves, arrange it to dress in silks, and never wear the same dress twice at sociables? Can anyone tell how men live and support their families, who have no income and don't work, and why others who are industrious and constantly employed, half starve?" The answer was simple enough. Items were procured by Jayhawkers or acquired at local street auctions. The auctions were usually held on Saturday in order to give the farmers in the surrounding countryside time to come in and look over the stolen merchandise. The plunder arrived almost daily from the different Jayhawker units that returned from plundering Missouri farms. Erastus Ladd said, "More than one anti-slavery raiding party had its origin in the town, and more than one Lawrence family possessed articles of dress, furniture, and livestock which could be characterized by but one word, loot."[42]

Richard Cordley admitted that Lawrence had prospered during the war because of the Jayhawkers' expeditions into Missouri. Cordley's fellow citizen Hiram Towne agreed. "Before this disaster, everything was going on as well as anyone could wish, everybody making money and the city building up very fast."[43] Commenting on the people of Lawrence, historian Albert Castel said that they were "either unable to drive these bandits out or were indifferent to their presence," and fellow author Lucien Carr called Lawrence a "mere fence-house for stolen property" once owned by Missourians.[44]

The enormity of the plunder staggered the imagination. Quantrill realized that there was no way to return such a huge amount of property to its rightful owners so he ordered it burned to keep it from being used by the people of Lawrence who acquiesced in its theft. It was a lucrative market. Many a Jayhawker became wealthy seemingly overnight from this nefarious traffic. Jennison stole so many pure-bred Missouri horses on his Jayhawker raids that when they were sold it was boasted that their bloodline was "from Jennison out of Missouri." James Lane got his cut of the profits from anything stolen by the Lane Brigade. Noted Redleg leader George Hoyt who kept his headquarters in Lawrence was known to live a life of leisure from the ill-gotten gains he made off the sale of stolen Missouri property.

Besides the vast amount of plunder that was kept in storage a great deal was also discovered in individual homes when they were searched by the guerrillas. Almost every house and building had some evidence of stolen property taken from Missouri. When each man among the guerrillas remembered how their own homes had been plundered by these Lawrence Jayhawkers and now they were witnessing the amount of plunder before their eyes, it only heightened their anger. They knew firsthand the devastating experiences of a Jayhawker raid. During such encounters nothing was overlooked that would benefit the Kansans' covetous yearnings for Missouri property. Gravestones that had once served to honor lost loved ones were carried back to Kansas and used for porch steps. When these stones were turned over and recognized by the raiders, it was an instant death sentence for those living nearby.

A large amount of the plunder stolen from Missouri was "on the hoof." Horses, mules, cattle, sheep, hogs, and oxen had been herded back across the border for years. During the raid citizens who had personally stolen or purchased stolen horses from the Jayhawkers were anxious to turn the animals out of their barns before they could be recognized. Evidence of this fact was seen as Lieutenant Hugh Dunn Fisher, chaplain of the Fifth Kansas Jayhawker Regiment, jumped from his supposed sickbed and ran to turn his horse out of his farm lot to keep it from being recognized by the guerrillas. His name was on the guerrillas' "Death List." If nothing else, this discovery alone would have guaranteed his destruction. Orders had been issued to kill him and under no circumstances to allow him to escape. Spies had been watching his house all night, and they knew Fisher was home in the evening and could not have gone away. His illness must not have been as serious as he had been letting on. After turning his horses loose, he ran to his cellar and hid in fear for his life. Fisher's two sons ran from the house and made for shelter in the nearby brush. The guerrillas allowed them to escape. Willie Fisher ran into militiaman Robert Martin who was already in uniform and carrying his rifle and cartridge box slung over his shoulder. When spotted by a squad of guerrillas, Martin was killed. Fisher was not harmed.[45]

Ironically, on a meager soldier's salary Fisher had just completed building one of the finest brick residences in Lawrence. For years before the war the Reverend Mr. Fisher had been one of the leaders in the free-state movement in Kansas. "He preached anti-slavery from the Methodist pulpits of Leavenworth and Lawrence until he incurred the thorough hatred of the proslavery element in Kansas and Missouri." Lawrence citizen Lawrence D. Bailey said that Fisher "was an ardent hater of slavery and entered upon his duties with zeal and efficiency." Fisher had taken a slave family of seven out of a steamboat load of slaves at St. Louis and brought them back to his home to live on his farm.[46] Especially due to Fisher the Methodist church in Lawrence was burned during the raid. It was this church that was adorned mainly with furniture and ornaments stolen from Missouri. Though made of stone, the interior was gutted by the flames.

During his Jayhawker raids Fisher advised Missouri Negroes to take the property of their white owners. Lawrence D. Bailey remembered, "In many cases he had advised the negroes to help themselves to the abandoned property of their rebel masters, and many a good span of mules or horses with wagon attached came out loaded with fugitive families, their bed and bedding and such poor remnants of food and furniture as they could get on short notice."[47] When the stolen property arrived in Lawrence, most of it was confiscated by the Jayhawkers under the dubious logic that the fugitives could not prove ownership. To Missourians, Fisher's actions were simply those of a criminal bent on plundering for his own selfish greed. To Fisher and those like him, it was simply explained as "liberating enemy property."

Quantrill's men were also anxious to get Fisher because he was one of the prime operators in harboring and organizing escaped slaves. Fisher was not only hated by Missourians but also by those in Lawrence who also didn't hold him in high esteem. He claimed the role of hero in nearly every skirmish and border dispute in which he was engaged. He was frequently in difficulty with his fellow clergymen, was a user of tobacco, which was in violation of the Methodist Episcopal Church Conference rules, was accused of mishandling and stealing church funds, and was not infrequently cited as a fraud and a liar.[48]

When the guerrillas went to Fisher's house, they found his family upstairs but did not find Fisher who had hid himself behind a pile of dirt in his unfinished cellar. Fisher himself stated: "Hardly had I secreted myself before four men, armed with revolvers, Jesse James leading the gang, ran into the house and, with oaths, demanded to know of my wife where I was hidden. Finally one of them seized a lamp, and they descended into the cellar, revolvers in hand, with orders to kill me on sight. Several times they were within a foot of me, but almost miraculously I escaped their search. Enraged at their failure, they went back upstairs and set fire to the house in seven places."[49] As the flames overtook the house, Mrs. Fisher poured water over the floor beneath which her husband lay hiding. As the guerrillas withdrew a short distance away and watched the flames engulf the house, Mrs. Fisher had her husband roll himself up in a carpet which she dragged from the building. Thinking it was just an excited woman trying to save some of her property, the guerrillas failed to notice that their quarry had escaped his just due.

Others were not as fortunate as Fisher. As the guerrillas chased wanted men through the town, many were seen to run into burning buildings to avoid being shot down in the streets and wound up being burned alive in the flames. Joseph W. Shultz, a Lawrence citizen, verified reports that many men were chased into the infernos of blazing buildings. In one instance Shultz's parents saw men chased into the burning carriage factory across the street from their home.[50]

Places of Refuge from the Raiders

To maintain maximum command and control over his men, Quantrill ordered them to keep their activities within the city limits. Therefore residents living on the outskirts of town were relatively safe, thinking the guerrillas were afraid of coming near their homes. Also to minimize losses Quantrill insisted that his men avoid places that might cause undue casualties. There was a deep ravine, wooded but narrow, covered with thickets and overgrown with underbrush, running almost through the center of the town. It was substantial enough to have a bridge built over it. Into this ravine many citizens escaped. Many of the militia, finding it impossible to reach the armory, tried to hide out there. The guerrillas often chased men into the ravine, shooting at them all the way, but did not follow them into the ravine itself. The only house searched near the ravine was that of Private John Read.

Another place avoided was a large cornfield on the west side of town where hundreds of men, women, and children sought safety. The cornfield soon filled with refugees fleeing the devastation of the killing in town. The guerrillas could have easily burned the field, but knowing there were women and children hiding inside, they declined to do so. The guerrillas knew many men had run into the cornfield carrying their weapons with them. They had no way of knowing just how many guns were hidden between the rows of corn. A sniper merely had to take a shot, move over a row or two, and be completely secreted from the raiders.

Lemuel Fillmore lived near the ravine. Hovey Lowman said Fillmore had ample time to escape, but instead at the first signs of firing he grabbed his pistols and was making his way to the militia rendezvous when he was surrounded by guerrillas and shot. Some wanted men who were not able to make it to the safety in the tall weeds of the ravine were able to hide in a little-known cyclone cellar in the center of town. Its entrance was almost totally hidden from view, and there several of them were able to seek shelter from the vengeance of the guerrillas.

An especially wanted man was First Lieutenant Abraham A. Ellis. He was a quartermaster in Lane's Brigade and had been at the sacking of Osceola, Missouri. When not serving in Company D of the Fifteenth Kansas Jayhawker Regiment, he spent time in his blacksmith shop in town. Though there were no eyewitnesses to the story, it was said that Ellis grabbed up his small child and hid in a nearby cornfield and would have escaped detection except that when the child started to cry Ellis was discovered and killed. Ellis's comrade-in-arms in the Fifteenth Kansas Regiment, John Z. Evans, was also found and killed. A counterpart of Abraham Ellis was Paul R. Brooks. He was one of the first persons sought. He had been the quartermaster of the Third Kansas Jayhawker Regiment in Lane's Brigade and had also taken part in the destruction of Osceola. Brooks owned a boot and shoe store on Massachusetts Street and a home on Kentucky Street, but fortunately he was visiting in Maine on the morning of the raid and escaped retribution although his store and all of its contents were destroyed. It was said that when he first arrived in Lawrence he "did not come to Kansas to save the territory, but to follow Horace Greeley's advice and the saving of it occurred to him after he arrived."

Another wanted man who thought it best not to be taken prisoner was William Hazeltine. Hazeltine owned a grocery business and bakery in town. Known as a radical abolitionist and "an active and zealous and energetic hater of Missourians," his name was naturally to be found on the guerrillas' "Death List." He had come to Lawrence with Sam Walker and the Ohio Emigrant Aid Society. Upon hearing the firing in town, Hazeltine bolted out his back door and made for the ravine just west of Vermont Street. He was pursued by a number of guerrillas who fired several shots his way. Just as he reached the edge of the ravine he tripped and fell down. The guerrillas assumed they had shot him and gave up the chase.

Other wanted men managed to escaped in whatever hiding places they could find. Sheriff Sam Brown hid beneath the floorboards of his house. He had served both in the militia and in various Jayhawker units. Three times the guerrillas set his house on fire, but each time Brown's wife successfully extinguished the flames.

Another house slated to be burned was that of Gurdon Grovenor. Grovenor had come to Kansas with the New England Emigrant Aid Company and had soon established a grocery business in town. It was said that he came to Kansas and "entered the border war with religious zeal." Grovenor's name was on the guerrillas' "Death List," and his house located in the 800 block of Massachusetts Street was listed as one of those "buildings to be destroyed." Grovenor was in demand as a speaker on what he termed the "evils of slavery" and the "shameless devils from Missouri." Grovenor's wife said that her husband was as much detested by the Missouri secessionists as was Jim Lane, commander of the red-trousered Kansas militia. Grovenor knew he could expect no mercy from the guerrillas. Before the guerrillas arrived at their house, Mrs. Grovenor made her husband get in the well, which she covered with the wooden cover just before three guerrillas stepped up to their front porch. One smashed in one of the front windows with the butt of a musket. After Mrs. Grovenor opened the door they proceeded to ransack the house then set it on fire in several places but left without molesting anyone.

Another contingent of guerrillas soon arrived. At their head rode a man wearing a red canna blossom in the band of his broad-brimmed hat. Mrs. Grovenor seized the bridle of the man's horse, demanding that he order his men out of her house. He removed his hat, bowed, and said, "William Quantrill, at your service, Mrs. Grovenor." "Fiddlesticks!" she snapped. "I know you, Charlie Hart!" "Is your husband home?" asked Quantrill. "I give you my word he is not in the house," she said. "You would never tell a lie," responded the gallant commander. Still seated on his horse Quantrill ordered his men to put out the fire and bring out the furniture. They obeyed. The furniture was carried from the house and the flames were beaten out before much damage was done. Before he left, Mrs. Grovenor gave Quantrill a piece of her tongue. "You should be ashamed. You stole that canna flower in your hat. The bulb was brought all the way from Massachusetts by my neighbor. She planted it in her yard, and you stole it!" With a smile on his lips Quantrill simply replied, "Such is the fortunes of war."

Shortly afterward, Captain Bill Anderson rode up and asked Mrs. Grovenor where her husband was. She replied that he had been taken prisoner. Satisfied at her answer, Anderson directed that the house be burned. Mrs. Grovenor pleaded with Anderson to spare the house as it was the only property she had. Her pleadings seemed to spark a cord inside the guerrilla leader. Before riding off, Anderson promised her that her house would not be burned. About an hour later, another party, under a different leader, came and seemed resolved to burn the house at all costs. For a long time Mrs. Grovenor talked in vain. At last she told the leader about the other party that had been there, described the leader of it so that he was recognized, and said that man had sworn that her house would not be molested. The leader of the second gang seemed very much surprised at her statement but seemed convinced of its truth by the full description she gave of the leader. He burst out with the remark; "If Bill Anderson spared your house, I should be ashamed to burn it!" and left with his whole party without another word. Anderson's vengeance must have been quelled by the time he rode away from Grovenor's house. Anderson claimed to have killed fourteen men. An old comrade of Anderson's said of him, "They claim for him such coolness under fire that he could strike any button on a man's coat that he wanted to." His comrade Jim Cummins recalled seeing him "in the dust and smoke fighting and cursing louder than any man I ever heard."[51]

Anderson had his own "Death List" with names that were important to him. One was that of William Edward Monroe of the Ninth Kansas Jayhawker Regiment. Monroe was responsible for arresting Bill Anderson's sisters in Kansas City, where one was killed in the jail collapse. When Anderson rode up to Monroe's house, all he found inside was Monroe's wife and two small sons. Corporal Monroe was away on a Jayhawker expedition. When Anderson asked for him specifically, a German neighbor woman told him the Monroes had moved out of the state. That was a convenient lie that proved fortunate for the Monroes since their house was not destroyed.[52]

Like the name Monroe on Anderson's personal "Death List," a name on Quantrill's personal "Death List" was John M. Dean, whom he knew before the war. Dean was in business with Ralph Dix and had a wagon shop located on Vermont Street. Dean was an early troublemaker who loaned his wagons to his fellow Jayhawkers to carry plunder out of Missouri. At the time of the Lawrence raid, Dean was the first sergeant of Company F of the First Kansas Regiment. Known as an active agent on the Underground Railroad, Dean was described as "a pompous, windy, shallow man who really believed in abolition." It was Dean who shot and killed Negro Alan Pinks before the war but was never prosecuted. Dean was able to escape, but his house was burned by a detail of four guerrillas.[53]

General George W. Deitzler was staying in the house of Governor Charles Robinson located on the far side of town, the last in the row on the west side of Massachusetts Street. Deitzler owned 160 acres one mile west of Lawrence but was on sick furlough. Deitzler had always been worried about an administration controlled by the likes of Lane and through his personal experiences had come to be his staunch enemy. Deitzler was the early leader of the Lawrence militia. He had been indicted in 1856 for treason for writing inflammatory newspaper articles. Quantrill had been acquainted with him when they fought against each other at the battle of Wilson's Creek when Deitzler was in command of the First Kansas Regiment. Members of the First Kansas were described at the time as "raw and undisciplined" troops. The regiment "robbed or plundered all, or nearly so, the farmers within a circle of five miles from their camp."[54] After being routed at Wilson's Creek by the Confederates, Deitzler's men retreated through Springfield but

General George W. Deitzler commanded the First Kansas Infantry Regiment during the battle of Wilson's Creek in Missouri. In 1863 Deitzler received a commission as a major general of Kansas militia. (Douglas County Historical Society)

not before taking the time to plunder the Springfield bank of $250,000. The guerrillas would have been able to capture two of the most wanted men at Governor Robinson's house, but Robinson was not at home and Deitzler managed to escape.

Robinson owned two farms; one of several thousand acres lay across the river. Before the raiders entered town he had gone to his barn at his Lawrence farm located on Mount Oread to take his horses to his hired man John Mack who needed them for haying. Robinson's barn on Mount Oread defied description. It was made of stone built into the side of the hill and was three stories tall. From the upper story it was possible to walk out onto the top of Mount Oread. The entire farm was surrounded by a stone wall fence. Robinson had risen early and was in his barn with his colored man Walker Johnson observing the approaching horsemen. Johnson remarked that it might have been Captain Earle's militia company coming in from their patrol, but when the column began firing their weapons they knew who they were. Robinson stayed on Mount Oread and was able to observe the entire raid. Back at the Robinson house, General Deitzler was looking out his bedroom window when a bullet came crashing through. Grabbing his pistol Deitzler immediately headed for the riverbank and hid among the tall grass until the raid was over.

Quantrill's Compassion During the Raid

While wanted men naturally met their fates, there were many instances of compassion during the raid that have been overlooked by historians. Catholic Bishop John B. Miege had just arrived in Lawrence the day before the raid and was staying at the home of Father Sebastian Favre to confirm several new members in town. The church's pastor was awakened by pounding on his door by a Quaker minister and his wife. Favre hid them in the basement of the church along with several others who were seeking refuge. Quantrill rode to the church and confronted Miege, explaining his mission there. After closely scrutinizing the occupants of the room Quantrill ordered his men not to molest those hiding there. The church and the people inside were spared by Quantrill's orders.

Normally Captain John Jarrette was not known to spare anyone wearing a Federal uniform. During the raid he saved five men who gave him a Masonic sign of recognition. Though wanted men were rarely released, there were many who received mercy from the guerrillas. Richard Cordley recalled: "In some instances they advised men to get out of the way. They burned houses, but were not unnecessarily harsh."[55]

After militiaman Hiram Towne had run away and hid himself in a cornfield west of his house, widow Emily Hoyt who was staying with Towne pleaded with the guerrillas to spare the house, and it was spared. Guerrillas had gone to Hoyt's house looking for Thomas Guest, but he had escaped with Towne. John Newman Edwards said that Cole Younger saved at least a dozen lives during the raid.

> Indeed, he killed none save in open and manly battle. At one house he captured five citizens over whom he put a guard and at another three of whom he defended and protected. Cole Younger had dragged from his hiding place in a closet a very large man who had the asthma. What with his fright and what with his hurry, the poor fellow could not articulate. Younger's pistol was against his heart when his old wife cried out: "For God's sake do not shoot him; he hasn't slept in a bed for nine years!" This appeal and the asthma together, made Younger roar out: "I never intended to harm a hair in his head." James Little took a wounded man away from a guerrilla, who was proceeding to

dispatch him, because the wounded man, in pleading for his life, had the accent of a Southerner. Andy Blunt, because a young girl gave him a cup of excellent coffee, saved her father, and George Shepherd rescued a wounded man and two children from a burning house because one of the children had given him a rose.[56]

Attracted by the boyishness of his face and a look in his blue eyes that seemed so innocent, a young girl came to Jesse James just as he was in the act of shooting a soldier in uniform that had been smoked out of a cellar. His pistol was against the Federal's head when an exceedingly soft and penetrating voice called out to him. "Don't kill him, for my sake. He has eight children who have no mother." James looked and saw a beautiful girl, probably just turned of sixteen, blushing at her boldness and trembling before him. In the presence of so much grace and loveliness he was a disarmed man. James replied, "Take him, he is yours. I would not harm a hair in his head for the State of Kansas."[57]

The guerrillas knew the women of Lawrence had many times joined with the men in the early confrontations and skirmishes and were known for making cartridges day and night for those fighting against the territorial laws and the proslavery party. Mrs. Samuel N. Wood and Mrs. George W. Brown were known to have hidden barrels of gunpowder and lead in order to make bullets for the free-state settlers around Lawrence. But despite this knowledge, many of Quantrill's men continued to show compassion on the women and assisted them in numerous ways.[58]

Lieutenant William Gregg took a squad of men to 744 New Hampshire Street to the house of militiaman Frederick W. Read. Read was a partner in a wholesale and retail dry goods store with William Bullene who undoubtedly sold plundered goods, while Read's barn was full of horses with dubious ownership. As a result, Read's name was on Quantrill's "Death List," and his house was slated to be burned. Upon hearing the firing in town, Read panicked. His wife followed him to the attic and covered him with a pile of bedding. Read had been drilling with his militia company the day before the raid and had left his gun in his store. His business was already in flames and his corncrib was on fire.

Guerrillas entered the house, pocketing jewels and keepsakes.

Gregg asked Mrs. Read where her husband was. She replied that he had gone East to buy goods. Gregg consulted his list and insisted that it was another man who had gone East to buy goods and that her husband had not left town. Mrs. Read then replied, "You seem to be an officer. Look at this house and that burning store and say if you have not punished us enough." Gregg concluded that enough damage had been shown and countermanded the order that Read's house be destroyed; in doing so, he saved Read's life. Gregg felt compassion for Mrs. Read and told his men, "Don't come here again today. This woman has been punished enough."

Gregg remained on the porch of the Read house for over a half-hour, making sure his order was carried out. Richard Cordley, an eyewitness of the raid, remarked: "Others again were as humane as men well could be who came on such an errand. They would allow the women to get out the furniture before they burned the houses, in some cases even helping them to lift heavy articles. In one or two instances they helped women take up the carpets and throw them out." An eyewitness stated, "The guerrillas sometimes expressed regret at the necessity of burning the houses; they were under orders."[59]

The people of Lawrence had long known that Quantrill should be greatly feared. Spy after spy had been sent into the city, and some of them even maintained residences there until the raid. The week prior to the raid, Mrs. Harriet M. Jones, whose house was on Kentucky Street on the hill below Mount Oread, observed a suspicious stranger who asked her husband for a job.

> We learned afterwards that he was a spy. My husband employed him and found that he was an excellent lather [a person who makes laths, wooden strips used in construction]. He worked for us three days and lived in our house. On the morning of the fourth day I went to his room to wake him and found that he had slipped away. We never saw him again until the day of the raid. That morning a man whom we have always thought to be him jumped from his horse just in front of our house and remained there until all the houses in the neighborhood were reduced to ashes. We saw him motion many times to members of this gang who were carrying torches to save the house where we lived.[60]

There were other men in Lawrence who were spared simply because they showed no special malignity toward Missourians in general. One man whose name was never identified escaped because his wife was quick to notice a love of flowers in the leader of the detail assigned to kill her husband. She saw a flower in the squad leader's hat and came out into her yard, which was ablaze with late August blooms. "Good morning," she said. "You've come to see my flowers." It was a surprise counterattack. The guerrilla halted to look about, with apparent enjoyment. "What do you think of them?" she asked. "They're fine ma'am," he said. "They are too pretty to be burned." And he turned to his men, "I'll shoot the man who touches them. March on!"[61]

The raid upon Lawrence was exactly the type of warfare that the Kansans were familiar with perpetuating. They had indiscriminately sacked and burned an untold number of Missouri towns, entirely wiping many off the map. Citizens of Lawrence suffered in a few short hours what the citizens of Missouri had been suffering for more than two years. But unlike Jayhawker raids into Missouri, only the residences and businesses of those outstanding enemies of Missouri and her institutions were being destroyed systematically during the raid. Guerrillas were indeed burning houses but ironically were being polite in the process. Raiders were removing their hats and speaking courteously to the ladies with manners and etiquette unaccustomed in Kansas.

Jayhawkers were used to burning houses and barns and killing all the livestock that couldn't be driven off, shooting the old men and young boys and raping the women and Negro servants. The acts of the men raiding Lawrence were nothing compared to the atrocities committed by the Jayhawkers in Missouri. Retribution for the widows and elderly citizens of Missouri in the guise of Missouri guerrillas came suddenly crashing down on Lawrence citizens because of their past criminal acts. After the raid, guerrilla John A. Workman was asked if he found anyone who confessed to plundering in Missouri. Workman replied, "Don't you know that every mother's son of them denied knowing anything about those deeds."[62]

The guerrillas' intimate knowledge of the town was most beneficial. They knew which buildings contained safes full of cash and valuables. A prosperous jeweler in Lawrence, David Prager, was roused from his bed by a squad of guerrillas and escorted to his store. Afterward, Prager noted that for some unknown reason he had the premonition that he would be spared, which he told his young wife who didn't expect to ever see him again. Prager did not take part in the border troubles and was not in the local militia, so his life was naturally spared. Upon arriving at his store, Prager was commanded to unlock the door. He informed the guerrillas that his hired man Alexander Marks sleeping upstairs with several other employees had the key to the safe. Prager was then ordered to "get home as quickly as you can," an order he hastened to obey. His only losses were his stock of jewelry valued at about $4,000.

Staying with Marks in the same building where they slept over the store was Jacob House and brothers Fred and Charles Eggert, employees in the firm of Duncan and Allison who occupied the same building. Wesley Duncan was a personal friend of James Lane besides being in the Lawrence militia. He was initially detained but escaped when his captors happened to spy a Negro who diverted their attention. Duncan ran to the home of Reverend Herron where both men hid under a bed.

Duncan Allison had decided to spend the night at his place of business since his wife had gone to the country to stay with her mother, Mrs. Benjamin Johnson, whose husband was owner of the Johnson House Hotel. Marks heard the firing of the guerrillas but did not realize the danger. "If we had, we could have made our escape as others did, by going down to the ravine in the brush, and when we did realize the danger, it was too late to escape, so we three remained in our room." The guerrillas rushed upstairs, demanding the key to the safe. Marks went downstairs and opened the safe for them. From the store one guerrilla demanded the best watch Marks had. After Marks handed it to him, he turned and left. Other guerrillas assigned to empty the safe spent their time taking everything from it.

After coming downstairs and seeing the destruction on the street, Marks recognized George Sanger who owned a soap factory in town lying dead in front of William Hazeltine's store. Sanger had been making his way to the militia rendezvous when he was shot down. Marks also discovered that James Eldridge and James Perine next door had been shot. With help from Charles Eggert he carried their bodies out into the street, expecting the building to be burned.[63]

The Conclusion of Quantrill's Mission

Quantrill's mission was coming to a close. At approximately 9:00 a.m. lookouts on Mount Oread reported seeing the dust of what looked like approaching Union troops in the distance, about ten miles away. Quantrill ordered his officers to collect their men and head to the east side of the South Park at approximately the same place they had entered the town. A wild Rebel yell was given as a signal to the guerrillas. The men came riding up, leading extra horses loaded with plunder. Altogether they took about three hundred fresh horses out of Lawrence. Most were to be used as replacements when the guerrillas' mounts gave out. Many men were simply leading them back to Missouri where they had been previously stolen. A few of the men had prudence enough to gather food for themselves for the return trip. Andy Walker said that many went hungry during the two long days in the withdrawal from Lawrence for lack of forethought.

Men assigned to acquire money from the stores and banks rode into formation with saddlebags stuffed with cash. Seventeen-year-old Martin Potts had his saddlebags full of money. Thomas Webb rode into formation behind Cole Younger. He had $3,000 he had loaded on a mule that was later killed on the return trip. George Todd had $4,000 tucked inside his uniform jacket. On the withdrawal from Lawrence, Todd's horse was shot out from under him. After jumping clear, he threw off his cumbersome uniform and lost the money in the process. Morgan Mattox said that guerrillas Charles Higbee and probably Benton Wood each had $75,000 they had taken from the banks. Hiram J. George got $30,000 in gold at Lawrence. In addition to these, Captain John Jarrette had $8,000 in his saddlebags earmarked for the widows and orphans of Missouri.[64]

Guerrilla James Milliken remembered, "None of Quantrell's men profited, in private gain, by the raids. We found many Confederate families in distress, and to these we gave money without stint. Money we obtained in raids was divided equally among the members of the band, and what they didn't give away was expended in the purchase of equipment and food. No Confederate family ever was preyed upon. They were paid liberally for what they could spare."[65]

Before leaving the Whitney House Hotel to rejoin his men, Quantrill turned to his friends and lifting his hat and with a slight bow said, "Ladies, I now bid you good morning. I hope when we meet again it will be under more favorable circumstances." Quantrill rode to the place where his men were waiting. After the town cleared of guerrillas, muster was taken and several men were unaccounted for. Quantrill assigned William Gregg to ride back with twenty men and round up anyone that was left. Quantrill told Gregg he would wait for an hour four miles outside of town where he would be searching for the last of the "wanted men" on his "Death List" before heading back to Missouri. After quickly riding through town, Gregg returned and reported that he could find no stragglers.

If there were any guerrillas left behind it was too late to mount another search to find them. Larkin Skaggs, one of the guerrillas from Cass County who had joined just before the guerrillas entered Kansas, was found to be missing. It was his first battle. Skaggs was a preacher whose church was forced to close because of the war. Skaggs had a brother named Willis. Willis was with Larkin in 1860 when the presidential election was held at Pleasant Hill, Missouri. Larkin wanted to shoot a man named D. P. Houghland who had voted for Lincoln, but Willis held his brother's arm and kept him from killing him.

While Quantrill was taking breakfast at Stone's hotel, Skaggs had entered and tried to take a ring from Lydia Stone, the proprietor's daughter. Quantrill yelled at Skaggs to leave her alone and get out. This incident only made Skaggs angry, and he vowed revenge. As the guerrillas were lining up in formation, Skaggs turned back to Stone's hotel where he demanded the occupants to step outside. When they did so, he opened fire, killing Nathan Stone and another man. The rest of the occupants ran back inside to avoid the bloodshed. Skaggs soon realized that he was left all alone, and seeing the predicament he was in, hurriedly attempted to ride away. By this time a number of citizens had come out from their hiding places. One found a gun and shot Skaggs before he could rejoin the rest of the command. Another man tied a rope around Skaggs' neck and the pommel of his saddle, then dragged the dead body through the streets, until

Larkin Skaggs joined Quantrill with Bill Anderson and fifty other guerrillas just before the Lawrence raid. As Quantrill's men withdrew from town he remained behind. Skaggs rode near a squad of armed men who shot him off his horse. (Emory Cantey Collection)

it was nude and terribly mutilated. The blacks sawed rings off Skaggs' fingers. His body was hanged and further mutilated by being cut with knives. A group of citizens scalped the corpse and made an unsuccessful attempt to burn the body. It was later thrown into a ravine and left exposed all winter. The body was never buried.

An accounting of the dead in Lawrence following the raid recorded 143 victims. There was also a reported property loss of $1,500,000 and a $250,000 cash lost. Intermittingly, explosions could be heard from the burning buildings caused by the large supplies of gunpowder kept for the militia.

Sitting in formation waiting for the order to move out, the guerrillas looked back toward the town. The scene in Lawrence defied description. Flames of more than eighty buildings reached toward the sky. Fortunately, the air was so still that the flames from the buildings did not catch fire to the ones next to them. The sight was horrible to every eye but those of the guerrillas. Harrison Trow remarked, "Smoke ascended into the air, and the crackling of blazing rafters and crashing of falling walls filled the air." A postwar account stated, "The town is burning and every street filled with suffocating vapors and the nauseous stench arising from pools of hot blood; and Lawrence can no longer be held by the guerrillas."[66] One building intentionally left intact was Bowersock's Mill. Quantrill had an indication that Price or some other Confederate command at some future date might invade Kansas and would have need of a good grist mill.

Accounts by Quantrill's men all attest to the fact that they had engaged soldiers. Bodies of the "wanted men" could be seen scattered in the dust of Lawrence's streets. William Gregg later wrote in his memoirs, "I have always believed that most of the men killed at Lawrence were soldiers," while Kit Dalton agreed by adding, "The flower of the army was dead, but the commanders, cowardly whelps, saved themselves by flight." Another account by guerrilla Lee C. Miller asserted, "At ten o'clock the town was in ashes and many, many Federal soldiers were slain." Scout John McCorkle said that Quantrill and his command had come to Lawrence to be avenged, and they were. "In this raid, a few innocent men may have been killed but this was not intentional." No home that was picked out as the home of a soldier's family or that of a Union man was left if it could be burned.[67]

As the guerrillas were gathering in their forces and taking muster, Quantrill conferred with his officers concerning the next stage of the operation. He had already decided the route he was going to take out of Lawrence. He would lead his column west out of town through the Wakarusa bottoms and across Blanton's Bridge. There were still several more important targets on his list that could be engaged on the way out of town, and these he assigned to separate companies that would ride parallel to the main body and seek out these places that had not been engaged earlier. Along the Wakarusa lived many men who served as conductors on the Underground Railroad. In the heavily wooded river bottoms, runaway slaves could easily be led out of Missouri and directed farther north. For years the men who aided these runaway slaves had been violating the Fugitive Slave Law by hiding them on their property and ferrying them on north into Nebraska or Canada.

One of the wanted men was Corporal Joseph Gardner, a Jayhawker with the Ninth Kansas Regiment who was living on Washington Creek, a branch of the Wakarusa River. Gardner had originally been a Quaker but had been disowned by the church for spurning the Quaker doctrine. In Lawrence, Gardner as well as his neighbors, Edwin Stokes and Horace W. Thompson, used their farms as stations on the Underground Railroad. Thompson had first come to Kansas in 1855. He had a trap door in his house leading to his cellar where he harbored fugitive slaves. Another neighbor John Armstrong also aided the Underground Railroad from his farm on Washington Creek. Only recently Governor Charles Robinson, Captain Samuel N. Wood, and Major James Abbot had given Armstrong money to start an Underground Railroad link to Iowa.[68]

Major James B. Abbot lived three-quarters of a mile south of Blanton's Bridge where he owned a corn mill and where his house was used as a way station on the Underground Railroad. During the raid, Abbot was in Lawrence hiding in a barn after fleeing the Eldridge House Hotel. He was an officer in the Kansas militia and served as an agent for the Kansas *Herald of Freedom*. He was also a good friend of James Lane and was eventually promoted by Lane as an officer in the Lane Brigade. Before the war he took part in the early border troubles and helped liberate free-state men who had been arrested by the legal authorities. Abbot's house was on the guerrillas' list to be destroyed.

In addition to Abbot's house, Captain John Stewart's cabin four miles south of Lawrence was also slated to be burned on the guerrillas' way out of town. Stewart had arrived in Kansas with the New England Emigrant Aid Company. He was one of the most wanted men among the guerrillas. Besides being a general traffic manager for the Underground Railroad, he had been with James Lane in the sacking of Osceola, Missouri. Stewart had led many raids into Missouri, plundering and killing as he went. Like Abbot he had been an active participant in freeing several free-state men from officers of the law after they had been arrested. When Captain Dick Yeager made a raid on Humboldt, Kansas, in May of 1862, Stewart captured twelve of Yeager's men near Emporia. Stewart had all the prisoners shot.

Another viable target was the farm of Abraham Rothrock, located ten miles south of Lawrence near the small settlement of Brooklyn northwest of Baldwin on the Santa Fe Trail, where Rothrock harbored runaway slaves in his house and barn. Rothrock was a minister of the Congregational Church of Wakarusa, and both his sons were in the Union army. The guerrillas planned to stop and burn his church before riding to his farm to search for him. Though being a Quaker and holding abolitionist views, he did not follow

Charles Higbee served as the treasurer in Quantrill's Partisan Ranger Company. Seen here in his red guerrilla shirt, Higbee was reported to have gotten $75,000 from the Lawrence banks to distribute to the needy citizens in Missouri. (Emory Cantey Collection)

the Quaker doctrine of nonviolence. Ironically, Rothrock's son, Private Hiram Rothrock of the Ninth Kansas Regiment, was in Missouri on a Jayhawking expedition while Quantrill was raiding Lawrence. Rothrock's neighbor and fellow Quaker Eliab G. Macy was also active on the Underground Railroad. On the way back to Missouri the guerrillas had orders to burn two houses belonging to Macy, one in Bloomington and another in Lone Star.[69]

An additional target was the house of Private John Ulrich of the Eleventh Kansas Jayhawker Regiment, the same unit that had been responsible for serving as the murdered girls' prison guards in Kansas City. Also on the list of houses to be destroyed was that of Thaddeus Prentice, a Jayhawker who often rode into Lawrence relaying important news. Other viable targets along the guerrillas' path was the home of Private Ansen Jardon of the Twelfth Kansas Jayhawker Regiment, who was known for his plundering operations in Jackson County, and the home of Private William C. Black of the Eighth Kansas Jayhawker Regiment, which had gained repute for their destruction of Independence, Missouri, a year earlier. All such houses of "wanted men" were to be put to the torch. On his way back to Missouri, Quantrill also wanted to find Philip A. Emery, a radical newspaperman. Emery had been an early perpetrator in plunder raids into Missouri before the war. Emery's wife said he often slept in his cornfield as the rebels were after him the same as John Brown and James Montgomery.

All the guerrillas were now finally gathered together and waiting. After Quantrill had issued orders to his officers with instructions for the ride back to Missouri, all eyes turned toward him as he rode to the front of the column. Many guerrillas had acquired fresh mounts, but Quantrill still rode the same horse out of Lawrence that he rode in on, a beautiful bay, weighing about 1,000 pounds, and it seemed to be of blooded stock. He pulled back on the reins, stopped, and turned to address his men. Quantrill's voice rose above the din. He expressed approval at the outcome of the mission, saying that he was well satisfied that all of his men had finally gotten their revenge for years of murder and destruction from Jayhawker raids. As for himself, he said he was "ready to die." In a few short words he told his men to expect hard riding and hard fighting ahead, but assured them that if they would stick together and obey his orders he would get them all safely back to Missouri. His last command before leaving Lawrence was, "All right, men. Four hours of this is all any man can stand. Formation! Mount! We all ride for Missouri in a body!" As soon as Quantrill raised his hat as a signal to begin moving out, the entire column of guerrillas raised up in their stirrups and three rousing cheers echoed from the ranks: "Gallant Colonel!" "Hurrah for Quantrill!" Quantrill then led his men back to the safety of Missouri. The great 1863 Lawrence raid was over.[70]

Epilogue

The greatest collusion and wildest sensationalized accounts by the Kansas press and their adherents began immediately after the raid ended. Kansas recruiting officer Captain Leroy J. Bean made a purposely false statement before a congressional committee, saying that the rifles in the city armory were rusty and of little use and were destroyed during the raid. The fact was that the rifles sent to Lawrence by General Ewing were the latest and most advanced rifles of the day. They were not destroyed during the raid, nor were they old and rusty.[1]

Historians began referring to Kansas during the time preceding the Civil War as "Bleeding Kansas." Noted historian Don Gilmore in his book *Civil War along the Missouri-Kansas Border* found that there were more Kansans killed in their state during this period by marauding Jayhawkers than by Missourians. In contrast, Missouri came to be known as "The Burnt District" due to the immeasurable number of homes destroyed by Kansas Jayhawkers who carried their criminal depredations across the state line. Eyewitness reports of Jayhawker raids in Missouri stated that one could ride all day without seeing one inhabited dwelling. The only reminders that homes had existed were the remains of blackened chimneys that came to be known as "Jennison's Monuments." Many Missouri communities were burned out of existence, and only their names have survived from accounts given during the war. Given these circumstances it was only human nature for the Missourians to want to strike back.

A guerrilla who took part in the Lawrence raid afterward remarked,

"You may be sure a great wail went up throughout the Northland because of desolated Lawrence, but never a damnation dissenting Puritan marred the platitude of his angular countenance by frowning on the atrocities that were daily being committed by Jennison, Lane and their bloody minions throughout the grief stricken portions of Missouri."[2] Likewise guerrilla Lee C. Miller observed: "There has always been a great howl about the Lawrence raid. But the howlers do not stop to remember that Kansas men killed more old and helpless men in Jackson County alone than we killed soldiers in Lawrence."[3]

The reasons for the Lawrence raid have never been addressed until now. Jayhawker attacks must be taken into consideration as much as Missouri partisan retaliation. If the accounts of the Lawrence raid contained a cardinal sin, it was the sin of omission. Rarely did Kansans of that day talk about their criminal proclivities. Omitted were any accounts describing their indiscriminate slaughter during their marauding expeditions through Missouri. Also omitted were their criminal acts and their criminal associations. What was known was that the men of Lawrence—whose behavior was unethical, whose nature was immoral, and whose actions were illegal—were reported as being merely peace-loving and law-abiding citizens. Included in these characterizations were the "ladies" of Lawrence, who were not opposed to wearing stolen silk dresses from Missouri or adorning their homes with "confiscated" furniture from their enemies across the border. And not least of all in post-war accounts was the most glaring act of complicity of omission that the military titles of the dead were rarely given. William G. Cutler provided an example in his book *History of the State of Kansas* when he wrote about a Lawrence victim, "Mr. G. W. Bell, County Clerk, lived on the side hill . . . " when in fact "Mr. Bell" was Captain George Washington Bell of Company F, Twelfth Kansas Regiment. As evidence, a photo survives of Bell in his officer's uniform.

Northern accounts of the raid state that there were no Redlegs in Lawrence the day the guerrillas attacked. Contrary to these reports there are several Southern accounts of the killing of many of the so-called Redlegs during the raid. It was a characteristic of Kansans that Jayhawker atrocities were never recorded except in understatements, such as the one in the report of a Jayhawker raid, "Independence was raided and the citizens were given a little touch of the misfortune of war." In actuality this statement meant that noncombatants were killed, houses were destroyed, and stock was driven off and herded back into Kansas.[4]

In trying to perpetrate the myth that Lawrence was a peaceful town full of innocent victims, there is rarely any notice given to individuals' association with Jayhawkers or Redlegs, nor were any citizens shown to benefit from business dealings in the stolen goods plundered from Missouri. The American legal system has always established that an accessory to a crime is as culpable as the perpetrator. So when the Jayhawkers returned to Lawrence with their plundered goods and were aided in their distribution and sale at public auctions held on the street corners of the city, the citizens of that city who participated in those activities were just as guilty as the marauders. Author Albert Castel has written, "The town folk acquiesced in selling and purchasing the stolen property." As evidenced during the raid, so much plunder was taken from Missouri that the buildings and warehouses in Lawrence were overflowing to the extent that many goods had to be kept out of doors in makeshift shelters until the weekly auctions were held.

Many contemporary accounts reveal that there were as many as 200 to 300 citizens killed during Quantrill's raid on Lawrence. Robert S. Stevens, who took an unofficial accounting of the dead and wounded, recorded 133 names of those killed in Lawrence; he also listed the wounded, including both white and Negro casualties. General Thomas Ewing's official report on the sack of Lawrence recorded almost the exact same number of casualties, listing 140 dead, including 14 from the Fourteenth Kansas Cavalry and 20 from the Second Kansas Colored Infantry Regiment, with 24 wounded. Captain Henry E. Palmer stated that 145 lives were lost in his account titled "The Lawrence Raid, Running Fight with the Guerrillas."[5] And Lawrence citizen Richard Cordley listed in his account, *Pioneer Days in Kansas,* 150 dead and 30 wounded. Cordley recounted that "one hundred and twenty-two were deposited in the cemetery, and many others in their own yards."

Other Lawrence citizens recalled almost the same exact figures. Matthew Shaw recounted: "My old memorandum book tells me there were 130 men killed and 150 houses burned."[6] Hiram Towne was quoted as saying he remembered there were 139 victims.[7] And Professor George M. McCleary, Kansas University professor, noted in his meticulously detailed research on the Lawrence raid that he found only 86 buildings destroyed in town.

Their wartime deeds paid dividends to many of the early border agitators. Kansas recompensed her "pirates of the prairies" with varied "rewards." Chief of all the Jayhawkers, James Lane, managed to stuff the ballot boxes and buy enough votes to secure reelection as Kansas' United States Senator. By 1863 Lane turned antagonistic toward President Abraham Lincoln and often feuded with his Senate colleague Samuel Pomeroy. By this time Lane was believed to be deranged besides being accused of financial irregularities. With an imminent scandal surfacing concerning corruption in the sale of Indian lands that threatened to ruin his career, Lane committed suicide in 1866.[8]

During the war Lane's underling Charles Jennison was court-marshaled for "conduct to the prejudice of good order and military discipline, gross and willful neglect of duty, defrauding the government of the United States, and disobedience of orders." He was tried and also found guilty of arson, robbery, and embezzlement, and sentenced to be dishonorably discharged. At the close of hostilities Jennison was elected to serve in the Kansas legislature and retired to live out his life on his three-hundred-acre farm, well stocked with the finest breeds of cattle, hogs, and game birds. His stables produced thoroughbred racehorses because, as one newspaper joked, "for some five or six years the Colonel enjoyed unusual facilities for selecting fast horses from numerous stables" and, as everyone knew, Jennison deserved a much-needed rest after having grown "stoop-shouldered carrying plunder out of Missouri in the name of Liberty."[9] In the end Jennison was so bad a man that even his wife had to part company with him. She left him after the war for keeping a house of ill fame at Fort Leavenworth, ostensibly a restaurant or eating house, with a "doggery" (a low grogshop) and gambling dive annex.[10]

Jennison's comrade-in-arms in the Seventh Kansas Cavalry was noted Redleg leader and former lawyer George Hoyt, who eventually returned to the practice of law. Notwithstanding his flagrant wartime activities he was ironically elected to the highest law enforcement position in the state and served as Kansas attorney general. Author Steven Starr wrote, "George Hoyt became the chief law officer of Kansas after being the former leader of what was nothing better than a band of highwaymen, arsonists, and murderers."[11]

Chief Justice Thomas Ewing resigned from the Kansas State Supreme Court in August 1862 in order to command the Eleventh Kansas Jayhawker Regiment. He was afterward promoted to brigadier general of U. S. volunteers in March 1863. After being found guilty by a military board of extortion and conspiracy to commit murder, Ewing was reassigned to an obscure post in Southern Missouri for the duration of the war. Soon after the war's end, Ewing moved to Washington, DC, to practice law. He traveled back to his native Ohio, where he remained active in political affairs and served the state as a Democratic representative to Congress. In 1879 Ewing was the Democratic candidate for governor of Ohio. Most infamously known for issuing the notorious Order #11 in reaction to the Lawrence raid, Ewing's actions were summarized by author Albert Castel: "The most drastic and repressive military measure directed against civilians by the Union Army during the Civil War. In fact, it stands as the harshest treatment ever imposed on United States citizens under the plea of military necessity in our Nation's History." Staunch Unionist General George Caleb Bingham toured Ohio displaying his now-famous painting depicting the horrors of Ewing's order. Ewing lost his bid for governor and subsequently moved to New York City where he died as a result of a streetcar accident on January 21, 1896.

When the Civil War broke out, James Blunt's involvement in politics as a committed abolitionist enabled him to get commissioned a brigadier general by Senator James Lane. Blunt was known for his bad temper and use of foul language besides having a reputation as a womanizer. After the war Blunt moved to Washington, DC, becoming a professional claim solicitor. The Justice Department indicted him in 1873 for conspiring to defraud the government. In 1879 he was committed to St. Elizabeth, the government hospital for the insane. Disease-ridden from syphilis, he died on July 25, 1881.[12]

The New England Emigrant Aid Society caused disharmony in

Kansas from its inception, and its disharmony reverberated for years afterward. In 1854 Daniel R. Anthony, Jennison's protégé, traveled to Lawrence with the first company of the New England Emigrant Aid Society. In June 1857, he located at Leavenworth, which city was his home for the remainder of his life. He was described as having only received a limited education and being by nature aggressive and radical. When the Seventh Kansas Jayhawker Regiment was organized in 1861, Anthony was commissioned a lieutenant colonel and served until he was arrested and charged with insubordination and relieved of command. He resigned on September 3, 1862. He was elected mayor of Leavenworth in 1863 and immediately began burning the homes of Southern sympathizers and chasing them out of town. He then turned the town into a "mere fence house" for stolen merchandise and plunder taken from Missouri. Most of the plunder was "on the hoof" and sold on the "black market" for his private use. General Ewing put the city under martial law and had Anthony arrested when he refused to maintain law and order in putting down the illegal traffic.

In 1864 Anthony was involved in a personal dispute in which he was wounded in a shooting affair, killing his assailant. Several years later he was again involved in a dispute; this time three shots were fired at him, one of the shots taking effect in the right breast, just below the collarbone, severing an artery. In the spring of 1866 Anthony was removed from the office of postmaster in Leavenworth because he refused to support the reconstruction policy of President Andrew Johnson. He was president of the Republican state convention of 1868, and the same year was one of the Kansas presidential electors. In 1872 he was again elected mayor of the city and was appointed postmaster of Leavenworth by President Ulysses S. Grant on April 3, 1874, and reappointed by President Rutherford Hayes on March 22, 1878. He served several terms on the city council and was nominated for mayor a number of times afterward, but was defeated.[13]

James Lane's political nemesis Charles Robinson witnessed Lane's downfall while trying to reestablish his own. While serving as Kansas' first governor, Robinson gained the distinction of being the first governor of a U.S. state to be impeached. As a leader in the

California squatters' riots of 1850, Robinson was severely wounded. He was arrested and charged with conspiracy, assault, and murder. Robinson was confined for more than ten weeks before being tried and found not guilty. Returning to Massachusetts he ventured to Lawrence with the New England Emigrant Aid Society. Robinson found himself arrested again during the Wakarusa War, this time for treason, the charge being "acting without authority, and defying the law." During this period Robinson angered many of his supporters with his passionate support for the Jayhawkers who were promoting violence against Southern sympathizers. In early 1862, Robinson was impeached for high misdemeanors and was accused of speculating in state funds. Although he was not convicted or removed from office, his political career was ruined. After losing his reelection bid, he left office on January 12, 1863.

Samuel C. Pomeroy was the financial agent of the New England Emigrant Aid Society. He was a member of the Osawatomie convention in May 1859 that organized the Republican Party in Kansas. On April 4, 1861, he was elected one of the first senators in Kansas. Pomeroy was reelected in 1867, but was defeated in 1873, partly due to charges of bribery brought against him by State Senator A. M. York of Montgomery County, Kansas. The charges were investigated by both the U.S. Senate and the Kansas legislature. The committee of the state legislature reported Pomeroy "guilty of the crime of bribery." The case was brought to trial in Topeka on June 8, 1874. After the bribery case against him was dismissed on March 12, 1875, Pomeroy returned to Massachusetts, dying in 1891.

Pomeroy's fellow agent in the New England Emigrant Aid Society was Martin R. Conway who followed him to Kansas. In 1859 he was nominated by the Republican convention to serve as the first U.S. representative in Congress from Kansas. Conway's part in the border troubles was writing the resolutions adopted by the free-state convention of June 9, 1857, in Topeka, which was labeled illegal by the president and Congress. Conway's personal difficulties continued for several years until in 1873, feeling a personal affront, he fired three shots, wounding Senator Pomeroy. When arrested Conway said of Pomeroy, "He ruined me and my family." Conway eventually lost his mind and in 1880 became an inmate of St. Elizabeth, the government hospital for the insane in the District of Columbia, where he died on February 15, 1882.

Sidney F. Clarke, who was James Lane's hireling since arriving in Lawrence, began his career by being appointed as the provost marshal general for the state of Kansas. He exercised his powers by hiring Redlegs to plunder the Missouri countryside with the understanding that he would share in a portion of their illegal gains. When operations slowed, Clarke's Redleg assistants robbed loyal Unionists as freely as they robbed those of questionable loyalty. For his part in the war the citizens of Kansas elected him to three terms as the state's only representative in Congress. Clarke's congressional career ended in 1870 when he was suspected of corruption. He returned to Kansas where he was elected to the state legislature in 1878 and made Speaker of the House.

Preston Plumb's military career began when he became an officer of the Eleventh Kansas Cavalry, being General Ewing's chief-of-staff. The Eleventh Cavalry was responsible for being the prison guards in Kansas City for the Southern women murdered in August of 1863 just prior to the Lawrence raid. During Plumb's Jayhawking expeditions in Missouri, citizens were murdered, women raped, and property stolen until Plumb became wealthy from the plunder taken. Plumb was further rewarded by the citizens of Kansas when he was elected a member of the State House of Representatives in 1867 and 1868, and served as Speaker of the House in the latter year. He later became prosecuting attorney of Lyon County, Kansas, and was president of the Emporia National Bank in 1873. In 1877, the citizens of Kansas elected Plumb to the U.S. Senate. He was reelected in 1883 and 1888 and served until his death.

On the other side of the border in Missouri following the war Quantrill's men never regretted the part they played in the Lawrence raid. After Appomattox the guerrillas sought to return to their professions and peaceful pursuits, simply desiring amnesty but instead only got it as paroled prisoners of war.[14] And while there is a monument to the 143 victims of Quantrill's raid located in Lawrence, there are thousands of monuments revealed in gravestones of victims from Jayhawker raids located in hundreds of cemeteries all over the border counties of Missouri. There is a basic philosophical difference between the Yankees and the guerrilla soldiers. The Yankees built massive stone structures to the memory of their fallen comrades, while the guerrillas were buried where they fell, scattered across the Missouri countryside, in fields, along bridle paths, and beside lonely trails. No one knew their final resting place. They were mourned by their comrades who carried their memories in their hearts. Noted guerrilla Frank James aptly stated, "They made their monuments while they lived."

Notes

Introduction

1. Cordley, "The Lawrence Massacre by a Band of Missouri Ruffians under Quantrill."
2. *Kansas City (Missouri) Western Journal of Commerce*, 1903, Kansas Collection, University of Kansas Libraries, Lawrence.
3. Younger Family Newspaper Clipping, KCMO Public Library; Appler, 108; Williams, "Quantrill's Raid," 143-49.
4. Lee C. Miller Memoirs.
5. Lowman, 70-71.
6. Cordley, *Pioneer Days in Kansas,* 212.
7. Alice Nichols, 255.
8. Jones.

Chapter 1: Knee Deep in Blood

1. Connelley, *History of Kansas*, 632-34.
2. Palmer, "The Lawrence Raid," 318.
3. Cutler, vol. 1, 193-94.
4. Edwards, 177.
5. Postwar letter from Fletcher Taylor to George Scholl, Emory Cantey Historical Archives Collection; *Westport (Missouri) Historical Quarterly,* vol. 5, no. 2 (September 1969): 10.
6. Edwards, 149.
7. Lee C. Miller Memoirs; *Confederate Veteran Magazine*, vol. 18, no. 6 (June 1910), Broadfoot Publishing Company.

8. William H. Gregg Manuscript.
9. Lykins. Following the Lawrence raid the injured girls who survived were not sent to Gratiot Prison but were instead banished from the border by the provost marshal of the district and not allowed to return to their homes during the continuance of the hostilities. Gathered from the provost marshal files in the National Archives.
10. Letter of Rev. Theo. M. Cobb to J. J. Lutz, Quantrill Collection, McCain Library and Archives, University of Southern Mississippi.
11. *Lawrence (Kansas) Gazette*, July 5, 1907, Kansas Collection, University of Kansas Libraries, Lawrence.
12. When Quantrill separated from part of his command in 1865, with John Koger and others going to Texas and Quantrill leading forty men into Kentucky, Koger had a bullet mold of Quantrill's in his pocket and forgot to return it. After the war the bullet mold was on display in the office of the *Oak Grove (Missouri) Banner*. Referenced in the *Kansas City (Missouri) Star,* December 23, 1910.
13. William H. Gregg Manuscript.
14. George Miller, 13, 32-36, 62, 87-94, 97-111.
15. *Houston (Texas) Tri-Weekly Telegraph*, December 30, 1863, and January 12, 1864; *Dallas Morning News* Historical Archive, October 18, 1929; Kansas Historical Collections, vol. 8 (1909-1910): 284.
16. *Grand Forks (North Dakota) Herald*, January 28, 1883.
17. *Confederate Veteran Magazine*, vol. 28 (June 1910), Broadfoot Publishing Company, 297.
18. *Reminiscences of the Women of Missouri*, 26-29.
19. William H. Gregg Manuscript; The Letters of Charles Monroe Chase in the *True Republican and Sentinel* of Sycamore, Illinois, dated Lawrence, Douglas County, Kansas, August 22, 1863, and Leavenworth, Kansas, August 29, 1863.
20. Banasik, *Embattled Arkansas*, 346.
21. George, *Biography of Captain William Henry Gregg,* 76.
22. *Dallas Morning News* Historical Archive, October 18, 1929; *Kansas City (Missouri) Star,* December 3, 1912.
23. *The War of the Rebellion: A Compilation of the Official Records of the Union and Confederate Armies* (Washington, DC: Government Printing Office, 1880-1901), ser. 1, vol. 41, pt. 2, 75. (Hereafter referred to as *OR*).

24. *Dallas Morning News* Historical Archive, October 18, 1929.
25. Ibid; Younger, 44-47.
26. *Lawrence (Kansas) State Journal*, December 11, 1862.
27. Edwards, 64.
28. *Dallas Morning News* Historical Archive, June 4, 1899.
29. *Blue and Grey Chronicle* 6, no. 1 (October 2002); *History of Vernon County* (St. Louis: Brown and Co., 1887), 269-311; Hagan.
30. Alice Nichols, 256.
31. The Letters of Peter Jackson Bryant, Kansas Historical Society, Topeka; *Lexington (Kentucky) Weekly Journal*, July 25, 1863; *St. Louis Daily Missouri Democrat*, September 8, 1863.
32. John A. Martin to his sister, Josephine B. Martin, Westport, Missouri, December 31, 1861, Josephine B. Martin Papers, Kansas State Historical Society, Topeka.
33. *Lawrence (Kansas) State Journal*, November 28, 1861.
34. John Speer, *Life of General Lane*, 252; Soodalter; "The Story of the Seventh Kansas," Kansas Collection, Kansas State Historical Society, Topeka, 16.
35. McLarty, 268-73.
36. Jacob Hall Family Papers, Jackson County (Missouri) Historical Society, Independence.
37. Jennison Scrapbook, Kansas Collection, Kansas State Historical Society, Topeka.
38. *The Old Settlers History of Bates County, Missouri* (Tathwell and Maxey, 1897), 40; Starr, 79-82, 100; Sheridan, pt. 3, 20.
39. Dalton, 59; Appler, 38.
40. Lowman, 40.
41. *Kansas City (Missouri) Post*, March 21, 1915; *OR*, ser. 1, vol. 22, pt. 1, 319-20; Parker, *Soil of our Souls*, 82.
42. Fisher, "The Lawrence Massacre"; C. E. Lewis to "Dear Bro.," Franklin, August 27, 1864, Methodist Historical Library, Baker University, Baldwin, Kansas; Lowman, 36.
43. Spring, 287; Edwards, 46.
44. Walker, 56.
45. Quantrill Collection, McCain Library and Archives, University of Southern Mississippi.

46. Walker, 56-57; Quantrill Collection, McCain Library and Archives, University of Southern Mississippi.
47. *Pleasant Hill (Missouri) Times*, September 5, 1924; *Independence (Missouri) Examiner*, August 30, 1929, and September 12, 1931.
48. Walter B. Stevens, 851.
49. Faxon Memoirs.
50. Lowman, 53.
51. Blunt, 211-65; Kansas Historical Collections, vol. 11 (1909-1910): 279-80.
52. Cordley, *Pioneer Days in Kansas,* 154, 156; Castel, 172.
53. Alice Nichols, 254.
54. *Westport (Missouri) Historical Quarterly,* vol. 1 (May 1865); Spalding, 92.
55. Speech by S. M. Fox at the twenty-seventh annual meeting of the Kansas State Historical Society, December 2, 1902, Kansas State Historical Society, Topeka.
56. Personal Recollection of Mrs. Sara T. D. Robinson of the Quantrill Raid, August 21, 1863, Quantrill Collection, McCain Library and Archives, University of Southern Mississippi; Spring, quoting Shalor Winchell Eldridge, *Recollections of Early Days in Kansas* (Topeka, 1920): 193, from Spring, 286; *Kansas City (Missouri) Star*, February 4, 1954; Deatherage, 634.
57. *OR,* ser. 1, vol. 22, pt. 2, 390, and ser. 1, vol. 34, pt. 1, 1004; A. C. Wilder, Letter to Captain Sidney Clarke, Carl Albert Congressional Research and Studies Center, Congressional Archives, Sidney Clarke Collection, Box 1, Folder 20.
58. *Lawrence (Kansas) Republican,* June 5, 1862.
59. Unidentified clipping, Jennison Scrapbook; "J. B. Hickok Deputy U. S. Marshal," *Kansas History, A Journal of the Central Plains,* vol. 2, no. 4 (winter 1979).
60. Palmer, "The Black Flag Character," 455-66.
61. General Blunt letter, Fort Leavenworth, June 9, 1863, Abraham Lincoln Papers, Library of Congress; Connelley, *Quantrill and the Border Wars*, reprint (New York: Pageant, 1956), 411-13; Palmer, "The Black Flag Character," 464.
62. *Lawrence (Kansas) State Journal*, March 12 and April 30, 1863.
63. R. C. Vaughan to J. O. Broadhead, Lexington, Missouri, May 8,

1863, in Broadhead Papers, Missouri Historical Society; Letter of Dan Holmes to his parents, Kansas City, November 15, 1861, Daniel B. Holmes Correspondence, Chicago Historical Society.

64. *Lawrence Kansas Free State*, May 7, 1855.
65. Colman; Cordley, *Pioneer Days in Kansas*, 67-68, and Chapter 14.
66. Cordley, *A History of Lawrence, Kansas*, 185; *Chicago Tribune*, August 25, 1863; *Rock Island (Illinois) Weekly Union,* August 26, 1863; *Weekly California (Missouri) News*, August 29, 1863; *Houston (Texas) Tri-Weekly Telegraph*, January 12, 1864.
67. *Lawrence (Kansas) State Journal,* April 17, 1862.
68. Robinson; Richard Hinton recalled the defensive posture of Lawrence: "The men and boys of Kansas, every one capable of carrying a musket, responded speedily to the call to arms," from Kansas Historical Collections, vol. 6 (1897-1900): 374.
69. Kansas Historical Collections, vol. 6 (1897-1900): 374.
70. Cordley, *A History of Lawrence, Kansas*, 251-52.
71. Colman; Cordley, *Pioneer Days in Kansas*, 67-68, and Chapter 14.
72. Cordley, *A History of Lawrence, Kansas,* 58, 170.
73. Winchell.
74. Lowman, 36-37.
75. Trow, 141.
76. Lee C. Miller Memoirs.
77. George, *Biography of Captain William Henry Gregg,* 76.
78. Voigt, 14; Cutler, pt. 3, 5; Thomas C. Reynolds Papers, Library of Congress.
79. Wallenstein; *Kansas City (Missouri) Star*, July 19, 1903.
80. William H. Gregg Manuscript.
81. *Houston (Texas) Tri-Weekly Telegraph*, January 15, 1864.
82. Sheridan, pt. 2, 314; Cordley, *A History of Lawrence, Kansas*; Douglas County (Kansas) Historical Society, Lawrence.
83. Edwards, 189.
84. *Lawrence (Kansas) State Journal*, August 6, 1863; Cordley, *A History of Lawrence, Kansas*.
85. Connelley, *Quantrill and the Border Wars*, reprint (Smithmark Publishers, 1996), 329.

86. *Lawrence (Kansas) State Journal*, November 6, 1862.
87. Ibid., April 6, 1863.
88. Ibid., May 28, 1863, and July 2, 1863; William H. Gregg Manuscript.
89. Dalton, 100.
90. Connelley, *Quantrill and the Border Wars*, reprint (Smithmark Publishers, 1996), 310-13.
91. *Kansas City (Missouri) Western Journal of Commerce*, August 27, 1863; *OR,* ser. 1, vol. 22, pt.1, 580-81.
92. William H. Gregg Manuscript.
93. Cummins, *Jim Cummins—The Guerrilla*, 57; *Louisville Kentucky Journal*, September 29, 1901.
94. William H. Gregg Manuscript; Dalton, 100.
95. James D. Richardson, vols. 1-2, 328.

Chapter 2: Brotherhood of the Blood

1. Article in the *Kansas City (Missouri) Enterprise,* reprinted in the *Herald of Freedom,* February 24, 1855.
2. Cordley, A *History of Lawrence, Kansas*.
3. Johnson, 429-41.
4. *Beaver Dam (Wisconsin) Weekly Republican & Sentinel*, September 16, 1856.
5. Article in the *Cedarville Kansas Pioneer,* reprinted in the *Herald of Freedom,* April 14, 1855.
6. Hoole, no. 1: 43-56; *Herald of Freedom*, October 21, 1854.
7. Unrau, 379-91; Cordley, *A History of Lawrence, Kansas*; Wilcox, 305; John J. Ingalls Letters, Kansas State Historical Society; Dick, 65-66.
8. Greeley; Cordley, *Pioneer Days in Kansas*, 60-61; *Herald of Freedom*, April 25, 1857; Cordley, *A History of Lawrence, Kansas*, 109; *Herald of Freedom*, April 14, 1855.
9. *Reminiscences of the Women of Missouri*, 271.
10. Article in the *Brunswick (Missouri) Brunswicker,* reprinted in the *Lawrence Kansas Free State*, April 14, 1855.
11. Spalding.
12. *Herald of Freedom*, May 5, 1855.

13. Recollections of Joseph Savage, Kansas State Historical Society, Topeka.
14. *Lawrence Kansas Free State*, March 31, 1855.
15. *Herald of Freedom*, January 15, 1855.
16. *Leavenworth Kansas Weekly Herald,* reprinted in the *Herald of Freedom,* April 14, 1855.
17. Aptheker.
18. *Leavenworth Kansas Weekly Herald.*
19. Hoole, no. 1: 43-56.
20. Letter of James B. Abbot to General James H. Lane, September 7, 1857, Kansas Collection, University of Kansas Libraries, Lawrence.
21. *Herald of Freedom*, February 16, 1856; George M. Beebe, Acting Governor, to President James Buchanan, dated Lecompton, Kansas Territory, November 26, 1860, Trans., Kansas State Historical Society, 1889-1896, vol. 5 (Topeka, 1896): 631-32; *Herald of Freedom*, January 12, 1856. Joel and Emily Grover's barn still stands today and is in use as Lawrence's Fire Station No. 4.
22. *DeBow's Review*, August 1856, 187.
23. *Herald of Freedom*, January 6, 1855.
24. *Leavenworth (Kansas) Herald*, December 8, 1855; Cordley, *A History of Lawrence, Kansas*.
25. B. F. Stringfellow of Platte County, Missouri, reprinted in the *Herald of Freedom*, June 2, 1855; *Lawrence (Kansas) Republican*, April 26, 1860.
26. *Herald of Freedom*, October 21, 1854.
27. Cordley, *Pioneer Days in Kansas*, 28.
28. Spalding; Cutler, vol. 10 (1907-1908).
29. Stewart.
30. Letter of E. D. Ladd to Samuel Ladd, September 17, 1854, printed in the *Marshall (Missouri) Statesman*, October 4, 1854.
31. *St. Louis (Missouri) Republican*, June 14, 1854.
32. *Liberty (Missouri) Platform.*
33. *Lawrence (Kansas) State Journal*, March 14, 1861, and May 16, 1861.
34. Cordley, *A History of Lawrence, Kansas*, 58; *Kansas City (Missouri) Times*, December 15, 1938; Jennison Scrapbook, Kansas

Collection, Kansas State Historical Society, Topeka; *Lawrence (Kansas) State Journal*, July 30, 1863; *Lawrence (Kansas) State Journal*, March 10, 1863; *Lawrence (Kansas) Republican*, May 9, 1861.

35. *Lawrence (Kansas) Republican,* October 17, 1861.
36. *Herald of Freedom*, April 12, 1856; Cutler, pt. 18, 1, and pt. 42, 2; John Speer, *Life of General Lane,* 233.
37. *Lawrence (Kansas) State Journal*, May 7, 1863.
38. *Herald of Freedom*, April 9, 1859; Ibid., August 14, 1862.
39. *Lawrence Kansas Free State*, March 17, 1855.
40. Anderson.
41. *Occidental Messenger,* reprinted in *Liberty (Missouri) Tribune*, June 23, 1854; John Speer, *Life of General Lane*, 194; *Lawrence (Kansas) Daily Republican*, February 12, 1859.
42. *Lawrence (Kansas) State Journal*, January 15, 1863.
43. *Herald of Freedom*, February 17, 1855; *Occidental Messenger,* reprinted in *Liberty (Missouri) Tribune*, June 23, 1854; John Speer, *Life of General Lane*, 194.
44. *Lawrence Kansas Free State*, January 3, 1855.
45. Article in the *Massachusetts Spy,* reprinted in the *Herald of Freedom*, January 12, 1856.
46. *Herald of Freedom*, August 15, 1857.
47. Robinson; Harlow.
48. Zornow, 67-74; Cordley, *A History of Lawrence, Kansas,* 35, 126.
49. Cordley, *A History of Lawrence, Kansas*, 57.
50. Personal Recollection of Mrs. Sara T. D. Robinson of the Quantrill Raid, August 21, 1863, Quantrill Collection, McCain Library and Archives, University of Southern Mississippi.
51. Cordley, *A History of Lawrence, Kansas*.
52. Duncan, 356; Martin, "Among the Sovereign Squats," 438-39.
53. Hoole, no. 2: 145-71.
54. *Herald of Freedom*, November 20, 1858; Albert D. Richardson, 116-20; Sheridan, pt. 1, 113-14, and pt. 3, 16; George M. Beebe to President James Buchanan, dated Lecompton, Kansas Territory, November 26, 1860, Trans. Kansas State Historical Society, 1889-1896, vol. 5 (Topeka, 1896): 631-32.
55. Fry; Cutler, pt. 42, 3; Fellman, 152.

56. Letters of William Smith and John Vansickle, Kansas Collection, University of Kansas Libraries, Lawrence; *Herald of Freedom*, July 9, 1859; *Lawrence (Kansas) Journal*, October 17, 1861.
57. Holloway, 512-14.
58. Fry.
59. Article in the *Michigan Free Democrat,* reported in the *Herald of Freedom,* January 19, 1856.
60. *Reminiscences of the Women of Missouri*, 271.
61. Cordley, *A History of Lawrence, Kansas*, 122, 163.
62. Robinson.
63. *Herald of Freedom*, January 6, 1855; Letter of J. B. Woodward to S. N. Wood, Kansas State Historical Society, Topeka.
64. Sheridan, pt. 1, 16-17.
65. *Lawrence (Kansas) Journal*, October 17, 1861, and December 19, 1861.
66. Notes from the General Court Martial, Camp Defiance, Kansas, January 20, 1862, H. Miles Moore Papers, Kansas State Historical Society, Topeka.
67. *Lawrence (Kansas) Daily Journal-World*, September 19, 1999.
68. Ibid.
69. Cordley, *Pioneer Days in Kansas*, 138, 157.
70. *Lawrence (Kansas) State Journal*, January 9, 1862.
71. Ibid., November 28, 1861.
72. Cordley, *Pioneer Days in Kansas*, 135-36.

Chapter 3: Damned and Deserved

1. Berneking.
2. *Lawrence Kansas Free State*, April 30, 1855; article in the *Kansas City (Missouri) Enterprise,* reprinted in the *Lawrence Kansas Free State*, January 31, 1855; Cordley, *A History of Lawrence, Kansas*.
3. Wells.
4. *Marshall (Missouri) Democrat*, June 26, 1861.
5. Letter of John Vansickle, Bourbon County, Kansas, December 28, 1858, Kansas Historical Society, Topeka.
6. *Kansas City (Missouri) Western Journal of Commerce*, August 2, 1862.

7. Greene, 448.
8. *St. Louis Daily Missouri Democrat*, September 1, 1863.
9. Kansas Historical Collections, vol. 6 (1897-1900): 371-82.
10. Anderson.
11. *Herald of Freedom*, May 30, 1857; Kansas Historical Collections, vol. 6 (1897-1900): 373.
12. Cordley, *A History of Lawrence, Kansas*, 24.
13. *Herald of Freedom*, January 19, 1856.
14. Article in the *Kansas City (Missouri) Enterprise,* reprinted in the *Herald of Freedom*, February 2, 1856; Robinson.
15. Kansas Historical Collections, vol. 6 (1897-1900): 371-82; John J. Ingalls Letters, Kansas State Historical Society, Topeka.
16. *Herald of Freedom*, October 29, 1859.
17. Cutler; Kansas Collections, Kansas State Historical Society, Topeka.
18. Ibid.
19. *Herald of Freedom*, December 17, 1859.
20. John Brown Collection, Kansas State Historical Society, Topeka.
21. Dalton, 97.
22. *Richmond (Virginia) Enquirer*, November 30, 1860.
23. Alice Nichols, 208.
24. *Herald of Freedom*, July 18, 1857.
25. Kansas Historical Collections, vol. 6 (1897-1900): 371-82.
26. *Herald of Freedom*, April 3, 1858.
27. John Koontz, Drew University. "James Redpath," *The Literary Encyclopedia*, June 13, 2003, The Literary Dictionary Company, March 22, 2006; Kansas Historical Collections, vol. 7 (1901-1902), Topeka.
28. *Macon (Georgia) Daily Telegraph*, October 31, 1890; *Kansas Historical Quarterly,* vol. 43.
29. Spalding; Alice Nichols, 273, 282-83.
30. Johnson, 436.
31. Kansas Historical Collections, vol. 6 (1897-1900): 371-82; Cutler, pt. 3, 8.
32. Kansas Historical Collections, vol. 6 (1897-1900): 371-82.
33. Robinson.
34. *Reminiscences of the Women of Missouri*, 272.
35. Elvira Scott diary, March 9, 1862, 97; Kempker, 287-301.

36. *Herald of Freedom*, October 13, 1855.
37. Martin, "Sketches of Kansas Pioneer Experience," 409.
38. *Houston (Texas) Daily Telegraph,* February 22, 1864.
39. Quantrill Collection, McCain Library and Archives, University of Southern Mississippi; *Leavenworth (Kansas) Herald*, December 8, 1855.
40. Article in the *St. Louis (Missouri) Republican,* reprinted in the *Herald of Freedom*, April 12, 1856.
41. Cordley, *Pioneer Days in Kansas*, 72.
42. *Lawrence (Kansas) Republican*, August 27, 1857; *Topeka (Kansas) Weekly Capital and Farm Journal*, January 25, 1894.
43. *Lawrence (Kansas) State Journal*, May 9 and August 6, 1863; Farren; Lowman, 36.
44. Cordley, *A History of Lawrence, Kansas*, 24.
45. Connelley, *Quantrill and the Border Wars*, 78; Alice Nichols, 270; *Herald of Freedom,* May 30, 1857.
46. Goodrich, 23.
47. Kansas Historical Collections, vol. 6 (1897-1900): 371-82, and vol. 7 (1902): 233; Cordley, *A History of Lawrence, Kansas*, 55; Hinton, "Pens that Made Kansas Free."
48. Lee C. Miller Memoirs.
49. Hoole, no. 1: 43-56.
50. Cordley, *Pioneer Days in Kansas*, Chapter 15; Cordley, *A History of Lawrence, Kansas*, 162.
51. *Kansas City (Missouri) Western Journal of Commerce*, May 29, 1858.
52. John J. Ingalls Letters, Kansas State Historical Society, Topeka; Cordley, *Pioneer Days in Kansas*, 80; J. Sterling Morton, "Centennial History," *Daily (Omaha) Nebraska Press*, July 5, 1876.
53. Thomas W. Higginson Collection, Kansas Collection, Kansas State Historical Society, Topeka.
54. Cutler, vol. 1, 153.
55. Stewart.
56. Cordley, *Pioneer Days in Kansas*, 64-66.
57. Monaghan.
58. *Herald of Freedom*, November 12, 1859; *Lawrence (Kansas) State Journal*, December 26, 1861.

59. *Lawrence (Kansas) Republican*, October 17, 1861.
60. Bailey, 23; Williams, "Quantrill's Raid," 143-49; Fisher, *The Gun and the Gospel*, 164; *Lawrence (Kansas) State Journal*, January 16, 1862.
61. Monaghan, 195-96; Britton, 148.
62. *Lawrence (Kansas) State Journal*, August 7, 1862; Banasik, *Missouri in 1861*, 226.
63. *Blue and Grey Chronicle*, vol. 6, no. 5: 6.
64. *Daily Lawrence (Kansas) Republican*, February 12, 1859, and October 17, 1861.
65. Charles Robinson to A. A. Lawrence, October 6, 1863, Robinson Papers, Manuscript Division of the Kansas State Historical Society, Topeka; *Lawrence (Kansas) State Journal*, April 4, 1861.

Chapter 4: Lawlessness Abounds

1. *Kansas City (Missouri) Times*, November 24, 1908.
2. Speech by S. M. Fox at the twenty-seventh annual meeting of the Kansas State Historical Society, December 2, 1902.
3. Margaret J. Hayes to her mother, Westport, Missouri, November 12, 1861. Margaret J. Hayes Papers, *Westport Historical Quarterly*, vol. 4, no. 1 (June 1968), Jackson County (Missouri) Historical Society.
4. Ibid.
5. Ibid.
6. Steinberg, 21; Miller, *Truman, the Rise to Power*, Truman Library Archives; Joanne Chiles Eakin and Betty Strong House, great-granddaughter of Jim Crow Chiles. "Walter Chiles of Jamestown"; Eakin, 52-55.
7. Bonnewitz and Allen, 43.
8. *Independence (Missouri) Examiner*, April 2, 1937; *Jackson County (Missouri) Historical Society Journal* (fall 1996); *Topeka (Kansas) Weekly Capital and Farm Journal*, July 11, 1889; *Reminiscences of the Women of Missouri*, 216.
9. Letter from Bingham to Rollins and Hall, February 12, 1862. James S. Rollins Papers, State Historical Society of Missouri, Western Historical Manuscript Collection, University of Missouri, Columbia; Niepman, 197-98, 208-10; Wilcox, 322-23.

10. *Reminiscences of the Women of Missouri*, 42.
11. Ibid., 35-36.
12. Ibid., 90-91.
13. *Independence (Missouri) Examiner*, December 28, 1914.
14. Report of the Headquarters Board of Officers, Kansas City, September 6, 1864. Thomas Ewing Family Papers, Library of Congress.
15. *Reminiscences of the Women of Missouri,* 125.
16. Jackson County (Missouri) Historical Society Archives, Box 93; "The Letters of Charles Monroe Chase," *Kansas Historical Quarterly*, vol. 26, no. 2 (summer 1960): 124-27.
17. Wilcox, 328; Edwards, 186; Hagan, 150; *Reminiscences of the Women of Missouri,* 263.
18. *Daily Journal of Commerce*, September 22, 1864.
19. *Reminiscences of the Women of Missouri*, 214-19.
20. *Liberty (Missouri) Tribune*, April 12, 1862; Roberta and Arthur L. Bonnewitz, 111.
21. Eakin, 25.
22. Roberta and Arthur L. Bonnewitz, 113.
23. Wilcox, 350-51.
24. *Kansas City (Missouri) Star*, no date, by son S. M. Barrett; Wilcox, 367-68.
25. War Diary of Fletcher Pomeroy, Kansas State Historical Society, Topeka; Rick Mack Historical Archives Collection.
26. War Diary of Fletcher Pomeroy. Kansas State Historical Society, Topeka.
27. *OR*, ser. 1, vol. 8, pt. 2, 448-49; OR, ser. 1, vol. 17, pt. 2, 53.
28. Senate Executive Documents, no. 26, 40th Congress, 2nd Session, 1.
29. Missouri State Education, Agricultural History Series, Missouri State University, Columbia.
30. Greene, 449.
31. The Richard Ely Selden, Jr. Letters of 1866 by Robert S. Barrows, Kansas State Historical Society, Topeka.
32. Tathwell and Maxey; Atkeson.
33. *Reminiscences of the Women of Missouri*, 250.
34. Welty, 155-69.
35. *Herald of Freedom*, March 22, 1856; *Kansas City (Missouri) Journal*, June 30 and July 23, 1863.

36. Daniel R. Anthony to Aaron McLean, December 3, 1861, in Langsdorgff and Richmond, vol. 24, no. 1 (spring 1958): 6-30, 198-226, 351-70, 458-75.
37. Unidentified clippings, Charles R. Jennison Scrapbook, Missouri Valley Special Collections, Kansas City Missouri Public Library.
38. *Lawrence (Kansas) Journal*, October 17, 1861.
39. *Olathe (Kansas) Mirror*, February 13, 1864; Bader.
40. Welty, 155-69.
41. Custer, 393-94; Ostrander, 134-35.
42. Charles Robinson to A. A. Lawrence, March 25, 1859. Letters of Charles Robinson, Kansas Room, University of Kansas Library, Lawrence; Cordley, *A History of Lawrence, Kansas*, 162.
43. Stewart.

Chapter 5: A Gallant and Perfectly Fair Blow

1. Trow, 145-46; Edwards.
2. *Houston (Texas) Tri-Weekly Telegraph*, December 30, 1863.
3. Frank Smith manuscript in the possession of the author.
4. Speech by S. M. Fox at the twenty-seventh annual meeting of the Kansas State Historical Society, December 2, 1902.
5. Langsdorf and Richmond, vol. 24, no.1 (spring 1958): 351-70.
6. Dalton.
7. Edwards, 190; Trow, 145.
8. Edwards, 188.
9. Quantrill Collections, McCain Library, University of Southern Mississippi.
10. *Houston (Texas) Tri-Weekly Telegraph*, January 29, 1864.
11. *Kansas City (Missouri) Times*, Tuesday, September 30, 1941; *Fort Worth (Texas) Star-Telegram*, June 17, 1920.
12. Rick Mack Historical Archives Collection.
13. William H. Gregg Manuscript.
14. Maddox, 75; Younger, 44-47; Ibid.
15. Willard Hall Mendenhall Diary, Western Historical Manuscript Collection, University of Missouri, Columbia.
16. Cummins, *Jim Cummins—The Guerrilla*, 26-27.

17. Ibid; Connelley, *Quantrill and the Border Wars*, 1910, reprint (New York: Pageant, 1956), 302.
18. William H. Gregg Manuscript.
19. Edwards, 186-87; *Reminiscences of the Women of Missouri*, 249.
20. Edwards, 174-75.
21. Interview with William Connelley on April 29, 1909, in Bartlesville, Oklahoma. Quoted in Connelley, *Quantrill and the Border Wars*, reprint (Smithmark Books, 1996), 262.
22. DeWitt.
23. *Lawrence (Kansas) Gazette,* July 5, 1907, Kansas Collection, University of Kansas Libraries, Lawrence.
24. Jackson County (Missouri) Historical Society *Bulletin,* vol. 16, no. 1 (March 1974): 8-9.
25. Edwards, 77-78; *History of Johnson County, Missouri* (Topeka, KS: Historical Publishing Co., 1918), 112.
26. Eakin and Hale, 273.
27. *Reminiscences of the Women of Missouri*, 270-71; Edwards, 247.
28. Frank Smith manuscript in the possession of the author.
29. *Jackson County (Missouri) Examiner*, May 5, 1905.
30. McCorkle, 78-79.
31. Ibid., 36.
32. *Reminiscences of the Women of Missouri*, 215-16.
33. Willard Hall Mendenhall's 1862 Civil War Diary, *Missouri Historical Review*, vol. 77 (July 1984), 444; E. A. Christie to Dear Pa, near Platte City, February 24, 1863, E. A. Christie Letter, University of Missouri, Western Historical Manuscript Collection, State Historical Society of Missouri Manuscripts.
34. Austin A. King to Major General John M. Schofield, St. Louis, May 30, 1863, John M. Schofield Papers, Library of Congress.
35. *Dallas Morning News* Historical Archive, October 18, 1929.
36. Younger, 50; Younger Family, Missouri Valley Special Collections, 1899-1936, Kansas City Missouri Public Library; *Knoxville (Kentucky) Journal*, November 20, 1889; *Dallas Morning News* Historical Archive, October 18, 1929.
37. *St. Louis (Missouri) Post Dispatch*, August 24, 1902.
38. Correspondence of Ben R. Hill, grandson of James "Woot" Hill, dated March 7, 1979, in possession of the author.

39. Hall and Hall; Family files of Martha Hill Davis, granddaughter of Francis Marion "Tuck" Hill, in possession of the author.
40. *McKinney (Texas) Examiner*, April 25, 1931; *McKinney (Texas) Daily Courier-Gazette*, August 7, 1933; *Dallas Morning News* Historical Archive, October 24, 1915.
41. Edwards, 459.
42. Atkeson; *Reminiscences of the Women of Missouri*, 248-49.
43. Doerschuk, 9-10.
44. *Liberty (Missouri) Advance*, April 1, 1910.
45. Connelley, *Quantrill and the Border Wars*, reprint (Smithmark Books, 1996), 262.
46. Fleming, 14-15, 19.
47. *Vital Historical Records of Jackson County, Missouri*, Daughters of the American Revolution, Kansas City, 1934.
48. *Dallas Morning News* Historical Archive, January 29, 1902.
49. Ibid., June 7, 1907.
50. *Independence (Missouri) Examiner*, September 12, 1931; *Biloxi (Mississippi) Herald*, April 9, 1899.
51. *Kansas City (Missouri) Star*, March 5, 1956.
52. *Reminiscences of the Women of Missouri*, 235.
53. *Oak Grove (Missouri) Banner*, October 8, 1898.
54. George, *The Georges—Pioneers and Rebels*.
55. Crittenden, 370-71.
56. *Dallas Morning News* Historical Archive, October 18, 1929; *Louisville Kentucky Journal*, September 29, 1901.
57. *Lexington (Kentucky) Herald,* September 3, 1911; *Miami (Florida) Herald Record*, October 11, 1914, from an article in *Collier's Weekly.*
58. By Frank Dalton as told to Garland Farmer, Douglas County Historical Society, Lawrence, Kansas.
59. *Kansas City (Missouri) Star*, May 2, 1882.
60. Wallenstein; *Kansas City (Missouri) Star*, July 19, 1903; *Lexington (Kentucky) Herald*, September 3, 1911.
61. Edwards, 176.
62. Eakin and Hale, 235; *Macon (Georgia) Daily Telegraph*, June 28, 1920.
63. *Dallas Morning News* Historical Archive, October 18, 1929.

64. Cummins, *Jim Cummins—The Guerrilla*, 8, 15, 42-43; Cummins, *Jim Cummins' Book,* 103-4; Goodrich, 54; Brant, 53.
65. J. Freeman to W. A. Brannock, Pleasant Hill, May 30, 1864, W. A. Brannock Family Letters, Jackson County (Missouri) Historical Society.
66. *Dallas Morning News* Historical Archive, October 18, 1929.
67. Connelley, *Quantrill and the Border Wars*, reprint (Smithmark Publishers, 1996), 302.
68. Hale, 77.
69. Connelley, *Quantrill and the Border Wars*, reprint (Smithmark Publishers, 1996), 203.
70. Margaret J. Hayes Letters, Jackson County (Missouri) Historical Society.
71. *Kansas City (Missouri) Post*, August 20, 1909.
72. McCorkle, 67.
73. *Liberty (Missouri) Tribune,* June 21, 1901.
74. Western Historical Manuscript Collection, University of Missouri, Columbia; Bruce Nichols, 37.
75. Bruce Nichols.
76. Civil War Letters of Webster Moses, Kansas State Historical Society, Topeka.
77. Daniel Holmes to his sister, December 21, 1861, Kansas Collection, Kansas State Historical Society, Topeka.

Chapter 6: Damned Yankee Town

1. McCorkle, 124.
2. Lee C. Miller Memoirs.
3. William H. Gregg Manuscript; Frank Smith manuscript, in possession of the author.
4. William H. Gregg Manuscript.
5. Cordley, *A History of Lawrence, Kansas*, 200.
6. *Kansas City (Missouri) Western Journal of Commerce*, May 23, 1861; Martin, "Memorial Monuments and Tablets in Kansas," 277-78.
7. Croy, 19; Frank Smith manuscript, in possession of the author.
8. Walker, 59.

9. *Lawrence (Kansas) State Journal*, January 1, 1863.
10. Ibid., December 4, 1862.
11. *Kansas City (Missouri) Star*, July 19, 1903, and April 24, 1907; from the journal of Samuel Hunt Davis, Douglas County Historical Society, Lawrence, Kansas.
12. Lowman, 49.
13. *Topeka (Kansas) Weekly Capital and Farm Journal*, July 26, 1859; Jones.
14. Quantrill Collection, McCain Library, University of Southern Mississippi.
15. Walter B. Stevens, vol. 2, 850.
16. Connelley, *Quantrill and the Border Wars* (New York: Pageant, 1956), 327-28; Trow, 147; Cordley, *A History of Lawrence, Kansas; Herald of Freedom*, June 28, 1860.
17. William Miller Reminiscences, unpublished (1913): 1-2, Kansas Collection, University of Kansas Libraries, Lawrence.
18. Hinton, "The War in Kansas and Missouri," 2.
19. "Lawrence—Today and Yesterday," *Lawrence Daily Journal World*, 1913, Watkins Community Museum of History in Lawrence, Kansas.
20. "Quantrill's Men Merciless," Douglas County Historical Society, Lawrence, Kansas; Frank Smith manuscript, in possession of the author.
21. Dalton, 100.
22. McCorkle, 125.
23. Shea; *Kansas Historical Quarterly*, vol. 24, no. 2: 144-50; *Greenfield (Massachusetts) Courier*, August 31, 1863; John Speer, *Life of General Lane*, 270.
24. Cutler, vol. 10 (1907-1908); Fry.
25. Cordley, *Pioneer Days in Kansas*, 137-49.
26. *OR*, ser. 1, vol. 3, 457-59.
27. McCorkle, 141.
28. *Recollections of Old Times in Kansas City, From the Journal of Mattie Lykins Bingham*, Jackson County Historical Society; *Kansas City Genealogist,* Missouri Valley Room, Kansas City Missouri Public Library.
29. *Kansas City (Missouri) Star*, February 24, 1894; Interview with

Andy Walker in the *Weatherford (Texas) Weekly Herald*, January 15, 1910; Trow, 147.

30. Colman, *The Massacre of the Union Cavalry Recruits,* Kansas Historical Society; *Lawrence (Kansas) State Journal*, July 31, 1862; Parker, *Soil of Our Souls*, 81.
31. Parker, *Soil of our Souls,* 81; Atkeson, 157.
32. Roster of the Fourteenth Cavalry Regiment, Kansas, 1861-1865, Archives Department, Kansas State Historical Society, Topeka, 215-19.
33. Cordley, *A History of Lawrence, Kansas*; Parker, *Angels of Freedom*, 182
34. William Speer, "My Story of the Quantrell Massacre," 306.
35. Sheridan, pt. 2, 199.
36. *Recollections of Old Times in Kansas City, From the Journal of Mattie Lykins Bingham*, Jackson County Historical Society.
37. "Recollections of Kate D. E. Riggs as told for her Grandchildren," in Henry Earle Riggs, editor and compiler, "Our Pioneer Ancestors, Being a record of available information as to the Riggs, Baldridge, Agnew, Earle, Kirkpatrick, Vreeland and allied families in the direct line of Ancestry of Samuel Agnew and Catherine Doane Earle Riggs," Ann Arbor, Michigan (Henry Earle Riggs, 1942), 210-17; Sheridan, pt. 3, 421.
38. William Speer, "My Story of the Quantrell Massacre."
39. *Lawrence (Kansas) Journal*, August 17, 1940.
40. Breihan, 103; Cordley, "The Lawrence Massacre," 98-115.
41. Lee C. Miller Memoirs.
42. Cordley, *A History of Lawrence, Kansas*; William H. Gregg Manuscript.
43. Cordley, *A History of Lawrence, Kansas*, 199, 203-4, 207.
44. "Lawrence—Today and Yesterday," The *Lawrence Daily Journal World*, 1913, Watkins Community Museum of History in Lawrence, Kansas.
45. Trow, 148.
46. Cordley, *A History of Lawrence, Kansas*; Frank Smith manuscript, in possession of the author; Lee C. Miller Memoirs.
47. Leverett W. Spring, *Kansas: The Prelude to the War for the Union*, Houghton Mifflin Pub., (Boston, 1896): 266, 270.

48. Eldridge, 184.
49. *Lawrence (Kansas) Journal World*, October 19, 1929.
50. Cordley, *A History of Lawrence, Kansas*, 206; *New York Times*, September 4, 1863.
51. Kansas Collection, University of Kansas Libraries, Lawrence.
52. Winchell.
53. Robert C. Stevens, 151-54.
54. Banasik, *Cavaliers of the Brush*, 25.
55. Winchell.
56. Cutler, vol. 1, 321.
57. McCorkle, 24-28, 76-84.
58. "One of the Sufferers" to S. N. Wood, Lawrence, September 2, 1863. Council Grove Press, September 14, 1863, Kansas State Historical Society, Topeka; Quantrill Clippings, Kansas State Historical Society, Topeka; *History of Tuscarawas County, Ohio* (1884): 463-64; John Speer, "The Burning of Osceola, Mo.," 305-12; Cordley, *A History of Lawrence, Kansas*, 197; Wallenstein.
59. "Lawrence—Today and Yesterday," The *Lawrence Daily Journal World*, 1913, Watkins Community Museum of History in Lawrence, Kansas.
60. McAllaster.
61. Cordley, *Pioneer Days in Kansas*, 190-98; Cutler, vol. 1, 322; Cordley, "The Lawrence Massacre," 98-115.

Chapter 7: A Just Retaliation

1. *Houston (Texas) Tri-Weekly Telegraph,* December 30, 1863; Shea, 14; Connelley, *Quantrill and the Border Wars*, reprint (New York: Pageant, 1956), 337; Banasik, *Cavaliers of the Brush*, 11; Roenigk, article by W. K. Cone, quoted by Roenigk.
2. Frank Smith manuscript, in the possession of the author.
3. McCorkle, 24-28, 76-84.
4. Cordley, "The Lawrence Massacre by a Band of Missouri Ruffians under Quantrill."
5. *Kansas City (Missouri) Journal*, August 29 and September 18, 1863; Cordley, *Pioneer Days in Kansas*, 231.
6. McCorkle, 24-28, 76-84.

7. Shea, 13; Dix, 8.
8. Frank Smith manuscript, in the possession of the author; George, *Biography of Captain William Henry Gregg,* 73.
9. Quantrill Collection, McCain Library and Archives, University of Southern Mississippi.
10. George, *Biography of Captain William Henry Gregg*; Burke, 233; *Herald of Freedom*, January 1, 1859.
11. *Houston (Texas) Tri-Weekly Telegraph,* January 12, 1864; *Houston (Texas) Daily Telegraph*, March 11, 1864.
12. Kansas Collection, University of Kansas Libraries, Lawrence.
13. Lee C. Miller Memoirs; Dalton.
14. Spring, 242; *Kansas City (Missouri) Post*, March 21, 1915.
15. Cordley, "The Lawrence Massacre by a Band of Missouri Ruffians under Quantrell."
16. Lowman.
17. Clarke.
18. Shea.
19. "Quantrell's Raid, Aug 21, 1863," Autobiography of Peter D. Ridenour—Who Survived the Raid—With Genealogies of the Redenour and Beatty Families (Kansas City, MO: 1908), 160-77.
20. Kansas Collection, University of Kansas Libraries, Lawrence; *American Heritage*, vol. 11, no. 6 (October 1960): 25.
21. Letter of Isadora Augusta (Johnson) Allison, Kansas Collection, University of Kansas Libraries, Lawrence; John Speer, *Life of General Lane*; Bradley, 80-81.
22. Kansas Collection, University of Kansas Libraries, Lawrence; *Kansas City (Missouri) Post*, March 21, 1915; *Kansas City (Missouri) Star*, September 11, 1905; Breihan, 114; Buel.
23. Per Merriam-Webster, to be "bucked and gagged" was "to be restrained by tying the wrists together, passing the arms over the bent knees, and putting a stick across the arms and through the angle formed by the knees," with a cloth tied tightly around the head and over the mouth to prevent speaking; Isley.
24. Lowman, 72-75; "Eyewitness Reports of Quantrill's Raid, Letters of Sophia Bissell and Sidney Clarke," *Kansas History: A Journal of the Central Plains* (summer 2005): 94-103.
25. *Lawrence (Kansas) Republican,* May 16, 1861.

26. *Lawrence (Kansas) Daily Journal-World*, April 2, 1948.
27. Ibid.
28. Cordley, *A History of Lawrence, Kansas*; Personal Recollections of Mrs. Sara T. D. Robinson of the Quantrill Raid, August 21, 1863, Quantrill Collection, McCain Library and Archives, University of Southern Mississippi.
29. Letter of Edwin Smith, Kansas Collection, University of Kansas Libraries, Lawrence; *Herald of Freedom*, June 4, 1860.
30. *Houston (Texas) Tri-Weekly Telegraph,* January 15, 1864.
31. A. C. Wilder, Letter to Captain Sidney Clarke, Carl Albert Congressional Research and Studies Center, Congressional Archives, Sidney Clarke Collection.
32. Cordley, *Pioneer Days in Kansas,* Chapter 9, 6; Cordley, *A History of Lawrence, Kansas*, 169; Bidlack, 119.
33. Letters of Edward and Sarah Fitch, Lawrence, Kansas, 1855-1863, *Kansas History* 12, pt. 2, no. 2 (summer 1989); Cutler, vol. 1, 323.
34. Riggs; Sheridan, pt. 2, 247; Edwards, 196. John Newman Edwards' account in *Noted Guerrillas* lists Peyton Long as the man who attempted to shoot Riggs.
35. Simons, 332-33; John Speer, *Life of General Lane*, 54.
36. William Speer, "The Story of the Quantrell Massacre."
37. *Omaha (Nebraska) Morning World Herald*, September 25, 1897.
38. *West Virginia Wheeling Register*, December 20, 1892, taken from the *St. Louis (Missouri) Globe-Democrat;* Cordley, *A History of Lawrence, Kansas*, 199.
39. Sheridan, pt. 2, 158.
40. Cordley, *Pioneer Days of Kansas,* 24.
41. *Kansas City (Missouri) Post*, March 21, 1915; William H. Gregg Manuscript.
42. *Lawrence (Kansas) State Journal*, February 21, 1861; "Death of Hon. Erastus D. Ladd," *Lawrence Daily Kansas Tribune*, August 27, 1872.
43. *Lawrence (Kansas) Journal-World*, August 21, 1961.
44. Cordley, *A History of Lawrence, Kansas*; Castel, *William Clarke Quantrill*; Carr.

45. Connelley, *Quantrill and the Border Wars*, reprint (Smithmark Publishers, 1996), 362-63, 386.
46. *Kansas City (Missouri) Times*, March 13, 1930; Bailey, 3, 32; *Omaha (Nebraska) Morning World Herald*, March 29, 1903.
47. Bailey.
48. Rev. Hugh Dunn Fisher Correspondence File, Methodist Historical Library, Baker University, Baldwin, Kansas.
49. *Omaha (Nebraska) Morning World Herald*, March 29, 1903.
50. *Topeka (Kansas) Weekly Capital and Farm Journal*, July 26, 1959.
51. Wallenstein; Shea; *Confederate Veteran*, vol. 4 (1896): 14.
52. "Lawrence—Today and Yesterday," *Lawrence (Kansas) Daily Journal-World*, 1913, Watkins Community Museum of History in Lawrence, Kansas.
53. Sheridan, pt. 1, 81.
54. *Blue and Grey Chronicle*, vol. 6, no. 5: 6.
55. Cordley, *A History of Lawrence, Kansas*, 245.
56. Younger, 52; Edwards, 197-98.
57. Edwards, 194. The identical reference is given in *A True Story of Charles W. Quantrell and His Guerrilla Band* by Harrison Trow as told to J. P. Burch on page 149, only the guerrilla is named as Frank James. Since John Newman Edwards names the guerrilla as Jesse James and his book *Noted Guerrillas* was published in 1898 while Trow's book was not published until 1923, I defer the referenced credit to Edwards.
58. Shea; Cordley, *Pioneer Days in Kansas*, 208-9; Cordley, *A History of Kansas*, 245.
59. Ibid.
60. Jones.
61. Alice Nichols, 257.
62. *Reminiscences of the Women of Missouri*, 254; *St. Louis (Missouri) Post Dispatch*, August 24, 1902.
63. Sheridan, pt. 2, 219; Letter of A. Marks to the Committee of the Semi-Centennial of the Lawrence Massacre, August 8th, 1913, Kansas Collection, University of Kansas Libraries, Lawrence.
64. Younger, 44-47.
65. Letter of James Milliken, Rick Mack Historical Archives Collection.

66. *Houston (Texas) Tri-Weekly Telegraph,* January 14, 1864.
67. Walter B. Stevens, vol. 1, 852; Trow; McCorkle, 126; *St. Louis (Missouri) Post Dispatch*, August 24, 1902; *Liberty (Missouri) Advance*, April 1, 1910; Fisher, *The Gun and the Gospel*, 189.
68. Parker, *Angels of Freedom*, 29.
69. Sheridan, pt. 3, 349.
70. Letter of E. D. Ladd to Samuel Ladd, September 17, 1864, printed in the *Marshall (Missouri) Statesman*, October 4, 1864; Shea.

Epilogue

1. The Lawrence Massacre, 2, United States, 50th Congress, 1st Session, House of Representatives, 14th Kns Cavalry, vol. report no. 1783 (Washington: 1882):1-3.
2. Dalton.
3. Lee C. Miller Memoirs.
4. Fox.
5. Transactions of the Kansas State Historical Society, 1897-1900, vol. 6 (Topeka: 1900): 317-25.
6. "Lawrence—Today and Yesterday," *Lawrence Daily Journal World*, 1913. Watkins Museum of History, Lawrence, Kansas.
7. *Lawrence (Kansas) Daily Journal World*, August 17, 1940.
8. Cutler.
9. Starr, 380-82.
10. *History of Clay & Platte County, Missouri* (St. Louis: National Historical Co., 1885), 722.
11. Starr, 216.
12. Blunt, 211; Cutler, 302-4.
13. *Kansas, A Cyclopedia of State History*, vol. 1 (Chicago: Standard Publishing Co., 1912), 79-80; Starr, 253.
14. George, *Biography of Captain William Henry Gregg*, 76.

Selected Bibliography

Books and Articles

Anderson, Melissa Genett. "The Story of a Pioneer." Kansas Collection, University of Kansas Libraries, Lawrence.

Appler, Augustus C. *Younger Brothers*. St. Louis: Eureka Publishing Company, 1876.

Aptheker, Herbert. *Abolition: A Revolutionary Movement*. Boston: Twane Publications, 1989.

Atkeson, W. O. *History of Bates County.* Topeka: Historical Publishing Co., 1918.

Bader, Robert Smith. *Hayseeds, Moralizers, & Methodists: The Twentieth Century Image of Kansas*. Lawrence: University Press of Kansas, 1988.

Bailey, L. D. *Quantrell's Raid on Lawrence.* Lyndon, KS: C. R. Green, 1899, 23. On file in Spencer Library, University of Kansas Library, Lawrence.

Banasik, Michael E. *Embattled Arkansas*. Wilmington, NC: Broadfoot Publishing, 1996.

———*Missouri in 1861: The Civil War Letters of Franc B. Wilkie, Newspaper Correspondent*. Iowa City, IA: Camp Pope Bookshop, 2001.

———*Cavaliers of the Brush*. Iowa City, IA: Camp Pope Press, 2003.

Barrows, Robert S. The Richard Ely Selden, Jr. Letters of 1866. Kansas State Historical Society, Topeka.

Berneking, Carolyn. "A Look at Early Lawrence, Letters from Robert Gaston Elliott." Kansas Collection, *Kansas Historical*

Quarterly, vol. 43, no. 3 (autumn 1977): 282-96.

Bidlack, Russell E. "Erastus D. Ladd's Description of the Lawrence Massacre." *Kansas Historical Quarterly*, vol. 20 (spring 1963).

Blunt, James G. "General Blunt's Account of His Civil War Experiences." Kansas Collection, *Kansas Historical Quarterly*, vol. 1, no. 3 (May 1932).

Bonnewitz, Roberta L. and Arthur L. *In Brooking Township*. Raytown, MO: Courier Printing Company, 1966.

———and Lois T. Allen. *Raytown Remembers*. Clinton, MO: The Printery, 1975.

Bradley, R. T. *The Outlaws of the Border*. Cincinnati: Cincinnati Publishing Company, 1880.

Brant, Marley. *The Outlaw Youngers: A Confederate Brotherhood*. Lanham, MD: Madison Books, 1992.

Breihan, Carl W. *Ride the Razor's Edge*. Gretna, LA: Pelican Publishing Company, 1992.

Britton, Wiley. *The Civil War on the Border*. New York: G. P. Putnam & Sons, 1890.

Buel, J. W. *The Border Outlaws*. St. Louis: Historical Publishing Company, 1881.

Burke, W. S. *Official Military History of Kansas Regiments: During the War for the Suppression of the Great Rebellion*. Compiled by J. B. McAfee. Leavenworth, KS: W. S. Burke, 1870.

Carr, Lucien. *Missouri: A Bone of Contention*. New York: Houghton, Mifflin & Co., 1888.

Castel, Albert. *Civil War Kansas—Reaping the Whirlwind*. Lawrence: University Press of Kansas, 1997.

———*William Clarke Quantrill—His Life and Times*, New York: Fell, 1962.

Clarke, Henry S. "Incidents of Quantrell's Raid on Lawrence, August 21, 1863." Kansas Collection, University of Kansas Libraries, Lawrence.

Colman, Cosma T. *The Massacre of the Union Cavalry Recruits, as told by Recruit Cosma Torrienta Colman*. Kansas Historical Society, Topeka.

Connelley, William E. *History of Kansas*. Chicago/New York: 1928.

———*Quantrill and the Border Wars*. Cedar Rapids, IA: Torch

Press, 1909, 1978. Reprinted by Pageant in New York in 1956 and by Smithmark Publishers in 1996.

Cordley, Richard. *Pioneer Days in Kansas.* New York: The Pilgrim Press, 1903.

———*A History of Lawrence, Kansas*. Lawrence Journal Press, 1895.

———"The Lawrence Massacre." *Congregational Record.* Lawrence, Kansas, vol. 5, nos. 9-10 (September and October 1863).

———"The Lawrence Massacre by a Band of Missouri Ruffians under Quantrill, August 21, 1863." *Directory of Lawrence.* Broughton and McAlister: 1865. Douglas County Historical Society. Lawrence. Kansas Collection, University of Kansas Libraries, Lawrence.

Crittenden, Henry H. *The Crittenden Memoirs*. New York: Putnam, 1936.

Croy, Homer. *Last of the Great Outlaws: The Story of Cole Younger.* New York: Duel, Sloan and Pearce, 1956.

Cummins, Jim. *Jim Cummins—The Guerrilla*. Kansas City, MO: Promise Land Book Co., 2004.

———*Jim Cummins' Book: The Life Story of the James and Younger Gang and Their Comrades*. Denver, CO: 1903. Reprinted in Independence, MO: 1999.

Custer, Elizabeth B. *Tenting on the Plains*. New York: Charles Webster & Co., 1887.

Cutler, William G. *History of the State of Kansas.* 2 vols. Chicago: A. T. Andreas Publisher, 1883. Kansas Historical Collections, Topeka, vol. 10 (1907-1908).

Dalton, Kit. *Under the Black Flag.* Kansas Collection, University of Kansas Libraries, Lawrence.

Deatherage, Charles P. *Early History of Kansas City.* Interstate Publishing, 1927.

DeWitt, Daniel. "List of Losses at Federal Hands, 1861-63." Jackson County Historical Society.

Dick, Everett. *The Sod House Frontier 1854-1890*. Lincoln: University of Nebraska Press, Bison Books, 1979.

Dix, R. C. "Quantrill's Raid—an Eyewitness Account" by Mrs. R. C. Dix. *Historical Quarterly,* vol. 1, no. 1 (May 1965): 8-11.

Doerschuk, Albert N. "The Hays' of Westport Who Came West With Daniel Boone." *Westport Historical Quarterly,* vol. 5, no. 2 (September 1969).

Duncan, Russell. *The Civil War Letters of Colonel Robert Gould Shaw*. Athens: The University Press of Georgia, 1992.

Eakin, Joanne Chiles. *Tears & Turmoil—Order #11*. Shawnee Mission, KS: Two Trails Genealogy Shop, 1996.

——and Donald Hale. *Branded as Rebels.* Independence, MO: Wee Press, 1993.

Edwards, John Newman. *Noted Guerrillas*. St. Louis: Bryan, Brand & Co., 1877. Reprinted by Two Trails Publishing, Shawnee Mission, KS, 1996.

Eldridge, Shalor Winchell. "The Quantrill Raid as Seen from the Eldridge House" as described by R. G. Elliott. Publications of the Kansas State Historical Society, *Embracing Recollections of Early Days in Kansas,* vol. 2 (Topeka: Kansas State Printing Plant, 1920).

Farren, Edward Payson. *Quantrill's Raid on Lawrence, Kansas: An Eyewitness Account.* Kansas State Historical Society, Topeka.

Faxon, Frank. Memoirs. Watkins Museum, Douglas County Historical Society, Lawrence, Kansas.

Fellman, Michael. *Inside War*. New York: Oxford University Press, 1989.

Fisher, Hugh Dunn. Manuscript. "The Lawrence Massacre." Kansas Room, Library of the University of Kansas, Lawrence.

———*The Gun and the Gospel*. Chicago/New York: Medical Century Company, 1897.

Fleming, Elvis E. *Captain Joseph C. Lea—From Confederate Guerrilla to New Mexico Patriarch*. Las Cruces, NM: Yucca Tree Press, 2002.

Fox, Simeon M. *History of the 7th Kansas*. Kansas State Historical Society, Topeka, vol. XI (1909-1911).

Fry, Alice L. *Following the Fifth Kansas Cavalry*. Letters of Alice L. Fry. Compiled by Two Trails Publishing Company, Shawnee Mission, Kansas. Kansas Historical Collections, Topeka, vol. 10 (1907-1908).

George, B. James Sr. *Biography of Captain William Henry Gregg, Confederate Officer, Quantrillian Officer, and good citizen*. Jackson County Historical Society.

———*The Georges—Pioneers and Rebels—David C. George and Nancy E. George, Their Life and Times. Oak Grove Banner,* October 8, 1898. Kansas City Public Library, 1965.

Goodrich, Thomas. *Black Flag—Guerrilla Warfare on the Western Border, 1861-1865*. Bloomington: Indiana University Press, 1995.

Greeley, Horace. *Overland Journey.* New York: C. M. Saxon, Barker & Co., 1860.

Greene, Albert R. *What I Saw* of *the Quantrill Raid*. Kansas Historical Collections, vol. 8.

Gregg, William H. Manuscript. Western Historical Manuscript Collection, University of Missouri, Columbia.

Hagan, George L. *Tales of Tragedy Trail*. Clinton, MO: The Printery, 1974.

Hale, Donald R. *We Rode With Quantrill.* Independence, MO: Blue and Grey Workshop, 1998.

Hall, Jacob. Family Papers. Jackson County Historical Society.

Hall, Roy F. and Helen Gibbard Hall. *Collin County—Pioneering in North Texas.* Quanah, TX: Heritage Books, 1975.

Harlow, Ralph Volney. "The Rise and Fall of the Kansas Aid Movement." *American Historical Review*, IV (1935).

Hinton, Richard J. "Pens That Made Kansas Free." Kansas Collection, Kansas State Historical Society, Topeka, vol. 6 (1897-1900).

———"The War in Kansas and Missouri. The Sacking of Lawrence. Pursuit of the Guerrillas." *New York Times,* September 4, 1863.

Holloway, John N. *History of Kansas*. Lafayette, LA: James, Emmons & Co., 1868.

Hoole, A. J. "A Southerner's Viewpoint of the Kansas Situation, 1856-1857." *Kansas Historical Quarterly,* vol. 3, nos. 1 and 2 (May 1934).

Isley, Elise Dubach. *Sunbonnet Days, as told to her son Bliss Isley.* Caldwell, ID: The Caxton Printers, 1935.

Johnson, Samuel A. "The Emigrant Aid Company in Kansas." Kansas Collection, *Kansas Historical Quarterly,* vol. 1 (November 1932).

Jones, Harriet M. "Survivor of Lawrence Massacre." Kansas Collection, University of Kansas Libraries, Lawrence.

Kempker, Erin. "The Union, the War, and Elvira Scott." *Missouri Historical Review,* vol. 45 (April 2001).

Langsdorf, Edgar and Robert W. Richmond. "Letters of Daniel Read Anthony, 1857-1862." *Kansas Historical Quarterly,* vol. 24, no. 1 (spring 1958).

Lowman, Hovey E. *Narrative of the Lawrence Massacre on the Morning of the 21st of August, 1863.* Lawrence State Journal Steam Press, 1864.

Lykins, Mattie. "Recollections of Old Times in Kansas City." *Westport Historical Quarterly,* vol. 1, no. 4 (February 1966).

Maddox, George T. *Hard Trials and Tribulations of an Old Confederate Soldier.* Van Buren, AR: Argus, 1897.

Martin, George W. "Among the Sovereign Squats." Kansas State Historical Society (1902).

———"Sketches of Kansas Pioneer Experience." Kansas State Historical Society (1902).

———"Memorial Monuments and Tablets in Kansas." Collections of the Kansas State Historical Society, Topeka, vol. 11 (1909-1910).

McAllaster, Octavius Warren. "My Experience in the Lawrence Raid." Kansas State Historical Society, Topeka.

McCorkle, John. *Three Years with Quantrill.* 1914. Reprint. Norman: University of Oklahoma Press, 1992.

McLarty, Vivian Kirkpatrick. "The Civil War Letters of Colonel Basel Lazear." *Missouri Historical Review,* vol. 44, no. 3 (April 1950).

Miller, George, D. D. *Missouri's Memorable Decade 1860-1870: An Historical Sketch, Personal—Political—Religious.* Columbia: Missouri Press, 1898.

Miller, Lee C. Memoirs. Western Historical Manuscript Collection, University of Missouri, Columbia.

Miller, Richard Lawrence. *Truman: The Rise to Power.* New York: McGraw Hill, 1986.

Monaghan, Jay. *Civil War on the Western Border 1854-1865.* Lincoln: University of Nebraska Press, 1955.

Nichols, Alice. *Bleeding Kansas.* New York: Oxford University Press, 1954.

Nichols, Bruce. *The Civil War in Johnson County, Missouri.* Shawnee Mission, KS: Two Trails Publishing, 2002.

Niepman, Ann Davis. "General Orders No. 11 and Border Warfare

During the Civil War." *Missouri Historical Review,* vol. 66, no. 2 (January 1972).

Ostrander, Alson B. *An Army Boy of the Sixties*. New York: World Book Company, 1924.

Palmer, Henry E. "The Lawrence Raid." Kansas State Historical Society Collections, vol. 6 (1900).

———"The Black Flag Character of War on the Border." Kansas Historical Collections, vol. 9 (1905-1906).

Parker, Martha J. *Soil of our Souls*. Lawrence, KS: Coronado Press, 1976.

——— *Angels of Freedom*. Topeka, KS: Chapman Publishers, 1999.

Reminiscences of the Women of Missouri. Missouri Division, UDC. Dayton, OH: Morningside Books. Reprinted in 2003.

Richardson, Albert D. *Beyond the Mississippi*. Hartford, CT: American Publishing Company, 1873.

Richardson, James D. *Messages and Papers of the Confederacy*, 2 vols. Nashville, TN: United States Publishing Company, 1906.

Riggs, Henry Earle. *Our Pioneer Ancestors.* Ann Arbor, MI: Ann Arbor Lithoprinters, 1942.

Robinson, Sara. *Kansas: Its Interior and Exterior Life*. Kansas Collection, University of Kansas Libraries, Lawrence.

Roenigk, Adolph. *The Quantrell Raid, Pioneer History of Kansas.* Manhattan, KS: Adolph Roenigk, 1933.

Savage, Joseph. "Recollections of Joseph Savage." Kansas State Historical Society, Topeka.

Shea, John C. "Reminiscences of Quantrell's Raid Upon the City of Lawrence, Kansas." Kansas Collection, University of Kansas, Lawrence; *Kansas Historical Quarterly.*

Sheridan, Richard B. ed./com. *Quantrill and the Lawrence Massacre: A Reader,* pts. 1-4. Lawrence, KS: Richard B. Sheridan, 1995.

Simons, W. C. "Lawrence Newspapers in Territorial Days." Kansas Collection, Kansas State Historical Society, 1926-1928, vol. 17 (Topeka, 1928).

Soodalter, Ron. "Captain Gordon's Infamy." *Smithsonian Magazine,* vol. 38, no. 3 (June 2007).

Spalding, Charles Carroll. *Annals of the City of Kansas and the*

Great Western Plains. Kansas City, MO: Van Horn & Abeel's Printing House, 1858.

Speer, John. *The Life of General James H. Lane,"The Liberator of Kansas."* Garden City, KS: John Speer Printer, 1896.

———"The Burning of Osceola, Mo. by Lane, and the Quantrill Massacre Contrasted." Transactions of the Kansas State Historical Society, 1897-1900, vol. 6 (Topeka, 1900).

Speer, William. "My Story of the Quantrell Massacre." Manuscript Department, Kansas State Historical Society, Topeka.

Spring, Leverett Wilson. *Kansas: The Prelude to the War for the Union*. Reprint 1907. New York: AMS Press, 1973.

Starr, Stephen Z. *Jennison's Jayhawkers: A Civil War Cavalry Regiment and Its Commander*. Baton Rouge, LA: Louisiana State University Press, 1973.

Steinberg, Alfred. *The Man from Missouri*. New York: G. P. Putnam's Sons, 1962.

Stevens, Robert C. *Land, Railroads, and Politics: The Careers of Robert Wadleigh Smith Stevens 1824-1893*. Attica Historical Society, Attica, New York.

Stevens, Walter B. *Centennial History of Missouri*, 2 vols. St. Louis-Chicago: S. J. Clarke Pub. Co., 1921.

Stewart, Watson. Personal Memoirs. Kansas Collection, University of Kansas Libraries, Lawrence.

Tathwell and Maxey. *The Old Settlers of Bates County, Missouri.* Amsterdam, MO: 1897.

The War of the Rebellion: A Compilation of the Official Records of the Union and Confederate Armies. Washington, DC: Government Printing Office, 1880-1901.

Trow, Harrison. *A True Story of Charles W. Quantrell and His Guerrilla Band*. Vega, TX: John P. Burch, 1923.

Unrau, William E. "In Pursuit of Quantrill: An Enlisted Man's Response." *Kansas Historical Quarterly,* vol. 39, no. 3 (autumn 1972).

Vansickle, John. Letters of John Vansickle, Bourbon County, Kansas, December 28, 1858. Kansas Historical Society, Topeka.

Voigt, Harry R. *Concordia, Missouri: A Centennial History.* Concordia, MO: Centennial Committee, 1960.

Walker, Andy. *Recollections of Quantrill's Guerrillas.* Shawnee Mission, KS: Two Trails Publishing, 1996.

Wallenstein, Marcel. "She Stood Up to Quantrill and Saved Husband." Kansas Collection, University of Kansas Libraries, Lawrence.

Wells, Thomas C. "Letters of a Kansas Pioneer." Kansas Collection, University of Kansas Libraries, Lawrence.

Welty, Raymond L. *Supplying the Frontier Posts*. Kansas Historical Collection, vol. 24.

Wilcox, Pearl. *Jackson County Pioneers.* 1975. Reprinted in 1990 by the Jackson County Historical Society.

Williams, Burton J. "Quantrill's Raid on Lawrence, Kansas—A Question of Complicity." *Kansas Historical Quarterly,* vol. 34, no. 2 (summer 1968).

———"Erastus D. Ladd's Description of the Lawrence Massacre." *Kansas Historical Quarterly* (summer 1963).

Winchell, James M. "The Sacking of Lawrence." *New York Daily Tribune,* August 31, 1863.

Younger, Coleman. *The Story of Cole Younger By Himself.* 1903. Reprinted in 1988 by Triton Press, Provo, Utah.

Zornow, William Frank. *Kansas: A History of the Jayhawk State*. Norman: University of Oklahoma Press, 1957.

Newspapers, Magazines, Periodicals, and Journals

American Heritage Magazine
American Historical Review
Beaver Dam (Wisconsin) Weekly Republican & Sentinel
Biloxi (Mississippi) Herald
Blue and Grey Chronicle, Independence, Missouri
Brunswick (Missouri) Brunswicker
Cedarville Kansas Pioneer
Chicago Tribune
Collier's Weekly
Confederate Veteran Magazine
Daily Lawrence (Kansas) Republican
Daily (Ohama) Nebraska Press

Dallas Morning News
DeBow's Review
Fort Worth (Texas) Star-Telegram
Grand Forks(North Dakota) Herald
Greenfield (Massachusetts) Courier
Herald of Freedom, Lawrence, Kansas
Houston (Texas) Daily Telegraph
Houston (Texas) Tri-Weekly Telegraph
Independence (Missouri) Examiner
Jackson County (Missouri) Examiner
Kansas City (Missouri) Enterprise
Kansas City (Missouri) Post
Kansas City (Missouri) Star
Kansas City (Missouri) Times
Kansas City (Missouri) Western Journal of Commerce
Kansas Historical Quarterly
Kansas Weekly Capital and Farm Journal
Knoxville (Kentucky) Journal
Lawrence (Kansas) Daily Journal-World
Lawrence Daily Kansas Tribune
Lawrence Kansas Free State
Lawrence (Kansas) Gazette
Lawrence (Kansas) Journal
Lawrence (Kansas) Republican
Lawrence (Kansas) State Journal
Leavenworth Kansas Weekly Herald
Lexington (Kentucky) Herald
Lexington (Kentucky) Weekly Journal
Liberty (Missouri) Advance
Liberty (Missouri) Platform
Liberty (Missouri) Tribune
Louisville Kentucky Journal
Macon (Georgia) Daily Telegraph
Marshall (Missouri) Democrat
Marshall (Missouri) Statesman
Massachusetts Spy, Worcester
McKinney (Texas) Daily Courier-Gazette

McKinney (Texas) Examiner
Miami (Florida) Herald Record
Michigan Free Democrat
Missouri Historical Review
New York Daily Tribune
New York Times
Oak Grove (Missouri) Banner
Occidental Messenger
Olathe (Kansas) Mirror
Omaha (Nebraska) Morning World Herald
Pleasant Hill (Missouri) Times
Richmond (Virginia) Enquirer
Rock Island (Illinois) Weekly Union
St. Louis Daily Missouri Democrat
St. Louis (Missouri) Globe-Democrat
St. Louis (Missouri) Post Dispatch
St. Louis (Missouri) Republican
The Literary Encyclopedia
Topeka (Kansas) Weekly Capital and Farm Journal
True Republican and Sentinel, Sycamore, Illinois
Weatherford (Texas) Weekly Herald
Weekly California (Missouri) News
Westport (Missouri) Historical Quarterly
Wheeling (West Virginia) Register

Archives, Libraries, Historical Societies, and Collections

Carl Albert Congressional Research and Studies Center, Congressional Archives
Chicago Historical Society
Congressional Record
Dallas Morning News Historical Archive
Douglas County (Kansas) Historical Society, Lawrence
Jackson County (Missouri) Historical Society
Jacob Hall Family Papers
Jennison Scrapbook, Kansas Collection
Kansas City Missouri Public Library

Kansas State Historical Society Collection, Topeka
Library of Congress
McCain Library and Archives, University of Southern Mississippi
Methodist Historical Library, Baker University, Baldwin, Kansas
Missouri Historical Society
Rick Mack Historical Archives Collection
University of Missouri, Columbia
Younger Family Newspaper Clippings 1899-1936
Watkins Community Museum of History, Lawrence, Kansas

Index

M

N